P9-CRE-474

More praise for *The Soul of Golf*

"A thrilling and revealing search through the fairways and roughs of America...Hallberg's inaugural round is described so poetically you can almost hear the Southern drawls of his three playing partners as they concede three-foot putts and reveal personal demons...*The Soul of Golf* is exciting, adventuresome, insightful. Ride shotgun with Hallberg and play a few holes, but don't spot him any strokes."

—Fort Worth Star-Telegram

"Vivid and captivating...An epic odyssey worthy of legend...It is difficult to imagine a more likeable and enjoyable companion than Hallberg on this journey to find the soul of golf."

—The Toledo Blade

"A gem of a book...In depicting his adventures with golfers and courses in such diverse places as Kiawah Island, Boone, N.C., and the Nevada outback, Hallberg delivers a humorous and marvelously descriptive travelogue."

—The Herald (Columbia, SC)

"Hallberg's odyssey around America is for those who might dream of leaving the rat race for a life on the links."

—San Jose Mercury News

"Perhaps only God, Tom Morris, or Carl Jung knows why we're so addicted to golf and willing to follow the game anywhere—but alas, they're not telling. Bill Hallberg, on the other hand, not only shares some of his unique take on the mystery but hauls us along with him on a joyful odyssey through the game's many places, both sacred and profane....*The Soul of Golf* elevates the golf road trip to a new level of adventure and, like all good travel stories, gives us a powerful glimpse of ourselves at our best—and worst."

—James Dodson
Author of *Final Rounds*

"A *Blue Highways* of golf."

—Waterbury Republican

"Although the mystique of golf remains an enigma, Hallberg's quest to discover its nature is well worth reading."

—Publishers Weekly

By William Hallberg

*The Soul of Golf
*The Rub of the Green

Edited by William Hallberg
Perfect Lies: A Century of Great Golf Stories

*Published by Ballantine Books

the soul of golf

william hallberg

FAWCETT COLUMBINE
The Ballantine Publishing Group • New York

Sale of this book without a front cover may be unauthorized. If this book is coverless, it may have been reported to the publisher as "unsold or destroyed" and neither the author nor the publisher may have received payment for it.

A Fawcett Columbine Book
Published by The Ballantine Publishing Group

Copyright © 1997 by William Hallberg

All rights reserved under International and Pan-American Copyright Conventions. Published in the United States by The Ballantine Publishing Group, a division of Random House, Inc., New York, and simultaneously in Canada by Random House of Canada Limited, Toronto.

http://www.randomhouse.com

Library of Congress Catalog Card Number: 98-96015

ISBN: 0-449-00297-7

Cover design by Kristine Mills-Noble
Cover photo © Brennon Jones

Manufactured in the United States of America

First Hardcover Edition: May 1997
First Trade Paperback Edition: June 1998

10 9 8 7 6 5 4 3 2 1

This book is dedicated to
Carl and Julie Hallberg
and to the memory of Jane Hallberg.
I'm humbled by their courage.

ACKNOWLEDGMENTS

I would like to thank Doug Grad for his brilliant editorial assistance, and my other supportive friends at Ballantine: Judith Curr, Linda Grey, and Emily Grayson. I am deeply grateful to my agent Barney Karpfinger for kicking all those lucky bounces my way. Thanks, also, to my golfing buddy Dan Mayo for keeping my mind on the game at hand. Finally, my deepest gratitude to all those wonderful people who traipsed the fairways with me this summer. Bless you all!

the soul of golf

CHAPTER 1

into the breach

There's nothing quite like cruising at dawn through Dixie, sober, alone, tired . . . listening to a wild-ass evangelist hyperventilate over lost souls and spiritual defectives like me. My prurient side wants to hear him out, but it's just too damned depressing. I flip the dial back and forth across the illuminated band. It's a pretty useless exploration, so I snap off the radio and concentrate on the broken dividing line sailing past. Fourteen golf clubs rattle ominously in the trunk. My car smells of stale coffee. I sense that soon my whole life may smell of stale coffee.

In the east, rust-colored clouds huddle over patches of woodland in advance of the emerging sun, which is only a horizontal knife blade at first, then a skullcap that slowly morphs into an orange dome, and finally a full, blazing circle. I flip the sun visor into position and don my Mafia sunglasses.

I'm launched . . . into the grat, flat, pork-rind belly of the South, where, if one can sparc the time, it's possible to buy pecan logs and firecrackers and peaches from roadside vendors or ascend into the brim of a two-hundred-foot-tall sombrero at South of the Border. Iris, my Plymouth Neon, veers onto the exit ramp, drawn to the irresistible tackiness of the place. I nose up to a huge concrete flamingo. The car next to mine is a pinstriped Dodge Caravan with a dog inside. All the windows are rolled down so the critter can breathe, but I'm sure he's a very warm little fellow.

I grab a takeout tortilla from one of the several garish eateries, then join newlyweds up there in the hat at high noon. The view is nothing too exciting: soybean fields and tobacco allotments, vast acreage decorated with white-flecked early cotton and the highway itself. Below, within the compound, is the Ferris wheel and the indestructible concrete wiener dog. (Pedro says, "You Never Sausage a Place!") Over there behind the curio shop and the burrito cafe is a miniature golf course with a Mexican motif. Olé! But it's stifling hot at South of the Border and nobody is playing golf.

Off again, down I-95, through Dillon and Darlington and Florence and Coward. In Hyman, South Carolina, is a truck-stop café (NASCAR SPOKEN HERE) where I can finally take a pee. Fifty-cent fluorescent condoms are for sale in the filthy rest room. I buy a package for novelty's sake only, then amble past the cellophane rows of boiled peanuts and Squirrel Nut Zippers to the Coke dispenser for yet another hit of caffeine. A slim, pretty girl with a poignant overbite looks me over from behind the cash register. With my eyes I tell her, Okay, I don't belong here—*I know* that.

"Ninee-fi cent," she says.

I dig five quarters out of my jeans pocket, place them next to the toothpick dispenser on the wounded glass counter, and tell her to "Keep the change."

"Can you play golf anywhere around here?" I ask.

"About a mile down the road," she says. "Cain't miss it."

Down the road is a mom-and-pop driving range cut out of pastureland. There are hand-painted distance markers planted in a field of coarse grass, bringing to mind a family cemetery plot. Plastic lawn chairs, one of which is occupied by a fat guy in purple suspenders, are situated randomly behind each of the marked-off hitting bays, where nobody is partaking except for one heat-resistant kid wearing a tank top and cutoff blue jeans. This, I surmise, is the Hyman golfing population, and for the likes of him, this patch of scruff is where it's at. I tell the hefty man that I'd like to hit a bucket of balls. "Two bucks," he says, and points me toward a wire basket filled with yellow range balls circumnavigated by black stripes so they look like Saturn.

I've hit maybe five easy wedge shots and already I'm soaked with sweat. The club is slippery in my hands, and droplets of perspiration hang from my eyelashes. Insects are chirruping in the desiccated weeds that hem in the little driving range. I'm being watched by the boy and the proprietor. At least I'm hitting the ball better than my arch-competitor in the tank top. I work through my irons, wedge through three iron (avoiding my two iron, of course), then it's *gonzo city*. The big tool. Out comes the driver and I'm nailing drives way, way past where somebody the caliber of, say, Mother Teresa would be planting her monster knocks. I imagine her in the next slot over, togged out in her buttery halter top. "You nutted that one, big guy," she says, blowing a smoke ring that hovers like a halo above her. "Whooeeee. You da man." And, wistfully, almost philosophically, she hitches up her Bermudas, tosses her clubs into the trunk of her car, and drives toward the hot horizon.

I rap a few last mediocre drives, then buy yet another Coke out of the driving-range vending machine. "Thanks a lot," I say, and sling my clubs over my shoulder.

"Come back," the fat guy says, and nods.

Despite having drunk about a half gallon of high-octane beverages already, I can't seem to wake up, at least not to the realities spiraling before me in the heat shimmer. Here I am, a middle-aged man with two kids, a couple of mutts, a Victorian cottage, and a girlfriend half my age named Gillian. But I'm going to leave everything behind in order to boogaloo my way across the continent and back, from sea to shining sea, in search of answers to golf's mysteries. Perhaps there's a wrinkled little man pulling a cart along some lonely fairway in North Dakota, and he's got the answers I'm looking for. Or maybe the answers reside in the mind of a little kid in Texas, a kid with supreme cognizance and prelapsarian purity of body and soul—not to mention an empirical swing crafted of pure wisdom. Or maybe *not*. As for the deeper meaning of the sport, I can say this much and no more: I do not have the answer. I know that I love the game, that it matters in ways that are inexplicable, that it owns more of my soul than I have ever admitted until now. If I triumph occasionally, it's because I hate with all my heart to taint the game with my incompetence. I'd rather walk off the course mid-round and bury my muzzle in the froth of a tall cold one than desecrate the game with a wretched performance. I admit to a truncated backswing with a borderline reverse pivot, a tendency to shank, and a jittery putting stroke. This adds up to a handicap that has been as low as five and as high as twelve.

Frankly, my nongolfing life is bouillabaise. I'm not coping well with the ambiguities of my own, present-day existence.

But never mind that; off I go to dissect the vast metaphor of golf . . . to probe the conundrums of the greenest sport known to man. Will I ever understand why we revel in the game's curious topography? Or why we will pay a month's wages to fly across the country or across the ocean to be humbled by a sacred patch of green earth? Will I come to know why we play a game so apt to bring us down? Or why we revel in our post-traumatic suffering? How is it that millions of golfers just like me persist in chunking and chili-dipping and shanking and hacking and duffing and diddling week after week on courses all across the republic? It's possible that I'll know less about such questions at the end of my journey than at the beginning, but maybe more about what it is to be a man in this realm. *Qué será será*, I say. *Qué será será*.

What is the strange pinging noise emanating from the region of my 2.0-liter engine? I stop the car and listen, then hop out to investigate. Fire ants have built a mound the size of a pup tent next to the mosquito ditch paralleling the shoulder. It's very wise not to insult their habitat, for these creatures will spill from their fortress, mighty tusks blazing, ready to kick butt and take names. I give a wide berth. Everything seems copacetic under the hood, so I buckle in behind the wheel, drop Iris into gear, and ease back onto the afternoon highway. The noise, I soon discover, is the result of an empty Pepsi can vibrating against a barrette under the passenger seat. Disaster averted. No turning back. Avaunt, then, past roadside crosses with plastic adornments, past JESUS IS LORD billboards, toward my destination.

I'm still looking for the first golf course of the day. Should one appear, I might be tempted off the highway for a quick nine with a couple of locals. But it's one scraggly farm after another, punctuated by scruffy little towns. Moncks Corner, Goose Creek, Oakley. At least now there are some signs for Charleston's motels and tourist venues.

* * *

Voluminous live oaks shade the highway now, and wetlands appear, with lean wading birds stalking the reeds and black waters. Up ahead a line of cars has stopped on the berm, their inhabitants ogling and pointing at what I can only presume is a gator or a human corpse floating beyond a tuft of aquatic grass. But I've got places to go, people to see, things to do, promises to keep and miles to go, and so on.

I would like to report that I've taken up lodging in a charming B & B on Calhoun Street near the Customs House. I would like to say that Miss Annabell Lee has given me fresh towels and a comforting smile upon my arrival. Fact is, I'm sleeping cheap at a Motel 6 on Phosphate Road. The pool outside my room is riotously multicultural. But it's only three o'clock in the afternoon and I'm a *turista* for the nonce, so it's off to the old city with me.

Call me sentimental, call me a hopeless romantic, call me pathetic if you wish, but I link up with a tuxedoed carriage driver near the old slave market. I give the top-hatted gentlemen fifteen dollars in exchange for the cliché tour of the Charleston environs. My traveling companions are a middle-aged couple from Murfreesboro, Tennessee, and their cheerless daughter, whom it would be my pleasure to hurl from her tufted leather seat onto the redbrick street. It seems that the dad has dragged his wife and sourpuss daughter to Charleston so he can play golf at the two great local courses—Harbor Town Golf Links and the Ocean Course—while the missus and child sniff potpourri in genteel gift shops. When I tell him that I'm destined to tackle the Ocean Course come morning, he says, "Good luck! That course kicked my ass."

By the time the tour is over, I've had my fill of gingerbread houses and slave quarters and Spanish moss and hurricane lore. Mostly, I'm starved, so I mosey up George Street in quest of Chinese food, for which I've had an inexplicable hankering all day.

The Great Wall is dark, cool, and ginger-smelling. I've never particularly cared for eating alone in restaurants. I always feel pathetic and lonely watching chatty couples and boisterous corpulent parties hoisting glasses around a circular table whilst I sit hangdog in my shameful corner. But I reckon I'd better get used to the experience, so I allow a very pretty young woman of Asian extraction to guide me, alas, to a shameful corner where I can adopt my lonely hangdog persona.

I'm more than a little bit aware of the peptic rumble I'm producing in anticipation of my moo goo gai pan. The restaurant, save for some exotic Chinese dining music, is quiet enough that I might just be disrupting the atmospherics of the place. I decide, finally, that I'm just paranoid; nobody seems to notice my existence beside the largest jade plant in North America.

I am *not* feeling well at bedtime. I am, in fact, feeling quite *un*well. I am a churning urn of fuming funk. A turning squirm of wormy punk. I enter the antiseptic bathroom, rip the sanitation strip from the commode, and close the door. No living human shall ever learn precisely what transpired in the privacy of that little room. But when I emerge, I see in the huge mirror above the desk cum dresser a man resembling Roderick Usher on a very, very bad day. "Cilantro," I moan. "South of the Border. Cilantro." Oh, vile, vile cilantro, bane of my existence. I am allergic to the stuff. I was lied to by the paper-hatted counter gnome at Pedro's Cafe. "No cilantro in this tortilla, right?" "Oh, no, sir. Cilantro, no."

If there's one thing in which I devoutly believe it's the calamitous ineffectuality of fervent prayer. However, in my gastric swound I pray like crazy to dear God that this terrible eruptive episode will end, that I'll be delivered in time to make Kiawah by ten or ten-thirty in the morning. It's a mundane supplication, I know, but I'm feeling bad. *Real* bad.

In desperation I drag myself to the motel parking lot, climb into the car, and drive one block to a Winn-Dixie, where I wobble up and down the aisles, using the shopping cart like a walker. I buy Pepto-Bismol and Alka-Seltzer and caffeine-free Coke, then drive back to the motel. I dose myself with palliatives and promptly rack out at around nine-thirty. For a while I just flop around on the mattress, feeling several billion miles removed from kith and kin, hearth and home, hammock and hacksaw. I miss my girlfriend and my mutts and even the mildew smell of my rug. My brain deteriorates. I imagine dire scenes from Hieronymous Bosch paintings; I'm the star of the show. Yours truly is naked and bloated and ill, but I've linked arms with other lost souls and we're groping toward oblivion. Flames lick at me from glowing cinders. Then the consortium of medicines starts to kick in. By midnight I'm feeling well enough actually to fall asleep, which I do assiduously.

It's almost eight o'clock in the morning when I realize that I'm Bill Hallberg and I'm prone in a twenty-five-dollar room on the outskirts of a grand southern city. The weather is fine, trucks are idling in the parking lot, children are crying next door, and all is right with the world. This is *it*, I tell myself. Into the breach.

To my utter shock and dismay, I learn from the motel clerk, upon dropping off my room key, that there is no Denny's in Charleston. *No Denny's!* This strikes me as something so impossible that I actually stop at a Howard Johnson's motel a mile down the road for a second opinion. "No kidding," I say when I get the sad news. I decide to press on toward Kiawah Island; maybe I'll spot an IHOP or an Aunt Becky's Pancake Shack along the way. Regrettably, even half an hour down the road, I've seen exactly nothing resembling a breakfast joint, so I settle on a McDonald's at the fringe of a strip mall in a town called Meggett. Which brings to mind maggot. Which makes my stomach turn over once or twice. In this queasy state I order tea and two plain biscuits with strawberry jam. These items I carry to my lonely hangdog corner of the restaurant. I can't handle the second of the two biscuits, so I shroud the thing in a napkin and exit the scene.

There's one thing the prospective golfer should know about Kiawah Island. When you get there, you're not there yet. It's ten o'clock in the morning when my front wheels make contact with the island bridge, and my tee-off time is eleven. I've shrewdly afforded myself a generous allotment of time for the greeting of golf operatives and the meeting of playing partners. There will, no doubt, be ample opportunity to hit a leisurely bucket of pristine, unringed shag balls . . . to stroke practice putts—lags and knee-knockers.

Ix-nay on that surmisal. It takes half an hour, punctuated by two gate checks and a deep cavity search, for me to achieve my destination at the distal end of this finger-shaped piece of real estate. There are billion-dollar homes and million-dollar cars from one end of the island to the other. I feel a teence outclassed behind the wheel of my dirty Neon. To my delight, there are also abundant bird paradises and wetlands populated by alligators and very smart reptile-evading herons. "Some *place*," I say to myself. Kiawah is probably a Seminole word meaning "I've got mine."

Finally, finally . . . a nicely carved biodegradable sign reading OCEAN COURSE. Thataway. I make a right-hand turn and travel another five or ten minutes before arriving at the beautiful gray-cedar clubhouse. It's twenty minutes before eleven, and I'm sitting on the asphalt of the parking lot at one of the classiest places east of the Pecos, sliding my feet into a very grubby pair of Nike Air winged tips. This is not a sight the well-heeled muckety-mucks would approve of. But hey, I'm running late. I snatch my sticks, umbrella, and tripod from the trunk and dash toward the clubhouse, ditching the whole mess at the bag drop along the way. "I'll put those on a cart for you, sir," says a college kid. I tell him thanks, and hustle up the steps to the pro shop, where I am to make contact with Brian, the pro, who has generously granted me a free round of golf. I'm embarrassed to be so late, but he's perfectly friendly and generous in his greeting. How does such a young guy wind up as head pro at the most beautiful course on the Eastern Seaboard? Hmmm. Nepotism? Mob connections?

Everything is transacted so efficiently, and all the hired hands are straight off the chorus line of Up With People. A happier workforce I have never seen. Within minutes I'm piloting my EZ-Go cart down a concrete path to the putting green, where my playing partners are getting a feel for the immaculate greens. Only then do I allow myself a chance to survey the gorgeous surroundings, which, in a strange way, fill me with awe and shame. This is the finest coastal landscape on the Atlantic, and *there's a golf course on it*! I honestly don't know how to feel. My golfish side is fiendishly delighted. My ecoconscious side shudders. This scene before me is the eerie, only slightly altered manifestation of a fantasy that has preoccupied me since I first laid eyes on the Outer Banks of my home state of North Carolina.

If you drive down this chain of barrier islands, hopping the Hatteras ferry along the way, you pass through sweeping dunes overlayed with sea oats arcing leeward and Johnson grass and scrub oak and ocean cedar. Between the dunes you glimpse emerald breakers stacked tall against the wind. And every now and then you must slow your car in deference to foot-deep sand that has blown across the two-lane road. Always, the landscape wants to heal over the intrusions man has made. Hurricanes sweep away entire seaside developments, beaches come and go in oceanic cycles, dunes shift, whales flounder onto shore at odd seasons, tidal marshes appear and disappear on a cosmic whim.

This is the most heartbreaking stretch of links-land I know of. Heartbreaking because there is no golf to be found on the whole, long, voluptuous trail, unless you count a little par three novelty course in Buxton. Never has there been land that yearned, in spite of itself, to be punctuated by emerald green, if only for a summer. My ecological conscience wrestles with my golfer's libido every summer when I thread my way from Coquina to Ocracoke. How beautiful it would be to play an illicit round of golf on such forbidden terrain. For a few ecstatic months, one could play the course, roam lush fairways framed in sea oats and ocean cedar, then, come October, let nature reclaim it. This course would be sculpted into the seaside dunes, nourished with indigenous waters.

Why does this sacred landscape provoke such sacrilege in me? Why do I imagine a golf course whose verdant fairways flow through the immaculate dunes and whose greens are pocketed low beneath the whistling oceanic bluster? I populate my links course with earth-toned golfers, myself included, who plod the evanescent Bermuda grass fairways, groomed daily by horse-drawn six-reeled mowers. No electric carts here. No condominiums, no billion-dollar mansions with Bentleys out front, no clubhouse, no caddie shack. Only a dusky tavern, nineteenth-hole way station where golfers hoist pints and recount their triumphs and tribulations.

And here it is before me, altered but intact. The Ocean Course. I don't quite know how to feel.

Exquisite marshes with segmented reeds and lily pads and sawgrass and hyacinths reach into the golf course from the island's interior. Then there are the dunes from which and upon which the playing surfaces are sculpted. Small gray signs flank the cart paths, warning golfers of this terrain's fragility, of dangerous snakes and spiders lurking in the bracken, of quicksand and fire ants and poison ivy and guerrilla snipers. Any shot straying from the straight and

narrow into *terra incognita* is forfeited to the ages, a healthy concession to the island's ecosystem, which is, at best, a reluctant host to a
golf course. This is links-land of the finest sort. Gentler, more so-
phisticated than the shaggy, primal moors of the Scottish and Irish
coasts. And more vulnerable to the give-and-take of nature.

The back tees at Kiawah, I've been informed, are reserved for
insane masochists, bungee jumpers, and survivalists. Nevertheless,
my scheme has been to play every course for all it's worth, suffer
nobly, blame my failures on the bossa nova with its magic spell, and
get on with my life.

The three fellows on the putting green are destined to be my
playing partners today. One of them is a pleasant-looking old gentleman with clear blue eyes and a jaunty white snap-brim cap. The
other two are forty-somethings like me, only more prosperous looking, evidenced by their hip sartoriality. We're talking Cal Klein and
Tommy Hilfiger here. Meanwhile, I'm decked out in brands of lesser
repute—specifically Trader Bay and Bugle Boy. I suspect that the
hundred-dollar greens fee will not provoke any serious belt tightening amongst this trio, and I'm suppressing an outbreak of class
envy. Using my Ping putter as a prop, I saunter toward the men who
will be joining me for the day's round, grateful that our foursome has
been prearranged. "Hi there," I chirp. "I understand you're stuck
with me today." My effortful congeniality has raised my voice a complete octave above normal, but the old guy is very friendly. He
extends his hand and gives mine a firm shake. "I'm Theodore. Glad
to meet you," he says. "This is my son Robert, and that guy there is
Mike." Handshakes all around. Obligatory self-deprecations. Yes,
we're all in over our heads, and yes, we hope not to embarrass our
ancestors. It's all part of the ritual: portray yourself as a total hacker,
so when you prove to be just that, the world forgives you. Mike is an
architect from Louisville, a bachelor, and a relative newcomer to the
sport. He's here with his brother's family, golfing, touring around the
city, getting away from business in Louisville for a week or so.
Robert, a trim, well-tanned fellow from Alpharetta, Georgia, who
looks nothing like his dad, wears a Byron Nelson–style straw chapeau. "Would anyone like to play the back tees today?" I ask. They

look back and forth amongst themselves as if I've invited them to partake in a rite of mutual circumcision. "I'll have my hands full from the blues," Robert says preemptively, "and the back tees would be a struggle for Dad." I nod, embarrassed for even broaching the subject. I'm only slightly disappointed to be compromising the full rigor of the course. Theodore cheerfully offers to play all the way back; in fact, he seems pleased not to be patronized in any way. This old guy *knows* he's not going to be hitting many greens in regulation, so what's a few extra swings. More golf for the money. That's my explanation for his enthusiasm.

"You're right," I say. "Who am I kidding?" I tell them. "Heck, I oughta be hitting from the ladies' tees." Guffaws. Chortles. What boffo fun. The more I think about it, the happier I am that somebody has gotten me off that foolish hook. Guys like me want to play the championship tees only because we're insecure. We *know* we're going to get taken to the cleaners, but if we're going to get clobbered anyway, we'd rather be clobbered by a big bully, not his weakling brother. It's much better for the ego. Mike says he's game for the back tees, but the die is cast in favor of the blues, which will be plenty tough on a breezy day like today.

"Why don't you put your clubs on my cart?" Mike asks. He seems like a nice fellow, so I unstrap my plaid bag and load everything onto his cart. We're two guys, Mike and Bill, Bill and Mike, heading into the fray.

A starter greets us with his clipboard when we arrive at the first tee. He gives us all the dos and don'ts of golf course protocol and tells us to hit away.

The first hole is more than the typical handshake that commences most rounds of golf. One must carry a long sweep of sea grass in order to reach the fairway, which puts Theodore at a considerable disadvantage. Or so I think. He's first on the tee and wastes no time in knocking his drive cleanly onto the distant fairway. "Well done," I tell him.

"That's always the hardest shot of the day," he says, and chuckles.

I don't feel sufficiently warmed up to use my driver just yet, and the hole is only 380 yards in length, so I opt for a cautious four wood, the most reliable club in my bag. But stage fright seizes me on the tee, causing me to strangle the grip, which in turn produces a nasty pull-hook. The ball sails high and left over a long dune that separates the cart path from the fairway. I'm secretly embarrassed that Theodore, who could be my grandfather, is sitting pretty in the middle of the fairway while I'm off in the boonies. "You can play it from over there," the starter says. "But you won't like it." When it's Mike's turn to make a spectacle of himself, he produces a fierce, high-arcing slice that's a total goner. The ball lands deep in a disapproving bog, where it is incubating to this day. His hasty mulligan skitters through the tall grass into a scrag of flowering something or other, stage left. Mike comes back to the cart, heaves a philosophic sigh, and climbs in. "Tough start," he says.

"Tell me about it," I say. This truly is no way to begin the assault.

Robert is the caboose. He's got a high-tech driver, which he uses to good advantage. His ball sails metaphorically over his father's ball and lands nicely in the middle of the fairway. I formulate a theory that the length of Theodore's drive divided by the length of Robert's drive will yield a result that inversely replicates the equational relationship between their respective ages. Ergo: $L1/L2 = A2/A1$. This morsel of pure genius I keep to myself.

Luckily, my ball is readily accessible, albeit forlorn, on a long patch of packed sand referred to as waste area. But my recovery shot to the friendly confines of the fairway will be blind. Out comes the Mizuno MST seven wood with its neat little runners on the sole. I swing nice and easy, sending the ball dutifully toward the unseen hole. Theodore yells down to me. "Hunky-dory. Just a little bit short of the green." Hope rises. Spirits soar. All that remains are a brilliant theoretical wedge stiff to the pin, a hypothetical one-putt, and the delusionary par. Pure fiction. Instead, I hit a thin approach to the back of the green, snake a putt six feet past the hole, and luck in from there for a bogey. But it could be worse.

Robert and his dad ho-hum their way onto the same green in three, take two putts each, and consider themselves lucky. Theodore's game is like a beautiful symphony played at low volume. All the attributes are intact, although a bit less dynamic than they must have been in his prime. Still, it's fun to watch a guy who makes the most of his skills and seems to enjoy every shot.

Mike, meanwhile, has thrashed his ball from a nest of wildflowers, but the thing only squirms into a thatch of Johnson grass a few yards ahead. Doom descends. He assaults the ball with a wedge, and it jumps onto the fairway. Then a five wood into the greenside sand trap, from which he hits a thin squealer through the putting surface and into the rough. His chip is fluffy, and his downhill approach putt tumbles twenty feet past the hole. I can see that his eyes are now fixed and dilated. Finally, a decent lag and a perfunctory tap-in. Poor fellow.

"Okay," I say. "We're all warmed up. Now we can start."

Number two is a gorgeous par five requiring a tee shot that carries two water hazards and averts another to the left of the landing zone. We are all dry after our drives. *Mirabile dictu!* Some of us are wounded or disabled, but we are all dry. Theodore is out there 180 yards again, short but sitting pretty. I've hit a decent four wood into the center of the fairway, around 215 yards. I hike across the manicured fairway to where my ball resides, next to a sprinkler head. A heron, big as a ptero-dactyl, wings low across the fairway, not ten feet from where I stand congratulating myself for my pretty tee shot. This phenomenon so dis-tracts me that I top my five wood, which costs me about one hundred yards of distance. For the first, and conceivably the last time of the day, all four of us are on the short grass at the same time. We are at varying stages of disintegration, but we're all on mowed grass.

It's the second hole on a perfect day in the middle of June, and I'm standing on my fantasy course next to a breathtaking marsh, ocean waves breaking against the shore to my right, clouds actually scudding overhead. There's beer in my cart, and my partners are gentlemen. Somehow, in spite of this preoccupying euphoria, I feel obligated by duty to play as well as possible. But I'm just too damned happy. Bogeys will not bring me back to earth; I could even remain airborne with a couple of double bogeys in the cargo hold. I know I may never get another opportunity to play Pete Dye's painful masterpiece. I can either revel in my surroundings or bear down and play the shots. I decide to let my next shot settle the issue. My four iron fades high above the sentry oak and lands twenty feet from the flagstick. Robert is also on in regulation. Theodore has methodically hit his shots down the imaginary dotted line, finishing everything off with a lovely approach shot to within seven feet.

A birdie for yours truly. "Lovely stroke," Theodore says. "You're a putting fool." My approach putt has actually gone where I command it, and I'm suddenly back to even par. Theodore misses his short putt, Robert makes a good par, and Mike stops the bleeding with a decent bogey.

Our first real opportunity for conversation occurs on the tee at number four, where we are held up by the group ahead, who seem to have found Moses' wicker cradle in the bull rushes. But first a nice group photo. I pose everybody in front of a giant, man-eating clump of pampas grass. I set the self-timer, hit the button, and dash into their midst. We drape our arms over one another's shoulders as if we're old navy buddies on shore leave. The shutter clicks, and we are immortalized.

"Theodore, do you mind telling me how old you are?" I ask, after I've put all of my photograph gear away. "You don't have to. Just wondering."

"Well . . . " He pauses for dramatic effect. "How old do you *think* I am?"

"Seventy-five," I say.

This pleases him no end. His eyes twinkle and he chuckles. "Eighty-six."

I'm glad to have given him the chance to surprise me. Then he's off and running with his autobiography. The guy, it turns out, has played golf all over the planet, for sixty-five years. He's seen Walter Hagen and Bobby Jones and Byron Nelson and Sam Snead. He's witnessed Open Championships at Baltusrol and Winged Foot. And now his son has brought him down from Cooperstown, New York, to play the Ocean Course. As much as my own father loves the sport, I doubt he has ever played a truly great golf course, and I'm ashamed for that admission, seeing how much this old fellow is enjoying himself. This would have been a meaningful experience for Dad. I imagine him and me and Robert and Theodore going around together. A little father-and-son outing. But it's too late for that now, a realization that briefly bums me out. Theodore is having more fun than anybody, playing his game, watching the birds and the swimming shadows. We're all tiny characters moving back and forth across a luminous canvas, and the golf is merely an excuse for making our appearance. I wonder if Theodore is wondering how many more chances he will have and if that tempers or enhances his joy.

It is the seventeenth hole at the Ocean Course on Kiawah Island. Theodore's game has faltered, mostly because he is a little tired out by the sun and wind and heat. But he's still happy as a man can be and good-natured about his shortcomings. We've struck up a kind of friendship, and now that his game has dwindled he is fully invested in my fortunes. I decide to let the rest of my foursome in on the fact that I'm writing a book about golf in America. It's too late to manufacture false gentility or retract the sacreligious utterances that have emerged from time to time. We are all exactly who we are, and that's a fine thing. Mike has made a handful of ebullient pars and a few peculiar dinks into the estuarial no-man's-land. Robert, who seldom gets a chance to play much golf, has come through quite nicely. I am nine over par after sixteen holes, and I'm looking at a very wicked par three alongside an alligator pond in which a reptile as big as a Chevrolet is floating. Mike gives the monster something to chew on; until the ball splashes, I'm convinced that the sphere will actually bean the critter. Theodore and son occupy the same greenside bunker after their shots. Due to my double bogey at fifteen, I bring up the rear, but that's okay by me. My seven wood, from the instant I hit the thing, is glorious. The ball sails high above the pond until the wind catches it and tosses it onto the green, only ten feet from the hole.

Another birdie for Bill Hallberg, brave, strong of heart, lucky as hell. Big numbers for everybody else.

The last hole we play for beers. Winner buys. But it's bogeys all around, so we're all shifting for ourselves, or so it seems.

The table on the terrace overlooks the ocean and the intervening holes. A waitress arrives with eight Heinekens on a cork tray. Mike has graciously and surreptitiously footed the bill for our refreshments and will hear nothing from the rest of us about reimbursement. "My treat," he says.

We all look pretty baked and maybe even a bit tired. But we're basking in the aftermath of a glorious battle well fought. It is here, sitting around the table with my new friends, that I learn something that gives the whole day a deeper meaning than I could have thought possible.

"Say, Theodore," I ask, aware that beer has rearranged the molecules of my brain. "You play with a regular foursome in Cooperstown?"

His eyes seem a bit glassy as he ponders my question. He takes a healthy sip of beer. I like it that an eighty-six-year-old guy can still knock back a brewski when the situation calls for it. "Well, yes I do. But I'm moving down to Georgia in the fall. My wife died last month, and I probably shouldn't be alone . . ." That's as far as his voice will carry him. He takes a very shaky swallow of beer, and a bit of it trickles down his chin.

Robert takes over the conversation, perhaps sensing that there might be a big emotional scene in the offing. "We're looking at some assisted living facilities near Alpharetta. That way Dad can get all the help he needs and be close by at the same time."

"That sounds like a nice arrangement," I say. But I know that it's probably not a nice arrangement at all as much as a sad necessity.

I imagine Theodore playing golf in the autumn gloaming with his old pals on a pretty course in Cooperstown. Yellow leaves are dropping from the maples onto the shadowy fairways and greens. He's got one putt to make before he has to say good-bye to everybody for the last time. It's a ten-footer, but they give it to him. "It's good," they say. "Pick it up." But he won't pick it up. He hits the thing ten feet past the hole. Then again, hard past the hole. Over and over, refusing to make that last putt.

So this round of golf has been about *that*. An existential finality has underridden all the good cheer and banter, and I was unaware.

The subject changes to me, my book, my itinerary. Our favorite courses. Our favorite beers. Holes in one. But underneath it all is that throbbing reality.

The time has come to say our own good-byes. Mike, who underneath his white cap is pleasantly bald, must go back to the condominium for one more night of family high jinks before returning to work in Louisville. Robert and Theodore will travel up to Alpharetta,

Georgia, to investigate assisted living facilities. And I must hit the road for parts unknown.

We stand at the railing as if we were the Royal Family, survey the unconquered links before us, then shake hands. I give Theodore a manly hug and head toward the parking lot, where my clubs, no doubt, will be leaning against the trunk of my car, polished, buffed, and properly rearranged.

CHAPTER 2

the duke of earl

My plan, if you could call it a plan, has been to plunge south-ward from Charleston, through Georgia and on into Florida, where old men play out their days on Spanish moss courses with ball-stealing monkey squirrels and impact-resistant armadillos that roam the fairways for the mere heck of it. But forecasts from Florida indicate shamefully bad weather for at least a few days, and days are a commodity I can't afford to squander. I ponder alternatives in the shade of a live oak behind a 7-11. There's the adventurous option of braving the Florida weather in hopes of leaping through an unlikely but not inconceivable window of opportunity or heading northwestward to the Smokies of my home state to revisit the scene of crimes committed against the game of golf by me and my late beloved cohort David "Duke" Earl. I admit that I've been lost in a globe of my own inevitable mortality since having left Theodore and his son to themselves at Kiawah. Maybe there's something about being alone and far from home that provokes such thoughts, but I'm now beginning to imagine the years trailing out before me.

Heading into the Appalachians will likely scare up the ghost of my friend, but it's a happy ghost for sure and a worthy one. On the other hand, traipsing the same Floridian fairways abandoned by my dad and his old pals a few years back is a prospect that seems almost too wistful to bear.

Before my mother's illness, when she and Dad were snowbirding in Sarasota, I'd visit them from from time to time at their rented, pantiled condominium alongside a manatee lagoon. While there, I indulged in the obligatory golf games with my dad and his retired friends at Misty Creek Country Club. I did my best to be charming and funny in their presence so my dad would have something to be proud of. And his pals seemed to be fond of me. There was Jeff (ceramic hip and a bad ticker) from Kingston, Ontario, and George (triple bypass, diabetes) from Queens, New York, and David (chronic excruciating headaches) from Milwaukee, Wisconsin, and a variously wounded cast of characters who rounded out the foursome on any given day. I looked forward to the perennial rekindling of friendships with these lovely gents, and I grew to like them enormously. Dad kept them abreast of my latest publications, and when anything of mine saw the light of day they would hurry to the bookstore to buy copies for family and friends. I was known as Carl's son the writer. All this fuss and feathers was a source of pride for Dad, although it embarrassed me, especially when he'd get so caught up in the adulation that, as seen through his eyes, my infinitesimal impact on the American literary landscape placed me with the luminaries in the writers' pantheon. I doubt that Jeff and George and Dave quite accepted Dad's interpretation of my importance. However, they went along with it; after all, they'd been up and down the pike a few times themselves and understood how it was with fathers.

But now, time has worked its erosive ways with everyone. Jeff has had two major heart attacks and can no longer leave his home in Ontario. George died of a ruptured aneurism two years ago, David, blinded and paralyzed by a massive stroke, hovers on just this side of his own eternal fate . . . and, of course, my father can no longer make the trip.

No matter which interstate highway I use to escape the South, I'll find markers of my own foolish mortality. If I bypass Florida, hugging the Gulf Coast, I can follow I-10 through Mobile and Biloxi, where I honeymooned with Vicki, on through Louisiana, into the town of Covington, where I got hitched in a small Episcopal chapel by a one-eyed priest, then into Baton Rouge, where I spent my early married years and where my son was born. Or I can take that more tempting, only slightly less sentimental, northerly route to the heart of the land, halting for a few days in the Smokies, where Duke and I hung out in the careless euphoria of high-altitude golf.

A decision has been made. The Smoky Mountains of my home state beckon. Westward Ho it is! I take a swig of iced Coke from a Big Gulp paper cup, and push in the clutch.

I-26 angles out of Charleston, then connects one hundred miles later with I-95, which eventually intersects with I-40, which I will follow to the mountains of North Carolina.

It's U.S. Open weekend, and Father's Day is Sunday. I've found jars of indigenous black currant jam and marmalade and wild clover honey to honor the occasion, and these items I've mailed to him, although I suspect that his presents will arrive one day late. However, the card I found at South of the Border is probably waiting in his mailbox. I have little doubt that on his day, Dad will be ensconced in that leather easy chair, within knob-twiddling distance of the Magnavox, rooting for the Golden Bear to make another run at a major. I'd like to keep driving all the way to Bowling Green. I could park Iris at the far end of Clark Street, sneak into the house while the TV screen is filled with golf, and nonchalantly assume my customary place at the far end of the sofa. "So, Dad, who's on the leader board?" I'd ask.

I wonder if he'd recognize the novelty of this moment or whether it would be integrated into a world that vanished, unbeknownst to him, twenty-five years ago when I went off to college. Perhaps I'm underestimating his lucidity.

At nine o'clock on the outskirts of Raleigh, I'm beginning to feel the effects of a long, eventful day. Lo, another Motel 6 beckons from the roadside. *Economy! Economy!* It's a famous exclamation. But who said it? Was it Thoreau? Tom Bodett? Ross Perot? Quiet comfort is a major issue for me at present—atmosphere is a feeble consideration. What I need is a hot shower and a sturdy mattress.

An Australian couple has taken the only available nonsmoking room, so I settle on a chamber last occupied by Joe Camel. But after half an hour or so I easily acclimate myself to the faint cigarette smell. One minute I'm sprawled on my king-sized bed in an air-conditioned room with the TV tuned to a Braves game; the next I'm waking from my coma, during whose oblivious hours the Friday-night baseball game has transformed itself into a Saturday-morning cartoon program called "Pinky and the Brain." It's a funny show once I focus in, and I enjoy lying in the dim morning light like a total wastrel. If this motel had room service I'd avail myself: a silver pot of java maybe, with double cream and Guyanese Demerara sugar, along with a couple of succulent crumpets, a wedge of pomegranate, a flagon of juice wrung from corpulent kiwis. And a Pop-Tart.

I'm a notoriously early riser, but for some reason I can't get out of bed until the lure of a Denny's heart-attack breakfast overcomes me. Here there are Denny's restaurants galore, two within one mile of each other. Now *this* is my kind of town.

The shower feels the way a shower ought to feel, and I can discern the slackening of my roostered hair under the hot stream of water. I haven't thought about golf since last night, but for no particular reason, the accidental, irrelevant dropping of a dime on the carpet reminds me that I failed to include a penalty shot in my scoring of number seven at Kiawah. But I can live with this blight on my soul.

I tell myself to stop thinking about golf. Somehow, though, the very admonition reminds me that the third round of the U.S. Open is on TV this afternoon. Do I really need to spend hours behind the wheel today? Is there a compromise that will place me in the snug, smoky confines of a sports bar at tee-off time? My new idea, suddenly, is to have a big greasy Grand Slam breakfast at Denny's, then drive as far as Winston-Salem to watch the tournament in a smoky pit with other junkies like me. Afterward, when the day's last putt has been holed, I'll drive mountainward until dusk or until I chance upon a Kozy Kabin in the foothills. *Voilà!*

Winston-Salem seems a ripe candidate for a sports bar, although I recognize the possibility that a televised NASCAR race might take precedence over golf—even the U.S. Open. In fairness, there is always a reasonable chance of this in Dixie, where many children

are named after engine parts. A guy in a Talledega 500 T-shirt with
a Confederate belt buckle does *not* persuade easily, and arm
wrestling over TV dibs with Richard Petty's arch goober is not on my
"gotta-do" list . . . but I'll just have to take my chances.

A miracle occurs, however. In the throbbing heart of Burlington,
hard by a Chevrolet dealership, I see the sign: *HOT SHOTS.* A jock
saloon for sure. Iris obeys my command, and we're soon parked
alongside a raised outdoor beer garden, empty on account of the
afternoon heat.

To my cynical delight the bar inside is empty too, except for a one-
armed denizen who masterfully consumes what appears to be a
cheesesteak submarine and a boat of fries. The bartender is a
graduate of Gold's Gym and is good buddies with a tattoo artist. But
he's friendly enough. He recommends a good local microbrew, and
after having taken possession of a mug of this beer, I assume
squatter's rights at a tall table in front of a suspended Toshiba. Greg
Norman is just teeing off as I lower my tongue into the foam, an idiosyncratic approach, granted, to making acquaintance with alien
beers. The tournament is taking place on Oakland Hills just outside
Detroit, a golf course I played when I was young and limber and fearless. Immediately thereafter I developed a physical tic that included
cringing, bed-wetting, and the involuntary grasping of my skull. I'm
better now, but I feel for the golfers who must contend with that
course under pressures that would implode a ball bearing.

The shadow of Beelzebub hovers over Norman; the curse of the
house of Cadmus radiates from his surfer hair. I feel sorry for the
guy. He's one of my favorite players on the tour, due, maybe, to my
fondness for tragic heroes. I don't want him to suffer, but I know he
must. The sparrow has fallen from the sky, the curious disorder of
the bat's entrails upon the rock reveals the curse of inevitable fate.
Unfortunately, within me lives a gloomy inclination, to which I here
admit, and it revels in the downfall of the great. When the Shark's
lips tighten, when his eyes search the heavens for explanation, when
his footfall shakes the green earth beneath him, I'm secretly gratified
that there are unknowable cosmic forces at work.

A young man and his wife enter the bar, pause at the threshold,

and gaze disappointedly in my direction, as if maybe this is *their*
table. It is definitely the greenside seat. I give them a come-and-
join-me nod, and I gesture toward the empty high chairs at the table.
The etiquette of the sports bar commands togetherness, after all. The
man points toward my table. "These taken?"

They bring their beers to the table and scoot out the chairs so they
can climb aboard. Then we shake hands. After three unsuccessful
tries at getting me to understand his name correctly, he despairs of
me and writes it out on a cocktail napkin. The three of us, Mike
NECZY . . . etc., his wife, Kim, and yours truly, are now the nucleus
around which the odd molecularity of the sports bar will grow. "Is
Steve Jones still in the lead?" Mike asks.

A hard-core. Some fun. "Yeah. Lehman's up there, too, and
Faldo."

"Isn't Jones the guy that broke his back or fractured his skull—or
something like that?" Kim asks.

"Ruptured his anterior pterodactyl bone," I say. "And his sar-
cophagus. Riding a dune buggy or some such nonsense."

I recognize that we're not ready for the unsheathing of my rapier
wit. So I take a huge swallow of Copperline Lager.

The expected horde of golf aficionados does not arrive. There are
a few couples eating burger combos and shrimp-in-a-basket, but
they pay little attention to the golf. Meanwhile, although we are inca-
pable of curing our own myriad golfing ills, Mike and I have identi-
fied the factors behind Norman's tendency toward self-immolation.
Kim suggests we send him an anonymous letter.

I've been quite a thirsty golf watcher on this nice June afternoon
in the dark cool confines of Hot Shots. Mike has been every bit as
thirsty as I; we are both better irrigated than most country club fairways. Alas, the round is over, Norman has faded from the leader
board, and God is perched bemusedly in his heaven.

Rather than endanger the masses by weaving down the highway
in my salubrious state, I decide to take up lodging at the Econo-
Lodge around the corner. But first, a candid photograph of Kim and
Mike standing in front of this saloon. "Smile," I say, and they oblige.
Mike, in particular, has been obliging steadily for at least the last

hour. I am also obliging ear to ear. We are a most obliging trio, although Kim comes by her good cheer unaided by vast quantities of gusto. "Give her the keys," I say, and he obliges.

"Let's tee it up sometime," Mike says.

I tell him I'd really like that. We shake hands and hug like comrades from Mike's ancestral home. These are good folks, and I feel lucky for having bumped into them.

Never has an auto-owning Homo sapiens negotiated a fifty-yard journey with more care than I exhibit. I'm awaiting the total abandonment of this service road by the driving population before I attempt the ten-second voyage to the motel parking lot. The prospect of standing one-legged at the conspicuous roadside and touching my nose for a member of the Burlington constabulary is not something I yearn for, nor is the obvious pecuniary fallout associated with a DWI. Then there's the little matter of public safety. Kim honks her horn and laughs as she maneuvers her car past mine.

After transacting this jaunt and paying for my room, I haul my stuff inside and hunker down for a lazy evening of reading and TV watching. I even manage an hour or two of work on my journal.

My proclivity toward greeting the daily dawn kicks in on Sunday morning. Actually, I have to wait around for dawn to arrive, but that's okay. A hot shower, a jolt of motel coffee, a quick perusal of the Raleigh *News & Observer*, and I'm fully stoked for what proves to be a psychedelic sunrise, all pink and orange and plum purple. Given my early start, I should arrive in Boone by midmorning, at which time I can make arrangements to play golf on Monday after the weekend crush has subsided. Sunday golf is something I've religiously avoided since my teenage years, mostly because I'm philosophically averse to any round that takes longer than childbirth. I intend to hit the practice range this afternoon, watch the last round of the Open, window-shop in Boone, then drive to the summit of Mount Mitchell to watch the sun fall off the edge of the world.

My recent high-fat diet and general lack of exercise are suddenly a concern to me. Ergo, I dig my Nike Air running shoes out of the suitcase, along with gym shorts and a gray T-shirt. Minutes later I'm slob-jogging down the service road, past Hot Shots, past the car lot, past Arby's and Wendy's and Hardee's, past the visible decline of Western civilization. I run like a weary escaped convict with hounds on his heels. I run to expunge the myriad poisons from my bloodstream. I run to be fit. To become one with the universe. I do it to become *immortal*.

I opt for a sensible, low-fat breakfast instead of the self-indulgent high-cholesterol fare I've been packing away since I left home. I grab bagels and cream cheese from the grocery store shelves and a carton of orange juice and a granola bar. Now I'll live forever.

Bill Hallberg, exercised, properly nourished, commands the wheel of his fast-moving gray Plymouth Neon. He inventories his little world. Weather: sublime. Engine: purring. a/c: up and running. CD player: operating full-blast.

Natalie Merchant sings "These Days" on the stereo, a song that always makes me want to love somebody, particularly Natalie Merchant herself. I play the song three times in a row, like some sort of foolish teenager with a broken heart. But my heart is not broken; it swells with expectation.

A few years back I made this drive to the mountains, although I detoured down to Charlotte so I could pick up Duke at the airport in advance of the much ballyhooed, long-awaited weekend golf outing. Our scheme, in theory, was to spend a night in Highlands, then, come morning, play Wade Hampton Golf Club, eat lunch afterward, play the Palmer course at Cullasaja, drive up the Blue Ridge Parkway to Linville, spend the night, play Banner Elk in the morning, eat lunch, drive to Linville Ridge for an afternoon round, then bust it to Charlotte so my pal could catch a Sunday-night flight back to New York City. Seventy-two holes in two days. A dollar a hole with carryovers and double bops for birdies. A bold plan indeed.

My friendship with Duke Earl began soon after my novel, *The Rub of the Green,* was published in the late eighties. He phoned me from his *Golf Magazine* office in New York to tell me that he loved the book and wanted me to take on a few assignments, to which end he suggested I come up to the city for a couple of days so we could talk things over. A week later we were drinking ale together in McSorley's on 7th Street in Manhattan, laughing like a couple of fools until tears rolled down our cheeks. My imitation of Gary Player's golf swing after he's eaten tainted shrimp in a New Orleans restaurant was particularly well received. I was quite proud to be the only American performing that delightful piece of mimicry at the time. Duke told one dozen golf jokes in a row without breaking stride. Our effortless, sudsy friendship began right then and lasted until his sudden, unexpected death in Paris two summers ago.

Duke was an anomaly in the world of golf, from the gold star embedded in his front tooth (a leftover from his days as a rock 'n' roll guitarist) to his counterculture politics. He smoked cigars, used persimmon off the tee, and laughed out loud at anyone who missed a putt of less than three feet. He had an encyclopedic knowledge of golf and its history, and his love for the sport manifested itself in beautiful, intelligent prose.

Unfortunately, Duke was not the best at making travel arrangements. But from his point of view, the more disorganized and unpredictable our adventure was, the more fun we would have. "So, where are we staying tonight?" I asked him as we turned onto the Cullasaja road just past Franklin.

"Oh, uh, we'll find something," he said, flashing his What Me Worry? smile.

"You were going to take care of motel reservations, remember? Jesus-peezus, Duke," I said.

"Relax, Hallberg," he said. "You're too tense."

So we sweatered up and resigned ourselves to a night in the car, in a field, in the middle of nowhere, under a sky filled with real stars, not gold ones.

We played our golf the next day, and after a warm night in a comfortable Boone motel, we played again on the day following. It was a season when my game was sharp and my enthusiasm was keen. Duke would nearly always hit his high, fading drive down the center, pick up his cigar, and watch me hit mine farther but less predictably toward the target. Our betting game became more lavish and Byzantine as we neared the end of our golfers' holiday.

Finally, on the fifteenth hole at Linville Ridge, Duke, lying two already, bet me that he could ricochet his chip shot off a greenside boulder and still make par. I gladly took the bet and doubled it. He set his cigar in the grass and, with no practice swing at all, hit a high, arcing beauty that landed directly on top of the boulder, made a grandiose vertical leap, then descended onto the brow of that same chunk of granite. The ball kicked directly toward the hole and stopped four feet from the cup. "That one's going to cost you big money, Hallberg," he said.

"You son of a bitch," I said. But there it was, the absolute finest shot in the history of golf. Duke's roaring laugh carried across the fairways. He was standing in the frail, late-afternoon light, leaning on his wedge as if it were a jaunty cane, his gold star smile catching the sun. That's how I'll remember Duke Earl. At that moment, at that time of life, in that way.

Boone is a nice college town with shops selling crystals and incense and discounted name-brand clothing. The pine-flanked post office across the street is a stone building where I buy a dozen stamps for the postcards I've purchased at a little store whose inventory includes bongs and lava lamps. My noonday arrival gives me a chance to gambol through the town, striking manly poses at those strategic moments when pretty coeds frequent the same sidewalk. I feel pathetic, almost pederastical, watching the way they move inside their baggy clothes. Somehow, though, I prefer the grungy ones to the immaculate Chi Omegas. I smile my sad caballero smile at these pierced, tattooed, green-haired specimens. I pause at storefront windows when they pass, as if I've just remembered a line from "The Waste Land." I suck in my gut and flex my irresistible buttocks. But I'm a mere fire hydrant, a parking meter, a chalkboard menu promoting inedible fare.

Enough of Boone with its unattainable women. Time avails itself, so I retrieve Iris from the community parking lot and drive out of town. The mountains are rife with kountry kraft stores selling whirligigs and gee-haw whimmy diddles. It's possible to buy fresh mountain honey in Mason jars and black currant jam hermetically sealed beneath paraffin plugs. At least a dozen log-cabin manufacturers dot the highway between Boone and Linville, my destination. It's hard to imagine how beautiful this terrain would be without all this squalid papoonery.

Just outside of Spruce Pine, I nearly tool past a hand-painted roadside placard: HILLSIDE GOLF. FAMILY FUN. I turn around in the driveway of a Baptist church and backtrack to the gravel road where the black arrow directs me up a slope.

Another little sign, this one nailed to a tree just where a tributary of the gravel road splits off to the right. I crunch up this tiny lane until I reach a gravel parking lot framed by fallen tree trunks and a split-rail fence. Off to the right is a house trailer featuring a white flag hanging from a bracket affixed to the door frame. On the flag is a yellow golf ball on an orange tee.

An ill-looking man in shorts is standing maybe twenty yards from this edifice, and he's whacking scruffy golf balls toward one of several telephone poles transecting the pasture before him. His swing is unlike anything I've ever seen. "You the proprietor?" I ask.

The man pauses and squints at me through very thick glasses. "He's out there mowing."

"Out there" is the rolling pastureland, upon which, unless I'm hallucinating, are a series of ovoid surfaces vaguely resembling golf greens. I excuse myself and race back to my car for the camera. This is the subterranean world I've been hoping to discover.

Indeed, dotted throughout the clover field are golf greens hardly bigger than those ubiquitous handmade quilts hanging from ropes in front of every roadside stand. There are red flags on poles in the exact geographical center of every green. Here and there are small, built-up AstroTurf platforms with hand-painted signs pounded into the ground. #1! #4!

It's a perfect day at the height of tourist season and a Sunday to boot. Yet the place is deserted, except for a flannel-shirted guy inching across the landscape on a riding mower. He must feel quite dejected to have created this humble little golf course with the sweat of his brow, only to discover that although he built it, nobody came.

I wander up the hill over to where he's parked his Toro. "Hello," I say, and give him a happy grin. My camera feels like a shamefully exposed appendage, and I'm embarrassed to be seen with the thing hanging around my neck. "How are you doing?" There he is, flalloping around on the landscape of his own disillusionment, and I'm here to record it with my extra-crisp Zeiss close-up lens. What a crass opportunist I am.

"Can I help you?" he asks.

"Well, I saw your sign a minute ago as I was driving by, you know. So I just thought . . ."

I'm a human being, a living, breathing corporeal entity, and I have taken the time to inquire about his project. "Name's Buck McCallister," he says. "Oh . . . hang on for a sec, will ya?" I watch him dip his coarse, ungloved hand into a fifty-pound sack of malathion and sprinkle these highly toxic granules on the ant mounds that dot the green. "There!" he says, and claps his hands together as if he were a baker and this was merely unbleached flower clinging to his skin. "What can I help you with?"

I tell him what I'm up to, and he launches into an account of how he retired from the California aircraft industry to return home to these mountains. He tells me how he bought out his brother's share of a twelve-acre inheritance so he could put his lifelong dream into action. So far it wasn't working out so well. If he has to, he'll just lease the property for grazing. He's made a dozen holes in one on his own course and more birdies than he can count. "Lot of guys come here after work," he says. "That's where I get most of my business. But it's been a struggle. I admit it."

I take his picture next to the number five flag. I get a shot of him raking the little bathtub-sized sand trap. Finally, he mounts his mower and I take one last photograph of him gazing optimistically toward his mobile home. Then we shake hands and say good-bye.

Here is a guy doing exactly what he wants to do. Family Fun. Hillside Golf. And yet, instead of feeling happy for him, I drive back down the gravel road feeling a little sorry for the guy. I wish that I had time to play a round of golf on the little course, even though the impact of my wedge on the unyielding AstroTurf tees would abrade the chrome from the sole of the club. I want to validate his faith, but

I can't. I stop at a trickling stream emerging from a corrugated pipe and wash off the malathion.

A handsome, carved Linville Ridge sign supported by stone pillars appears at the roadside just a few miles past Buck McCallister's humble golf course on Highway 221. I drive up the paved road, which meanders past granite gates and massive flower beds and mailboxes replicating the houses in front of which they stand sentinel. After stationing Iris in an empty parking place outside the clubhouse, I stroll down a flagstone walkway to the pro shop. Bill, the club professional, remembers me from a few years back, or says he does, and when I give him the particulars of my mission, he generously agrees to let me play the course in the morning, free of charge. It's a truly beautiful layout and the most altitudinous course east of the Rockies. Frankly, I'm not sure what I would have done in the event of his turning me away, although I envision a minor, ex officio golfing adventure beginning and ending beyond the ken of the power structure. "I'll put you with some PGA guys who are teeing off at eight-thirty. That okay with you?"

"Sure thing," I say, and thank him. I consider the prospect of going round the course with a trio of scratch golfers who resent my shabby game and wish me ill. I secretly vow to play like a god tomorrow, thus winning them over completely. They'll buy me lunch in the clubhouse and name their children after me.

I find myself driving twenty-five miles back to Boone, mostly because I've remembered the Japanese steak house on the bypass. The Mikado. The grill-side eating arrangement promotes conviviality, and I'm feeling sort of isolated from the world at the moment.

I hold up one lonely finger when the hostess greets me at the door. "Only *one*?" she says. "Okay, sir, follow me."

I sit at a table occupied by members of what I can only guess is a women's soccer team. It's either that or a battered wives' club. They're all drinking Asahi beer, so I order one for myself, hoping to thus ingratiate myself. My subtle beer-bottle-down-the-hatch salute goes unnoticed. Their collective karma, something like a zone defense, is impenetrable, and I shrink into my own little bunker while shrimp fly end over end into our personal chef's corrugated hat.

Come morning I'm once again eating bagels and cream cheese. There's a three-day supply by my reckoning, but that's okay by me. I can just loll around this room in the comfy Best Western motel and smack my lips if I please.

Linville Ridge actually has a shoe room where members and guests can slip out of their New and Lingwood loafers into Gucci soft spikes. A young man, sensing that my fingers have made contact with the plastic lace-tips of my Rockport Striders, escorts me from the parking lot to the aforementioned Shoe Room, thereby averting a scandalous situation. Fine by me. A free round of golf. Who am I to complain about such details?

The young assistant pro behind the glass counter gives me a key to an electric cart and points to the driving range. "You can warm up if you like. Hit till you're happy," she says.

The rising sun illuminates a monstrous hotel atop Grandfather Mountain, high above the driving range. It is a blight of unimaginable proportions. How that thing slipped past Earth First! and the Sierra Club is beyond my comprehension. Even a chicken liver like me might have chained his carcass to a backhoe if it meant preserving what would otherwise have been one of the most magnificent spots in all of the Smokies.

Perhaps the anger and depression wrought in me by this ugly building is the primary explanation for the stranglehold I have on the grip of my wedge when I toe the first immaculate range ball into position. Whatever the reason, my inaugural shot is a shank, a sidewinder, a nonsequitur. This is a very bad omen. *Relax,* I tell myself. *Not so steep.* But my next shot is also right of right. Duke Earl would be howling with laughter right now.

In minutes the two pros from Dover will join me here on the range, and I will be revealed as a hacker. The more anxious I become, the more the symptoms ingrain themselves. I need quaaludes with a

Prozac chaser. A lobotomy and a vasectomy. I press a tee into the ground just an inch or so outside the golf ball. My goal is to hit the ball while leaving the tee in place. This, at last, I accomplish. Then again. Until my confidence finally returns, my pulse slows to normal, and I regain cruising altitude.

John and Art show up ten minutes later, just as I'm toweling the wet grass from my irons. "Hey, Bill," Art says. "This is John." I shake hands with both of them, and we chitchat about the weather and the beautiful terrain before us. "You played here before?" John asks. He's a trim, nice-looking fellow with glasses.

"A few years back," I tell him.

"We're counting on you to keep us on the straight and narrow then," Art says.

I watch them hit a few iron shots, expecting to witness a sort of clinic on proper tempo and swing plane. In fact, John has a very good swing. Art, a large crew-cut guy, is crooked off the tee, yet brutally long. He chunks his first few shots, though, and quite a few thereafter. My heart leaps with joy.

"So . . . you guys are PGA pros?" I ask.

They both get a good laugh out of that. "Do we *look* like PGA material to you?" Art says, and hits another one fat.

We're three jolly goofs, carting to the first dewy tee, beyond the mammoth stainless-steel sculpture of a golf club inverted and rammed shaft-first into the earth by the hand of God. The first fairway is silvered over with dew, and the sun is in our eyes. We take turns watching each other's drives sail into the blinding horizon. Mine is dead center, a miraculous outcome considering how nervous I am. Art's first ball is a lawn ornament for the big Tudor house surrounded by impatiens and zinnias. The shot is so thoroughly off course that Art doesn't even ask for a mulligan. He tees up another ball and off it goes, into the trees, but in play. "Beautiful, Art. Just beautiful," Art mutters. Golfers tend to address themselves in the third person, maybe because they prefer not to share the same skin with people who hit balls into flower beds. John belts a long drive into the wet rough on the left side of the fairway. Not quite pride-bending enough to merit a reprise. And . . . we're off!

* * *

Art is a professor of education at Appalachian State here in Boone, and John manages a public golf course just outside of Boone. How they were transformed into PGA professionals by the Linville Ridge staff is beyond our comprehension, but I'm so thoroughly grateful for the error that my mood is buoyant enough to keep my game afloat. At least through the front side.

It is over beers at the turn when I discover that both men are boomers like me, single through circumstance, and at opposite sides of the political spectrum. Art hunkered down in a Catholic seminary during the Vietnam War, adopted the guise of a priest-in-the-making, subverted the dominant paradigm like so many young men of his generation, and grew into a gentle academician with an unruly golf swing. John prefers not to discuss politics, but I gather he's at the other end of the teeter-totter from his pal. We all love our beer, though, and we all love our golf. *Salut!* We're shuffling out of the snack bar when we see former Miami Dolphins football coach Don Shula at the head of a table filled with Shulas of all ages. It would be crass and impolite to hit him up for an autograph, but I nod toward him as I pass, and he nods back. Hey, it was a *moment*.

Everything from here to the coast is down below. It all tumbles away to the east. And there are some shots on this course that, if you overclub them just slightly, will cause the ball to bound all the way to Ocracoke. The course is heart-stopping at times, especially when the green hangs just beneath the sky. Duke loved this course, maybe because we were both on our games that afternoon a few years back, all even in our betting, drunk on the whole idea of golf and friendship.

I'd like to say that I've been in contact with Duke's spirit throughout the round thus far, but it's not the truth. My mind has been on my game, which surprises me. All in all, I've played well, with only one half shank to apologize for. Art, despite his erratic play, has been a joyful companion, and John's wry cynicism is a good counterbalance to his partner's abounding zeal.

Unfortunately, my recollection of that round with Duke is too muddled, perhaps by all the beer we drank on that day, or the beer I've drunk today, or by the simple passage of time. Except for a few

fleeting echoes, I can't seem to summon him from the hemlocks and
maples.

But in the tree-lined tunnel between the fourteenth green and the
infamous ricochet hole, I hear his voice so clearly that I stop the
cart. And the voice says, "God, Bill. Ain't it *great*?"

Then, when Art and John and I emerge from the trees, we see
that the fifteenth hole is completely dismantled. The fairway has
been stripped bare, and the green, which is just a pile of gravel,
has been relocated farther down the slope, most likely to accommodate the whim of some sorry clubhouse faction who couldn't hit the
hole in regulation. Damn them, neither could I, but there's virtue in
striving for the unachievable, or so I've told myself at the end of every
cursed round for my entire life. *Nothing* of the original hole Duke and
I played remains. "Man, will you look at that?" I say.

"Pars for everybody?" Art proposes.

"Sounds good to me," John says.

They zoom on ahead to the sixteenth tee, but I linger for a minute
or two, watching men in hard hats maneuver big yellow machines
back and forth across the muddy incline. My chest hurts, and my
jaws begin to ache. I'm trying to extract the poetry from the irony
here, but it's a painful task, believe me. Somehow, though, I can't
seem to abandon the place just yet because I sense the presence of
my friend. I can even smell the smoke from his Garcia Y Vega cigar.

The Duke of Earl has been hiding from me all day long. The bastard. But what did I really expect, after all? That he would meet me
in the clubhouse bar for a commemorative beer? Or concede me my
tap-in at eighteen? Frail hope, indeed. Then I realize, of course, that
what is lost is lost forever, as every golfer knows. Lost as surely as a
ball in the ocean. My pilgrimage has been a vacant exercise finally,
born of wistful longing for something past recovery.

Or so I tell myself . . . until I see him there, sitting on that jutting
piece of granite just above the scar in the hillside, smoke curling
from his stogie, gazing at the limitless trees and mountain peaks. I
ease up the cart path toward the yellow boulder, closer, closer,
riding the accelerator like an artist. I'm finally near enough to see
that the figure is not my friend at all, but a working stiff in a hard

hat, smoking a cigarette, scrutinizing what is most likely a topo-map of the construction zone. But it's okay. It's just as well . . .

I'm even glad he's only an anonymous guy like me. And pleased, upon reflection, that the tee, the fairway, the green, that all of it has been so thoroughly transformed. The *original*, the magical hole where Duke made his killing, will exist forever unaltered in my imagination, and Duke's laugh will echo against the trees for all eternity. That's plenty good enough for me.

CHAPTER 3

black and white
and green

I've driven only as far as Waynesville tonight because I'm not
ready to be weened from the bosom of my home-state mountains.
There's a Comfort Inn just north of town, on the Maggie Valley
Road. I can be found at poolside, fondling a contraband double dose
of Schaefer beer (cleverly concealed in a Big Gulp cup), taking
furtive sips of the cold, tongue-biting brew. My arms and legs, as
seen in the mothy halogen lamplight, are the color of red Georgia
clay, while my belly and feet are more akin to Carolina beach sand. I
look like a two-tone Edsel. In the swimming pool, a girl about ten
years old is playing a game called "Shark!" with her water-winged
kid brother. The rules of the game require that the little fellow
splash as best he can across the pool, cognizant that at any moment
his sister will rise from the depths and bump his abdomen with her
skull, at which point he must scream "Shark!" (This is a variation on
the game called "Pickerel!" we culturally deprived Ohio kids played
growing up.) Anyhow, it's a fascinating thing to watch, and the rules
seem pretty easy to follow. A very heavyset woman whose legs are
even whiter than my belly is supervising the aquarian activities,
although her gaze falls more than occasionally upon me, as if at any
minute I will be offering felonious candy to her treasures.

The children in the pool make me wish I could reel in Garth and
Rachel, whose far-flung summer activities will preoccupy them until
my return from this quest. I miss my kids a lot, and I feel selfish for
having ditched them in favor of this adventure, but they claim they'll

be just fine, and they're rooting for me to bring home the bacon.
Garth is in Governor's School, a residential study program for brainy
teenagers located in Winston-Salem. Rachel is at Camp Cheerio for
a few weeks, kayaking, Indian-style canoeing, riding the obligatory
zip line, studying Indian lore, creating art from indigenous stones
. . . then she's off to her maternal grandmother's house for the balance of her exile. I'll try to phone my kids again tonight, but reach-
ing them is, I've discovered, no easy task. Instead, I leave messages
with various functionaries, write letters, jot cryptic notes on postcards: *"I did not stay here." "You never sausage a place." "I had a
date with this ski bunny."*

Inertia has a major hold on me for the moment. It's nice sitting
here at the cusp of night with the black mountain peak looming
against the ashen sky. When the kids aren't splashing, you can hear
crows laughing over in the community garden. Spending a couple of
easy days here on the brink of the Appalachians is a real temptation.
However, I *will be* strong in my resolve to push on! " 'Scuse me while
I gird my loins." "Hand me that pitching wedge will ya?" Off I will
go, *toute de suite,* into the wild green yonder.

Okay, a confession is in the offing. I'm nervous about my next stop
because I'm so very, very white. I am the detestable crème inside the
much-maligned Oreo cookie, and I'm going to Atlanta, Georgia,
"The City Too Busy to Hate," to juxtapose my honky sensibility with
the African-American mind-set. In other words, I intend to seek out
a venue where *I* am the minority element in this game of golf, which,
if it weren't so green, would be blinding white. I will, in a four-hour
time frame, and within the meager boundaries of a single round of
golf, arrive at profoundly definitive conclusions regarding the subtle
but meaningful distinctions between the black man's golfing experience versus that of his white counterpart—i.e., yours truly. Either
that or I'll have a helluva grand time with some guys who have a lot
more melanin than I do.

I live in Jesse Helms country, where Bill Clinton is a Commie
traitor and a drug runner and a threat to our American way of life.
Jesse is a patriot hero, protecting us from homosexuals and liberals
and secular humanists and welfare scum. Pickup trucks equipped
with gun racks and Confederate license plates and IMPEACH HILLARY

bumper stickers rule the road, while tobacco and kudzu hold dominion over the surrounding countryside. Continuing our tour of Down East, you might note the myriad species of Baptist churches coexisting in this neck of the woods: Southern, Primitive, Reformed, Missionary, Free Will, Southern Primitive Reformed Missionary Free Will . . . and every permutation in between. In the Midwest, where I was raised, African-Americans pretty much confined themselves to the big cities. I arrived at this astonishing, wide-sweeping conclusion by observing a quarter-mile section of an Ohio bean field and, seeing no black faces during my ten-minute observation period, concluded that farmers of color are a rarity in this vast agricultural region. Around then, I also went to Detroit a few times to see the Tigers play, and I saw a lot of black folks. Thus, I'm pretty confident of my opinion on racial demographics. On the other hand, integration in the Carolinas is achieved on a kind of patchwork basis. Streets and blocks rather than 'hoods and ghettos, as far as I can tell. Generally, life goes amicably forward in this fashion. Blacks and whites joyfully participate together in high school sports, in softball leagues, in double sculls rowing competitions and wine-tasting seminars.

Golf, on the other hand, is a whole different bag of shag balls. With only a few exceptions, country clubs are completely white, or very nearly so. No black man or woman would be turned away at the gate if a member were to extend an invitation for a round of golf, but the more modest public courses in small rural towns and big cities are the habitat of the African-American golfer in the South.

I claim that my failure to join one of the local country clubs is based on principles of rectitude and virtue, but that's never been put to the test because I can't afford the initiation fee, let alone the dues. So my smug morality bears scrutiny, most of all by me.

About Atlanta I know very little. Just the pre-Olympic hype about billion-dollar construction projects and the sprucing up of tourist sites like that big subterranean shopping zone. My instincts tell me that there are sections of this city where African-American golfers have their own courses.

I could be totally adrift on this notion, but I sense it with my keen socioethnic nose. So tomorrow I'm driving to Atlanta in quest of a golf course where *brothers* rule the fairways and where albinos like me are as rare as speckled owls.

When I dial the number that theoretically activates the hall phone in Garth's dormitory, the line is busy, as it has been for the last one hundred forty-four hours. Meanwhile, Camp Cheerio's phone is nailed to a tree on a deserted island in the middle of Lake Wenowakahacheekagonawa. Only after I've let the thing ring four score and seven times do I despair of the whole mad idea of speaking with my daughter before many moons have passed. My girlfriend Gillian, on the other hand, picks up right away. She's glad to hear from me but sad to report that my cable has been disconnected on account of nonpayment. She's, however, bailed me out once again, and it's now possible to watch programs about King Tut and Machu Picchuan llamas. She wishes I were home. She misses me. I tell her I must kill many buffalo before I return to teepee. She is heap sad. Squaw a little bit pissed, too, that me let cable bill go past due.

I hit the sack at eleven-thirty, wondering if I should have checked in on Dad. Or Mom. Or my sister Julie. Or any other of the infirm. There's always the possibility of receiving upsetting news when I speak with them. Somebody has taken a fall, one of them has a new dire symptom, Dad has gone exploring and nobody quite knows where he is. I feel guilty for the omission, and my sleep is troubled by shame.

It takes many cups of Denny's coffee to get me up and running in the morning. The poor waitress doesn't even ask anymore if I want a refill. I'm just a regular stop along the way for her. Little does she know, but her tip will be *mucho generoso*, and there will be wild rejoicing hours from now when she returns home to inform her little family that Baby Lou can get that operation after all.

At the Georgia border are a bevy of carryout liquor stores. I know I've drunk too much beer in the past few days, and I commit myself

anew to abstinence in order to regain some of my mental acuity. Iris
slows momentarily as we roll through this zone of temptation, but I'm
Brett Strongheart, full of resolve and weak coffee. One orphaned can
of Schaefer rolls back and forth in the Igloo, a rebuke for all my
recent self-indulgence.

The mountains are a thing of the past now. Air is thick and hot
and humid. Pines have replaced the maple and hemlock trees so
abundant in the high Appalachian forests. The towns are more tuned
to the local mind-set than the resort communities of the Smokies
with their specialty shops and B & Bs and art galleries and workout
gyms. Here in Georgia, a few miles above the junction with the interstate, you can find Seed n' Feeds and IGAs and old hardware stores
with brooms and scythes and hog troughs on display out front. The
noteworthy new dimension of this scene is the presence of black
people on the sidewalks. The atmosphere reminds me of my own
town on the Pamlico Sound, and I take comfort in the familiarity.

I'm beginning to resent the interstate highway system. The driving
is soulless and boring, so much so that no particular CD, no selection from my Books on Tape inventory, nor any wild sexual fantasies
from my extensive mental gallery can compensate for the tedious,
never-ending thump of expansion joints passing beneath the car. I
just want to hurry down I-895 to Atlanta so I can begin the process
of interjecting myself into the subculture.

Atlanta, like Kiawah, starts long before it begins. In this case
there are factories and industries of every dimension and every conceivable level of ecological affrontery. Always in the distance, never
nearer, is the skyline of this city, ballyhooed on hundreds of billboards, most of them featuring Olympic themes. I can't help wondering what will happen after the frantic preparation for the games is
over, when the last eight-dollar julep has been consumed and all the
leftover Izzy dolls have been burned.

Finally, in Atlanta, satiated by a cheese Whopper and a Coke, I
cross the restaurant parking lot to the bank next door. An equation
blinks in my brain: *Banker = Golf. Golf = Banker.* An armed guard
opens the door for me and smiles. (This *is* the big city!) Do my eyes
deceive me, or is that not a young black woman working away inside

a small glass office at the far corner of the bank? I need only ask *her* where Atlanta's black population plays its golf. She will tell me, and I will go there. That's how simple the issue is, as I see it.

I knock softly on her doorjamb, and she looks up from her paperwork, smiles politely, and asks if she can help me.

"Well, I've got a good one for you." (Huge disarming smile here.) "I'm doing a book about golf in America, and I'm trying to find a golf course whose clientele is black. Public, private. Doesn't matter."

"Let me understand you. You mean a *blacks-only* golf course!" she says. "A course where *only* blacks can play?"

Time to backtrack. "Not *exclusively* blacks. Just mostly. Or almost mostly. You know . . ."

"You mind telling me why you're looking for a black golf course? You don't look black to me, honey."

I want to tell her that my grandparents came over on slave ships. That my name is Kunta Kinte, that I can slam-dunk, that I dig Snoop. "I'm exploring the American golfing experience," I say, "and obviously . . ."

"And you need to play golf with some black folks to round it out. That it?"

"Well, uh," I say. She's figured me out in no time flat. Here I am, the blue-eyed son of Vikings, and I'm just sort of wondering if I might do this little hit-and-run experiment with some black linksters who happen to have adopted whitey's game.

"Tell you what," she says. "Here's a phone book. There's an empty desk. Let your fingers do the walking. If I was you, I'd call the Chamber first. They might could help you out. But, as for me, you're talking to the *wrong* source. I don't know a *thing* about golf."

A lady at the Chamber of Commerce hands me off to a subordinate, who in turn suggests that I go toward Stone Mountain. He is pretty sure I'll find what I'm looking for there. Very sure.

A plan of attack takes shape in my white man's brain: I shall seek this mountain of stone, locate an indigenous banker bearing proper markings and characteristics, then schmooze with this banker until he yields up desired information, i.e., where in this baking metropolis does one find a course (public or private) frequented (primarily, exclusively) by dark-pigmented human beings?

Eastward I go on the busy inner-city highway, following signs to Stone Mountain. Finally, I swerve onto an exit ramp, which deposits me on Industrial Parkway. I turn right, as I must, and immediately I spy a bank into which go, and out of which come, *African-Americans*! Hosanna in the highest!

This has been *une pièce de gateau* so far, if a bit awkward. After parking Iris as near as possible to the glass front door of the First Bank of Atlanta, I check my complexion one last time in the rearview to make sure I'm still a white guy, then hop out of the car and enter through said front door.

Everybody working in this place is black. And female. All of the bank officers are busy with clients, so I wait in a line behind a very thin guy with two canvas bags filled with change. Foolishly, I assume that the coins are denominated and wrapped. But when his turn comes he opens the drawstring throats of the bags and pours out enough coins to buy a thousand-year supply of fluorescent condoms. This is *not* working out as planned, so I search the lobby, hoping to spy an officer who isn't busy with a customer. No cigar. I stay put, though, because this teller looks friendly and I may earn some points for showing patience. I forge a mask of tranquillity and watch as the two of them, bank teller and numismatist, sort through the change. Ten minutes later she's forking over a dozen twenty-dollar bills.

"Help you?" she asks me after the skinny guy has split the scene.

"I'm looking for a public golf course, please. One where African-Americans play." My expectations, I know, have become ever more ambiguous. Soon I will be asking for a golf course where a black guy might have played once.

"Oh . . . you want Browns Mill. That's what you want. Know how to get there?"

"Not a clue," I tell her, but I'm ebullient.

"Easy as pie. Get back on 85 and go right through Atlanta heading south. Okay? After the airport, start looking for the Cleveland Avenue exit. Take that until you get to Browns Mill Road. Take a left and you're right on top of it. My daddy plays golf there."

"Bless you," I say. "Thank you *so* much."

"Good luck," she says, and smiles a beautiful gold smile.

My evening's lodging shall remain a mystery, except to say that I've been in a kind of rut lately. I can tell you that the room is clean and comfortable and dirt cheap. Many trucks are parked lengthwise out by the chain-link fence. There is no bidet in this room nor is there an Edwardian phone with a sterling mouthpiece. No mint under the pillow. No *New York Times* will be folded outside the door in the morning. That should give you a hint. But my lips are sealed.

The best news is that, at last, I've made contact with my son. It was a total fluke, but he happened to pick up the ringing phone as he was heading out to the dining hall. We talked for ten minutes, at which point he said that he would be late for chow if he didn't get a move on, so I told him I loved him a lot and gave him an exact time and date when I would phone again. During our brief chat, I learned that he's gotten heavily into Ginsberg and Kesey. I also think maybe he's found love there on the grounds of Old Salem. Lucky boy.

That I've troubled over what to wear to my rendezvous is an embarrassing admission. My abundant soulfulness will just have to speak for itself, unaided by emblems of liberal solidarity. (No X hats for *this* guy, and no color coordinating with the flag of the African National Congress, either.) I select khaki slacks and a black polo shirt. If there's a message implied in that combination, it's too subliminal, even for me.

It's only a ten-minute drive down the interstate to the Cleveland Avenue exit and only a few miles from there to the Browns Mill section of the city, where I stop at a 7–11 to get a cup of coffee. It's a warm, sunny morning, and I'm well rested and generally in love with the world. The golf course is visible on the other side of a barbed-wire chain-link fence and the players I see out there are indeed African-American.

The neighborhood here is shady and bustling but disorderly and strewn with trash of every description. Car axles, Pampers, stereo turntables, pizza boxes, empty bottles of Wild Irish Rose. The buildings flanking the convenience store are boarded up, and metal bars cover the windows of the few businesses that manage to stay afloat. I'm not shocked by what I see here; it's not much different from scenes I've encountered in my own town. You get a sense, however, that around this corner is a similar scene, and around that corner, and the next, until you come back to the same storefront and begin again. There are a thousand similar blocks in this city, though, with a million young men drinking beer at eight o'clock in the morning. Golf seems such an obscenity at the moment, and I'm embarrassed to be so conspicuously dressed for that purpose. There are young men squatting against the storefront, drinking from cans concealed inside paper bags. (Apparently, nobody's ever clued them in on the Big Gulp ruse.) But they're friendly when I tell them good morning, and I'm sure I could bum a cigarette if I asked them.

The presence of a white guy roaming the aisles of a neighborhood store like this is not a total novelty, I gather, but I sense that I'm at least unusual. Maybe it's because I'm so out of place, or in spite of that, or maybe because these people are inherently pleasant . . . for whatever reason, almost everybody smiles at me and says "good morning." A guy even slimmer than the Stone Mountain coin man stands next to me at the Bunn-O-matic coffee machine, and we're taking turns grabbing packets of sugar from a stainless-steel bin. "I need some jet fuel," I tell him.

"I hear ya," he says, and hands me an extra sugar, just in case.

The checkout clerk operates from behind a bulletproof shield plastered with notices: WE ACCEPT WIC, FDC, FOOD STAMPS. NO PERSONAL CHECKS ACCEPTED. NO CREDIT ACCEPTED. CLERK CANNOT OPEN SAFE. I can barely see her on account of the hand-printed admonitions. She grins when I shove a fifty-dollar bill through the little mouse tunnel where cash transactions occur. (There's a separate hole for coupons.) "You got anything larger than a fifty?" she laughs.

"I can give you quarters and dimes," I say.

"No problem," she says. "This is fine," and very surreptitiously, very observantly, slides my change through the hole. "I'd spend that quick if I was you," she tells me. It's a code I can't quite penetrate, but I sense that it's a kind of friendly warning.

There's a nice spot beneath a tree in the Browns Mill Golf Course parking lot, and it's there that I eat my cheese crackers and sip my hyperglycemic coffee. I watch golfers, most of them black, pull in, open the trunks of their cars, extract clubs and coolers and assorted golf accoutrements, then sit on the railroad ties to lace up their spikes. Honestly, I'm just a little bit disappointed not to be the only Caucasoid on the scene, but if this is the way it is, this is the way it is.

I transform my blatant honky face into something more boldly cosmopolitan and shamble to the pro shop to see about imposing myself on somebody's fun. There's a young black fellow operating the cash register, and he's announcing tee-off times into a microphone connected to a loudspeaker out by the putting green. "Good morning," he says. "You have a time already?"

"Well, no I don't. I was hoping you could work me in with a twosome or a threesome. That sound like a possibility?"

"Shouldn't be no problem at all."

"Do you suppose you could put me with some golfers who are, uh, *black*? It's a long story, actually, but if you could . . ."

"Lemme see what we've got out there," he says, and runs his finger down a column of names. "Hmmm . . . hmmmm . . . hmmmmm." Then he presses a red button on the microphone and informs one of the groups below that they've got company. "All set, if you don't mind a threesome," he says, "but you'd better kick it in gear because they're already on the tee." I thank him profusely, pay him the modest greens fee, and shake his powerful mitt, an act that causes a mysterious metacarpal crunching sound. He tells me to have fun out there. Then I dash across the parking lot to get my golf bag and shoes from the trunk of the car. In my sophomoric brain I manufacture a song that goes to the tune of "Marching to Pretoria." I hum it softly as I lace up my shoes: "I am golfing with some *black* guys, some *black* guys, some *black* guys . . . la la la." My nervousness has apparently tweaked the latent dunce in me.

They are sitting on the bench at the first tee, watching the group ahead hit their second shots toward the first green, a modest par five. I cruise up in my golf cart, feeling suddenly like a total interloper. Both of these fellows stand up and walk across the tee to introduce themselves. I customarily forget the names of people whose hands I shake, but I hone my concentration this time. Luther is a sixtyish fellow with a very strong, barrel-shaped body, and his friend Harry is smaller but quite substantial in his own way. They are cheerful and welcoming. I decide to tell them right away that they'll be immortalized in a golf book, and they give me a *That so?* look.

"This is a comedy book, I take it," Luther says. " 'Cause my game is a joke." Harry laughs heartily, and so do I. "We better get our butts in gear," Luther says, nodding to the parade of golf carts forming on the cart path leading to the opening hole.

Luther and Harry both use Big Bertha drivers; in fact, they both employ the complete line of Big Bertha weaponry. It's an unusual coincidence, for sure, but I don't spend much time interpreting what this means, if anything. Harry waggles over his Top-Flite, takes a quick backswing, whips the club downward, and hits a high draw, short but decent. He has one of those swings that looks like the *before* in a *before*-and-*after* promo for a swing trainer. But the ball goes where it's supposed to go. Luther, despite his size, is not a huge driver of the golf ball, but he's out there on the cut-grass, too, past Harry. Due to lack of warm-up, I feel like a rusty farm implement when it comes my turn. This is definitely a four-wood moment, as there's no sane rationale for dragging out the big war club at this junction.

A very curious, very secret, very shameful truth seizes me as I waggle nervously over my ball, and it is that I do *not* want to play my best today—*not* that I want to be a total duffer, a *white* duffer, an effigy of white dufferhood. I just don't want to swagger onto their turf like a WASP golfing god and evidence some imaginary genetic predisposition toward this largely Anglo-Saxon pastime. White men can't jump; black men can't putt, and so on. I'm making way too big a deal of this, I know. Maybe the importance of the occasion has mutated beyond itself because I've allowed the transformation to occur; the matter has simply become too large in my mind. It dawns on me that I've been swimming in a smaller pond than I'd ever imagined, and this is the proof of it. Years ago, I went to a golf course in Toledo with my dad to see an exhibition match, among whose participants was Charlie Sifford, the only significant black player on the pro tour at that time. He wore yellow slacks and chomped a cigar, even while he was striking the ball. I recall how curious it was to me then, seeing a black man playing golf on fairways and greens normally forbidden to him. I recall that the caddies were black like him, even his own caddie. Everyone clapped and cheered wildly when he sank a putt or curled a five iron around a dogleg, as if he had performed a feat of magic. There was an undertone to the experience that I couldn't put my finger on at the time. Now, in some curious way, the subliminal truth of that experience is struggling inside my brain.

I'm standing on the tee in front of two black men, who are just men like me, after all, yet I feel like an alien from the Planet Zork.

Somehow, my swing passes through this fog of realization, connects with the ball, and sends it down the center of the fairway, beyond Harry's ball, beyond Luther's ball. "That's a heck of a nice drive, Bill," Harry says.

"The blind pig finds the ear of corn once in a while," I say.

We're three American golfers tooling down the cart path of a nicely wooded public course on the tattered margin of a huge southern city, almost, but not quite, beyond the reach of that real world on the other side of the hurricane fence. My golfing partners don't really belong to that world, of which they are no doubt weary. They've occupied it, of course, and surely it occupies *them*. Which may explain why they would leave behind their beautiful, predominantly white Peachtree City Country Club course so they can play a round of golf on this humble track on the border of chaos. They must surely be reminded of their native Motown with its Halloween arson and junkie killings and blighted street corners where young men hang out in front of convenience stores and drink beer and smoke and watch the world go by without them. Luther and Harry worked in Detroit's city park system, where they learned to play golf on the hardpan municipal courses. Finally, they had enough of it and retired together to the Deep South, mostly so they could play golf year round and live out their friendly lives together.

I'm quite a lucky American golfer through the first half-dozen holes. A couple of misguided ten-footers, their errant courses corrected by the vagaries of a brown fungus, tumble into the cup for pars, and I'm dead level with three holes to go on the front side. Luther and his best pal Harry are locked in a good-natured competition that has raged unabated since they moved to Peachtree City from Detroit ten years ago. They hole out every putt, even lip-hangers, and meticulously record their scores. I feel left out, keeping my own score, playing my game, racking up routine pars while they happily slalom their way from tee to cup. But on number seven, after Luther has hit his usual two-hundred-yard drive down the center and Harry has whacked his tee shot into the first cut of rough on the left, the world changes. My mind is on some absurd bit of imagery having to do with Vietnamese cuisine. Why, on the seventh hole of a golf course, miles from a decent restaurant, would my golfer's brain wrap itself around the sensory attributes of tran bien chicken? Honestly, I'm thinking about a plate of Vietnamese food served to me once at a restaurant in Washington, D.C.—the smell of it, the luscious caps of mushroom and perfect slivers of ginger-flavored chicken. And that accounts for the fact that my golf swing goes extravagantly awry, sending my ball clean over the chain-link fence, where it takes a huge Wallenda hop on Browns Mill Road and bounds over to where my beer-drinking acquaintances are holding forth in front of the convenience store.

It would be better for all concerned if the string of expletives hurled by Bill Hallberg into the steamy atmosphere of Atlanta went unprinted. Know, at least, that I couldn't stop myself once the dam broke. I slammed my bastard four wood against the hard-baked ground, cursed the day I bought the thing, berated God and motherhood and goodness and light, then wrapped everything in a scatological cocoon and hurled all of it into the mad heavens.

When I turn around to elicit a little bit of empathy from Harry and Luther, they're totally spasmodic. This is definitely the happiest moment of their lives. I've just duck-hooked my golf ball into the lap of soul brother number three at the hangout on Browns Mill Road. I have just trashed a perfect round of golf. I have embarrassed myself before God and country. But for Luther and Harry, this is the merriest event in the history of Christendom. If they weren't holding each other up, they'd fall down laughing. Tears roll down their cheeks, and they've got their hankies out.

Then a bolt of cosmic truth nails me from an odd angle, and I laugh, too. This is my catharsis. I can't outrun my fate nor exceed my humanity. Nobody in the history of golf has hit a shot more crooked than mine, nor with a more poetic outcome. A member of the chorus by the 7–11 holds my golf ball aloft as if he were a bleacher bum and a moon shot from Ken Griffey, Jr., has landed at his feet. "Better tee up another one," Luther says, but he can barely get the words out.

That my provisional ball also sails out of bounds is just a goofy denouement. I take yet another ball from my zipper pocket and I *throw* this one over the fence. "Damn this game to hell," I say.

And now we are bonded. Harry and Luther and Bill. No pretenses to hide behind, no worries, no particular expectations. Each shot is just a question with ten wrong answers.

At the turn, Luther shares lemonade made by his wife. He tells me how, on the day of his open-heart surgery, she crashed the car on the drive to the hospital and broke her leg. All the Peachtree neighbors made casseroles and mowed the grass and visited them both in the hospital. "That was the most wonderful thing, Bill. Just wonderful. I'm not going to tell you I haven't encountered some prejudice from time to time, but there's a lot of good people out there." He offers me a ham sandwich, but I'm not really hungry.

My game comes totally undone after the turn. A couple of lucky pars come my way, but mostly it's a dreadful mélange of bad judgment and incompetence, spiced with misplaced bravado and mild insanity. But I'm having way too much fun to care.

Harry, on a par three near the end of our odyssey, hits a beautiful five wood to within ten feet of the cup. The ball holds its line beautifully against the wind and very nearly lands in the hole on the fly. "Great shot. Awesome," I say.

"Almost an ace," Harry says. "That would be my *second* one."

"Don't ask him about the first one," Luther says. "You'll be sorry."

"Let's have it," I tell him.

"Well, a couple of years ago I went in to see the doctor for some problems I was having. They gave me tests, you know, scans and the like. Then when I went back a week later, they said, 'Hey, you got prostate cancer, and we've got to do surgery right away.' "

"Yeah, but he had a golf game next day," Luther says. "And Harry isn't going to miss his golf game for nothing. Right, Harry?"

"Right. So anyway, next day I'm playing at Peachtree and I get the first hole in one of my life. I think that's God's way of compensating."

It seemed like a pretty bad trade-off to me, but I could see Harry's side of things. "So anyway, I had surgery on the day after that, and I haven't had a minute's problem since."

"I'm sure glad about that," I tell him.

On the last hole I've shanked my approach into the tall rough short and right of paydirt. Harry and Luther have already landed their shots on the green, but I'm foraging in the spinach for mine. They take pity on me and hustle down the slope to help me in my search, but we're really in no hurry to find the thing because doing so will mean that the round is over. We're just three guys, after all, having a day of it on the golf course.

There comes a time, though, and it has arrived. Luther pulls a ball from his pocket and drops it in the rough. "Hit this one," he says. I take my mountain-goat stance and dink his Top-Flite into the greenside bunker. This incompetence is another source of mirth for my pals. In fact, they seem eager to witness any new species of foolishness I can manufacture out of my pancake lie in the sand. I certainly don't wish to let them down, so I dig to China with my cockamamy sand wedge. Wind throws granules back over me. The stuff is in my hair, clinging to my sweaty skin, it's inside my shirt . . . The ball has only relocated on the precarious upslope of the trap. I slug the ball again, and this time it floats up onto the green, fifteen feet from the cup. Luther looks at Harry. Harry looks at Luther. These men who wouldn't concede a drop of rain to each other say in unison, "That's good."

I pick the thing up and thank them.

After drinking some more of Luther's lemonade in the parking lot, I take their pictures. Then Luther takes one of Harry and me. Then Harry takes one of Luther and me. Then, using the self-timer, I snap one of this happy trio we've become. Luther to my left, Harry on my right. We've got our arms around each other, and we're grinning like there's no tomorrow.

CHAPTER 4

on the bayou

I know only to steer Iris toward the setting sun and keep my foot on the gas pedal. Beyond that, my strategies have lapsed into a desultory snarl. I'm sad to report that there's no sun at the moment, just black udders drooping from the shaggy margin of an endlessly rainy sky. I'm tired of flat cropland and pine barrens and trailer parks and palmetto scrag and exits to little freeway towns whose Indian names I can't pronounce. Cusseta. Notasulga. Letohatchee.

I'll tell you, though . . . there's really nothing better on the planet than Krystal hamburgers for healing a wounded soul. They're succulent fare for a hungry misanthrope like me. We're talking basic road food here, let's face it, but sin is a virtue when you're in the dumps. Ergo, none of that dairy-protein vegan trip for yours truly—specifically the goat cheese/tabouli/soya pup platter, with a ginseng enema for dessert. *Au contraire.* Five or six of these tasty little fellows and a bag of greasy fries washed down with a hearty high-fat milkshake rich in lipids and high-fructose additives. There's your cure for *weltschmerz.* I'm sitting in this depopulated burger joint in Opelika, Georgia, at two o'clock in the afternoon, and it's raining to beat hell, raining big skinny pillars from the gutters to the bushes below. I'm working on burger number four, listening to bored Krystal employees speculate on how they'll find money to bail Bobby out of jail. A country-and-western suicide ballad oozes from a speaker overhead. I'm having a lovely day.

Nobody in Georgia is golfing right now; according to radio weather reports, this soggy weather system has blanketed the entire state, and the risk of hydroplaning into a tired roadside cow has chased me off the highway and into this low-budget eatery.

For the moment, at least, I don't want to think about golf except in the purest mechanical sense. For example, what would provoke a normally straight hitter like me to hit a ball so crookedly that the thing winds up in the lap of misery's apprentice in the weary outback of Atlanta, Georgia? Honestly, I'm pleased to know that my Ultra 90 Competition has found a home with *him* rather than eternal rest in an ignominious sewer drain or the bowels of a fetid golf course pond where fish go belly up, a place frogs steer clear of. I'd really like to check back in four or five years to see what's up with that ball and its new owner. Maybe the fellow will have found a nice job so that he can enjoy an occasional Saturday round at Browns Mill with his buddies. I imagine him teeing up a golf ball at the seventh hole, maybe hooking it over the fence for old times' sake and watching the thing bounce into the hands of another young man . . . who would in turn . . . Well, *there's* a frail hope. Does life ever actually work out so poetically?

I guess I'm feeling a little bit sad because these newborn friendships I've been hatching for the last several days will never mature. Of course, I'll send Christmas cards to Luther and Harry and maybe a copy of this book when it comes out. But I would like to have gone home to Peachtree City with Luther, say, and met his nice wife, tussled on the carpet with his dog, and maybe just played a quiet round of golf with my new buddy on his own course. I yearn for real, enduring friendship, not these forlorn excursions that end before they begin.

This neurasthenic mind-set could explain why I'm pondering a geographical tangent into the bittersweet realm of my foolish past. I drag my greasy finger across the atlas . . . through Alabama and Mississippi on into Louisiana. Bogalusa . . . Folsom . . . Tickfaw . . . finally, Baton Rouge, home to James Gordon Bennett, my deepest, dearest friend.

In the fall of 1978, I was a new instructor, crushing rocks for the Department of English at Louisiana State University, poor, happy in my poverty, happy in my marriage, content to live in a climate so humid it was kind of hard to tell sometimes when it was raining and when it wasn't. I lived with my wife in a small unairconditioned bungalow on Wisteria Street, around the corner from a K&B drugstore, which sold its own brand of beer for ninety-nine cents per six-pack. The consumption of more than two or three of those specimens at a sitting was ill-advised, but sometimes I took the plunge anyway, then paid dearly for my foolishness. I was a very thirsty young pauper, and, most months of the year, Baton Rouge was the world's largest sweat lodge.

In those days I wore my hair long, my ties thin (when I wore them at all), my shoes scuffed, and my politics emblazoned on my denim sleeve. I hadn't touched a golf club in four years because the overtones of that sport were inconsistent with my liberal worldview. In other words, my old MacGregor Tourney irons gathered dust with the rusty bikes and broken tools in my galvanized steel garage. Golf, as I saw it then, was a hive of moral abominations: sexism, racism, elitism, right on down the list. For good measure, I also believed the sport was inimical to the health of the planet. I'd convinced myself of these assumptions. *Almost.*

From time to time, however, I had illicit autumnal dreams in which I was standing on the brim of a blustery hillock on the Old Course. On one side of me was the bay of St. Andrews, its whitecaps tattered by wind gusts, while on the other were fields of yellow gorse and ivory-colored heather. Before me, the monstrous Hole o' Cross double green where I had, during a youthful summer abroad, made an unforgettable birdie going out and yet another coming home. In this dream I was always in street clothes, without my golf clubs, completely alone in the fragile October light. The ball sat beautifully on the firm turf at my feet, but I was helpless to do more than gaze wistfully at the thing.

I would wake up in the morning, aching to drag my clubs from their hiding place, dust them off, and drive to any old golf course for a quick, egalitarian round. I always swallowed the impulse with my morning coffee, though, and let my yearnings dissolve in the busy hours of the day.

It was about then that I met James Gordon Bennett V, a collateral descendant of the famous *Herald-Tribune* editor. Jim was working on the chain gang with me at LSU, poisoning youthful minds with mutinous politics. He was permanently holed up next to me in a warren set aside for the stoop laborers; we were untenured and carried our books and papers in canvas bags like Macy's shoppers. I didn't like him much at first, maybe because he wore devious-looking black horn-rim glasses and wing tips. Or perhaps it was because he had attended Johns Hopkins and Stanford, while I had earned my degrees at humble midwestern land-grant universities. Most likely, though, it was because he was so much like me in the ways that counted. He was young, newly married, poor, son of an air force colonel, and a *writer*. It was later that I learned of his love for golf, and that made all the difference. For the first few weeks of our acquaintance, though, we hardly spoke, eyeing one another warily in the hallway. Then, one afternoon as we were defacing freshman compositions in our separate cells, the fire alarm sounded, chasing us out of the building and onto the lawn outside. We peons stood together in a knot by a trash receptacle. "I hope the friggin' place burns to the ground," Bennett said.

"We are a *tiny* bit weary of grading freshman papers?" I asked.

"We are," he said, "most egregiously weary. I'd rather be golfing."

Golf. The objective correlative. The missing link. The *je ne sais quoi* of a *qu'est-ce que c'est* world. A week or two later we were merry linksters, traipsing the boiling late-summer fairways of the LSU golf course, wet towels on our egregiously weary heads, carrying our clubs in Sunday bags, slurping iced tea from thermoses.

We played twice a week for four years, just Jim and I, on blue-collar public courses weaving through oil tanks and city zoos and cow pastures and raised industrial pipelines ... on city-park courses with train tracks dividing the front nine from the back. But our mainstay was the somber LSU course, where drunk college kids with astronomical handicaps and baseball grips chopped their way through eighteen steamy holes, drinking contraband beer provided to them by fraternity brothers who zoomed up the boundary road at odd moments in beer-laden, flatulent convertibles, then disappeared into the watery distance. Nobody over thirty could survive the heat, and since electric carts were *verboten*, the course belonged almost exclusively to Jim and me and our inebriated yahoo compatriots.

* * *

I commit the last two hamburgers to the trash bin and push out into the gloom.

It feels good to have a destination, even considering the very real possibility that Jim and Carolyn have fled with their kids to Durango, Colorado, or Dublin, or even the Dolomites. Summer heat wins out over everything in Baton Rouge, and the only way to address the problem is not to address it at all but to flee to cooler climes.

Again, I'm behind the wheel and, again, on cruise control. In the beverage holder is the omnipresent nonnutritional beverage. As I close in on a road-hogging school bus, a handful of little kids smear their faces against the rear window and roll their eyes around cartoonishly. I lean over the steering wheel and give them my crazed literary genius face. Soon there are a couple dozen kids staring out at me. Enough of this diversion. I press the accelerator, which activates Iris's mighty thrusters. I blow by the bus as if it were just a lame Zamboni. The kids race to the side of the bus to see what other neat trick I might have for them. In passing, I offer them "Eleanor Roosevelt on Acid," but they don't really get that one and seem sort of let down by the effort. They wave pathetically, and I wave back.

I'm skipping the part about the interminable miles of pine trees and cotton and more cotton and pine trees. I'm totally bypassing the soporific soybean fields and mind-numbing sameness of the Dixie highway. Furthermore, I'm sparing you my philosophical musings on how the big red clay farms were once enormous plantations made prosperous by slaves and so on.

I drive like a hellion through the doom, stopping only for gas and M & M peanuts (mostly for the cheerful yellow wrapper). I play Nirvana at full blast and sing along as best I can. God and the saints are offended by the noise I make. A ten o'clock arrival is possible, the threshold of discourtesy by any reasonable standard. But I will bring flowers for Carolyn and beer for my pal Jim. All will be well.

* * *

Only after I have crossed the Pearl River into Louisiana does my headache subside. I've been gulping aspirin with my cream soda, wishing the late-arriving sun would duck below the horizon, pronto. At the Poplarville cutoff I hop onto a two-lane road that meanders through paper-mill country and swamps with amputated cypress trees and potbellied fishermen casting lures from johnboats into the lily pads. I find a Cajun station on the radio. It's Dewey Balfa singing a song I have named "Petite Louise," which is suddenly my favorite song in the world. *Ton jambes, ton bras sont court . . . ah la la.*

Just south of Bogaloosa, beyond the paper mill and upwind from the formaldehyde stench of pulp grinders, is a white Louisiana French cottage with tall green shutters and a cut-glass door. Out front, a spreading live oak from whose mammoth limb hangs a battered, dismembered motorcycle at the end of a heavy chain. The yard is a wilderness of cogs and axles and car doors and tree stumps embedded with axes and knives. In the waning light this is the finest thing I have ever seen, so I stop the car on the roadside to take a picture. I've just erected the tripod when a dirty pit bull charges from behind a rusty porch glider, leaps the ditch, and, teeth bared, zeroes in on the interloper. I know I'm just a headline now, an obituary in the hometown paper. I scream "No!" and instinctively thrust my palm toward him like a Barbara Woodhouse trainee. The dog skids to a halt just shy of the dividing line and sits down. *Sits down.* "Good boy," I say. *"Bon chien."* My heart is in tachycardiac mode, and I feel I must sit down, too. But the tableau before me is irresistible. Americana in the background, canine in the foreground. I fix my shaky camera to the tripod's bayonet mount, gather the scene into the frame, and press the cable release. *Violà!* Art! I take the photograph again and again, using different exposures and apertures. I zoom in, then back off. The light will soon be gone, and I know I will never be here again, a realization that reminds me in some strangely poetic way of my mortality. Too bad, I tell myself, that life is not filled with moments where the world is in such crisp focus. "C'mere, pup," I say. The dog slinks toward me, and I offer him a sniff of my knuckles. He gives my fingertips a cautious lick; I pet his grimy head. He leans against my shin and gazes up at me like a lover. "Good boy!" I say. "What a good boy. *Quel chien merveilleux. Frère Jacques. Chevrolet coupé. Allez reservoir. J'ai mangé la fenêtre.*" He seems to dig French *beaucoup*. For the first time since Browns Mill, my spirits are on the upswing.

I pack up my photographic gear and begin the last push to Baton Rouge. The illuminated love-starved dog dwindles in my rearview mirror.

At ten o'clock I exit the interstate onto Capitol Boulevard. I've been here a million times, and there's no doubt in my mind that Bennett's house is just a three wood and a five iron from where Iris idles at the traffic light near the Bombay Bicycle Store. We're close to paydirt, I know it. If I can just locate the Perkins Avenue intersection, the rest will be easy. Unfortunately, I drive in the wrong direction for a mile or so, through garish behemoths on dime-sized lots. I realize I've entered the twilight zone; I reverse my route but fail again to see the street sign I've been looking for. Everything is bewilderingly familiar, and I feel like my dad must feel when he gets lost coming home from the Kroger store. This *should* be a snap, but it isn't. I realize after ten minutes of frustration that I simply can't remember how the streets work in this city. Then I see it. Right down Government Street. The K&B drugstore. My Star of Bethlehem.

I *ought* to know my way to Bennett's house from here, but the landmarks have shifted, the facades have changed. One-way streets have replaced the easy old two-way avenues. I should phone him anyway to let him know that I'm dropping in unexpectedly. A parabola wearing a white baseball hat walks out of the drugstore. "Sir, do you happen to know where Cedardale Avenue is?" I ask.

"Couldn't tell ya," he says. His little car rocks when he climbs inside.

I stand in a moth swarm beneath security lamps outside the drugstore, waiting for the phone to ring. "Hello," says a voice I know all too well.

"Hey, Jim. I'm in Baton Rouge."

"Who is this?"

"Who do you *think* it is?" I ask.

"Bill. My gosh. You're in town?"

Jim and Carolyn and I sit at their fifties-style antique chrome-and-Formica dining table drinking Red Stripe beer. Matt and James are asleep in one of the bedrooms down the hall. We talk for a long time about our kids, our vacations, the scandals thriving at our respective universities. Bennett's hair is grayer now, the horn-rims have been replaced by contact lenses, and he's developed a charming little potbelly. Nothing major, mind you, just an inverted mixing bowl there above his belt buckle. He still wears his trademark button-down shirt with the long sleeves rolled up. Unfortunately, he can no longer play golf on account of severe tendinitis in his right elbow. I offer a pornographic explanation for the ailment, and he laughs. "You're probably on to something," he says. Sometimes it takes you about three beers to remember what good friends you are. Alas, Carolyn has an early morning ahead of her, so at around midnight she says, "Well, fellas . . ." But we two reprobates last until two o'clock in the morning, filling in the years that have elapsed since last we were together, digging deeper and deeper into the vault of secret truths that unite us.

"A damn shame you can't swing a golf club," I tell him. "But you can still be my gallery, right?"

"Absolutely," he says. We finish our beers and turn in for the night.

I've been given his son's—my godson's—bedroom. There are clean sheets on the bed and fresh towels folded on the chair. It feels good to hit the hay in familiar surroundings for a change.

For some godforsaken reason I'm up with the sparrows. After a while, it comes to me that I'm now in the Central time zone, which helps explain my aurorean inclinations. After a quick shower, I get dressed in my last clean shirt and some blue jeans that barely pass the sniff test. Down the street then and around the corner to the Coffee Call, an old haunt renowned for its beignets and café au lait. A team of dedicated scientists could probably find my DNA still hovering in the fragrant air.

There's powdered sugar on my muzzle, I know it, but I'm so thoroughly enjoying my morning paper and nostalgic coffee that I don't even bother with a napkin. It's crazy how the seams of one present-day moment can so neatly join with those of the past. All the intervening rift of years with their baffling history simply vanishes and you're right where you are doing exactly what you're doing. This is the misshapen logic that swims through my coffee-and-chicory brain on a Wednesday morning in the Bayou State. I'm so thoroughly lost in time that I half believe I could walk out the door, hop in my old Rambler, and drive back home to the little house on Wisteria Street where Vicki is safely asleep.

"So what's the plan?" Jim asks when I walk in the door an hour later.

"Don't know exactly. I was thinking of heading down to Fat City. Could pick up a game of golf with some yats at one of the public courses in Metairie. That might be a hoot."

"Carolyn says to tell you there's a golf course at the leper colony at Carville. Sounds like it might be up your alley. Interested?"

"Oh. *Desperately*," I say, and laugh.

That evening we're sitting in Felix's Oyster Bar. It's the Bennetts and yours truly staring at a large oval platter filled with butterflied crab claws. The largest bottle of Tabasco in the hemisphere is going round amongst us; our lips are swollen, our eyes watering. We're in a new, totally visceral culinary dimension, something eons removed from the pedestrian meat-and-potatoes world I grew up in. The restaurant has no atmosphere at all, unless you count smoke and pinball racket and the clink of silverware. The table is Formica, the chandeliers are cheesy wagon wheels, the beer pitchers are corrugated plastic numbers that kill the beer's effervescence. On the other hand, the food is brilliant and bountiful and dirt cheap. This is the most popular eaterie in the city, a favorite with the governor, the local Mafia, the tuxedo crowd, and the working stiffs.

Almost precisely when we've chomped the last morsel of flesh from our claws, Paula, our waitress, appears with heaping plates of steaming, fiercely aromatic crawfish étouffée. You wouldn't think

that little kids would go for exotic, highly spiced seafood, but Matt
and James dig in like this is their last meal on earth. We grown-ups
show barely more restraint. We've got Miller High Life to punctuate
our assault, and we make the occasional guttural noises normally
associated with farm animals. What little conversation we make has
only to do with the food before us. We are cave people, modified and
defined by the food we eat.

I've done exactly nothing of a professional nature to merit this little
side trip to Baton Rouge. I've befriended a soiled watchdog, penetrated the inner sanctum of Carville, renewed old friendships,
quaffed vast amounts of beer, eaten the meat of myriad crustaceans,
and slept extravagantly well in a bed belonging to a little kid. So, on
the morning after, bolstered by aspirin and Tums and coffee and
beignets, motivated by rising panic and moral obligation, I decide
crassly to manipulate my professional connections in order to
wangle a round of golf on the Bluffs, one of the most highly praised
new courses in the state of Louisiana. A strategic phone call to the
right source, a gratuitously selective, highly interpretive injection of
autobiography, a plaintive appeal and, *voilà*, I'm an honored guest,
the fourth member of a quartet of linksters.

The immediate by-product of this arrangement, scheduled for one
day hence, is the ongoing consumption of still more crustaceans,
more mollusks, more cross-sectioned appendages of cephalopods
simmered in roux, spiced with pepper sauce and filé, the whole
steaming mess heaped onto king sized beds of white rice, chased
down with cold Dixie beer and tumblers full of Pimms with cucumber rafts and, finally, strong coffee. The site of this terpitude is New
Orleans, to which Jim and I have been transported by Carolyn, our
chauffeur and our savior. The scene varies from one hole-in-the-wall
restaurant to another, up one wrought-iron side street and down the
next horse-clop boulevard. There's jazz at Buffet's Bar, sleazy sax
music at Jackson Square, weird organ music issuing from the cathe-
dral. All of it tumbling together into a huge, noisy gumbo that causes
the mind to swim.

Carolyn drives us home at midnight. I stare at the fuzzy road
ahead while Jim snoozes in the backseat. No observer could imagine

that the two passengers have a golf date at nine o'clock in the morning.

Morning arrives like a blacksmith's hammer. I sit on the edge of the bed wondering why I've compressed so much decadence into such a short span of time. I will die an early death if I continue this way. My epitaph will read HE LIVED LIFE TO THE HILT, AND THEN SOME. Jim and I are destined to drive to the Bluffs, allowing enough time for obeisance at the pro shop and a little bit of socializing with my fellow linksters, maybe a bucket of practice balls, some work on the putting green. But I sense that my eyes have shrunk to BBs beneath my anvil skull. My hyperbolic hangover, complete with auras and cosmic rotation, is the worst I've had in years.

Fact is, I'd rather chew the balata off a Maxfli than play golf today. The very idea makes me shake my sorry head. I am a normal, responsible human being, a loving father, a competent professional, a hard worker. Yet my recent squalid behavior trails behind me like the aftermath of a garden slug.

Bennett hears me stirring around in the kitchen, and he emerges from the bedroom looking none too fresh himself. But he's one of those stoics who, if his arm were caught in a thresher, would politely suggest that somebody hit the kill switch. I've already downed a few Advil, and I'm coveting the lonely remaining capsule in the plastic bottle. "I'm really not up to this," I tell him.

"Want to cancel?"

I decide to squeeze one more day of wear from my wilted linen slacks and my black polo shirt. Luckily, my underwear situation is splendid, and I have a couple of pairs of new socks to boot [SIC]. I appear sufficiently duded up to avoid shame in the presence of gentry.

Jim offers me another hit of joe, which I do not need but accept anyway. Perhaps by taking in vast amounts of stimulants I can achieve a higher, more meaningful plane of existence, thereby gaining insights into the mysteries of golf, mysteries heretofore beyond my ken. We carry our mugs to the car; it is time to begin our trek toward St. Fran-

cisville and the ho-hummery of country club golf. Along the way, after
having discovered the diuretic effects of coffee and relieving same in a
patch of woods adjacent to a Cajun cemetery, we get to talking about
sex—particularly as it comes to bear on golf's intricate topography. I
reveal to my friend the wondrousness of late-night, coed skinny-
dipping in the dark waters of the Bowling Green Country Club quarry
in defiance of huge warning signs erected by the Austrian greens-
keeper, George. And of wordlessly, urgently surrendering my virginity
to a girl named Pam on the damp, fragrant frog hair of number six green
beneath a star-filled midwestern sky, with sprinklers whispering all
around us. For a teenage boy, drunk on golf, those greens and fairways
were almost holy places, and making love on such hallowed ground (or
anywhere else, for that matter) was a sacrament. I remember distinctly
that the pin was cut back left, and I recall having three-putted the
green earlier that day. But, had I *not* missed that second putt, I
wouldn't have bumped into her coming around the corner of the city-
park bathhouse that afternoon. Nor would I have bought her a cherry
snow cone, nor kissed her icy red lips over behind the tractor shed. I
recall, too, that out of modesty we kept our shirts on while we made love
and said not one word to each other afterward. Instead, we held hands
and walked each of the nine holes from tee to green, laughing every so
often out of nervous shyness. Only after she had surreptitiously unlocked the side door of her parents' house with a key extracted from
beneath a geranium pot did I say "Good night." I kissed her quickly,
and then she disappeared into the dark reaches of her house.

The drive leading up to the enormous Louisiana-style clubhouse is
flanked by beds of impatiens and caladiums. "Bucks," Jim says to me.
   "Big bucks," I agree.
   "I wish I could play. Damn . . . ," he says.
   "It's not too late," I tell him.
   Sherry, the clubhouse assistant, finishes transacting the sale of an
argyle golf shirt and an Alien sand wedge to a wheezing gentleman
who, in about a year or two, will be romancing an oxygen bottle.
Sherry gives me a nice smile and rotates a registration book so I
can sign my name and address, just in case I vandalize one of the

bent-grass greens in a fit of pique or shatter a millionaire's picture
window with a misguided fairway wood. I am then directed toward the
driving range, where a few golfers are already warming up and toward
which I am subsequently chauffeured by James, my aide de camp.

Hoping that none of these noisy dolts are in my group, I tip over
the yellow wire basket and drag a ball into position for what I hope
will be a graceful wedge shot. Not to be. Swing number one results in
a divot the size of a dish towel, which my sidekick, doubled over
with laughter, fetches for me and tamps back into place with his New
Age sandals. "Caught that one a bit thick, didn't you?" A few cautious cut shots and one extremely thin flop shot later, and I realize
that my mental game is wanting. Too much caffeine, too much beer,
too little sleep, too many worries. I need a week of unbroken monas-
ticism. I could go for twenty-four hours in a sensory deprivation tank
with the dials set on *high* and cucumber tuffets on my eyelids. I
should just mosey on back to the parking lot, saddle up Iris, and let
her bear me and Jim back from whence we have come.

I'm a buffoon on the driving range. I turn my attention to the
putting green, where, I soon learn, my playing partners are honing
their strokes. They have apparently been forewarned that I am
theirs, for no sooner have I dropped a few Ultras next to a practice
hole than they stride up to meet me.

Ollie is an African-American guy who, beneath his white panama
hat, is wearing very large horn-rimmed glasses. I have to admit my
surprise at encountering a black golfer on a very private golf course
in the Deep South. Ollie is the *only* black golfer on the course, alas,
but I'm grudgingly pleased that the trail has been blazed. My own
relatively large hand disappears inside his grasp. I give him my most
jovial grin. "Good to meet you," he says, and introduces me to Dick,
another smartly clad fellow of retirement age, but exceptionally trim
and athletic-looking. The last member of our group, Jimmy, is a wiry
version of Andy Williams. He's a pretty short fellow with a white
mustache and a forward-leaning aspect that lends an air of aggres-
sion to the way he patrols the putting green. He cans a ten-footer,
then joins me and Ollie and Dick. We banter about the golf course
and its architect, Arnold Palmer. We chitchat about the vulnera-
bility of bent grass beneath the wilting Louisiana sun. It's all pre-

liminary to the real issue at hand, that being, How good a golfer is this Hallberg fellow anyway?

Ordinarily, I am an eight handicapper, but today my game feels rickety and weird. "I'm playing to about a twelve," I tell them, trying to discern from the angle of their eyebrows whether this is good news or bad. "Well, Jimmy is about a three, and Ollie here is a four," says Dick, "and I'm about a five." My nightmare from Linville Ridge has been realized; I'm playing golf with people who actually know how to play the game. I will be revealed as a duffer. My knees quiver inside my slightly rumpled khakis. I'm such an obvious nonsequitur to this trio that Jimmy suggests we play a four-way bet, with yours truly receiving strokes on all the odd holes. Two-dollar bets with double bops for birdies. I'm shamed to be so outclassed. Bennett, sotto voce, says, "Yer fucked, buddy boy. Hope you brought lots of dough."

On the first tee, a beautiful little par four riding the crest of the namesake bluff above Thompson Creek, Ollie and Jimmy and Dick produce high-tech weaponry from their leather touring bags. I, with my scuffed Ram persimmon four wood, feel like a complete nebbish in the presence of these aging stallions. "Where's your titanium driver?" Dick asks me.

"Oh, uh, I'm holding out for radioactive plutonium," I say. "Some little guy in Oak Ridge makes them in his basement. They glow in the dark. Very useful."

I'm the very soul of wit. Which has no bearing on the lugubrious fact that I'm still holding a scuffed, dented, back-weighted anachronism versus their space-age drivers. I am invited, by virtue of the traditional golf tee flipping ceremony, to hit first. I cast a wry glance in Bennett's direction, then turn my attention to the problem at hand, to wit, the propulsion of a dimpled orb toward yon green. I take a couple of practice swings, then address the ball. My drive is surprisingly accurate but anemic—an old man's drive. But my senior partners say "Well struck" and "That's the ticket" because I'm straight down the middle. Faint praise, considering what comes next. It's Ollie's turn. With his custom-fitted titanium bazooka, he launches one that, midflight, has a nice overhead view of my white flyspeck below. He's outdriven me by a good fifty yards.

This is not a particularly long or difficult opening hole. But I'm obliged to stand mid-fairway with the same four wood in my hands, ready to confront doom. "Hit it square, Alice," says Bennett. I've got a serious case of nervous flop-sweat; beads of perspiration hang from my eyelashes and the tip of my snout. My practice swings inspire serious doubts. The ball, when I finally pull the trigger, is a malevolent crooked squealer, hell-bent for Thompson Creek, into which it plunges from a very high altitude. I'm lonely and embarrassed, angry and dejected, damp and hung over. Then I hear from afar the sound of charity and mercy. "Take your mulligan from *there*." It's my lovely friend Dick yelling back to me. He has wisely edged farther toward the tree line for protection, as have the other big hitters.

"You sure?" I holler back. I drop another ball onto the Bermuda grass at my feet. This time my skulled fairway shot skitters onto the green, far, far from the flagstick. I am, however, more than pleased to be on the dance floor, despite being twenty miles from the music.

I manage a miraculous par on number one, which keeps me nominally at pace with Jimmy, Ollie, and Dick. Ollie suggests I hit one experimental tee shot with his driver at number two. The grip is built up to accommodate his arthritic hands, but what the heck, I'm game. Because there is nothing at stake, I take a nice relaxed swing this time, and the ball sails many miles down the fairway. "Damn," I gasp, feigning a heart attack. "What a *club*." I do the classic reach-for-the-wallet move. "Name your price. I must own that stick."

"Better try mine first," Dick says. His is a jumbo Taylor Made Burner Bubble titanium-headed number, the immensity of which conjures a shovel more than a golf club. I tee up another ball and again drill a screamer way out beyond my wondrous first drive. For some unknown reason, Jimmy does not partake in this exhibition, but I'm just as happy not to press my luck.

"You really need to upgrade, my friend," says Bennett.

"I know," I tell him. "Just can't afford five hundred clams right now."

"Tell me about it," he says. I know it's killing him not to be out on the links with us, suffering nobly. Tendinitis, as a rule, doesn't engender the sympathy that, say, a brain aneurism or congenital heart failure might. But I know how much he loves to golf, and I can easily put myself in his place. He looks a bit silly in his sandals and

black Hathaway button-down shirt, but I let him take a few putts on
the second hole. He's always had a nice touch around the green, and
he rolls a forty-footer to within eight inches of the cup. I'm sure that
my new friends are a little disappointed that Jim is sidelined instead
of me, especially when I leave my approach putt seven feet short,
then miss that one for a double bogey. So I'm down six dollars after
two holes. This is going to be a most unremunerative experience.

After a solid hour of public humiliation, I accept the bit and
bridle of ineptitude. My game happens to stink today, and there is
nothing to deodorize it. Rising slowly within me, is a curious sense
of relief. I think of my childhood, of hiding from my sister in the dark
closet while she counted to ten. Always, there was a moment of
exquisite joy when the door flew open and the light rushed in and I
was found, as I am now found. Jim, who at first seemed let down by
my poor play, has assumed a kind of bemused acceptance. Maybe
it's easier for him to roam the frustrating sideline because things
have gone so badly for me.

I reassure myself with the abiding fact that no round I've played,
good or bad, has altered the course of my existence in the slightest.
Nobody has loved me more when I've played well. There is actually
something about failure that evokes empathy from sensitive wit-
nesses, and now that my partners know the hopelessness of the
cause, they respond to my abject humanity. A *seven* on a par four! A
score so ignominious that it doesn't even have a nickname. Had I
missed the little knee-knocker, I'd have made a *snowman*—an eight.
Now that, at least, has a sort of cachet. Dick buys me a consolation
beer from the beauty queen who roams the course in a golf cart laden
with iced-down Dixies. Ollie suggests a reconfiguration of the lop-
sided betting game, which I have subsidized until now, but out of
pride I veto the proposal. Jimmy has three-putted for a bogey just to
make me feel better. He's no match for me, though. What can one do
but laugh when a ball decides to ricochet off a green bench, then
bound into a backyard carp pond? A garage window shatters, a
garden gnome is beheaded, a sleeping dog is awakened by a severed
branch. The absurdity of this game has dawned in all its blazing
glory. I'm a middle-aged Ohio guy, slaloming humid fairways a thousand miles from home, and I'm getting my butt kicked by men old

enough to be my dad. They outdrive me, outputt me, they even out-
think me.

Poor Bennett is taking my failure to heart. He traverses the fairway
like a sympathetic elf and hands me a wedge for my approach to the
par five. "Can you get home with that club?" he asks.

"Probably not," I say, "but what's to lose?" Here at number eight
is where the predictable irony kicks in. Again, the blind pig finds his
ear of corn.

"Hmmm," he says, and does a funny thing with his mouth, which
communicates serious doubt. I take my existential stance over the
ball, feeling as if I am God staring down at a pale, obedient planet; I
hurl the tiny globe into a parabolic arc whose terminus coincides
roughly with the flagstick. The aftermath of this mystical act draws
applause from my gallery of one. "You pulled that one from an ori-
fice, big fella," Bennett says. "It's a tap-in birdie for sure." Even my
hosts are celebrating my elevated fortunes. They try to convince me
that the last few hours are only a bad dream; everything from here on
out will be glorious. They flag down the beer cart once again so Ollie
can buy me a reward for my recent triumph.

A triple bogey with a birdie chaser . . . what a curious smorgas-
bord my game is. With one swing, I've fought back from a thirty-
smacker deficit to a mere eighteen. Maybe I won't have to write a
check after all.

The climbing sun seems to lift my hangover through the top of my
skull. Perhaps the birdie and the lucky par closing out the front side
have alleviated my suffering for good. The beautiful alien world
around me and the dramatis personae animating this bit of twisted
theater have achieved a new clarity.

While the last nine holes are less than sterling, my game is much
improved. Forty-seven blows on the front and forty-two on the back.
By the grace of God I have broken ninety, but barely. Jimmy, Ollie,
and Dick are all in the mid-seventies—and they're *disappointed.* We
stand on the threshold of the nineteenth hole, tallying our wins and
losses. I've been damaged to the tune of twelve dollars, a sum so
small that I can convince myself that the forfeiture of same is a mere
hiccup.

I'm grateful for Bennett's sake to be sitting en masse at a round table in the clubhouse bar. At last he's one of us now, partaking fully in the ritual rehash that finishes off any worthwhile day on the links. I've been aching to ask Ollie how he came to belong to a club so thoroughly white. He seems like part of a huge conspiracy in reverse taking place before my eyes. First, Harry and Luther and their comfortable assimilation into the ostensibly white world of Peachtree City. And now Ollie, who seems to be the most popular man in this very Caucasian golf club. "I learned to play in the service," he says. "And mostly I played with whites, but I've got no taste, as you can see." He slaps Jimmy on the shoulder. "Don't know why I'm the onliest one here, except that there just weren't that many blacks playing golf when I got interested in the game. Everybody here treats me just great, though. These are all my friends," he says with a sweeping gesture. I'm waiting for some huge truth to descend, for a siren to sound and streamers to fall from the ceiling. I'm the victim of a gargantuan practical joke, right? Ollie has been shipped in from some "muni" in Fat City, just to fake me out. But no. It's not a joke. "This is the New South, right here," Ollie tells me. "If a black man has the money, he can join this club, and he'd be welcome, I assure you."

Bennett, the army brat, has played all the military courses on which these gents learned the game, including a few in Korea. They seem to like him, and I'm glad to sip my Coke and listen to their friendly banter. Somewhere in the flow of conversation is an invitation, agreed to by all, that we should reunite in November for another round of golf, a fivesome this time. To that end, Ollie hands Jim a card with the name of his orthopedist. The wing needs fixing, for sure, and I think Ollie has a vested interest in the well-being of our injured friend.

It's almost time to hit the trail, and the conversation tapers toward a polite conclusion. I promise the fellows that I will treat them kindly in my book. I hint that Jimmy may be transformed into a statuesque black woman for the sake of readability, an idea that Ollie approves and Dick seconds immediately.

It would be nice to sit around and shoot the breeze with these gents for another hour or two, but because I must leave for Texas later in the afternoon, I suggest that Bennett and I get a move on. Everybody stands up, and we shake hands and pat each other on the back like old chums, which we seem to have become. I drop a couple of fives on the table to cover the drinks, but Ollie snatches them up and stuffs them in my back pocket. "On me," he says.

They walk Jim and me out to the parking lot, shake our hands once again, and close our car doors like bellhops at the Plaza. We roll down the windows of the stifling car, back out of the slot, and ease out of the parking lot. "See ya," I shout.

Today, I've played the game of golf badly indeed, but it avails absolutely nothing to have done so, or not done so. The issue has always been far deeper than that. We are mortal men from different walks of life, Ollie and Dick and Jimmy, and Bennett, too, and we've had a fine time of it on the links, which has been the bonding element between and among us. They've watched my theatrical suffering, and they know exactly how much and how little it all means. Even the miraculous birdies provoke a joy that is disproportionate to the moment. It's all about things that hover beyond the boundaries of the golf course. The greens and traps and fairways are just little arenas where we can grieve for our mortality and rejoice for exactly the same reason. The futility of the buried lie, the gleaming opportunity of a perfectly placed drive posing in the middle of the fairway, the frustration of the putt left shy of the hole . . . all of it is really about something else. Back there at number eleven, standing ankle-deep in sand, staring down at my fried-egg lie, I was thinking about the size and shape of a grave and why we are not buried standing up. There's no good reason for such an anomalous thought, but there you have it. My ten-foot putt at number fourteen was my bargain with God. If it fell, my sister Julie would be miraculously cured. I gazed through my own sweat at the hole, praying that the ball would tumble in, that she would be saved. Alas, the ball circled the hole and hung obstinately on the lip.

Jim and I watch the flat Louisiana countryside roll by. Neither of us has much to say, at least not out loud. I'm thinking about him, what a fine friend he is to be so attuned to my fortunes, trivial and

profound. In an hour I'll be on the road once again, heading westward toward some fine adventure. When I arrive at my destination,
I'll be different on account of everything that has attached itself to
me here and because of those parts of myself that I'm leaving behind, including a perfectly new golf ball at the bottom of Thompson
Creek.

CHAPTER 5

lone star sonata

I'm sitting on the hood of my car, staring at a bundle of orange clouds overhanging the emu ranch and the catfish farm across the highway, waiting for the wrecker. This is not a happy moment for a man on a mission. "Damn . . . damn . . . damn!" I say, loud enough to spook the emus. My windshield is spiderwebbed from the impact of a cattle heron now lying dead in the middle of the northbound lane. With any luck, Iris will be restored to health by noon tomorrow and I'll be up and running, but for now I can only cross my fingers and read meaning into the shapely, brooding thunderheads. Maybe things have taken a turn for the worse back in Ohio. Maybe Dad has walked into a cornfield, never to be seen again. Maybe Mom's tumors are growing, boiling like malignant clouds. Maybe Julie's marrow is on fire.

Gerald arrives in his AAA behemoth, slides a harness beneath my rear axle, hoists poor wounded Iris into position for the trip into Shreveport, and kicks open the passenger door of the truck so I can hop in. He's a jocular fellow, this Gerald, a chain smoker, golfer, a midnight rambler, a paintball hero, a papa, a hubby, a recovering alcoholic. (An AA-AAA?) His accent is softly Cajun, although we're one hundred miles north of his ethnic stomping ground. "Hit a fuckin' bird, did ya? Four, five times a week I get a call from some poor asshole who's tangled with one of them big ol' bastards. Yer lucky, though. Sometimes they wind up a bloody mess in the front seat. The birds, I mean. *Then* there's hell to pay, I guarantee. Mmmmm . . . mmmmm!" His eyes are in mild disagreement over which direction is true north, but he doesn't wear corrective glasses. He offers me a Harley-Davidson cigarette, a cup of water from his cooler; he invites me to play a round of golf with him on Friday afternoon at his municipal course. If he had a teenage daughter he'd offer her hand in marriage.

"Could you take me to a Motel 6 after we drop the car at the body shop, please?" I ask.

"You sure you don't want to stay at the Marriott downtown? Real nice hotel, if you ask me. Rooms are big and clean, and they got an indoor pool and big screen and a bar. You drink?"

"I've sort of sworn it off for a while," I tell him.

"Good," he says. "Stuff'll get you."

And I *have* sworn it off. I perceive my former self as the very emblem of sloth and dissipation. I've jogged exactly once since leaving home, and the only weights I've lifted have been cleverly disguised as beer mugs. I swear an oath on the soul of the dead heron that I will abandon my evil ways. Nobody is *forcing* me to guzzle brew or stay up late or eat high-fat foods or eschew meaningful exercise, both physical and mental. It's not that I *want* to destroy my liver and kill my brain cells, although I've obviously oriented myself in that direction. My self-diagnosis includes mild depression born of familial concerns and angst brought on by the nonexistence of a functional golf swing. When I look in the mirror I observe the extent to which my derelict lifestyle is taking its toll. I'm hollow around the eyes, and droopy. Things are going to change, believe me. Things are going to change.

We deposit the car inside a chain-link compound behind the body shop, after which Gerald takes me and my luggage and my sticks to the Motel 6 near the junction of Highways 49 and 20.

It would be worthwhile, I suppose, to take a cab into Shreveport city, hike around the business district, perhaps treat myself to a healthy, low-fat meal at a Chinese restaurant, then take in a movie. Option number two has to do with locating a driving range where I can rehabilitate my ailing golf game. However, I have a yearning to be totally alone tonight. I haven't checked in on the folks back home in several days, and while I greet this responsibility with mixed emotions, I need assurance that everyone is hanging on okay.

For supper I eat a healthful McDonald's salad in my room. I watch

Peter Jennings, then pit my intellect against those of the current *Jeopardy* contestants. I'm getting my butt kicked by two school-teachers and a helicopter pilot, all three of whom know the place where Anne Boleyn was incarcerated prior to beheading. After downing my tea and some complimentary Saltines, I phone Dad to find out how the world is turning. "Hi, Bill," he says, as always. I dread the day when his memory crumbles completely and I become a strange voice at the other end of the line. "Where are you?" he asks.

"I'm in Shreveport," I tell him.

"Shreveport? What's in Shreveport?"

"*I'm* in Shreveport, Dad. Killed a cattle heron with my car. My window got shattered."

"A cattle heron?"

"That's right. A cattle heron. Flew right into my window and smashed it."

"Where did you say you are?"

"Shreveport, Louisiana. How's Mom doing?"

"I just took her down some soup. She's been in bed all day."

"Is she feeling okay?"

"About the same."

"About the same as what, Dad?"

"Not too good. Where are you?"

Room 123, Motel 6, Shreveport, Louisiana. The very tightly woven brown commercial-grade loop carpet breaks right to left if you're aiming for the door. An unrepaired cigarette burn interrupts the line between the bureau and the threshold, but that's the rub of the green. The housekeeping staff will be apprised of same come morning. I drop a nickel near the door and three new golf balls over by the bureau. The game is this: if I can roll two out of three putts to within a foot of the coin, Julie and Mom will be spontaneously cured of cancer and my dad's brain will again function normally. This bet has manifested itself in a hundred different ways over the last several months: *if* I can run six miles without stopping . . . *if* I can write for four hours without getting up for a beer . . .

I line up the first putt carefully, but I'm distracted by the glaring

swag lamp hanging over the Formica table to my right. I click off the
light and reset myself over the ball. Because a bead of sweat has
formed on my cheekbone, I'm forced to step away for a moment. The
stakes are too high to take chances. My hands tremble as if this were
the last hole of the Masters and the putt before me were for the whole
shebang. I settle my Ping B61 blade behind the ball, then let my
eyes follow the imaginary dotted line to the target. Finally, I stroke
the Ultra gently toward its fate, which, *hell and damnation,* happens
to be snug against the doorstop *two feet* past the nickel.

The deal changes. It's a mutual thing between me and God. We're
talking *one* out of *two* now. This is a good cause, after all, and He's a
lovely fellow. I hone my concentration to the imperatives—line,
speed, especially the peculiar topography of the carpet itself. There
is no choice but to succeed. God is reckoning the bet in earnest now.

Unfortunately, the next putt catches the break too high and gains
speed as it descends toward the nickel. Again, I am outside the
perimeter. The deal is *off.* Sorry, God, but I'm backing out. Predesti-
nation, I recognize, is a bitch to overcome. How can a guy win
when the answer is already in the envelope? With my putter I take
an angry one-handed swipe at the remaining ball, sending it
careening into the corner, from which it ricochets at a high rate of
speed against the a/c housing. The ball comes to rest within six
inches of the nickel. The bargain is restored. I have rescued
my family from woe and misfortune. The "Hallelujah Chorus" and
the pyrotechnic bombast of the "1812 Overture" collide in my ebullient skull.

Now I am as hungry as a warthog. Will my fingers seek the fateful
buttons of the phone, summoning oleaginous disks to my motel
doorstep? Be strong, family hero. Resist the lure of hydrogenated
cheese and processed pepperoni.

Iris, I'm told, will be completely rehabilitated by noon, as promised.
This is a source of joy unbounded, and I'm inspired to seize the front
end of a beautiful, hot Louisiana day and mold it to my pleasure. I
check the Yellow Pages, hoping to find a nearby driving range where
I can install a new and improved downstroke forged in the feverish

flames of uneasy sleep. I know I'm releasing only partially into the ball, an error that not only costs me distance but often induces an embarrassing blocked push that sends the ball to the right of its target. Over and over again in my dreams, the handsome new swing reveals itself. The imaginary ball sails up and into the majestic clouds, then drops tight to the pin. I'm eager to recapture this stroke, which abandoned me about the same time I divorced myself from golf. Quid pro quo, I reckon.

Indeed, there is a facility, Putt-Putt Golf & Games just a mile or two away, featuring batting cages with mechanical pitchers, football, basketball, a driving range, and, of course, Putt-Putt. I check out of the motel and wait alongside my worldly belongings for a taxi.

So, I've done a poor job of exploring the idiosyncrasies of various locales where my travels have taken me. My only excuse for this embarrassing truth is that I'm eager to vacate the Deep South, where everything is all too comfortably familiar. I add another resolution to my growing list: henceforth, I'll paint myself with local color.

This driving range is no bargain at all. A large bucket of yellow balls requires an investment of ten dollars, but I swallow hard and pay at the window. I will practice wisely, thinking my way through the process, pretending to know enough about the mechanics of a golf swing to be an effective tutor to myself. Never mind the young brunette two slots over with her khaki shorts and saddle oxfords. "Just pull the church-bell rope, Bill." "Let the club head do the work." "Keep your mind on the task at hand." "Align the shaft with the target." "Stay in rhythm." The trick is to amalgamate the clichés into a comprehensible truth. The trick is to separate subtext from pretext. The trick is . . . the trick is . . . The thesis of my prac-tice, the guiding principal, is to bring the hands down vertically from the top, tugging the church-bell rope, then releasing the club head into the ball, allowing the right hand to roll over the left on the follow-through.

Before hitting even the first ball, I swing the club rhythmically, again and again, so that the blade passes over the same broken tee. How odd and dislocated I feel. And how totally alone here in the humid barrel of the boot of Louisiana, pretending that my golfing skills are at the core of my sensibility.

The young woman has left the scene, and I'm riveted, finally, to the task at hand. The practice session is paying dividends. Old muscle memories have been reawakened, and the swing feels natural again. No shanks, no self-defensive snap-hooks, no block-outs veering to the weak side. Just a few fat ones, but this is not the sort of mistake that will devastate a round. Even my drives, when I finally get around to hitting the big stick, are true and surprisingly long, considering the thickness of the morning air. There may yet be hope for the young vagabond from North Carolina.

The taxi picks me up at the driving range parking lot and I'm whisked onto Hollywood Avenue, past strip malls and Taco Bells and used car dealers. Then right on Linwood, into the commercial clutter of the city, where the body shop is located.

"All set," Gary the installer says. "No problems at all." Iris is in fine fettle, equipped with a spanking-new windshield indistinguishable from the original. The repairs, minus the deductible, are totally covered by my insurance, and all is well. Shreveport impresses me as a no-nonsense, straight-up, honest-to-goodness city.

I have rolled through the hazy Louisiana flatland into the Lone Star State, the beginning of a new region where there are no crawfish farms to speak of or emu ranches or llama sanctuaries. Suddenly it's cattle country, pure and simple, minus the suicidal white herons. Texas seems tough and uncompromising compared to Louisiana, where atmosphere and lifestyle are everything. *This is what it is; take it or leave it. We can get along just fine without the likes of you. But have a good time anyway. Ya hear?*

I have absolutely nothing upon which to base this assertion, except for the state flag flapping in the hot Texas breeze at the welcome station a few miles west of the border. The middle-aged woman at the counter hands me a complimentary state map. "Welcome to Texas," she says. Her "T" would propel a sesame seed through a brick wall.

In Kilgore, just twenty miles from the Louisiana border, all the McDonald's employees look like Rangerettes. The whole town looks like Rangers and Rangerettes. This is a good place for Yankee tourists to buy a pistol or a Stetson or a hand-tooled leather saddle, although this is technically not quite cowboy country. But it *thinks* it is, and that's good enough. Rebellion seizes me, and I abandon the golden arches in favor of an indigenous eatery specializing in Texas barbecue, plenty stringy and tough as floss. I order a passel of the stuff, some hush puppies, slaw, and a barrel of unsweetened tea, which I carry on a tray to a long communal picnic table centered by a big lazy Susan crowded with hot sauces and hot peppers in bottles and lethal spices with skull-and-crossbone labels. I'm joined at my table by Garth Brooks and Travis Tritt. Or possibly their dead ringers. I feel conspicuously dull in my gray T-shirt, walking shorts, and neoliberal sandals. I assert my masculinity by spritzing my barbecue with liquid fire. The effects of this act of pure lunacy include weeping, gasping, frantic guzzling, and coughing. I note in my distress that none of the cowboy trio has chosen to embellish his luncheon fare with inflammatory sauces. *Greenhorn,* they seem to say. It's probably a little joke played on tourists by the Kilgoreans.

After having twice taken advantage of the free refill policy, I carry my iced tea to the car and, before engaging the transmission, sip copious amounts of the icy liquid to quell the burning sensation in my gut.

My destination is Fort Worth, where I've choreographed a golf outing with some friends of my Aunt Harriet, a musician whose primary instrument is a relatively obscure Baroque item called the viola da gamba, or, as I translate it, the *leg fiddle.* My golfing partners will be Harriet's friends Andy, a clarinetist with the Fort Worth Symphony and Fran, a retired pediatrician and until their knees gave out, an old tennis partner. Although Harriet's schedule demands that she be in Wisconsin for the nonce, I've been invited to occupy her long, one-story house, in which I celebrated Christmas thirty-five years ago as a little kid but have not visited since. My recollections are surprisingly vivid, although I can't quite explain why that is. I remember the Bechstein grand piano in the living room, the big picture window overlooking a ravine, the music studio with the post horn hanging on the wall—and the smell of her cats, Vivaldi, Rienzi, and Balzac.

The landscape between Kilgore and Fort Worth is not so different from north Louisiana, save for the singular reality that the latter is definitely *not* the former. I feel as if I've finally entered an unknown realm, with one tiny beacon of familiarity on which I fix my compass. On the outskirts of Dallas, I fill up with gas and phone Harriet's house on the off chance that her daughter Connie is in residence. To my surprise, Harriet herself picks up the phone. "Harriet? Can that be you? What are you doing home?" I ask.

"Well, I delayed my trip so I could play golf with you, Bill. I couldn't imagine missing a chance to see you."

"Wonderful," I say. "What a surprise . . ."

Her splendid directions guide me perfectly to her front walkway, which is lined with the fossilized remains of ammonites. In fact, the predominant landscape motif is the crustaceal remains of prehistoric mollusks. This is, no doubt, Uncle John's doing. He's an unusual man, to be sure, and I can easily imagine his joy at finding a treasure trove of defunct Mesozoic critters, there for the taking in a farmer's newly plowed field. "Well, hello, Bill," Harriet says, and laughs. She is the happiest woman on earth as far as I can tell.

I give her a big smooch. "Well, fancy meeting you here," I say.

"You need to call your mother and dad," she says. "They'll be thrilled to know you're here."

"I phoned them last night," I say, feeling a bit guilty for begging off. "Maybe I'll ring them up later."

"Tell me about your trip," she says. "Would you like a Coke?"

We sit in her living room between the Bechstein and the big picture window, which is just as I recall it, even to the backyard water oaks with their down-hanging mistletoe. I give her the highlights of my adventure thus far. Theodore and Harry and Ollie and Jim. The kamikaze bird, the incendiary barbecue, the New Orleans gumbo and beignets, and the myriad anonymous cheap motels. I've actually had one roll of film developed in Baton Rouge, and I hand her a stack of color prints. The photograph of Theodore and his son is especially nice, but most of them are forgettable wish-you-were-here snapshots. She studies each of the pictures with more interest

than they deserve. I do my best to provide an accompanying anec-
dote when she seems to expect one, which is often. But that's Aunt
Harriet for you. Everything fascinates her—even cheesy images that
only barely capture the queer odyssey on which I've been embarked
for the past ten days. She wears her hair conveniently short, and her
attire is a reflection of her laid-back approach to life. She is far too
polite *not* to laugh at even my feeblest attempt at humor, and when I
actually concoct some amusing, wildly hyperbolic spin on things,
she's a goner. Tears roll down her cheeks, and her hands fly to her
face to camouflage the fact that she's totally out of control.

Connie drops by with her four-year-old son just as Harriet and I are
heading out the door for a drop-of-the-hat dinner date. I haven't seen
Connie since she was a toddler, although I would recognize her anywhere. We retreat back to the living groom, where we make awkward
conversation for a few minutes, then play a game of Drop-the-Ball-in-
the-Wastebasket with her son. He's a boisterous little fellow, prone to
temper, but a good boy nevertheless. I get a kick out of abetting his
efforts to toss the ball into the basket. He wouldn't know Howard
Cosell from Mr. Rogers, but I do a fairly obnoxious play-by-play of his
activities as he runs full-tilt across the room with the intent of slam
dunking: "He skies. He scores. The Horned Frogs *win!*"

That evening, after dinner at a Mexican restaurant and a stroll
around the terraced fountain downtown, Harriet and I attend a symphony concert held under the stars at the municipal park. She seems
to know nearly everyone in attendance, and at intermission I shake
hands with several dozen of her friends, all of whom seem to have
read my novel. My guess is that they were coerced into doing so by
my escort, but I'm flattered just the same. It's a beautiful breezy
night, a perfect night for a Mozart concert, flavored with champagne
and Danish cookies. I detect a sweet, possibly illicit smell wafting
from a copse of trees just over my right shoulder. We sit on the grass,
we two, and stare at the black trees against the blue-black sky,
taking it all in. Violin music threads through the high branches and
sails toward Ursa Major, which is visible despite the predominating
light of the illuminated city. Harriet is not performing tonight, I suppose because she had planned to be on vacation about now. But here

she is, next to me, and in her place onstage a straight-backed college girl who tilts her head beautifully when she plays, like a Modigliani figure. I'm sure I can hear the sound of her cello gliding solemnly beneath the soaring violins like a lugubrious current prowling the floor of the animated sea. In spite of the exquisite confluence of cool evening air and the strains of classical music, I can't help feeling a bit wistful about my mother, ensconced in her musty bedroom at home, watching endless C-SPAN and Larry King programs while I sit in the clover and revel in the warm tones of the string section. Or my father, watching a Tigers game alone in his ticking, humming living room. Or Julie, braving it again through yet another run-in with chemotherapy. And to think that my mission, above and beyond the divertimentos and allegros, is to play golf with a handful of the odd beings who inhabit the fruited plains of America. What an odd juxtaposition confronts me on this day and all days yet to come.

When the concert is finished and the blankets are being folded, the sky explodes with fireworks and cannonades. Nobody seems inclined to take even a solitary step from this glorious, convivial, sulfurous venue, least of all Harriet and me. Finally, when the last wisp of smoke vanishes from the face of the moon, the masses commence their march to the parking lot on the opposite side of the park. Harriet latches onto my elbow, and we march forth like June/December lovers on the heels of a grand summer evening.

I command the remotest of the bedrooms, far down the carpeted hallway. There are the obligatory clean towels and extra pillows, the mark of a four-star hotel. But I'm too tired to take a shower or even to get out of my clothes for that matter. I lean my head out the door and wish Harriet, who has also turned in for the night, pleasant dreams. Then I flop onto the mattress and wait for sleep to come.

Which it does, without notice.

I have visited the dark, dreamless abyss, death's first cousin, a slumber so profound that I can't even claim to have enjoyed it, save for the fact that I feel refreshed when I awaken to the sound of the street sweeper at 6:00 A.M. So as not to rouse Harriet, I quietly twist the latch and let myself out the front door into the cool, fresh Texas morning. My electric coffeepot and a tin of Colombian coffee are hiding somewhere in the clutter that fills my trunk. I locate first the coffee, then the percolator amongst the shoes and the Frisbee and the poncho and the shag balls. With my discoveries, I stroll the dim morning sidewalk (alongside which gleam the myriad white fossils), bearing the means by which I will, with the mere addition of tap water and electricity, perform alchemy.

Imagine sitting on the front steps of a pleasant house on a cool Texas morning, a mug of hot black coffee cradled between your palms. The magpies are squabbling in the neighbor's yard, an army jet rumbles two miles overhead, every now and then a distant garbage truck clanks and wheezes . . . lights go on in houses up and down the block . . . sprinklers kick into action, car engines turn over, a kid on a Trek mountain bike flings rolled-up newspapers onto the driveways. Ah, life. Your mystery is no mystery at all. It's only the beautiful, quotidian humdrummery that lifts up this world and moves it along. I sip the coffee carefully to avoid burning my lips. Caffeine radiates within me, and the dusky dregs of sleep melt away. When my mug is empty, I tiptoe into the kitchen for a refill, which I consume while reading the morning paper. I can hear Harriet stirring about down the hall. My hope is that she is as rested and content as I am.

She appears in the kitchen a few minutes later wearing powder-blue shorts, a navy sleeveless top, and a white snap-brim. *Très sportif.* "Good morning," she says. "I trust you slept well?"

"Very extremely well," I say. "Like King Tut."

"And you're ready for some golf?"

"Absolutely," I tell her. She fusses about the kitchen, helps herself to a cup of coffee, makes some whole-wheat toast, feeds the cats, washes out a pan, throws away an empty milk carton, and generally does what needs to be done. She's humming some tune that sounds vaguely familiar to me. Harriet is a charter member of the Fort Worth Early Music Society, so most likely it's Italian Baroque. If I dare to ask, "Is that Baroque?" she will say, "Why? Does it need fixing?" (she's a hopeless punster), and, anyway, I've been informed that most early viola da gamba music was written by Italians.

"Well," she says, "Fran and Andy are going to meet us on the putting green at nine o'clock. So, depending on whether you want to practice or not, we can leave now or a little later."

"No hurry," I say. "I'm enjoying the newspaper." A lot has happened since I left home. Plane crashes, mass starvation, O.J. depositions . . . wonderful stuff.

Harriet takes the time to practice her gamba, which is less than a cello and a heck of a lot more than a viola. She tells me that an eighteenth-century non-Italian composer named Carl Friedrich Abel is responsible for the sonata, which is poignant and plain-spoken. I'm embarrassed to admit that six years of piano lessons have had no audible impact on my life. And given the marginal benefit of innumerable golf lessons and instruction books, I can only conclude that I'm immune to edification of any sort. I play a passable blues harp, but only in the privacy of my automobile. Often, I'd much rather blow a few tunes on the harmonica than listen to a CD.

The Pecan Valley Municipal Golf Course is overrun with golfers of every imaginable size, shape, hue, and gender. Texas has been suffering drought conditions, and while the watered fairways are holding their own, the parched roughs are looking rather scraggly. Even the live oaks growing on the rolling terrain look desiccated. Setting aside the dire implications of yet another cloudless summer day, the weather is propitious for golf, and it's no surprise that hackers and scratch golfers alike have converged on this pleasant patch of turf bordering the Trinity River. Harriet and I extract our shoes and clubs from the trunk of her car, don the former, and hoist the latter onto our shoulders for the short hike to the ranch-style clubhouse. There's a considerable queue at the counter inside the pro shop, which gives me a chance to ogle a barrel of used golf clubs, one of which is identical to the number that Dick tempted me with at the Bluffs a few days ago. I could fly to Bali for the price of that slender implement; I could buy Rachel a cashmere jumpsuit or subsidize Garth's yearning for a steel guitar. I heave a sigh and tell myself again what a rare and beautiful wood persimmon is. Harriet offers to handle the greens fees, which would minimize my overall expenditures, but the idea is unconscionable, given that she's already delayed her trip to Wisconsin on my behalf, fed me, entertained me, and provided a roof and a bed. "My treat," I tell her.

We find a patch of shade under a big oak tree and loosen up while we wait for the rest of our foursome. On account of her ailing knee joints, Harriet has been forced to relinquish her beloved tennis in favor of golf, a sport she has played for only one year. Meanwhile, her pal Fran can no longer see well enough to whack a fuzzy yellow ball over a net, and she, too, has adopted golf as her new recreational pastime. Before even venturing onto the links, Harriet practiced her golf swing for weeks at a local driving range. "Well, I didn't want to embarrass myself, now did I?" she says, taking a few practice swings. Her motion is simple, compact, and graceful, and for that reason she should be shunned by those among us whose wild flailings are more Baroque than even the curliest Italian leg fiddle sonata.

A living, breathing Italian-American comes huffing up the steps from the parking lot. He hustles toward us, carrying his clubs like a suitcase. "Sorry I'm late," he says. "God, so sorry. Hope I didn't keep you waiting. Gosh."

"You're Andy," I say.

"Oh, yes. Bill! Wonderful to meet you. I *loved* your book. Gee, this is *great*. Got caught in traffic. I've heard so much about you."

"All lies," I tell him. "A pack of *foma*."

I like this guy already. He's built like an athlete, but he's possessed by an artist's personality. The hair poking from under his white cap is slightly wild, and his manner is frantically earnest and sweet-natured. This is no lame presumption on my part but an instinct that I will, on this occasion, trust wholeheartedly. Andy is a clarinetist who has been known to join Harriet in performance, namely, the little-known and oft-forgotten *fugue mal à deux* for licorice stick and leg fiddle. I like him slightly less when I discover that he's owner of, yes, another high-tech space-age driver. I'm calculating whether or not to take the big plunge and join the cheaters with their Big Mama War Hawk Tommy Gun Hammerhead Bertha Bubble drivers or whether to piddle along with my biodegradable museum piece. Hmmm . . .

"One moment, please," I tell them. " 'Scuse me. Be right back." I hurry into the pro shop, a prisoner of my limbic system, an hombre filled with frenzified lust for a magical driver of my own, a wand that will lift my faltering golf game to a new level. I know the club I want, and, salivating over the possibility of a meaty endorsement contract from the manufacturer sometime in the future, I pluck the Taylor Made Burner Bubble titanium driver from the barrel. It is so beautiful that I want to kiss it, caress it, lick it. The head is annealed with a brown metallic paint that, at first glance, might fool the observer into believing that the thing is made of wood. But it is most decidedly a twenty-first-century item. Because the club is slightly used, the cost is a little less excruciating than it might have been. So I carry my treasure to the counter, hand the pro my Visa, and wait nervously for the approval to come through. This is as close as a man can ever come to giving birth. I indulge in anticipatory Lamaze breathing. I imagine cute names for my bubble-shafted baby. Killer. Ooono. Blaster. At last the transaction is complete, and I shake hands with the pro, as if he were the physician attending delivery and I the proud papa. I exit the shop cradling my bundle of joy with its neat leather head cover. If I had a box of cigars I'd give a stogie to everybody. On second thought, it would be wise to not reveal the dimensions of my crass jealousy, the telling factor behind my self-indulgence. Harriet and the rest are on the putting green, sorting out the vagaries of Bermuda grass, so I take the opportunity to slide the driver into my bag, unbeknownst to them.

I extract my putter, a few clean golf balls, and mosey over to the practice area. "Fran, wonderful to see you again," I say. "So glad you could join us. You're looking well." I give her a big Texas hug.

"It's been a long time, hasn't it?" she says. "Fifteen years, is it?"

"You were just a schoolgirl," I say. "A maiden."

"I was sixty!" she says, laughing. Fran wears thick lenses to compensate for her faltering eyesight. She has a friendly, cheerful face and, like Harriet, sensibly coiffed hair.

Since Andy and I will be playing the back tees together, we share one cart, while Fran and Harriet commandeer another. Electric conveyances are an element of modern golf that I deeply regret. The player is disconnected from the elemental side of his sport: the contours of the course, the mild exertion of an uphill climb, the leisurely interaction with the elements. There are a few advantages, though, like the conviviality bred by sharing the same vinyl seat with another of one's species, the obvious virtue of a fiberglass roof that shields one from the onerous rays of a midsummer sun . . . Then there's the little matter of transporting multiple canned libations for the purpose of consuming same as the situation demands it. But weighing it all in the balance, I'm of the old school, the Scotch/Irish holistic version of the game.

A loudspeaker announcement informs us that we're on deck, so we motor through a tunnel of locust trees to the first tee, where the foursome ahead of us is already scooting up the cart path in their battery-powered buggy. The unfortunate fact is that in mixed foursomes, men always hit first because the women's tees are forward and in peril from the masculine tee shot. So it's the clarinetist and the flouncy pedant with honors by default. The first hole presents a genial green fairway thrown into relief by blond rough. In the distance, a mile past the flagstick, is the levee that runs alongside the Trinity River and prevents flooding—a remote possibility these days. Thirsty rabbits nibble dew-soaked grass up by the bunkers, wisely beyond our reach. "Swing away," Andy says. Harriet and Fran are spectating from the shade of their golf cart back by the ball washer. "Aim for the rabbits," Harriet laughs. "But don't *hit* them." I'm reminded of the rhyme she used to recite to me when I was a kid:

> *"Mother, may I go out to swim?"*
> *"Why yes, my darling daughter.*
> *Hang your clothes on a hickory limb*
> *But don't go near the water."*

I feel like a golfer today, clear-headed, focused, eager to play. It's amazing what eight glorious hours of oblivious sleep can do for the old psyche. "No rush at all," Andy says. "We've got foursomes on top of foursomes today." I seize the opportunity to swing my new club twenty or thirty times, being careful to remember: *loose grip* and *deep take-away*. The titanium driver is an inch or two longer than my two wood, which induces a much flatter swing—not a bad thing for a dangerously upright player like myself. Finally, almost unconsciously, I step up to the ball, let my body relax, allow my eyes to close slightly, press my hands slightly forward, ease the club head slowly backward, with my hands as far as possible from my body, let the shaft of the club fall into a horizontal plane at the top, pull my hands down, break my wrists into the ball, meet it solidly at impact, keep my eye on the spot vacated by the ball, allow my right shoulder to lift my head, then watch the ball soar long and straight, right at the trio of jackrabbits. Oh, joy eternal. Manna from heaven. At last I've found a club that might actually make a difference in my game.

"Beautiful drive, Bill," says Andy. He's the kind of guy who would rejoice in any good shot, the way he would revel in a beautifully sustained note played by a fellow member of the orchestra.

"A rarity," I say. "Must have done something wrong."

"Nonsense!" Andy says.

My golf swing has been charitably described as truncated, abbreviated, compact, and anal-retentive. This is *not* necessarily by choice, but rather a manifestation of, shall we say, skeletal impliancy. Andy's swing, however, which happens with no fanfare and little preparation, is *huge*. The shaft actually eclipses parallel on the backswing, a feat that equates roughly to putting both of one's feet behind one's head. I should have expected nothing else from so effusive a man as he. His ball sails high and long down the left side of the fairway, where it bounds on the hard ground and rolls down toward the green. "Isn't this a grand day?" he says.

"My, yes," I say. "It's an awesome day."

We escort Fran and Harriet to their tee box, fifty or sixty yards ahead. Fran tells us not to expect much, even before she tees up her ball. "Oh, I get it. You're going to play with our minds before you take our money, eh?" I tell her.

"I'm just a beginner," she says, and squints happily at us three onlookers.

"You're a *ringer*," I tell her. "A sandbagger. You're wearing that pink blouse just to lull us into a false sense of security. Uh-huh."

Fran sets up nicely over the ball, rivets her attention to the task at hand, takes a surprisingly limber swing at the ball, and knocks it nicely down the fairway. "Beautiful shot, Fran," Harriet says. Fran gives a shrug, and says, "I'll take it."

"Now . . . you want to see something amazing?" Andy asks. "Just watch your Aunt Harriet hit a golf ball." She plants her tee in the ground, balances the yellow ball on the concavity, then steps away for a moment to survey the fairway. Next, she steps up to the ball and bisects the fairway with it. Not long, but dead center and totally respectable. "Isn't that remarkable?" Andy almost whispers. "She does that every damn time."

On the first hole, I toss a nice seven iron onto the middle of the dance floor, while Andy's approach trickles down the embankment next to the green. Harriet and Fran don't have quite enough power to reach the green in two shots, but their little chip shots come to rest inside of ten feet, and they're putting for par. Andy, recognizing the distinct possibility of becoming a comic character in a widely distributed golf book, falls victim to a mild case of stage fright, an endearing phenomenon with which I completely identify. To wit, he doesn't quite get himself parallel with the upslope and therefore dinks his chip shot onto the fringe. I know he's thinking "Shit hell and damnation," but he's too much the gentleman to utter the words. Lying three! To his credit, Andy's meticulously analyzed approach putt nearly snakes into the hole, and we unanimously concede his tap-in. Then it's my turn in the spotlight. I'm aware that the dew will be a factor this morning. By my reckoning, the line is slightly left to right and the putt will be much slower than the carpet of a Motel 6. When I finally stroke the putt, however, it is a stray cat that breaks in the *opposite* direction. To make matters worse, I have rammed the putt with approximately twenty-five-thousand foot-pounds of force, sending it almost seven feet beyond the target. A lovely read on all counts. I try hard to look merely bemused, but deep down I'm fuming at my own stupidity. "Oops," I say. "I must be illiterate, 'cause I sure can't read a putt."

I'm still away. This time, I vow to ram the little bastard into the hole where it belongs, giving the ball no chance to deviate from its destiny. I give it a solid whack, and it scurries toward the cup and plunges in. Kudos from all.

Fran and Harriet barely miss their par putts, but they're far more philosophical about the vicissitudes of golf than I am. Perhaps I need psychological counseling. Or a consistent golf game. But what the hey. I'm even par after one.

For the next several holes, Fran and Harriet taunt us machos with their consistent play. Andy and I have become more and more flamboyant, discovering arboreal reaches heretofore unexplored, visiting the crawfish pond bottoms with our tee shots, losing golf balls in the middle of the blinding morning fairway. We make our share of pars, but there is at least one snowman on the card, and it belongs to me. The good news is that Andy and I, by virtue of our communal suffering, have bonded like prisoners of war. He obviously loves the game at least as much as I do, and, like me, he aches when his golf shots betray him. He heaps blame on himself for his frailties. "That's so stupid, Andy," he says to himself. "Use your *brain*, man," he says. Maybe golf affords us the opportunity to vent our personal misgivings in a harmlessly metaphorical way. I can't bring to mind any more opportune context for self-flagellation than the golf course.

Andy waxes romantic about the great courses he's played, and he seems to understand *why* they're great. He wants to play Kiawah and Augusta and Cypress Point with me someday. He promises me a round of golf on Colonial in Fort Worth. But it's the eclectic banter that's most appealing. Golf is the background music to a wide-ranging conversation about politics ("Bunch of bums!") and academia ("Bunch of bums, mostly!") and an odd jumble sale of ideas that deserve comment. At the turn, our quartet stops for sodas, which we sip in the shade of that enormous live oak by the clubhouse. Harriet and Fran are nine and eleven over par respectively. Andy and I are tied at forty-two each. My game, at least from tee to green, is much improved, possibly due to my practice session in Shreveport. My improvement may be attributable to the dead cattle heron. My putting has been atrocious, but so has everyone else's. The greens are crusty and unpredictable, and thus blameworthy.

A strange undercurrent has threaded through the day, and until the tenth hole I've been unable to put my finger on just what it is. Harriet is sitting on the sun-soaked bench next to Fran. We're waiting for the fairway to clear, chatting about cats and Garrison Keillor and strange deaths. Her posture, the tilt of her head, even her uncontrollable laugh penetrate me in a powerfully wistful way. All day, it's just been a strange note thrumming up and down my spine. Then, at that moment, the distant image coalesces for reasons I will never know. I'm suddenly washed over by a recollection buried in a deep vault at the core of my brain. What I recall is the one and only time I ever came anywhere close to playing the game with my mother, who had been trying to learn golf, mostly to please my father. After supper one night, she and I walked up our street to the little university course, pulling our carts behind us, anticipating a few holes of unsanctioned twilight golf. But we never swung a club that night. Instead, we sat on a green bench next to the tee box at number four, watching purple martins swoop through the cool air, feasting on mayflies. It was an amazing thing to see, their glorious frenzy, the way the low-hanging sun illuminated them against the dull eastern sky. We sat on the bench like lovers, taking it all in, hardly saying a word. But she could barely restrain her happiness at the confluence of exquisite imagery and the company of her son.

I see my mother in Harriet. I almost hear the familial blood coursing through her veins. My impulse is terribly romantic and slightly preposterous. I want to throw my arms around her and tell her how much I love her, half expecting a miraculous spiritual transference to occur in the aftermath. But I *do* love Harriet, on her own terms, in daylight or twilight or the dark, star-filled Mozart night.

Only on the fourteenth hole does Harriet's game falter. Her tee shot runs into a sinister thicket of indigenous scrub, too ornery to deserve a name. The rest of us linksters, safely in the fairway, can only empathize with her plight. She takes a drop, meticulously measuring two club lengths from the thorny tangle, and drops the ball in the long rough. Her recovery shot leaps from misery into chaos. "Oh my goodness," she says. "Drat!" She slugs the ball again, and it trickles onto the fairway. To recount the diabolical remainder of her activities on this hole would be a cruel task, which I will sidestep. Her score for the hole is a two-digit number, and that meager information will just have to do. I feel ashamed to have made a routine par.

Fran keeps plugging away, making bogeys mostly, canning almost every putt of less than ten feet in length. Andy and I manufacture enough good shots to convince ourselves that life is worth living. And Harriet recovers her game completely in preparation for the grand finale.

None of us is anxious to see the last hole looming before us, literally or metaphorically. But here we mortals are, on a public course on the plains of Texas, gazing at the abundant live oak that marks the conclusion of a fine and, alas, a finite morning on the golf course. Fran has provided the baseline melody, with Harriet riding the same notes but one octave higher. Meanwhile, Andy and I have provided an interesting scherzo to enliven and complement the mix.

There isn't much time to luxuriate in the shady sanctuary of the nineteenth hole, at least not for the likes of us. Harriet must catch a plane to Chicago, Andy has a rehearsal, and Fran has family arriving from out of town. I dash into the clubhouse to buy four cans of Coke, and we sip our drinks as we make our way to the parking lot. Andy and I trade addresses and phone numbers, exchange invitations for future golf games, then, reluctantly, part company. He's a lovely guy, and I wish I could haul him around the continent with me. "See you soon," I tell him, and shake his hand vigorously.

"Damn straight," he says.

Before I have a chance to assist her, Fran has already slung her clubs into the trunk of her car. I give her a hug. "See you in about fifteen years," I say.

She laughs. "Well, I hope it's a lot sooner than *that*."

"Oh, it will be," I tell her. "I promise."

She and Harriet, old friends, embrace and wish each other well. Harriet will be in Wisconsin throughout the summer months, and Fran will be without her regular golf partner for the first time since she adopted the sport. Somehow, this seems like a significant realization for both of them. I can see it in their eyes. I imagine that when you get to the stage in life where you can actually *see* life's eighteenth green looming in the distance, with dwindling holes between you and your end point, you begin to reflect on the conduct of the sport, its odd topography, and its curious relationship to the world beyond the game.

Fran carefully backs her Oldsmobile out of its parking place, and Harriet, captain of the ship, follows her out of the lot, onto the shady drive that leads to the road that will take us back to the house where Iris is already packed and ready for the next leg of this adventure.

CHAPTER 6

how the west

was won

I'm slowly baking at a picnic table alongside I 40 in the stovepipe of
Texas, not far from the dusty town of Wildorado, at six o'clock P.M.,
eating hot chicken noodle soup with a *spork*! I'm eating this hot
soup on the hottest day of the year, wondering if I could ever feel more
disassociated from golf than I do right now. Considering my mission,
this is a frightening concept. But the parched landscape, the scrawny
jackrabbits nibbling at sagebrush, the bleak emptiness of the terrain,
the total absence of compelling topography make me feel estranged
from the living, breathing world I've left behind, but especially the
green world of golf. This leg of the trip seems more like exile than
adventure. If I'm going to be in the West, I want real cowpokes and
box canyons and cactus and howdy-do saloons and adobe dwellings—
not this endless dearth. I'm keenly aware of moving farther from home,
farther from the things that matter most to me, into a realm where golf
becomes at once a nonsequitur and categorical imperative like eating
and sleeping and dying. I'm riding into a searing wasteland where the
rivers are dry and trees are vestigial and the natives are as weathered
and shrunken as the trees.

A plastic *spork*! Hot soup. It's totally insane, I know it. But hey,
I'm starved, so, unless I'm game for a bowl of Rice Chex with curdled
milk and a rotten apple, my menu is limited to things in cans.
Furthermore, I've lost my only spoon. What's a man to do?

Which might explain why I'm hunkered in this picnic shelter staring
at a sun-bleached dog turd at the foot of a yucca tree, mind-tripping

93

about frozen sorbet and cool cucumbers when, in reality, I'm sporking poultry-flavored swill from a two-pint saucepan and drinking sulfur water from a metal cup. *Yippee ki-yi-yay* and so on. I'm *not* a boffo buckaroo, to be sure. I've got to admit it, I'm seriously cheesed off at myself for not stopping to eat real food in Amarillo while I had the chance. This logical lapse is a sad commentary on my judgment and preparedness. I've neglected to realize how desolate this part of the country is. Did I really expect the golden arches or a big orange hamburger totem tall as a geyser to sprout up from the dust? Whatever hopes there were of coming across even a roadside burger stand have gone a-gloaming. Soup anybody?

The little saw teeth at the business end of my plastic, hybrid, good-for-nothing plastic spork make the process of eating soup more than a little awkward. Odd thing is, nobody seems to pay much attention to a guy eating soup on the hottest day of the year. They're all too busy walking their dogs, complaining about the heat, poring over road maps, hot-footing it toward the rest rooms, nibbling on sandwiches. Your basic rest area activities.

Cars and trucks blast down the highway, as if fleeing the unbearable terrain. My aim is to get out of the Alamo State by dark, but miles are *big* out here, and I might not make it to Tucumcari until nightfall. But I will make it.

After soup, I use the nearby pay phone to call my daughter, with whom I've spoken only once in the last two weeks. I miss her terribly and worry that she's homesick. I've postcarded her every day so far, but what can you say in three square inches? Gillian reports that Rachel has phoned home several times, and all's well, but the kid misses her pups and her friends . . . and her dad. I wonder if she feels as dislocated as I do. She's a sensitive girl and takes the world more seriously than she ought to at her age.

The Camp Cheerio telephone rings approximately fifty-five times before a child named Rachel picks up the phone. But it's not *my* Rachel. This one seems so dull and inattentive that I feel as if I'm hollering into a canyon. "Her name's what?" she asks.

"*Rachel*. Same as yours. You sure you don't know another Rachel there at camp?"

"I dunno her," she tells me. "Everybody's at assembly. I'm sick."

I ask her to deliver a message to my daughter. The message is as
follows: "Tell Rachel Hallberg to call her dad tomorrow morning at
seven-thirty *your time* at the Motel 6 in Tucumcari, New Mexico." I
urge her to repeat the message, but there are too many syllables for
her, and I recognize the futility of this conversation.

In my frustration, a goofy, theatrical impulse seizes me suddenly.
I suspect it will have a cathartic effect on my wounded psyche. I
have a strange feeling that if I don't do this one thing, my connection
with the sport of golf will evaporate completely in the dry heat of
northwest Texas. I mosey over to my car, pop the trunk, and extract
my titanium driver, along with a tee and an old golf ball from my
bag. I carry these items with me to a patch of ground near the picnic
area, where, after several failed attempts, I manage to get the teed
ball to stand up in the soft sand. That accomplished, I take a good,
solid stance. There's an oil derrick a-hulking in the distance, and I
use it as my target. The sandwich eaters and dog walkers and map
readers pause for a moment to see what this blond guy is up to. I
waggle the club a few times to heighten the suspense, gaze purpose-
fully toward the whatchamacallit bobbing away on the horizon, purse
my lips, draw the club back, then hurl the club head into the ball at
warp speed. It's as nice a drive as I've hit on the entire trip, and at
least as meaningful. A couple of onlookers clap, Bill's Brigade, but I
don't acknowledge the applause. I content myself with the knowledge that the old Titleist will decompose over the years or perhaps
the dimpled egg will *hatch* and a new, mad golfer will be born.

An hour later, cumulus clouds fill the new windshield, as if, at long
last, Texas might just get some rain. Should the skies open, I'd be
happy for the folks of the Lone Star State, but displeased for my own
sake, as I'm not a good rainy-day driver. Not by a long shot. Out of
boredom, I tune up and down the radio's frequency band, searching
for NPR, a weather report, or anything that will reestablish the existence of a world beyond these tumbleweed plains sprawling on
either side of the highway. Instead, I find a broadcast of an Amarillo
Dillas baseball game. The Dillas are locked in a pitchers' duel with
the Lubbock Crickets. I imagine myself as a young minor leaguer in
a Crickets uniform, pounding my glove in center field, in a quaint,

old-fashioned stadium, in the faded heart of a small forgotten city. I'm not thinking about whether to hit the cutoff man or even whether to wing the ball to home plate should a Texas-league double land at my feet. Instead, I'm contemplating my relevancy to a universe where a kid like me stands on a patch of grass in northwest Texas while, ten thousand miles away, Rwandan refugees scrabble around in the mud like crows for corn kernels. A minor-league ballplayer relegated to Lubbock does not often ponder such matters. If a fly ball were to come my way right now, it might just hit me on the head. But that's the way it is when you're so far from everywhere. The mind wanders ... After the game I imagine getting totally drunk and having sex with the manager's daughter on the dark, vacant pitcher's mound. A part-time security employee discovers us, and I'm subsequently traded to a team in Vancouver, British Columbia, where, in my spare time, I learn lawn bowling and acquire a taste for fresh salmon. The Vancouver Salmon. The Vancouver Spawners. The Lumbermen. I can't see how a cricket mascot has much more appeal than, say, a cockroach or a silverfish. Why not the Lubbock Road-kill. The Dust. The Loners. This speculation, I realize, isn't fair. I happen to know that Lubbock has a respectable symphony orchestra and a major university to its credit. But even that is a strange thing to contemplate.

I listen to a few innings of ball between the Crickets and the Dillas while lightning crinkles the radio signal and the sky blackens in the distance. It does my heart good to know that happy people exist in this neck of the woods. They have well water to drink and food on the table and baseball games on the radio and symphonies to attend and college football games with their glorious festoonery. The soft, almost nonexistent rain, the cheerful play-by-play banter emanating from Amarillo, the steam rising from the highway, even the wet roadside rabbits lend a new poignancy to this land. Now I can almost imagine a golf course, greener than green, sprawling amidst the shallow mesas silhouetted against the darkening sky.

The first really intimidating drops of rain hit my windshield just inside the New Mexico border, a milestone that should fill me with joy. The barrier to my happiness hangs like a gray curtain between a pair of gothic sandstone formations up ahead. The western sky has turned slate gray, almost black, and night has descended, suddenly and emphatically, from the cloud-choked heavens. My headlights illuminate the endlessly silver pavement.

I admit to a deep, primal fear of driving alone in the dark, especially on the open road. The symptoms of this inexplicable, unfocused dread include the sensation of cold fingers wrapping slowly around my spine. This is an embarrassing thing for a grown man to admit, but there you have it. My mind fills with worry, and I fall prey to every species of grief and woe. Add rain to the bargain, and my distress evolves into a panic, wherein my hands clutch the steering wheel so tightly that driving becomes difficult. I hear death rattles and fearful cries and weeping that outweeps the most heartsick chorus imaginable. I am so undone by the foreboding darkness and the unrelenting rain that I drive eighty miles per hour, hoping that in this wilderness there will be an overpass beneath which I can park my car, fire up the Coleman lantern, and extract what cheer I can from the glowing mantels until the rain ceases. Or, failing that, maybe I can drive at breakneck speed right through my own fear into a realm of relative tranquillity.

So here I am, quaking behind the wheel of my car, steering directly into dense cones of furious atoms, concentrating on the center line of the highway, but expecting an apparition to block my progress at any moment. I know the blatant truth behind my fear, and it has everything to do with dying on the open road, alone, in the dark, in a place far from home, unbeknownst to my children.

I hear my mother's voice, calming me, but since the voice seems to come from the grave, I'm only more frightened. Poor Gillian has observed my irrational performance on more than one occasion and won't allow me to get behind the wheel at night, unless my route includes traffic lights and streetlights and the soft congenial glow of illuminated buildings.

I do not die on the open road and am, in fact, rolling down the brightly lit commercial strip at the eastern edge of Tucumcari. I feel

transformed in ways difficult to describe. I'm Columbus at Hispaniola, Balboa at the Pacific Ocean. My endorphin level is so high from
the recent ordeal that I feel obscenely happy easing into a parking
space outside the office of the Motel 6 right alongside a customized
Dodge van with tinted windows and North Carolina plates. The overhead mercury vapor light paints everything purple. The driver's side
door of the van opens and out comes a friendly-looking bald fellow
wearing a white polo shirt adorned with a Pinehurst logo. "Hi there,"
I say. "Where in North Carolina are you from?"

"Charlotte," he says. "You a Tarheel?" He's in danger of being
hugged and kissed by a congenitally heterosexual male.

"I'm from Washington. Old Washington. The Pamlico Sound Washington. I teach English at East Carolina University."

"No kidding," he says. "My son will be enrolling there this fall.
Small world, eh? What's your name?"

I introduce myself to Robert (which I presumptuously diminish to
Bob) and his wife, who emerges from her side of the van slightly
rumpled and road-weary. I shake her hand, too, and we play a fast
and furious game of "objective correlative," which yields up a dozen
or more points of convergence. His college roommate at Duke was
from Washington, his middle daughter went to Miami of Ohio, as did
I, and we're both golfers, Bob and I. When he discovers that we have
Kiawah's Ocean Course in common, he says, "Tell me the God's
honest truth. What did you make on that par three . . . is it number
seventeen?"

"Birdie," I say, grinning. "Total fluke. Should have been in the
alligator hole with my tee shot, but Fate intervened."

"Damn. I made *seven*. Completely ruined my score." He laughs,
as if this abomination were the greatest joy of his life.

For some reason, even when he asks, I don't want to explain what
I'm doing here in Tucumcari, alone, my car full to the gizzard with
personal effects. I don't want to alter the delicate molecular structure of our momentary friendship. "You going to play some golf on
your trip?" he asks.

"Oh, sure," I tell him.

"You ought to look up my dad if you get out to Tucson. He lives in

one of those golf course retirement places. Sun City. He's got pan-
creatic cancer, so it's harder and harder for him to get out and play.
But he still does his thing, you know?"

I tell him I'm sorry his dad is sick. "But it's great that he can still
golf," I say, wishing the same were true of my own dad, with his
fractured vertebrae and his fused right wrist and his disordered
brain. So . . . Bob has driven cross-continent to play golf with his
pop. What a good son he is. Maybe a better son than I. It's quite
easy to imagine them together, cruising up and down the saguaro-
lined fairways carpeting acres of Arizona desert, reminiscing.

"Yeah. He's been waiting his whole life for the time when he
could retire to Arizona and play golf every day. He's out there six
months, then, bam. This."

I can only shake my head in commiseration. The doomed rub of
the green. We go into the office together, the three of us, and get registered. Then, after grabbing the required luggage from our vehicles,
we exchange addresses, phone numbers, and wish each other well.

Once I've established territoriality in Room 211, I sally forth,
yielding to my growling innards, and allow myself the pleasure of
one very unhealthy meal before returning to the path of righteous-
ness. I happened to see a sign for a Denny's as I was coming into
town, and I have every reason to believe that by driving eastward
down the main drag, I will happen upon said eatery and I will feed
my angst with a sampling of their succulent fare, as in a couple of
burgers, some greasy fries, coleslaw, and a milkshake. My one lousy
meal, a bowl of chicken swill, has not served me well—physically or
spiritually. And, frankly, a healthy salad is not sufficiently evil to cut
the mustard. Denny's it is, health be damned.

Feature me in the company of famished truckers and jackbooted
telephone linemen and lonely pioneers, snarfing down my grub in a
most unseemly way. We men are a fraternity of gobblers and gulpers,
so even the most guttural activities will not be raising many eyebrows. "Piece of pie?" waitress Linda asks when she determines that
I'm at long last losing steam.

"Sure, why not? What's good?" I say omnivorously.

"Apple's good. Cherry. They're all good."

"Apple, then."

"À la mode?" she asks, her pencil poised over the little order tablet.

"À la mode!" I exclaim. Grrrrr. And a bucket of lard to go, please.

I feel like a Macy's Turkey Day balloon after I have finished. I am replete to the nth power. And a little bit ashamed, although not for very long. By the time I've unlocked my motel-room door and flipped on the light, my burdensome moral terpitude has diminished to near weightlessness and I'm perfectly happy to flop on my queen-sized bed and watch HBO. Two naked women are chasing a fully clad young muffin down the hallway of what appears to be a four-star hotel. I am highly enthusiastic about the dramatic possibilities of the scene. The fugitive hastily unlocks his room, leaps inside, and slams the door. There's a lot of tittering out in the hallway. I wonder if, given my two-week hiatus from intimacy, I would run quite so fast as this foolish escapee. The plot of this movie is so utterly vacuous that even the promise of fleshier scenes is insufficient to keep me tuned in. However, my hypothalamus has been seriously tweaked, and I'm filled with unspecified longings that must, for the time being, go unanswered.

I'd like to report a highly portentous dream of golf with naked female caddies and bacchanalian frolic on the verdant fairways. Or possibly more terrestrial fantasies having to do with fairway-splitting drives and one-putt greens. But whatever dreams I've had are the stupid, surrealistic things in which selected English graduate students bowl canteloupes down a concrete driveway toward a cardboard likeness of Angela Lansbury.

How is it that a man who's ingested probably three thousand calories in one squalid sitting is starved on the morning after? Believe it or not, William Hallberg, golfer, writer, father, lover, and dutiful son and brother is beastly hungry. A neon sign flashes in his brain: DENNY'S. DENNY'S. DENNY'S. What a sad, pathetic, and unimaginative human being is this Hallberg, whose id says to his ego, "Man, you're headed for an early grave."

Ego says to id, "Hey, do I look fat to you? I can't weigh more than 175. So bugger off, will ya?"

"It's your life, chump," says id. "Might read up on cholesterol and heart bypass surgery, though. You're destined to have Porky Pig's aorta grafted to your ticker, big fella. Go with a bran muffin and Butter-Me-Not spread. Think *heart-smart*. Trust me on this one."

"Fuck off," says ego.

"Oink," says id. "Oink. Oink. Oink."

Superego has been cooling his heels for long enough. "The both of you, shut your gobs, will ya?" he says. "I've got no time for hooey."

"Bacon, please," I say, "and two eggs sunny-side-up, hash browns, and toast. And coffee . . . with Half and Half." My ego seems to have beaten the crap out of my id somewhere between the motel and the restaurant. But I'm ashamed of myself for being such a weakling in the face of temptation.

"So, you want the Grand Slam breakfast," she says. Her tag says Nancy. "That one comes with pancakes."

"Oink," I say. "Oink. Oink. Oink."

Guilt and shame have copulated in my brain, replicating themselves one hundred times over. I can't bring myself to eat the mountain of food on my plate, much as I would like to. The eggs stare up at me with their google eyes, but I can't return their loving yellow gaze. Instead, I turn toward the gumball machine, inside of whose transparent globe are brightly colored sugary orbs, each containing myriad calories. I nibble unbuttered toast, sip coffee, surreptitiously fondle my gut. "More coffee?" asks Nancy the waitress.

"Fill 'er up," I tell her. "Thank you very much."

"You're not going to eat your breakfast?"

"Guess I'm feeling a little bit off my game," I tell her.

"Can I get you something to settle your stomach?"

"I'm okay, really. I'll just drink my coffee."

She scurries off, then returns a few minutes later to give me another shot of java. I think she feels a little bit guilty that my four-dollar breakfast is going to waste, so she's placating me with copious amounts of joe.

Finally, I've sipped my last sip, and she gives me my tab. Bless her Tucumcari soul; she's charged me only for toast and coffee. "Say, that was awfully nice of you," I say.

"Sorry it didn't agree with you," she says. "I hope you have a wonderful day."

"I was wondering, Nancy. Would there by any chance be a *golf course* in this town? Kind of a long-shot question, I know, but I thought I'd ask."

"Actually, there *is*. Now let me see if I can think to tell you how to get there." She sticks a pencil into her copiously stacked, highly teased hair and stares at the ceiling fan as if the answer were spinning around up there. "Okay, go straight through town, okay? And cross the railroad tracks, okay, and start looking for a little brown sign that says GOLF COURSE. It'll be on your right, the sign, but it's teeny and easy to miss. Turn at the sign, okay? And you'll see other signs if you pay attention. That's the best I can do. I'm not a golfer," she says.

I tell her "Thanks" and watch her swish toward another table with her omnipresent coffeepot. Unbeknownst to her, she will be receiving her largest tip of the day, if not the week, from William Hallberg.

Seven-thirty comes and goes. I sit on the mattress of my motel room, only half expecting the phone to ring. It's nine-thirty North Carolina time, and Rachel is probably tracking deer or building a teepee by now. I dial my sister Julie's number and let the phone ring for a while. Maybe she's been in contact with this elusive daughter of mine. It's getting harder for Julie to walk these days, although she usually keeps her portable phone near at hand. She finally picks up and says hello. "How're things?" I say. It's a nice omnibus phrase that allows her to tell me about her health status without my specifically asking. As ever, she says "Fine," even though things are not so fine at all. The cancer has spread to her sternum, leg bones, hips, and spine, which bends her into the shape of a question mark. Her hair is gone. Her weight is down, and her esophagus has ceased to function properly. Which means that every couple of months doctors

insert an inflatable device down her gullet. She takes Dilaudid for
the pain and a space-age drug called Taxotere for the cancer, but
this drug, like all its predecessors, lost its efficacy after her first or
second run-in with it. When her red blood cell count plunges, the
doctors transfuse her. When her metabolism shuts down, they irri-
gate her. When her Hickman shunt fails, they insert another, just
below her clavicle. Tolerating the various treatments has become
increasingly difficult as Julie's health worsens. The tumor marker,
which functions like a species of Dow Jones average, has begun
climbing again into a numerical realm considered ominous by her
medical team. But Julie, amazingly, will keep whacking her bass
drum until the batteries run down. Of that I'm certain.

"How's the trip going?" she asks. "Meet some real characters?"

"Everybody has been wonderful so far. No jerks, no terrible bores.
I'm having fun, but I feel so damned far away."

"Want to trade places?" she laughs. I feel foolish for complaining.

"Did you get your test results back?"

"Well . . . the marker jumped up to 580. I spent all day yesterday
feeling sorry for myself. I'm over that nonsense. Dr. Burger is going
to try a new course of treatment. Something called Novalbine. He's
very hopeful."

"You scared?" I ask.

"Sure I'm scared. But Dr. Burger's nurse says this is no time to
panic. There's new stuff coming out all the time."

"That's right," I tell her.

"Have you talked with Mom or Dad?"

"Afraid to," I say.

"But you call anyway, don't you?"

"Yup."

We chatter away for a while longer. She wants to know what her
niece is up to, but I really can't tell her. I promise that I'll make sure
Rachel phones her if, by some miracle, I should hear from her
myself. And Julie makes the same promise to me. One reason for my
staying in Motel 6s has to do with being accessible in case of an
emergency. One need only call the 800 number and ask where
William Hallberg is staying and somebody named Veronica or
Keisha will say, "Why, he's in Tucumcari, New Mexico, today!" I

give Julie my itinerary for the next week or so, but it isn't much more than a geographical guessing game.

Finally, reluctantly, I have to tell my sister good-bye. Each of our conversations seems momentous. I want her to know how much I love her, but when I make the attempt to put the feeling into words, it always comes out as mere banter. My hope is that she knows, in spite of my ineptitude, what my feelings are.

The golf course is exactly where Nancy said it would be, at the end of a series of ever-narrower gravel roads cutting through the scrawny vegetation. The sky is perfectly clear, and the air is so dry that despite the heavy rain, Iris kicks up a rooster tail of dust in her wake. The land is more assertive than I had imagined, more exotic than the desert plains of northwest Texas. Here there are arroyos and buzzards and rock formations and native dwellings. There's nothing *pretend* about the western trappings here. The adobe buildings were not erected by an engineering firm from Chicago in order to achieve an effect. The clay is native, and the architecture is integral to the climate and financial means available to the inhabitants.

The parking lot outside the humble clubhouse is vacant save for an old red Ford pickup. Nothing would make me happier than to play a quiet round of golf alone on this surprisingly green course in the middle of no-man's-land. In front of the clubhouse is a row of no-frills pull-carts, there for the taking. The clubhouse does not open until eight o'clock. I decide to loiter for half an hour on the putting green until the golf course manager arrives. A persistent banging sound emanates from the toolshed behind the clubhouse, the sound of metal on metal. Out on the second or third fairway is a single man, an old fellow, piloting his cart along the rough. I've taken a couple of dozen practice strokes on the beautiful bent-grass greens when a black gentleman in coveralls comes out of nowhere to greet me. "Good *morning*," he says, smiling. "You can go on ahead and play if you want. I'll get you a scorecard, and you can pay when you're done. That sound good to you?"

"That's great," I say. If I can get on the road by noon, I should make Santa Fe by late afternoon, which will give me time to explore the environs. "You've got some beautiful greens here," I tell him.

"You know," he laughs. "Everybody says that. But to tell you the truth, I wouldn't know to compare. I've been here thirty years, and I've never set foot on any golf course but this one. And you know what else? I don't even play the game. How about that?" He gets a huge kick out of telling me this.

"I hope you won't mind my asking, but are you the only black guy in this town? I mean, I haven't seen too many black folks around here."

"Name's Sam by the way," he says, and offers me his big mitt to shake. "Am I the only black man in Tucumcari? Well, I 'spec I am, but there's a black girl works at the restaurant downtown. I started working here with Vista way back in the early sixties, and then the job went full-time. So here I am. Learned everything by the seat of my pants." He's got identical gold borders around his front teeth.

"Well, you're good at your job, Sam. And I appreciate your assistance."

"Any time. You *enjoy* yourself now," he says, and strides back to the shed from whence he came.

And I do enjoy myself. The course is a trim, crisp, honest track with a clear concept of reward and punishment. The narrow, close-cropped fairways roll gently through corridors of oak trees, all of the same vintage, all of the same size and shape. Unruly shots will conflict with the limbs and branches of the aforementioned trees, so accuracy will be at a premium on every hole. I can't recall ever having seen finer greens than these, nor smaller, more diabolically contoured putting surfaces. There is a preferred landing zone on every shot, on every hole, on every fairway, on every green. I confess that I was expecting a tricked-up little novelty item designed to placate tourists and fools. Instead, on pure whim, I've stumbled onto a course as pure and honest as springwater.

If you look hard, you can see beautiful orange mesas, traced against the western sky. The air is freshened by the previous evening's rainfall, and the temperature is nearly perfect. I feel like the luckiest guy in the world to have the course nearly to myself on such a pretty morning. The experience is all the sweeter when I realize that by afternoon, the temperature will be brutal. There are jackrabbits munching grass everywhere I look, but I'm more than happy to share the fairways with them.

I warm up at the first tee for a long time, working out the road stiffness that seizes me every morning when I wake up. It feels good not to be stultified by a massive breakfast binge of the sort I've indulged in for the past week or so.

Sam has mounted up, and he's riding his Jacobsen mower down the first fairway, the blades raised like the wings of a mechanical butterfly. I will be putting on newly cut, lightning-fast greens today, which pleases me no end, as I am a bit of a yipper from time to time. There's joy in knowing that your putt will very likely reach the hole despite your timidity. The trick is not to give the putt a mind of its own; if that occurs, there's hell to pay, the currency of which is self-loathing and despair. Not to worry . . . brave, undernourished William Hallberg welcomes the challenge before him.

My drive on the first hole is so straight and long and accurate that I wonder which dead pro's ghost now inhabits my body. I'm right on the irrigation line, two hundred sixty-five yards out. For a moment, I let myself believe that if there was only myself to please, nothing to live up to, no outside pressures, I could play the game beautifully. I'm walking up the number one fairway, pulling my cart along the springy turf, dreaming that the game, the day, the world belong only to me. My swing feels loose and graceful, almost—yes—artistic. Well, not artistic. But competent. Up ahead, Sam finishes the last few swaths with his orange Jake mower and replaces the pin in the cup. He waves his hat in the air, and I signal him with my eight iron. "Thank you, *Sam*." After waggling over the ball for a few glorious seconds, I flick it greenward from my perfect lie in the fairway. I'm almost disappointed that the game has become so remarkably easy. A companionable crow flaps onto the green and craps not far from my ball, but I don't mind; it's just biology, after all.

My Ultra is fifteen feet above the cup on the top shelf of the green. I'm ogling a slick little downhiller that cannot and will not stop anywhere near the hole. Position is *everything*, and I am seriously disadvantaged. I lay the pin off to the side and read the putt carefully, as if there were really something riding on it. It looks straight as a laser to me, but wickedly fast. I line myself up carefully, let my eyes glaze over with concentration, relax my arms and hands. Ready . . . steady . . . *go*. I barely touch the ball, just enough to get it creeping toward the hole. The thing is actually gathering speed as it bears down on its target. I *know* that the putt is going to fall. It is as certain as toast in the morning . . . but damn if the little critter doesn't do a little pirouette around the rim of the cup and scoot back in my direction about six inches. *"Damn,"* I say. *"Ya little bastard child."* But the expletives are purely for the gallery, which has flown off toward God knows where. Truth be told, the young pro from North Carolina is quite pleased with the outcome. He taps the ball nonchalantly into the hole, simply for the delicious clatter it makes inside the cup.

Now, why is this such an important event in my life? Is it because I get to march up and down the metaphorical fairways, hopeful that for once the forces of chaos will submit to my sudden mastery? Today might be the day when potential finds realization, when failure and bad luck take a long hike to oblivion. Or maybe not.

I birdie the third hole, a slightly doglegged par 5. Testosterone drips from my pores. I have reached the green in two massive, crowd-pleasing strokes, followed by a handsome approach putt and a tap-in for my bird.

Number four is a pretty little par three with a cattail pond along-side and tufts of pampas grass guarding the back of the green. Sam is in the middle of things as I approach the tee, but I'm glad for him to finish his work before I hit my tee shot. The sun is high enough now for its rays to tumble through the tree branches, mottling the fairway before me.

After Sam is finished mowing, he plants the flag in its socket, mounts his mower, and glides stage left to bear witness to my tee shot. How odd it is to imagine that something as inconsequential as his presence would have any bearing whatsoever on the mechanics of a golf swing. But I can feel the tension building in my fingers, wrists, forearms, and shoulders. *Relax, Bill. Loosey-goosey.* I grit my teeth and try to command the arrival of a meditative state. Yonder is an anomalous Tucumcarian of African descent, a man I will probably never lay eyes on again in this mortal life, a fellow who will, in a matter of a few days, forget my name and the atoms that substantiate me. Yet, in his presence, I'm transformed, undermined, and thrown off track. I try to replicate my mind's-eye diagram of proper uptake, downswing, and follow-through. Again and again I replay the image until it seems fixed in my brain. Only then do I dare hit the ball with my four iron. And how shall I describe the flight of my ball? Majestic? Inspiring? Grandiose? Hyperbolic? Hmmm . . . let's try gut-wrenching. Goofy. Deformed. Misbegotten. What has occurred is unspeakable in the presence of fellow golfers. The S word. Rhymes with stank. Crank. Hank. Bank. Why prevaricate? It is the dreaded shank!

Sam is laughing so hard he nearly falls off his tractor. My ball is lying out of bounds in some unmentionable scuzz that grows like lesions on the desert floor. I hurriedly, blindly tee up another ball and swipe angrily at the thing. This one flies majestically, inspiringly, grandiosely, hyperbolically onto the green, six feet from the cup. I am redeemed. I am as redeemed as a dog-food coupon. I am risen from the dead, hallelujah. Strike up the flipping band. Undaunted, unwithered by mockery, Hallberg strides up the fairway, past the frog pond, onto the green. With his gallery of one looking on, he perfunctorily cans his short putt and salvages bogey. "Good recovery," Sam shouts over his newly revved up mower.

"Thanks," I say.

Then, for no apparent reason, he kills his mower's engine. "Say. You know what?"

"What?" I ask, smiling.

"Today's my last day on the job. I'm retiring as of five o'clock this afternoon. I been here from the day this course opened."

I let go of my pull-cart and walk up to where he's sitting in the bucket seat of his mower. I shake his hand firmly. "You did something great here. You ought to be damned proud of yourself."

"I appreciate that," he says. "I really do." A gust of wind lifts the collar of his coveralls. I can hear the snap of the flag back on the green. Maybe it was the wind that made Sam's eyes water. Maybe, but I doubt it.

I bogey the next two holes. At number eight I spend too long in a greenside bunker and take a double. But all the while I'm thinking of Sam and what it must be like to walk away from something he's poured his whole life into. He's fed it, watered it, fertilized it, groomed it, brought it to maturity. Now he'll be the only black retiree in this small New Mexico town.

At number nine, my last hole of the day, I loft a pretty seven iron onto the green, twenty feet from the cup. The putt is uphill all the way, slightly left-to-right and into the freshening wind. A rabbit grazes on the long grass growing around a fence post nearby, and an iridescent crow hobbles along the rough to my right. Gravel crunches under car tires in the parking lot, and leaves rustle overhead. All of my senses are invigorated by the world around me. The ball is the pinpoint in the middle of the world. My task is to apply my putter blade to the dimpled posterior of this tiny globe, thereby altering the geophysical center of the known universe swirling in perfect symmetry around the tiny white sphere before me. No mean feat.

I station my feet just so. My eyes become unfocused, eliminating one unnecessary factor from the task with which I am charged. This is a quest born of blind faith and instinct. I know the line to the hole. Speed is no issue, as I will *not* be leaving the ball short of the hole. I have only to trust myself and stroke the ball smoothly. When I'm ready, I draw the putter blade back, slightly to the inside, then square to the ball at impact, and on down the imaginary line to the target. The ball runs, runs, falters, teeters, tumbles into the cup. A perfect birdie on a perfect day in the middle of June.

CHAPTER 7

golf in the
new age

"Dad," Rachel asks, "where *are* you?"

"The Land of Enchantment," I tell her. "How about that?"

It's nigh onto three in the afternoon, and I'm in Clines Corner, New Mexico, in a smelly phone booth, where I've resided for at least half an hour while the phone makes busy signals in North Carolina. I'm adamant in my determination to get through to my daughter, even if that means taking out a mortgage on this vertical, see-through coffin. When the line finally clears and the phone rings, I endure a moment of fear that the dim-witted Rachel will answer. *"Please, God, not her,"* I mutter. I'm in luck, though. A sensible young girl named Amy picks up and says, "Hello." Not "Hey," not "Hiya," but "Hello." When I ask her if Rachel Hallberg is anywhere about, she says, "I'm looking right at her."

I haul in a huge lungful of air and expel it. "Really? No kidding?"

Which brings us to where I interrupted myself.

"What's the Land of Enchantment?" Rachel asks. "I forgot . . . Arizona?"

"Sorry. Arizona is the Land of Leaping Lizards," I tell her. "Guess again."

"Seriously. Where *are* you?"

"New Mexico. Specifically, Clines Corner, which is mostly a truck

110

stop that sells Indian jewelry and meteor fragments and insulting baseball hats. But I'm closing in on Santa Fe."

"I want to go there," she says. "Take me sometime?"

"Sure," I say.

"What've you been doing, Dad? Anything vaguely interesting?"

I give her a hyperbolic account of the time between her last post-card, mailed from Shreveport, and the present. She's particularly interested in the dead heron, for purely sensational reasons, I sur-mise. But I'm anxious to find out if *she's* having a good time and whether she's homesick. "I learned to bottom-roll a kayak," she says. "It was cool."

"That's outstanding," I say. "You'll have to teach me the tech-nique. Any other triumphs? You ride the zip line?"

"Yeah, but the lake is *so* cold. Froze my buns off."

We yammer away like a couple of old biddies, mostly enjoying the fact that we're actually talking to each other. She sounds content and healthy, which alleviates some of the guilt I've been contending with since the day I left her behind. "You're going to your grandmother's house when? Remind me."

"Day after tomorrow," she says.

"God. That soon? Mercy!"

"Yup, Grandma is going to pick me up on Sunday." Rachel's maternal grandmother is a fine person, really, but a very serious smoker. And Rachel is an antifuliginous crusader in a state where tobacco is sacramental. Rachel's grandma rents a summer place in the mountains near Highlands, North Carolina, and she has agreed to house and feed my daughter while I travel the fruited plains.

"You sure you're okay with this arrangement?"

"I'm fine, Dad. Stop worrying."

"The cigarettes won't bother you?"

"I'll go out on the porch when she lights up."

"You're a good soul, you know that? I love that about you. I love *you.*"

"Love you, too."

"Hey, listen. I'll call you at your grandmother's house on

Wednesday at eight-thirty P.M. your time, barring some unforeseen circumstance. And if I can't call you then, I'll call you the next day. At eight-thirty. Got it? If you need me, call the toll-free Motel 6 number, and they'll tell you where I am. I'm relying heavily on the hospitality of Tom Bodett these days."

"Sounds good."

"Have fun, now . . . and remember . . . 'Just say no.' "

"Sheesh," she says. "Give me a break." Then, a slightly cynical "I love you."

It feels wonderful knowing that she's healthy and happy. But her well-being throws other, more ominous matters into relief. I'll try to concentrate on the positives for as long as possible.

I duck inside the Clines Corner trading post on the off chance that I will find a gift for Rachel. The moccasins are tempting, and there is a showcase filled with nicely carved Navajo and Hopi fetishes, some of them priced at well over one hundred dollars. But I'll be in Santa Fe before long, and I don't wish to jump the gun, so I settle for a pack of sugarless gum and a few postcards.

The gum becomes useful when I begin the ear-popping climb into the mountain range in which Santa Fe is nestled. The scrubland on either side of the two-lane road is filled with boulders, some of them big as Airstream trailers. The plant life becomes more varied at the higher altitudes. There's the omnipresent sagebrush, of course, but interspersed are real trees. Aspen and larch and juniper. Tucked into the foothills are the first signs of real wealth I've seen since Fort Worth. Large adobe houses hide amidst the rock formations at the end of dusty little roads. I can only guess that water lies beneath the inhospitable terrain.

The speed limit is now approximately two hundred miles per hour, judging from the fact that Iris is the slowest car on the road and she's doing a cool seventy. Cars honk at me, as if I'm in violation of some unwritten minimum speed law. Heavy clouds, swollen with rain, hang over the high peaks in the west. I suspect false pregnancy, however; after all, this is New Mexico, and it is the first day of July. This state, like Texas, is in the midst of a terrible drought, which has diminished the water table and necessitated harsh conservation measures. This fact I have learned by listening to the radio as I burn rubber toward my New Age destination.

A peculiar whim seizes me as I roll down Cerrillos Avenue into Santa Fe's business district. I'm hungry for some human contact, and I'm bored with the Motel 6 scene, so when I happen upon an unpretentious, elongated adobe youth hostel, I take the plunge. Iris veers into the parking lot, which is already crowded with compact cars bearing antiestablishment bumper stickers, and Harley hogs with spangled gas tanks, and VW buses that seem to have escaped from the sixties unchanged. Except for Iris's rugged roof rack and the messy interior, I might feel a trifle self-conscious about driving a car with original paint and matching hubcaps.

The hostel's office is not an office at all but a counterculture community center where the inhabitants of this way station can make use of the hot plate, microwave, or washer and dryer. Some fellow in the corner, near the bookshelf, is playing Beck on his boom box, and a coterie of disciples groove to the avant-garde music issuing from his machine. There is a desk, but no one is in attendance. I ask a beautiful-looking young laundress, "What's the deal?"

"He'll be baaaack soooon," she sings, and tosses her amazing black hair over her shoulder. She floats toward the dryer, inside of which tumbles a mélange of tie-dyed garments. I wish I were stoned out of my gourd. I'd sit on the floor, bathed in the aroma of patchouli and ginseng, listening to Beck and watching this beautiful druid's clothes spin magically behind a circular window. At this moment I have never heard of golf. There are no clubs in the trunk of my car. A birdie has feathers and lives in a sycamore tree.

So I wait, happily, embraced by a crazy brand of spirituality, the memory of which is sweet as the smell of cannabis. I occupy an overstuffed chair next to an empty stroller. Within a few minutes, a bespectacled fiftyish fellow, pleasantly unkempt, emerges from the bathroom labeled GENTLEMEN. "Can I help you?" he asks.

"I need a room for a couple of nights," I tell him.

"Sign here," he says. "Twenty bucks a night."

"Beautiful," I say.

"Peace," he says, and hands me a receipt.

The room is, well, spartan. The bed is not a bed so much as a cot of the sort one might find in the federal pen at Leavenworth. But what the heck, I'm in Santa Fe, among beautiful New Age people, and if I think hard enough I can levitate above the lumpy mattress, thus averting the otherwise inevitable damage to my lower back. I unroll my sleeping bag, cram my suitcase beneath the bed, and carry my shaving kit over to the pedestal sink, above which hangs an unframed mirror. I look shaggy and unusual, especially for a golfer. I wonder about the impact of my voluminous hair on my credibility as a serious linkster.

On the spur of the moment, I cross Cerrillos Avenue to the hair cuttery, where I receive, at the hands of a young woman named Rosa, the worst haircut of my life. After I've entrusted my fate to her and she has worked her evil magic, she spins me around in the chair; I see in the mirror *not* William Hallberg, pseudoliberal, neo-eco-radical, but a functionary of the Christian Coalition. This is not a happy moment for a man possessed of a high level of vanity, a man who prides himself in his benign pseudo-revolutionary sensibility. *Fucking A. Fucking A, B, C, and D!* I say to myself.

Well, now I look like a golfer for sure. Or a narc. My opportunities for insinuating myself into a possible lovefest at the bunkhouse have gone a-glimmering, however. My very presence would throw a pall over the summoning of ancient spirits. Moral: "Over the ears" apparently means "above the ears" in Santa Fe, New Mexico.

There's plenty of daylight left, and I'm feeling a mite peckish, so, avoiding even an accidental glimpse of myself in the rearview mirror, I drive into the city center in order to scope out the environs and feed my murmuring gut.

Santa Fe's business district is a great place to go totally broke in no time at all, especially if you're an artsy sort of guy, which, setting aside ridiculous stereotypes, I am. I spent a year rehabilitating a condemned Victorian cottage on the Pamlico Sound, and I've filled it with egregiously un-Victorian decor, including a coffee table fashioned from an enormous cross section of Adirondack burl. My hearth is ballast stone, deposited on the Pamlico shore by English trading ships in the early eighteenth century. Thus, when I lay eyes on the myriad shops with their abundant, exotic inventories of wonderful mission furnishings and Native American crafts, my salivation factor is at flood level.

Among my peculiar interests is artwork by painters from the Santa Fe school, especially Georgia O'Keeffe and Marsden Hartley. The first shop I come to after having deposited Iris in a Park N' Pay on Water Street is, in fact, a gallery selling high-quality reproductions of their works and beautiful posters of lesser value. I sniff around the place for a while, lamenting my relative poverty but enjoying the fantasy that I am sizing up inventory with the prospect of acquiring some of the aforementioned specimens. Even the contemporary artists of the region seem worth admiring.

I'm hungrier than I am stupid, so I push on down the block to the town square, where I experience coincidence number one of my odyssey. There I am, ogling unaffordable turquoise jewelry in a store window, when somebody taps me on the shoulder. It is none other than my English Department colleague Jim Wright, whose office is next to mine. "What the *hell* are *you* doing here?" I ask, shaking his hand, then giving his wife, Lucy, a hug.

"Are you here alone?" he asks.

"Well, I've hooked up with a male prostitute, but he's wandered off somewhere," I tell them. Side-splitting guffaws ensue, commensurate with the character and quality of my witticism. Truth be told, Jim only snickers and Lucy just looks confused. "Actually, I'm doing a book that combines golf with travel. So, voilà! I've traveled to here; now I must find a golfing adventure.

"Taos Country Club," Jim says. "Carved right out of the high desert. It looks beautiful. Lucy and I saw it yesterday."

"Hmmm . . ." I say. "Tempting." Jim and Lucy are visiting a friend of theirs in Santa Fe but will be leaving in the morning. "Man, I still can't believe I bumped into you folks. This is unreal. You had anything to eat? I'm on the prowl for chow. Why don't you join me?"

Lucy tells me that they've just eaten at the Plaza Court, a

good Mexican place, which she heartily recommends. I think they're a little worried about becoming idiosyncratic characters in whatever mischievous prose I might concoct vis-à-vis this adobe wonderland. I bid them farewell, promising that I will try my best to capture the essence of our chance encounter. "You, Jim, will be incarnated as a seven-foot Watusi, and Lucy, look for a Roller Derby queen."

Instead of eating Mexican, I locate a handsome bar called the Cock and Bull. The place is empty, which should send up incendiary signals that this isn't one of the sought-after venues for the ingestion of comestibles. I'm interested only in bulk and nourishment, plus a sampling of the local microbrews. Seated at the counter are a bedazzled woman and a grizzled old wrangler who seem to be in love judging by the billing and cooing. The barkeep abandons his wet towel and strolls over to my desolate table to see what I have a hankering for. I indicate the barbecued beef sandwich, famous onion rings, side salad (for health), and a Sierra Nevada lager. "Ah, heck, bring me two of those, okay?" I tell him.

I eat like a polite savage in my corner of the bar. I'm a little bit embarrassed at the mountain of food on my plate, and even more embarrassed that it will be absolutely gone when I get up from this varnished table. The clink of my silverware resonates off the high tin ceiling. I've just speared a monster onion ring with my fork and have bitten approximately one hundred fifty degrees away from the circumference of the thing when a beautiful young flaxen-haired woman pushes through the door. My chewing ceases. Never in my life have I wished *not* to be sitting behind a plate of such singularly unhealthy food. She is, herself, unutterably beautiful and remarkably healthy—no doubt, a runner, a sun worshipper—and a vegetarian. Only a vegan could grow such blindingly shiny hair.

Indeed, she orders something at the counter from the man with the wet towel. He goes to a glass cooler and finds a half bottle of Chablis, which he gives her, along with a blown-glass wine goblet. She takes her wine to a table at the opposite corner of the bar from mine; she might be offended by my gnawed sandwich and corpulent rings. She gazes into space while she sips her Chablis, as if she's calculating when the moon will be in the seventh house. Only after the bartender brings her a salad festooned with sprouts and assorted greenery does she refocus. My appetite disappears—but not my thirst. I gulp the lagers, leave money on the table, and stride out of the bar affecting a sensitive male persona. But she's too busy nipping endive from the tip of her fork to notice.

I shamble to the crowded plaza, where a sort of reggae New Age band is doing its thing on a stage at the north end of the square. There are marimbas and xylophones and bongos and guitars and Inca flutes, the confluence of which is wonderful. Most everyone is dancing to the music, either alone or in clusters. I wonder why so few actual couples are partaking. I find some space near a small obelisk near the center of things and stand on the stone bench that surrounds it. Because I am hopelessly anal-retentive and genetically midwestern, I am unable to let myself go the way most of the citizenry has done. I recognize the young woman from the bunkhouse laundry there, near the stage. She is lost in the music, dancing like a gypsy, looking absolutely gorgeous. "Okay, everybody," says the lead singer, a joyous, djellaba-clad black man with a shaved head. "We're going to do a rain chant now. And I want everybody to join in the chorus. So, all of you, repeat after me: *'We woka nonay woka aynonay.'*" The crowd replicates the chant as if they were all born multiculturalists. Then the band explodes into a highly energetic infectious number that sends the crowd into a frenzy. I've graduated from toe tapping, to clapping, to a species of overhead hand waving that I recall from my groovy youth. When it comes time for the refrain, the volume softens and, under the direction of the man in white, the crowd sings the chant perfectly, again and again. Then the music soars, sending even the moths into a frenetic swirl. This cycle continues for at least twenty minutes, until the first drops fall from the sky. An enormous cheer resonates off the adobe storefronts, and the dancers throw their arms around one another. Lightning cracks in the distance, and the band hurls itself into one last chorus. The heavens open, and rain pours down on us all. Three lean, bra-less jeans-clad women remove their T-shirts and wave them over their heads, not ten feet from where I am standing. This is the greatest

town in North America; I'm sure of it. The cloudburst scatters most
of the crowd, except for the topless nymphs and a handful of
voyeurs. I dash down the street to the parking garage to liberate Iris
from confinement.

I drive southward again, down Cerrillos Avenue, until I notice a
Cineplex. One of the movies is *Tin Cup*, a golf movie about a down-
on-his-luck driving range pro. My novel *The Rub of the Green* has
been making the rounds in Hollywood for a few years, and while a
few moguls have sniffed at it, none has yet taken the big plunge. On
a pure whim, and not a little jealousy, I steer into the theater parking
lot, pull into a slot, and get out to investigate. The feature begins at
nine-fifteen, and my timing is superb. I'm a complete sucker for
movies about knuckleheads who triumph over their own frailties and
who, with some dumb luck and a little help from their friends,
achieve success in a tempestuous world.

I munch unbuttered popcorn and watch Kevin Costner's character
hone his rusty game. Halfway through my pack of Jujyfruits, he's
managed to triumph over adversity and has had excellent sex with a
very attractive young woman. So, here I sit, alone in a darkened theater in Santa Fe, New Mexico, with glutinous matter stuck to my
teeth and an irrelevant neon condom hidden in my wallet. I have no
intention of being disloyal to my girlfriend, but should a fit of total
self-destructive insanity seize me, I believe that a glow-in-the-dark
rubber is surely the way to go. Ah, the stuff of dreams . . . Well, at
least the movie has spiked my interest in the game of golf, and for
that I'm grateful. I actually *want* to tee it up tomorrow.

I check in briefly at the bunkhouse common room and discover
that nobody's home, save the desk jockey, who's watching Ted
Koppel on his little color TV. I bid my host a good night and clomp
down the walkway to my cell. I brush my teeth very aggressively,
then slide into bed.

Taos Country Club, I've learned, is not only open to public play but
has an exceptionally fine layout, carved into the high desert just
south of its namesake. So I set out early in the morning from Santa
Fe, stopping at a downtown bakery for a Danish and a large cup of

coffee to get me up and running. I'm on the heels of a terrific night of sleep, the kind of sleep that happens about as often as a total eclipse of the moon. For a significant part of the night, I wallowed in the REM cycle, dreaming bizarre dreams of public appearances on the Letterman show. "So, Bill, you've written this crazy book about golf, and now you've cracked the late-night talk-show scene. What's your biggest fear about being in the public eye?"

"Well, Dave, my biggest fear is that I will accidentally say the word 'fuck' on national . . . oh, *fuck*! I just said *fuck*. FUCK!" Considering the character of my wacky dream, I awaken remarkably refreshed.

The drive up to Taos follows the Rio Grande, which tumbles over smooth pebbles and between slick boulders. The river twists and turns, through canyons and open land, through pinched evergreen notches; it has fallen inexorably from its headwaters, located in the San Juan range upstate. The two-lane road passes beautiful little split-rail ranches, hemmed in between the river and the craggy mountainsides. I take advantage of a pull-off to park Iris and walk down a dusty path to the streambed, where I remove my shoes and socks and dangle my feet in the surprisingly cold water. Between Espanosa and Pilar, an impoverished trailer-park town, is the Camel Rock casino, owned and operated by the Navajo who inhabit the nearby reservation. The building is modern, and the parking lot is full, even at seven-thirty in the morning. Gamblers are a hard-core breed, but no more incorrigible than your average golfer, I suppose. Omnipresent tamarisk trees line the banks of the Santa Fe, a sad fact of life considering that they are alien to North America, a sort of horticultural experiment gone wrong. They've overgrown every river in the southwest. I'm happy to see aspen, the first of the trip. Trout fishermen in waders cast their flies upstream, although the ongoing drought has reduced the water level considerably. I worry about the trout, swimming with dorsal fins poking through the surface, especially when the river widens and shallows out.

After driving for a blissful hour through beautiful evergreen mountains, I come upon a plateau that stretches for miles in all directions. The road bisects this rangeland perfectly, and I barrel toward Taos, which is barely visible at the foot of a mountain range. Every so often, I encounter an adobe mansion big as a hotel; then, half a mile down the road, a battered shack with a disabled pickup out front. The ratio between the former and the latter tilts toward the former the closer one comes to Taos. Then, when the town is just a mile or two in the distance, there appears a sign for the Taos Country Club. I'm instructed to turn left down a narrow gravel road, at the end of which is a temporary-looking building surrounded by newly poured foundations and backhoes and sand-filled dump trucks. Construction workers stand beneath the awning of a trailer smoking cigarettes and drinking coffee from Styrofoam cups. Their day is soon to begin.

As is mine. The temporary clubhouse is chockablock with the usual golf equipment, umbrellas, clothing, and souvenirs. The pro is a friendly young fellow named Jack, who wonders whether I've made a tee time—not such a bad idea on a beautiful summer day at the height of tourist season. "My plan is to link up with a two-some or a threesome. Sort of barge in, I guess you could say." I tell him that I'm doing a book on golf as it's played in America, which isn't really quite *it*, but it's a workable entrée. I'd prefer that my partners be tourists, like me. Handicap is not relevant, nor is gender, ethnicity, or country of origin. I've pretty much thrown the door wide open. Jack says that the round is complimentary and that he'll be glad to pair me up with one of the groups who have already made a tee time. "Why don't you go on out to the practice green, and when I get you fixed up, I'll contact you." He gives me a handsome pewter divot fork as a keepsake and asks me a few more questions about what I'm up to. He politely suggests that he's heard of me, but I'm sure he's thinking of Gary Hallberg, the touring pro. It happens all the time. I promise to send a copy of this book to him when it comes out.

I've been killing time on the practice green for a lot longer than expected, but my putting has needed attention. Lately, three-footers have been giving me fits, mostly because that putt ought to be a sure thing. I'm relatively cool once I move out to the *maybe* range. And I'm absolutely sanguine from twenty feet out. Then, curiously, my neurosis returns on the long lag putts. It's a crazy phenomenon, for sure, and the only cure is to get comfortable with imperfection. Not every knee-knocker is going to go in. Three putts are part of being mortal. Furthermore, God will not judge me based on my putting stroke. He's far more concerned about the neon condom in my wallet than he is about my mastery of the short putt. Nevertheless, I roll about one hundred twenty very short putts—two-footers, tops. After all, a three-footer is not much longer than a two-footer, and a four-footer is . . . well.

After about half an hour, two fiftyish fellows, one gray-haired and lanky, the other short and stout, approach me on the putting green. "Are you Bill Hallberg?" the tall guy asks.

"I sure am. Are you my new golfing buddies?" I ask.

"Looks that way. This is Harry. I'm George."

We take care of the formalities quickly—all the traditional disclaimers. I tell them about the project I've undertaken. Harry cringes when I mention that they will be characters in the book, but then he laughs. "Imagine that," he says. They seem like extremely pleasant fellows. George has been a golfer for only five years, while Harry has been playing the game since childhood, albeit infrequently of late. Out of the corner of my eye, I watch them take a couple of dozen practice putts each. George brandishes a new Odyssey putting wand with a space-age insert purported to add feel to every putt. I have my doubts, of course, but it's a handsome stick, and it pleases me that he's willing to take the game so seriously. His stance over the ball is a little suspect, but some of that has to do with his being around six-feet-four. My snap judgment is that Harry is more resistant to the seductive wiles of the game. His practice strokes are perfunctory, and his reaction to the worst of them is stoic. George is over there working on ten-footers, exhorting himself to concentrate. "Rats," he says when he leaves a putt short. "Come on, George. Get it to the hole."

The golf course is beautiful in the morning light. All the swales of this desert links course are thrown into relief by the low-hanging sun. In the distance is the Santa Fe range, black against the morning sky. Before me the emerald, treeless fairways flow through sagebrush and Indian paintbrush and ocotillo. There's only the faint tinge of mountain forest to remind us that this desert floor is only one of the several ecological strata defining the region. "What a great day," George says when his name is called over the loudspeaker. "Guess we're up."

I ride alone in my topless electric cart, while Harry and George commandeer their own. While we're waiting at the first tee, George tells me about his last golfing adventure, in Durango, Colorado. "Nicest course I ever played," he says. "They must have poured a king's ransom into that place." I gather that George is sufficiently prosperous to live the good life, judging from the fact that he's renting a small villa in Taos. He's hosting his pal Harry and his wife for a weeklong visit. "Yesterday morning Harry and I were the first ones on the course. It was just beautiful, wasn't it?" Harry nods, and surveys the magnificent terrain. "Not a sound except the birds. And there were deer and rabbits and desert mice all over the fairways."

It seems George and Harry grew up together in Brooklyn, attended Catholic school together, then went off to different colleges. But they've been like brothers their whole lives. Harry has been victimized by corporate downsizing and, at age fifty-four, is looking for work. "It's pretty damn frustrating," he says, "at this point in life to try for a new job. I still haven't adjusted to unemployment." My impression is that this visit is intended as a morale booster for Harry, although I wonder if his recent bad luck will be more apparent, juxtaposed against George's big plans, which include a possible retirement in the Taos mountains. "Harry's a good man," George says. "Somebody will grab him soon."

When the fairway is clear, George steps onto the tee. He takes a few lavish practice swings with his Big Bertha driver, then addresses the ball. His swing is brisk and truncated, but the ball scoots down the fairway about two hundred yards. "There you go. That'll work just fine," I say. When it's Harry's turn, he eschews practice swings and takes a flat, vicious swipe at the ball, which results in a warped-looking drive that sails out over the sagebrush to the left, then curves back into the fairway, dead center. "Nice drive. A very unusual flight path, I'd say." Harry gives me a wry smile. He knows that his swing does not resemble the Platonic ideal, but so long as it works, he seems satisfied.

We're at 7,800 feet here in Taos, my first really high-altitude golfing experience. I tee up an Ultra DPS and have a look down this fairway, whose landing area is quite generous, but woe unto him who strays from the friendly confines. Dense fescue rough defines the green bent-grass carpet and, beyond that, *death*—a very serious sagebrush infestation, exacerbated by thorny species of desert scrub. No man will return alive from a safari into these wilds. There are warnings on the scorecard. Rattlesnakes, scorpions, venomous spiders, and other unpleasant varieties of wildlife await marauders. Undaunted, I decide to let out the shaft, partly to impress myself and partly to test Leonardo da Vinci's conjectures on the aerodynamics of dimpled orbs. I can feel my jaw clenching, my grip tightening, my gaze narrowing. A voice in my brain says *"Now!"* I drill my tee shot straight down the middle. A miracle. All the contrarieties of a bad golf swing have canceled each other out. I don't give a turkey's toe-nail for how I looked in the process of having blasted this tee shot or whether I've split a gut or soiled myself—or burst an aorta, for that matter. The ball is out there at least a good three hundred yards, the longest drive of my life, not counting a wind-aided boomer on the concrete fairway of a course in northern England. It's all I can do not to get an erection so manly is my drive. "God A'mighty," says George.

"That won't happen again," I say.

Unfortunately, Harry's fairway shot is a sidewinder that skitters into the desert. He puffs out his cheeks, drops another ball, and chops it up the fairway. I know it will be a long day for him. Meanwhile, I loft a wedge onto the green, ten feet left of the flagstick, and George finds the bunker.

It's a lame hope indeed, but I can't help pulling for Harry to experience transmogrification. Nothing short of that will rescue his game. He seems to enjoy the rapturous sunshine and the pure air, but golf is no panacea for his deeper concerns. There are issues so big that golf can't touch them, at least not the kind of golf he's destined to play. He needs divine intervention, a hole in

one, a miracle, like the Atlanta Harry's bizarre quid pro quo—a
cancer diagnosis on Thursday, an *ace* on Friday. The swing just
isn't there for this Harry, though, and his brain is not fully
engaged in the task at hand. But George is having the time of his
life, making pars and bogeys, with an occasional double bogey
tossed in for comic relief. He believes in the miraculous proper-
ties of his new putter, in the virtues of big-headed titanium drivers, of solid-core golf balls. He's having the time of his life. "Now,
this is fun!" he says. I'm playing with my usual inconsistency.
Mostly pars, but a few ugly patches as well. And I'm pulled in
opposite directions. I'm happy that George is having one of those
memorable rounds upon which God smiles from on high. But I'm
also rooting for Harry to do something extraordinary, something
beyond his capability.

Beginning at number six, George manufactures five straight pars,
the first time in his entire golfing life that he's had such a run.
Twenty-footers are snaking into the hole, badly bladed approach
shots are skittering onto the green, drives are rescued conveniently
from oblivion by ball washers and trap rakes. In fairness, he's
playing his game as well as he can, urged on, perhaps, by the
prospect of literary immortality. "I'm picking up," Harry says after
his second fairway shot vanishes into the brush. We're on number
twelve. I've hit a drive, tilted by the freshening breeze into the sagebrush beyond the mounded rough. Maybe, by virtue of dumb luck,
my ball will have found one of the rare openings in the dense cover.
Not bloody likely, but what the heck. It's worth a gander. So I park
my cart near the hem of the rough and hop out to explore. William
Hallberg, master of the game, is only five over par after eleven, and
there is some hope that he will break eighty, disallowing obliquities
such as this one, of course.

I'm only a few feet into the bracken, searching in vain for my
errant ball, when I hear a distinct, heart-stopping rattle. Etiquette
suggests that one should remain stationary in the presence of a
coiled, unhappy rattler. But I do a grandiose, Olympian Fosbury
flop clean over a sizable sagebrush specimen into the relative
safety of the adjacent rough. This is the moment of transcendent

joy for Harry. He has never seen a man gain such altitude so quickly, and he's laughing out loud from the safety of his golf cart. "See a snake?" he asks.

"Hell, yes," I say. "He's in there, all right." I can still hear him rattling. I get down on my hands and knees so I can get a glimpse of the rattlesnake I know to be coiled beneath the pale green foliage. My eye catches a flash of something yellow caught in the low branches of a sagebrush. I refocus, crawl a few feet closer, adjust my angle of observation, and see that the dreaded pit viper is nothing more than an M&M's wrapper snagged in some sagebrush and rattling in the breeze. "It's a damned *candy wrapper*," I shout. This bit of news finishes Harry. He's a total goner. Having accepted his miserable golfer's doom and dropped temporarily out of the fray, he's now the happiest fellow on the golf course. And I'm so pleased to be the agent of his merriment that I break into laughter so painful that tears roll down my cheeks. "Peanut M&M's. Very dangerous. Highly venomous peanut M&M's."

Harry, whose mysterious burden is suddenly lightened, plays in admirably. He makes very big numbers on several of the holes, but he seems to be enjoying his dufferhood. George, meanwhile, has come back to earth, and, due to a triple bogey at number twelve, my chances of breaking eighty have gone very much by the boards.

Almost without our having realized it, the sky has gradually filled with purple clouds, dense as boulders. We've just hit our tee shots on number seventeen when lightning illuminates the mountainsides, miles in the distance. But the clouds overhead are undeniable, and the first drops of rain tumble down on us. My umbrella is locked safely inside Iris, so I'm vulnerable to whatever is in store. Which is a good drenching. We three wet golfers whack-and-run our way up the penultimate hole, and we manage to hit our tee shots at eighteen before the downpour begins. It's every man for himself now. I whack a slippery one up the fairway, neglecting any semblance of protocol. We're standing in the fairway, intending to hit our third shots onto the par four concluding hole, when a lightning bolt lands perilously close to us. "Pars for everybody," I scream. "Let's haul ass."

We clamber into our carts and hurry to the clubhouse. We will get no wetter than we are at present, but the flashes and thunder are intimidating. When we dash into the clubhouse with our dripping clubs, the pro tosses us towels. "Have fun out there?" he asks.

"It doesn't get any better than this," I say.

We three golfers stand at the picture window, watching the rain pelt down. The workers have long since abandoned ship, and there are ever more linksters steering their carts toward home base. Upon arriving, soaked and bedraggled, we are given free beer from the clubhouse cooler. The mood is highly festive. Survivors all, we gulp our brew and laugh at ourselves.

When the rain lets up, which it soon does, I tell my friends that I must away. As warmly as possible, I shake the hands of Harry and George. "It was a wonderful day," I tell them. "Hope the world treats you both right."

"Good luck with your travels," says George. "Send us a copy of the book. Don't *forget*, now."

I promise them that they won't be forgotten and dash into the dwindling rain with my golf clubs, which I hurl into the trunk. Without removing my golf shoes, I drive out of the muddy parking lot, onto the muddier road, and away from Taos Country Club. Harry, I realize, has made exactly one par, that being on the last hole. But it's something to build on.

By eight o'clock, the rain is gone and the sky has cleared. The square is empty tonight. No band, no magicians, no Indian dancers. Just some skateboarders and a couple of painters capturing the velvety evening light. I eat a delicious chicken chimichanga at the Mexican restaurant recommended by Jim and Lucy. Afterward, I purchase locally made turquoise necklaces from Rosemary Black Crow, a Navajo street vendor. One for Rachel and one for Gillian. "Beautiful stones, aren't they?" she says. And they are. For Julie I buy beautiful Mexican painted plates and for myself a silver ring. Garth will have to wait. He's a hard one to shop for. My gift for Mom and Dad is nothing you can buy, so they are taken care of.

I duck into the community room of the bunkhouse to see what might be afoot at ten o'clock at night. Just a couple of wearly travelers waiting for their clothes to dry. Only mildly disappointed not to have happened upon a sixties-style love-in, I amble down to my quarters and fall onto the bed, hoping for another good night of sleep before I head into the high mountains of Colorado.

rocky mountain, hi!

It's a strange thing, driving east again. I feel defeated almost, aiming Iris's prow toward the rising sun ... but eastward it is because that's the way the highway takes me. Eastward for a while, then gradually northward toward Pueblo, then Denver and on into the tall mountains. I want to play golf above the clouds in air so thin the ball wants to fly forever. My new friend George mentioned, almost in passing, that Mt. Massive Country Club, the most altitudinous golf course in America, sprawls at the feet of its namesake and Mt. Elbert, the monarch of all Colorado mountains. I want to take my stance at the highest point of Mt. Massive Country Club and tee up a ball so lively as to be outlawed by the USGA. With my bubble-shafted titanium driver, I'll take the swing of my life and send the ball into orbit around the moon—a grandly sentimental, utterly foolish tribute to my dad. I'll retrieve the ball, even if that means violating the moon to get the thing, and when I pass through Ohio on the last leg of my journey, I'll make my father a gift of it ... his trophy for teaching me all there is to know about the rub of the green.

I'm sorry to be leaving Santa Fe. It's one place on this earth where, as a tourist, I have not felt like an outsider but rather part of the congenial hum. My morning drive takes me into spectacular sun-filled valleys, through which flow streams that shine like mercury. The population—what there is of it—is scattered ... a homestead now and then, a trailer, a ranch, a shack with zinnias in the yard. Nothing you could quite call a settlement, except for a mobile-home outpost called Glorieta and the historic neighboring town of Pecos, stomping grounds of the legendary Judge Roy Bean. The town isn't much, but I stop long enough to photograph the old jail and buy postcards at a little curio shop, which just happens to sell gas, or vice versa. But that's the way it is in this beautiful outback. Specialty shops are nonexistent around here, and everybody has a sideline. There are signs in front of most of the few humble houses along the roadside. Ranchers sell firewood. Loggers board cats and dogs. Veterinarians raise chinchillas.

As I cruise on toward Las Vegas, New Mexico, I can't help thinking about Harry and George, but especially Harry. I wonder what yesterday's round did for him. It must have been painful in a way, that juxtaposition of careless leisure against his own worry and fear. Too bad the fellow doesn't love the game of golf because he could make it matter if he really wanted to. He could make it matter, then escape into that existential realm where bad lies are offset by lucky bounces and all the rules are written down and humans must accord one another their due. Golf doesn't kid us or deal us killing blows. We make a snowman on one hole and a deuce on the next. That's the nature of the sport. I was rooting for Harry to make a birdie somewhere along the line . . . or a par . . . or even a decent string of consistent bogeys. But the game wasn't ready to yield to him just yet nor he to it.

Maybe Harry will soon land a job befitting his talents. Maybe his daughter will find a good job of her own and move out of his house and into her own apartment. Maybe he will buy a magic putter that will unlock the door to the game and golf will come to mean something to him. He deserves a good bounce, either way.

The land between Las Vegas, which I bypass, and the Colorado border is less inspiring than that which precedes it. I feel as if I've never left Santa Fe, although I'm filled with anticipation for the snowcapped mountains that await me later in the day. Natalie Merchant keeps me company most of the way. "Noah's Dove" tends to get me all wistful and pathetic. But sometimes it's good to hurt for no

damned reason at all. I tell myself that anyway, as I roll through
unpopulated, inhospitable territory toward the uppermost reaches of
New Mexico.

Just inside Colorado, the mountains suddenly reappear. Big,
craggy fellows, covered with fir trees. There are chalets perched
among the conifers and the first brown-and-white pictographs indi-
cating the proximity to ski resorts. In a pretty little town called
Trinidad I stop at the tourist information center to get myself a free
map and maybe some information on the golfing scene. A nice old
lady, obviously a volunteer, flusters through file cabinets and looks
under counters for a golf brochure she is quite sure is still available.
"Oh, dear! I'm so sorry. I can't seem to find it. I'm so dreadfully
sorry," she says. I'm afraid she's going to cry so disappointed is she
in her inability to put her arthritic hands on the item in question.

"Really, it's not a problem. Don't worry about it. I'll just stop at
the Chamber of Commerce in Denver." I give her a friendly tap on
the shoulder. "Wouldn't mind a map of Colorado, though."

"Now *that* we have in abundance," she says. "Here, take a
handful of them."

"Really, I just need one."

"Shoo . . . shoo, shoo, shoo," she says, laughing.

And off I go with maps aplenty.

I've been in this state for less than half an hour and already I'm
willing to don a plaid shirt and clunky boots for TV spots extolling
its many virtues. Unsightly billboards are few and far between, but
the roadside is rife with stone picnic shelters and scenic overlooks.
Ominous signs threaten litterers with hefty fines, chemical castra-
tion, and possible decapitation; plucking wild posies and sucking
minerals from rock formations can mean time in the hoosegow;
transporting runaway convicts is a massive boner with dire consequences. It pleases me no end to see said convicts, orange-clad,
swarming around big, yellow roadside trucks, picking up trash from
the tall grass.

My flirtation with the mountains is all too brief. I've been teased
by an isolated cluster of minor peaks, and now, once again, I'm confronted with grim, hot, dusty plains. Even Natalie Merchant is

unable to soften the harshness of these surroundings. I stare at the onrushing highway through tinted glasses, wishing stupidly for rain.

Pueblo shimmers in one-hundred-ten-degree heat, bleached and foreboding. Of course, my perception is that of a man driving at a high rate of speed through the industrial corridor on the outskirts of town. Somewhere beyond the grain elevators and petroleum tanks and rusting factories is a bustling downtown filled with happy Coloradans. But it's a hard thing to imagine at the moment.

An hour later I arrive in Colorado Springs. It's here that the high mountains make a dramatic return. Pikes Peak with its snowy skullcap looms beyond the endless, symmetrical residential developments marching in formation up and down the walls of the valley. Here, in this basin, myriad golf courses appear, contradicting the arid terrain that rejects greenness in all its manifestations. It's comforting to see rolling fairways again and blue-green spruce trees and zinnia beds and beige sandtraps after days and days of desert landscape.

Still, the heat is oppressive when I exit my car in the parking lot of a Kmart. I'm in serious need of a spoon, an item that cannot be purchased in its orphaned state. One must adopt an entire family of silverware in order to gain custody of a simple spoon. I stomp out of the housewares section toward the aisle where camping equipment is on display. I find a stainless steel knife/fork/spoon trio in a plastic holster, a lovely item, especially considering that the knife neatly doubles as a bottle opener.

The air outside is searing and my thirst is great, so, after paying for my purchase, I march down the awninged walkway to the asthmatic courtesy door of a Kroger's. Open Sesame! Posthaste I go to the beer cooler for a sixer of Coors. Then, obligatory Beer Nuts. Deeper into the great, cluttered maw I go. In a mad frenzy, my arms dart autonomously toward the rainbow shelves. I'm pitching merchandise into my cart like a "Beat the Clock" contestant: Pringles, Wonder bread, bologna, Kix, Peter Pan, Yoo-Hoo, Oreos, Cheez Whiz, milk . . . a bag of ice. And Triscuits. Exactly nothing that I've appropriated is vaguely healthy for a middle-aged American male, save for the ice. Gillian would be ashamed of me for shopping unwisely, so I hurry to the produce section, where I grab a Granny Smith apple and a one-pound bag of carrots. Redemption. The freckled checkout clerk smiles at me when I arrive at the cash register. "You're a *man*, all right. My husband came home with almost the same junk last night."

"Cub Scout leader," I tell her, flashing the grin of a solid citizen. Jiminy Cricket whispers obscenities into my ear. I *am* ashamed for the lie, and I *am* undisciplined, but it's too late to backtrack now. "You know those boys . . ." She's not buying any of it, but maybe she senses she's hurting my feelings because she lets up on me.

Just outside of Larkspur, I stop at a rest area, where I commandeer a shady picnic table. The air is hot but nothing like the convection oven of northwest Texas. Because birds have made a toilet of the varnished tabletop, I use my bath towel as a place mat. For lunch I eat a bologna and Cheez Whiz sandwich (rejecting mayonnaise on account of its high-fat content), chips, Oreos, and a scraped carrot. I wash everything down with a double dose of Yoo-Hoo.

I am sated. I am replete. And bound for the Mile High City.

It's been my intention since the outset of my journey to spend a day in Denver, so I find a Motel 6 on Arapaho Road, just on the southern flank of the city. At exactly three o'clock in the afternoon, I register at the office, carry my cooler and suitcase into my poolside room, and get into my orange swim trunks. Motel regulations require swimmers to take a cold shower before immersing themselves in the pool. The shower water, when I pull the metal chain, is riveting in its coolness—so frigid that my brain has room for only this one concept; I can barely muster the intellect to let go of the chain. I wonder if the chaise-lounge women can read my lips. *Jesus, Mary and Joseph!* I say. Purified, I walk dripping to the edge of the pool, wait for some water-winged kids to clear out, then dive otter-style into the deep end. I swim one full lap underwater, break the surface, then rest my elbows on the concrete deck. The water feels delicious, revivifying. I'm tempted to engage the half-dozen kids in a friendly game of "Shark!" but they're too busy diving for pennies.

The sun feels good on my pale belly, which, despite my wretched dietary habits, seems less formidable than it did ten days ago. I'm the only adult male poolside at present, which makes me feel slightly lurid and suspect. It's the times we live in, I suppose, or perhaps it's my own paranoia, but I believe that the moms, with their peeled-spud complexions, are concerned about the likes of me. I'm reading a *Time* magazine and drinking another can of Yoo-Hoo; I fit the profile.

At five, when the rates go down, I ring Bowling Green to see what's up with Mom and Dad. I haven't even bothered to get out of my wet trunks. I feel worn down from all the driving and heat and golf and worry and sun and weird food and beer. The phone rings once, and Dad picks up. "Hi, Dad, it's me, Bill."

"Just a minute," he says. I hear him mumbling something. I think he's telling Mom that I'm on the line. And, indeed, I hear her voice at the other end. "Hello?"

"Well, hi, Mom. You must be in the living room with Dad. Or are you both in the bedroom?"

"Dad made some delicious stew and coleslaw. He's still a good cook, aren't you, Carl?"

"I'm taking a break from the golf today," I tell her. "Sort of golfed out, if you know what I mean. I need to rest."

"That's good, honey. Get some rest."

"How are you doing, Mom? You getting up out of bed?"

"Oh, a little. But I'm weaker. I can tell."

"You've got to get up and move around, Mom."

"I would if I could. But I'm feeling pretty wobbly."

"I know, Mom. I understand."

We chat about the Santa Fe scene and my experience with the deadly M&M's wrapper at Taos. But it's clear she's losing energy for conversation, so I tell her that I love her.

"I love you, too, honey," she says, her voice breaking. Then, suddenly, there's a dial tone. She has hung up the phone. It happens sometimes. At the end of a paragraph of conversation, one or the other of them will punctuate by hanging up the phone, without warning, for reasons I can only imagine. Still, I feel injured by the abrupt termination of our chat. And sad somehow. I suppose I need that nominal reassurance that she's still living and breathing, talking, hearing, and attentive. I want to imagine that she still enjoys the singing of their ancient canary and the shockingly red begonias on the patio and the smell of Dad's unpredictable stew. Every phone call home seems momentous in my mind. When will Dad slip through the gate into incomprehension? And when will Mom just melt completely away? What can I say to aid them on their separate journeys? Only that I love them.

I take a very hot shower, an immorally long hot shower, during which my mind conjures images of my mom, wearing her favorite bathrobe, going into the flames. My chest aches at the thought. I turn my face up into stinging water. I can't manage to stifle a sob, the sound of which resonates inside the fiberglass shower. It is so alien and disconnected from what I know of myself that I'm almost frightened by the sound I make.

I slide into a pair of khaki shorts, leather flip-flops, and a gray T-shirt, gulp down a quick consolation beer, then abandon this vale of tears in favor of a jaunt into downtown Denver. An RTD bus deposits me at Union Station, not far from Sixteenth Avenue, where the Tattered Cover, a marvelous, eclectic bookstore, is located in a historic brick building with creaky wooden floors and high ceilings. It feels great to be poking through the bookshelves, slipping a volume out from between its neighbors, reading liner notes and blurbs and opening paragraphs. Or ogling pictures of nude volleyball players and harelipped Chinese children in blue hospital pajamas.

Finally, I find three books I'm looking for. One is the collected poems of Philip Larkin, a crusty Englishman who, in his own beautifully grumpy way, understood the world's truths, not that he could abide them. He *hated* golf, but for that he must be forgiven. To offset my affection for a man with such a singular blind spot, I select a coffee-table book on Bobby Jones, my notion of an American hero. The text is minimal, and the black-and-white photographs evoke an age I never knew. But it's a perfect gift for my father because its antiquity connects with the strongest part of his brain. Finally, a hardcover novel, *Snow Falling on Cedars*, by David Guterson. The seductive cover and the lovely, clean first paragraph capture me. I carry the books up to the teller and give her a hundred-dollar bill. "Could you double-bag them for me?" I ask.

"Be glad to," she says, and smiles beguilingly. "I hope you enjoy them."

A book is a wonderful prop if you're dining alone, disguised as a

thoughtful intellect. You feel less a loser if you've got something
upon which you can fix your gaze besides the gay restaurant traffic
from which you are excluded. Fact is, I'm once again seated at a
table by myself in the funky bowels of the City Spirit Café, not far
from the bookstore. I give waiter John my order—a sensible salad,
stuffed mushrooms, and tea—then let my eyes fall upon a Larkin
poem called "Churchgoing." The wistful depiction of a lonely
English country church visited by a lonelier traveler brings me
down, so I aim for something possibly sexier and thus uplifting. The
next poem, however, is hardly cheerier than the first, so I opt for the
Bobby Jones book.

The LoDo section of Denver is a fine place to walk when the sky is
no longer blue but you are. The shops stay open, the sidewalks are
crowded, the people seem high-spirited and healthy. Because I've
already far exceeded my daily budget, I content myself by window-
shopping and making poignant eye contact with solitary young
women who scurry up and down the sidewalks.

Although I've slept the night away like a domesticated hound, getting out of bed in the morning is more difficult than I can ever
remember. My joints ache, and my temples seem to be bookended
by marble tombstones, so I gulp a couple of Advil in hopes of molli-
fying my mysterious ailment. A subsequent hot shower helps matters, as does a large mug of home-brewed, homeopathic coffee with
lots of milk and sugar.

By the time I've checked out of the motel, I'm in at tournament
level once again. I reckon I've fallen victim to a mild case of psycho-
somatosis—a privilege accorded to lonely wayfarers like myself.

Onto I-470 I go. Onto the great southern loop, the chin strap of
the Mile High City. Off to the right, through the bird crap on the passenger window, looms the gauzy metropolis beneath a veil of smog.
The eastbound lanes are choked with morning commuters, yet Hallberg sails smugly along, his radio tuned to NPR. The gas gauge suggests that Iris needs refueling, but that will have to wait until Denver
is a fait accompli.

A mistake has been made. A mistake has been made by me. For
reasons unknown, the entire chain of mountain towns on I-70 is

without power. Thus, the gas pumps at every station are temporarily defunct. I have the option of joining flocks of other cars parked at odd angles in front of the 7–11s and Texacos, or I can drive all the way back to Denver, or I can roll the dice and push toward Leadville. My instincts tell me to play it safe, but I'm a greedy fellow. *Andiamo,* into the great unknown I forge with my finite fuel supply, trusting fate and the accuracy of my gas gauge. There's probably fuel enough to get me to Idaho Springs, and if necessary I'll wait there until the juice returns, invigorating disabled pumps from Golden to Silver Plume. Along the way to Idaho Springs, high in the delirious mountains, I come upon a roadside buffalo herd within a vast compound. I slide over to the berm, dismount, and walk to the densely touristed fence with my camera. There are hundreds of buff out there, shaggy fellows, and calves, and cows with udders less copious than those of domestic cattle. They graze among the mountain spruce and aspen on grass so tall and green as to defy credulity. This is the first real buffalo herd I have seen in my life, and I'm more thrilled than I care to admit at the sight of them, big and ornery and oblivious creatures that they are.

But I have a golf date to keep, so I press onward, toward the clouds.

Idaho Springs fulfills my every hope. At eight-thirty in the morning, the electric current is once again humming in the thick high-tension cables overhead and digits twirl inside the lens of the BP pump like cherries in a slot machine. It's a wonderful sight, this visible diminution of my money supply, inverse to the climbing fuel level in my tank.

At the Loveland Pass, just a few miles up the road, the elevation is nearly twelve thousand feet and there's *snow* on the ground. After parking Iris on a gravel turnoff, I climb out of the car to revel in the fact that I'm more than two miles above the Atlantic, where I dipped my toes just a couple of weeks ago. The air is so cold that a sweater is obligatory, and it takes some deep digging to locate one at the bottom of my suitcase. Snow seems to pack beautifully here at the thermal cusp of North America. One perfect snowball hurled against a granite facade at roughly seventy-eight miles per hour yields a handsome white bra cup plastered against the stone. One more well-placed shot, and, voilà, I've created my dream girl. I breathe in the thin mountain air, then exhale plumes of fog, a strange and wonderful phenomenon considering that this is the second day of July. Maybe there's a high-altitude corollary to rapture of the deep, which would explain the joy I feel at being here at the highest four-lane pass on the continent.

I veer off the highway at the Leadville exit, and stop long enough to phone the Mt. Massive Country Club to see about getting in a round on short notice. Jeff, the course manager, answers the phone. When I explain the nature of my mission, he not only invites me to play as his guest but happily agrees to join me. With the possible exception of my inaugural round at Kiawah, this is the most excited I have been over the prospect of playing golf. I'm imagining a quaint, old-fashioned little course, something like Tucumcari but one mile closer to the sky.

The mountainsides along Route 91, the Leadville road, have been gouged and blasted and pummeled to oblivion by various mining operations, which, over a century ago, fueled the economy of Leadville, making it one of the most prosperous and boisterous cities in Colorado. However, after the mountains had been gutted, the mines shut down, and the town all but surrendered to poverty and abandonment. Then, when there was more plywood than glass in the downtown windows, Leadville's proximity to the interstate and the high peaks slowly enhanced its prospects (but sadly, *not* the land-scape through which one must pass in order to arrive there). Now, according to the promotional brochure, there are "abundant charms to be savored by residents and tourists alike." In order to savor these charms, one must follow the meandering road past one species of geo-logical blight after another, through half-baked reforestation projects wherein scrawny saplings are invited to find footing in slag and riprap and soil corrupted by extraction chemicals. For the sake of ironic contrast, gorgeous snowcapped peaks, Elbert and Massive, gleam against the distant western horizon—which makes the corrupted roadside scenery all the more difficult to bear.

Before making my appearance at the golf course, I decide to get some coffee and doughnuts in Leadville, maybe find a comfortable room, and generally get the lay of the land. I've done my level best to rationalize the aforementioned landscape, which has taken some of the steam from my enthusiasm. I keep telling myself that men and women prospered in the wake of the mining operations; furthermore, useful metals are not created in a bakery, after all. I'm trying . . . believe me, but the tree hugger in me is saddened.

I am, nevertheless, pleased by the town itself from the moment I pass beneath the banner advertising a huge arts and crafts weekend upcoming. The wide, clean main street is lined with an odd assortment of shops and saloons and hotels and offices, some of them beautifully restored and others still neglected. The Delaware Hotel, home of Baby Doe Tabor, world-famous dance hall chanteuse, and dowager heiress, is a beautiful old building, its original Gay Nineties ambience faithfully preserved. Inside, there are brass planters with feather palms, and chandeliers, and floral carpet, and burnished wood furniture. It's no Motel 6, but what the hey. I register at the desk, and the young woman behind the counter gives me the key to Room 13. "Check-in is at one o'clock, but we'll make an exception just this once." She winks at me, and I give her a comprehending nod. I haul my suitcase up the carpeted stairs, unlock the door to my room, and find a mahogany four-poster, a marble-topped washstand with a ceramic basin, a rocking chair, and a couple of faded black-and-white photographs of stern, high-buttoned settlers. I'm pleased with the change of pace. Of course, I miss the brown industrial-grade loop carpet and the Formica bureau and the airbrushed prefab paintings found in my favorite chain motel. But I'm holding up in light of that disappointment. I make a mental note to call Gillian when the phone rates go down to apprise her of my whereabouts, just in case . . .

After biscuits and coffee in the Delaware's coffee shop, I stroll onto the cool, elevated sidewalk. The temperature can't be higher than sixty degrees, but the midmorning sun is gloriously warm on my shoulders. To find the golf course, one need only find a numbered side street, then aim toward Mount Massive, which is precisely what I do. Along the way is a beautiful old cemetery with weathered stones and overgrown burial plots. There are elegant old three-story

Victorian dowagers, badly in need of paint but charming in their dis-
repair. Then, farther out, humbler, nearly identical cottages,
probably belonging to the common miners in days of yore. Beyond
the city limits are the gorgeous log houses and stone mansions
belonging to the new settlers, who have seized the opportunity presented to them by the gorgeous terrain and the availability of vast
uninhabited tracts of land. In ten years this region will probably
resemble Aspen or Vail or any of a number of trendy resort communities. A pity, I think. But inevitable. The evergreen forest sweeps
up the mountainsides, dwindling near the snowy crown of the high
mountains that dominate the landscape.

The Mt. Massive clubhouse is not at all massive. It's a straightforward wooden structure of recent vintage like thousands of such
buildings at myriad municipal courses across the country—with
one notable exception. This humble cube gazes upon snowcapped
mountain peaks and the breathtaking sweep of blue-green forest.

Iris feels right at home amidst the handful of humble, battered
vehicles nosed against the split-rail fence at the boundary of the
parking lot. I pull my golf clubs and shoes from the trunk one more
time and deposit this kaboodle on the deck overlooking the tiny
putting green. Jeff greets me before I'm halfway through the door.
Perhaps there's a sign hanging around my neck: OBSCURE AMERICAN
AUTHOR. "You made it," he says. "Good to meet you, Bill." Jeff is a
big, sturdy fellow who looks more like a snowblower salesman than a
golf operative. He's wearing some highly habituated blue jeans and
a button-down plaid shirt—not exactly traditional golf attire. Already I like the guy.

"God, what a setting," I exclaim. "And not a half bad day for a
round of golf."

"Can I offer you a beer?" he asks. A man after my own heart. Of
course, decorum camouflages my fervent desire for a tall, midmorning brewski, but, as the sun is not yet over the yardarm, I
politely demur. I settle for a can of Coke and a Slim Jim, a true pioneer breakfast. Jeff introduces me to his assistant, Tom, who will be
manning the counter while I traipse the links with my new best
friend. Tom hands me a package of tees, a green plastic divot fork

with the words MT. MASSIVE COUNTRY CLUB printed on the thumb plate, and a bucket of very grubby range balls. "Go on out and hit a few," he says.

I'm standing by the door holding my bucket of oyster-colored range balls in one hand and a Coke in the other. The Slim Jim pokes from my chest pocket like a number two pencil, while the dangerous divot fork and the lethal golf tees are squirreled in the change pockets of my khakis. "So where has your trip taken you? Anywhere interesting?" Jeff asks. He leans casually on the glass counter, a Coke can all but lost in, yes, another *huge* mitt. The world teems, I think, with huge-handed mutants.

I provide an edited account of my most recent adventures in New Mexico, multiplying by a factor of twelve the number of topless women celebrating the drought-busting rainfall. He shows a genuine interest in the details, albeit fabricated, of this luminous moment in my humdrum life. In turn, he shows me a schematic of the additional nine holes planned for Mt. Massive's near future, one more concession to progress, I guess.

The driving range, an isolated bit of acreage located across the road from the clubhouse, is one of the strangest I've encountered in all my days of golfing. A long, narrow AstroTurf carpet is laid down directly over the rocky irregularities of what appears to be a species of tundra indigenous to this landscape. The artificial turf is lumpy and much abused by adamant hackers and low handicappers alike. Nonetheless, I roll a handful of grungy spheres onto the rug and bump a few wedges into the rocky wasteland before me. I can view the entire majestic world of tree and granite and snow, awesome and bewilderingly beautiful, but I'm blooping cruddy spheroidals into a field of lichens and weird purple succulents that look as if they would explode when stepped upon. The practice range provides comic relief more than anything else, although I've managed to untangle some of the road kinks that have nearly become part of my identity.

By the time I return to the clubhouse, Larry and Harvey have arrived on the scene, and Jeff introduces us. Larry is a forty-something like me, with long blond hair hanging from the perimeter of his white baseball hat. "Ha. Gooda meetcha," he says. The accent is so purely

Alabaman that he doesn't even need to tell me where his roots are. But it's a nice reminder that I, too, am connected to the South, perhaps more inextricably than Larry. Harvey is an older fellow, seventy maybe, and a retired widower. He has a neat little pencil-thin mustache and a hat he might have stolen from Theodore back at Kiawah. Because Jeff is technically on call today, he and I will ride in an electric cart, while Larry and Harvey use pull-carts. My preference would be to walk the fairways, but I'm the guest, and the round is complimentary. Am I going to complain? Not likely.

Larry, I can tell, has been playing a lot of golf lately. His skin is the color of an NFL football, and his blond mane is bleached almost to whiteness. We wait at the first tee together, watching a very beefy fellow in striped tube socks, cutoffs, and a Grateful Dead muscle shirt flail at his teed-up golf ball. The ball is destined to slice, which it does, wickedly, deep into the mountain spruce bordering the first fairway. The hole is a relatively short one, but the green, flanked by nasty little pot bunkers, is hardly bigger than a motel bedspread. "Why don't you let us cut in front of you guys? We'll be out of your way in no time," Jeff suggests.

Apparently this quartet of hackers are regulars out here, and they're glad to step aside while we hit our tee shots. I decide to save my titanic drive for a more appropriate moment. Still, my shot is a good one, well struck but surprisingly short considering the thin air and the right prevailing wind. But I'm situated nicely on the fairway, a short iron shy of the green. "Damned nice," Jeff says. "Good ball. Excellent position." Larry nails one into a row of maples lining the left side of the fairway. The ball knocks against limbs and branches. Twigs and branches fall from a tree, then the ball. He is a dead duck, snookered by the fat trunk of a well-placed tree.

"*There's* trouble," Jeff laughs.

Harvey uses an iron off the tee. "I can't hit the woods," he says. "They all go right. Can't tell you why. Think it's up *here*," he says, and taps the side of his skull. His tee ball sails down the fairway, one seventy-five. When Jeff steps onto the tee, I can tell he's a crusher. His swing is big and limber and practiced. But the ball, when he strikes it, draws toward the left-hand rough and dodges into the patchy turf in the shade of the magnetic maple trees.

It's hard to describe how geared up I am to play golf on such a
beautiful day with good fellows in the high mountains of Colorado.
My clean bunker shot at number one spins to within a foot of the cup
for a tap-in par. My partners make bogeys and doubles, and I'm up a
quarter on each of them. They're good-natured chaps, and their
woodsy adventures are all part of the game. Furthermore, I have a
sneaking suspicion that either Larry or Jeff, on any given day, would
make toast of me in a head-to-head competition. Even Harvey, who
will use his putter from anywhere on the golf course, has a knack for
getting up and down from pinecone stymies and hellhole bunkers.

Okay, I'm pleased to be holding my game together, if only for the
sake of my personal pride. It's fun to play well on alien terrain. I
have little in common, really, with any of these fellows, aside from
the green ground we share momentarily. Larry seems to have made
enough money setting up computer programs in Las Vegas gambling
casinos to have retired early to these mountains, although the dis-
covery of Leadville and the resultant population pressures have
tempted him to push farther into the wilds of Colorado. Jeff was an
itinerant ski bum who fell in love with the mountains, lost his heart
to a young woman, and picked up the game of golf by pure necessity.
By working long hours during the golf season, managing the clubhouse at Mt. Massive, he could ski in the wintertime. A perfect solu-
tion, and an enduring one. Harvey lives alone, half a continent from
his sons. His habitat is the golf course, where everybody seems to
know and like him. In a matter of ten minutes, I've fallen in with
these fellows. They include me in their wagers, and taunt me while I
crouch over my knee-knocker. "Pressure's getting to him," they say.
"Writer boy got a case of the nerves."

I like the everyman golfing population at Mt. Massive. There's no
dress code, no expectation of superior play. The course is solid and
tough and idiosyncratic. Number two is a strange golf hole, so odd in
its configuration that even the locals want to see it go. Imagine a
blind par three, straight up a hill between fifty-foot spruce trees.
Only after a greenside bell rings the all-clear do the players below
hit their tee shots. My seven-wood shot is one of those rare efforts

that stick in the brain for a lifetime. The ball flies perfectly through the opening, disappears against the snowcap of Mount Elbert, then tumbles out of the sky. "That's *gotta* be awful damned good," Larry says. "I might could take that one myself." He waggles for a minute over his ball. His own high draw nips the high branches of the tallest spruce and plunges earthward like a wounded quail. He will need to scramble for his par. Harvey doesn't have the might to loft the ball all the way to the mysterious green, but he drills a two iron into the hillside and watches the ball climb the incline and race over the crest of the hill. "Little bastard," Jeff says, then lets fly. His tee shot is a high, soaring beauty that nearly replicates mine.

By dumb luck, my ball has come within a few feet of going in the hole. Jeff is sitting pretty on the back of the green, while Larry and Harvey have tricky little pitches up to the top tier where the pin is located.

I want this birdie. I want this birdie in the worst possible way. I'll sell certain of my body parts for a birdie. My partners make their tries at the shifty golf hole, and when everybody else is accounted for, I take my turn over the ball. It's a dead-straight putt, slightly downhill, a total irrelevancy. If the club head makes contact with the ball, the thing will run to the hole. Aim is everything. I stare at the white cup liner, then my ball, back and forth until Jeff says to hit the damn thing. Finally, I pull the trigger, but it's a misfire for sure. The ball skids left of the hole—a dreaded pull. "Shit happens," Jeff says.

"I flat yanked it," I say. "Ah, well . . ."

We all have our moments. Larry launches a beautiful seven-iron to within five feet of the cup on the par three fourth hole, then cans the putt for a beautiful deuce, which earns him a couple of skins from each of us. However, on the short fifth hole, Harvey punches one onto the green and snakes in what was supposed to be a lag putt for a birdie. He takes off his snap-brim and mops his bald head in disbelief.

My time comes, too, but in a most unexpected way.

I can't help noticing that the ball carries less well at this altitude than it did in Taos, which completely confounds me. Jeff explains that the ball needs air to gain loft and, having gained loft, to *sail*. The aerodynamic function of the golf ball's dimples are compromised once the point of diminishing returns has been achieved, which happens to occur at around seven thousand feet, or so he tells me. And I believe him. So there will be no memorably long drives at Mt. Massive.

"May as well be at sea level," Jeff says.

In defiance of known gravitational and aerodynamic laws, I'm determined to blast my drive at number eight, a relatively short par five. It's an eagle I'm after, which will bring me to level par and immortality. I absolutely lean into my drive, but it's smothered and consequently veers toward a dense patch of spruce trees. There's every reason to think that the ball is consigned to oblivion. But it ricochets, possibly off the brainpan of a squirrel, back onto the fairway. "Lucky bastard," Larry says. "Lucky Yankee bastard." But he hasn't seen luck yet because my gut-busting fairway shot, belted with a *driver*, bolts straight down the dotted line, lands just short of the apron, and rolls onto the green, ten feet from the flag. A birdie is a foregone conclusion. An eagle might just be flapping his wings. After Jeff makes his birdie—the hard way, from the sand—I anchor myself over the ball. *Square the blade*, I tell myself. I dispense with the frenetic head movement and concentrate on a grass blade a few inches down the target line. Then I let go. The ball rolls directly at the cup, holds its line quite nicely, then suddenly balks and halts at the lip. I've left it short. "Call the damn sheriff somebody," says Jeff. "Too bad."

I cap my round with an ugly seven on the last hole, but I've had too much fun to worry over it. My game has improved, I've made good friends, I've basked in mountain sunshine.

We sit at a round Formica table after our round is complete, just talking. Larry, I discover, is a marathon runner. Moreover, he does centuries—one-hundred-mile races up and down mountain roads in high altitude and freezing temperatures. This is the last thing I would have expected from a man who retired at age thirty-eight. I'm half expecting Harvey to apprise me of his world heavyweight boxing title, but he's mum on the subject. I have a sudden urge to fabricate some marvelous bit of fiction about myself—my stint as a Hollywood stunt man, for instance. Finally, when the last swallow of beer is gone, I promise my friends that I will shave a few strokes from their scores when I tote them up for public consumption. To that end, I claim the following scores on behalf of our foursome. Jeff—36. Larry—37. Harvey—39. Bill—30!

I have to say good-bye to my pals. They're flattered when I tell them that this has been the most enjoyable round I can remember. "Come back anytime, Bill," Jeff says. "Let me know, and we'll play some of the other mountain courses."

"I like this one just fine," I tell him.

It's after five by the time I return to the Delaware Hotel, and, because it's cheaper, I use the pay phone in the lobby to ring Gillian back in North Carolina. She picks up right away. "Hi, sweetie," I say. "How's tricks?"

"Bill," she says, her voice quavering. "Now listen to me. Rachel is going to be *fine* when this is all behind her, but she's had a very bad trampoline accident. At her grandmother's house. Or at a friend of her grandmother's. I'm not sure. Anyway, Bill, she apparently snapped the two large leg bones down near the ankle. There's some other damage, too. Metatarsals. Other bones. They're calling it a compound fracture. A very serious break. But she's already had surgery, and she's in recovery."

"Oh, God!" I say, feeling a sudden exaggerated pull of gravity. I sit down, almost involuntarily on the cushioned bench. "Damn it . . ." I say. "Damn it . . . *damn* it." Without my quite realizing it's happening, my eyes go all watery, and light from the prisms of the lobby chandelier swims in a thousand directions. I'm sitting in a public place, talking on the phone at the bottom of a well-traveled staircase, trying not to visualize the accident, but my mind veers in that direction. "Where is she, Gillie? How do I reach her. What's the number at the hospital?"

Gillian gives me the phone number, which I scratch onto the back of the Mt. Massive scorecard with the little pencil. "I'll call you back if I can't get through. Wait . . . I'll call you either way. Sit tight. Okay?"

I ring the number of the hospital switchboard; they connect me to Room 211. Rachel's grandmother picks up. "It's Bill. How's Rachel?"

She tells me that the surgery went well. Pins and screws, possible skin grafts forthcoming. A terrible jigsaw break. But the surgeon was wonderful, and everything, she repeats, went very well. "She was in a lot of pain, poor kid, and she was asking for you the whole time." This is almost more than I can bear. I'm out in the boondocks drinking beer, whacking a golf ball around the mountainside while my daughter is screaming in pain, surrounded by strangers. "You want to talk to her? She's just coming out of anesthesia."

"Yeah, *please*. Can I talk to her?"

"Dad," Rachel says, and starts to cry. "I'm so sorry."

"It's okay, sweetie. It's okay. There's nothing to be sorry about except that you're hurt. I'm coming right home."

"I'm going to be fine. If I need you to come home, I'll tell you. There's nothing you can do."

"I'm coming home."

"Please don't. I know how you hate trampolines. This was all my fault."

"Nonsense, sweetheart. It was nobody's fault."

"Please, do your book stuff. I'll feel horrible if you don't." She's crying again, and there is so little I can do to comfort her. "Just call me every day? Will you?"

"I'm coming home, Rachel."

I sit at the window in Room 13 of the Delaware Hotel watching the light fade over the rooftops. Sometimes, I realize, you think you've got a birdie in your hip pocket; then your approach shot hits a sprinkler head and the perfectly struck ball kicks out of bounds, or into a pond, or into God knows what species of misery. A simple three-foot putt, destined to fall, drifts off course and slides by the hole. Golf is just like that . . .

The sky is nearly black above the Leadville rooftops when the phone, suddenly, rings.

CHAPTER 9

forever and
ever, amen

I have left undone that which I ought to have done. I have failed to
call Gillian back after promising I would. Nevertheless, my heart
plunges when the phone rings on the night table: bad news can
come from any angle these days, although by considering matters
rationally I should know who is calling me here in this faraway place.
"Bill," she says. "Is everything okay? You didn't call me back."

"Oh, jeez, I'm sorry, Gillie. Really, I am. Yeah, sure, sure . . . everything's as good as can be expected." I clear my throat and rub my sore
eyes. "Sorry, sorry, sorry for not phoning you to say so. That was incon-
siderate of me."

"I imagine your brain isn't quite in gear right now," she says.
There's a trace of an English accent that shapes her words and
makes her seem even farther away than North Carolina. "Don't worry
about it," she says. "I understand."

"There's no excuse. Forgive me?" She says that Julie has phoned
my house to find out how's tricks but that it seemed unwise to give
her the word on Rachel's accident just yet. I agree that it's better for
Julie, with her own medical exigencies, to remain unapprised for the
time being. Better for the dust to settle first.

"You were right not to tell her, Gillie," I say. "Right now it looks
like Rachel will have a long way back. She's fairly drugged up. But
surprisingly on top of things."

"I know. She just phoned me here a minute ago."

"She did? Rachel? Why?"

147

"You forgot to give her your phone number there at the Delaware Hotel. *And* she wanted me to twist your arm . . ."

"Not to come home, right?"

"Not to come home . . . *right.*"

"I've booked a flight from Denver tomorrow."

"Cancel it. You don't want her to think she's ruined your trip, do you? She already thinks she's let you down by doing something . . . how did she put it . . . *ill-advised.*"

"I want to be there."

"I know you do, but she wants you to carry on."

"This is such a bummer. God!" I twirl a golf tee on the night-stand. It points unambiguously westward. "Okay. I won't come home."

"Good boy," Gillian says, and I hear myself laughing at this canine praise.

She's a good soul, this Gillian, and I tell her so. She says she loves me, and I honestly believe she does. "Bye, sweetie," I say.

The cost of a room at the Delaware includes breakfast. Despite the turmoil of the last dozen hours, I'm one hungry pilgrim, explained by my having eaten only a frosty doughnut and three inches of a Slim Jim during the last thirty-six hours. Hispanic cooks and college-girl waitresses scurry from table to table in the hotel's pleasant dining room. "Am I too early?" I ask at the threshold of the sanctum sanctorum. A beautiful young woman, probably a summer employee, politely informs me that breakfast begins at seven. She does, however, hand me a conciliatory *Denver Post* to occupy me for half an hour while my stomach turns over like a silver-dollar flapjack.

Breakfast is worth the wait. Homemade rolls, cheese grits, over-easy eggs, Canadian bacon, pineapple, and coffee. Lots and lots of coffee, poured and repoured by the darling of the ages. "One more cup and I should be at tournament level," I tell her, and she laughs. There is not one dental filling in that beautiful mouth of hers. Not one blemish on her heartbreaker face. Some lucky boy out there somewhere, a very young, very lucky boy, will win her perfectly sweet heart one of these days. How odd it is to imagine that I could be her father. The whole idea of fatherhood has consumed me since news of Rachel's accident. Fatherhood and loving relationships and responsibility. I need practice, I know. Over the past few years I've allowed self-indulgence to swell inside my middle-aged soul. Beer, lust, bad food, inertia, fiscal irresponsibility . . . and now golf. Perhaps this one colossal immersion in the greenest of games will be the end of it for me. But I doubt it.

After tucking a memorably large tip beneath my gold-rimmed breakfast plate, I wave to the restaurant staff and exit the scene.

Rachel answers the telephone when I ring her hospital room. I need reassurance before climbing behind the wheel of my car for a bizarre lurch into the vast nothingness of southern Nevada, my next destination.

"Hi, cutie. How you doing?"

"Dad. Where are you? You're not in North Carolina, are you?" Her speech is sleepy-sounding and hoarse.

"Gillian told me I shouldn't come home. That you would prefer that I not do that. You still feel that way?"

"I'm fine. I'm taking a lot of pain medication, and Grandma will take good care of me. All the young doctors are flirts. I kind of like it. I have a sore throat."

"Did they tube you?"

"Tube me?"

"Put a tube down your throat when they knocked you out."

"Don't know. Will you find me something turquoise? I like Indian jewelry."

"You got it," I say. "Turquoise . . . jewelry . . . for . . . Rachel. Know how turquoise got its name?"

"Turkey. Turquoise used to come from Turkey."

"Smart girl."

"Thank you."

"I love you, Rachel."

"Love you, too. Call me?"

"Every day!"

At eight-thirty I'm blasting through the mountains at a high rate of speed. I want to make Austin, Nevada, before nightfall. There will be no more night driving for this Ohio-born lad. I'll sleep in a haymow with a Nubian goat before I reprise my nightmare voyage into Tucumcari. Which means taking full advantage of Iris's massive booster rockets and speed limits so generous as to make the West a spectacular blur. I've filled my tank in Leadville. There will be no gambling with the regional power supply today. My cooler is throbbing with unwholesome foodstuffs, chewable Americana. If a volcano blows, postmillennial anthropologists will find me preserved in an ocean of pumice, an Oreo clamped between my teeth, a Yoo-Hoo cradled in my petrified hand.

It's a troubling thing for an acrophile like me to decend, however gradually, from the highest reaches of the Rocky Mountains. The altitude at Vail is barely seven thousand feet, much higher than the highest point in my home state but fully a mile down from the Loveland Pass. The snow is gone from the mountaintops, and the ski slopes look like golf fairways corrupted by guy wires and scaffolds. I stop in Vail only long enough to pee at a tourist information center and make one circuit of the shopping area. There's plenty of merchandise I'd be happy to own—signed Tiffany lamps, paintings by Jasper Johns and Willem de Kooning, carved marble gargoyles—but the price tags are astronomical and my Visa account is bloated to bursting. I buy a pack of Big Red cinnamon gum at a Rexall and two postcards. There at the magazine rack I see a woman in cat sunglasses and a Cassini scarf. I know she's somebody famous, Faye Resnick maybe, or maybe not. But when she wipes her nose with a lipstick-stained handkerchief, my interest fades.

Time avails, even in Vail, so I rescue Iris from the meter maid and her ticket book. We cruise up a corollary side street past million-dollar cabins with shock-collared collies in the front yard and Range Rovers in the driveways, onto the service road, which crosses the Colorado River via a beautiful stone bridge and ultimately feeds onto the interstate a mile or two west of town.

Twice along the way, I'm halted by flagmen whose job it is to prevent travelers from driving headlong into boxcar boulders that have tumbled down the mountainside for the express purpose of frustrating the westward insinuations of wanderers like me. I chew my Big Red gum and watch the Colorado pour toward its rendezvous with the Cane five hundred miles downriver. Hot air blows through rolled down windows of the car. I exit the car and sit on the fender for a while, then walk up the center line to ascertain the nature of the holdup. "Rock slide," a trucker says from his high window. "Happens all the goddamn time," he says. "Rock slide or a jackknifed semi. Either one or the other. I'm bettin' rock slide, figurin' the rain kicked some ass here last night."

Finally, a puff of brown exhaust from up near the front of this stalled parade—a sure sign that a big truck up there is finally in motion. Time to scoot back to the cockpit, time to get the show on the road, time to roll. On past Eagle I cruise. Eagle and Gypsum and Silk and Rifle, into the brown, hot deserts of Utah.

By one o'clock I have completely abandoned the moist evergreen mountains, which now fill my rearview mirror when I summon the heart to steal a glance. I've entered an eerie geometrical world of Art Deco rock formations, staircased and flat-topped, like Busby Berkeley sets. The foliage, what there is of it, is now more horizontal than vertical and less green than gray. Maybe I'm merely softening to alien landscapes because I can't help thinking how beautiful it is, all of it: yucca, dwarf piñon, ocotillo, globe mallow, Gilia, primrose, prickly pear . . . even the omnipresent sagebrush. The delicate spring blooms, save for a few stragglers, have withered under the oppressive sun. Even so, sand, more than sun, rules the eastern Utah landscape. Sandstone mesas, windblown dunes, sandblasted arches, and rust-colored arroyos. I am confronted with a decision. I can, if I wish, detour down to Moab and Arches National Park where Edward Abbey, friend of packrats and rattlesnakes, held forth in his lonely trailer while he wrote his *Desert Solitaire*. Or I can press single-mindedly toward the next link in this mysteriously green chain. I have been so much the golfer, the consumer, the jovial inebriate that I yearn for even a taste of abnegating desert wilderness.

Highway 191 drops south off the interstate and dwindles into the shimmering horizon. After a few miles on this road, I wonder if I've blundered into a nuclear testing zone, so flat and dry and uninhabitable is the landscape. But inertia carries me forth, through the desolate wasteland, until, at last, I see what I've been looking for traced like dusty thunderheads against the inner wall of the southern sky. These are the formations that Abbey came to love. Delicate Arch. Courthouse Towers. North and South Windows. They are, at best, only suggestions of themselves from this distance, but my heat-congealed blood is once again flowing with excitement.

I bypass the park entrance for now in favor of a reasonable lunch in Moab, which seems to have made few concessions to the tourist trade. The southwestern motif pervades: adobe shops painted mustard or rust or tan or brown. Decorative hitching posts. Saloons. There are several emporiums specializing in beautifully crafted Navajo jewelry, far superior to the baubles I fondled in Santa Fe. Finer merchandise by far than the humble necklace I purchased from Rosemary Black Crow. I locate a comfortable, rusticated restaurant with bean-sprout possibilities, and I eat my Mexican salad within its dusky confines, serenaded by canned mariachi music. Then, to the jewelry store, where I spend half an hour pointing at various bracelets and pendants that might please Rachel. Finally, I settle on a beautiful turquoise and silver bracelet, delicate enough to complement her slim wrist but substantial enough to make a statement. Five turquoise ovals sit in a perfect row, each in its own silver nest. The piece seems inauthentic, somehow, a concession to a mainstream sensibility, but it is unusual and very pretty. The selection pleases the Navajo girl who waits on me. She gently places the bracelet in a cotton-lined box and includes a card with a brief biography of the artist, William Nighthawk.

The drive up into the Arches is heart-stopping. I want to halt the car at every scenic turnoff to admire the massive, tormented monuments to the elements of nature. But I've narrowed my quest to Delicate Arch for its defiance of geometry and gravity itself. If I am to absorb one phenomenal image, it will be the pale afternoon moon viewed through the arch's impossibly large portal, rainbowed over by the thinnest of sandstone fins.

Iris is the only car parked in the small lot at the mouth of the Delicate Arch Trail, a good bit of luck. Observing the clearly posted admonitions forbidding violation of the cryptobiotic crust (formed by a very gluey species of cyanobacteria), I march toward my goal. The frail moon is over my right shoulder at this time of the afternoon; camera in hand, I stroll through a nice cluster of piñon pine toward my destination. It's possible to stand directly beneath the arch, but, aside from the novelty of a choreographed hold-it pose, the value of the experience is better realized by finding just the right perspective. So, I march on past the arch, into its formidable shadow. The span is incredible and so impossibly thin in places that I wonder if its support derives from its own uplifting beauty. Now, from this wonderful angle, the moon floats like a stage prop within the arch's blue window. I snap the photograph, feeling almost irreverent. One picture will have to do. The imagery before me is all I could want, and I spend a good long time standing alone in the shadow of the formation. The smell of Utah juniper fills the hot high desert air. Or is it primrose? The wind makes a whistling sound in the crevices at the base of the enormous fin, and there's also the sound of sparrows squabbling over a bit of scrap. All in all, a beautiful confluence, and one I won't soon forget. When a band of Asian tourists arrives with their Nikons and tripods, I begin the trek back to my car.

For two hours I haven't once considered whether I should be carrying a sixty-degree wedge in my golf bag. Or whether my putting would improve with a modified forward press. Nor have I, except in a very abstract, highly spiritualized way, dwelled on the painful vicissitudes of my family life. Instead, I've been reconstituted as what I truly am: an amalgamation of minerals no more impressive than sandstone but ordained by the cosmos to think and to marvel and to wonder. A very waxy conclusion to be drawn from a simple jaunt into the wilderness. Maybe a cold beer will dissolve my romantic notions, but I hope not. It's a risk I'll have to take.

I need to find out, in the midst of this wonderfully bewildering trek, what the game of golf means to me. Why, aside from fame and fortune, am I blazing across the uninhabited, uninhabitable dry plains of the American Southwest with a set of golf clubs knocking in the trunk of my car and a new sleeve of Ultras competing with road maps for space in my glove compartment? How odd it is to be minding my traffic lane, listening to an REM song about swimming naked at night and all the while rehearsing a truly immaculate golf swing at a driving range in the back of my brain. As often as I ponder the more meaningful realities of my existence, this recurring motif intrudes. A man, not unlike the fellow driving this car, is swiping a golf ball from a patch of pristine turf toward the dome of the universe, again and again and again. But I am inside the skin of that man, and I can feel the corded grip in my hands. Golf is a game of odd shapes and peculiar motions, with tangible goals, and pitfalls to thwart your progress. The challenge of golf is a fine and wonderful reason to play the game. However, the striking of the ball is the thing, the all-consuming, central Platonic element in my affection for the game. Maybe because it's so damned difficult to bring an iron blade down and into the ball at such a precise angle, cutting away that little apron of turf underneath and watching ball, then divot, fly out against the sky. The feel of it, the percussive heft of a golf ball meeting the grooves of a club face just so, just there. Punitive, inexorable, perfect.

As a child I'd lie in bed swinging golf clubs in my dreams, waiting, even in my sleep, for daybreak so I could race across the street to the golf course with my sawed-off sticks and a few balls rescued from the ignominious pond that caressed the seventh green.

I grew up in a part of the Midwest where I couldn't drive twenty miles in any direction without seeing at least one golf course or a sign urging me to TURN HERE for eighteen holes of championship golf. Discounts for juniors. Public welcome. How could I *not* think about golf, even in winter when the game waited, latent, beneath the snow. Now, in my forties, I am just coming back to the game that once owned my heart. The driving range is again open in that roped-off section of my brain. I'm swinging the club again with a limber, elegant perfection I can never achieve in real life.

There's nothing out here to remind me that golf is other than a dream. Just cactus and harsh stone outcroppings and abandoned shacks and endless, endless road. My plans have changed due to my excursion earlier in the day. I can't make Austin, Nevada, before nightfall. A more realistic objective is Ely, seventy miles beyond the western border of Utah. I hate to admit it, but I'm happy to know that a Motel 6 is waiting for me with its puttable carpet and its hot shower.

Daylight holds until 10 P.M. at this time of the year, and I'm certain of arriving before the dread of night seizes me again.

With a beer trapped between my denim thighs, I gobble a peanut butter sandwich and gnaw a scraped carrot while cannonballing along Highway 50 at exactly five miles over the speed limit. The interstate is a fond memory; now it's two-lane road all the way to California. Western Utah is more agrarian than I had imagined, but less agrarian than, say, an agrarian region ought to be. In the farm town of Delta, I fuel up at a rockabilly malt shop *cum* gas station where Mormon kids hang out, sipping Cokes and leaning into and out of car windows. I gas up with ethanol-enhanced fuel, buy myself an icy Coke, and roar off toward the brooding horizon. Now the land heaves up and tilts, and the road begins to slither. I'm getting very, very edgy. There's no energy left in me for another night in purgatory, and I worry that I've miscalculated the distance to Ely.

No one should endure a description of my emotional state, wheeling through mountain curves in fierce rain with translucent animal eyes staring through the premature darkness from the roadside. Know only that I can't discuss it further, except to say that upon arriving in Ely at shortly before midnight, I sat immobilized in my car for half an hour, parked under a floodlight outside the Motel 6. I stared at the floodlight until the ghost of it clung to my retina like a pall. When I finally gained nominal control of myself, I went inside the office and all but wordlessly registered for my room.

So, here you shall find me. I've turned on all the lights in Room 115, snapped on the TV, filled the tub with hot water, and climbed in with a beer to keep me company. There's no way to adequately explain this disorder of the mind that occasionally grasps my psyche in its cold, wet claw. If it's fear of death, it is a fear that takes me only when I'm alone, only at night, only on the empty highway.

Now, having drunk one beer and part of another, I can melt into the warmth, which I fortify with hot water whenever I please. It doesn't matter who sat in this tub before me. Any infectious fungus

spores swimming the shores óf this salubrious tub can have their
way with me for all I care. My headache is subsiding, my aching
jaws relax, my hands unclench. At last, I am returning to myself.
Exhaustion is the typical aftermath of an "episode," as my friends
like to call it. When it is all over, I lapse into a slumber so profound
that it hovers all night on the brink of oblivion.

At six-thirty in the morning, I feel as if I've traveled ten thousand
miles and fifty days to get here. And, as ever, I'm famished. Not far
down the road toward town, I find a perfect restaurant with vinyl
booths and yellowed newspaper articles and Elvis plates on the
walls. A middle-aged waitress with jet-black hair calls me sweetie
and brings me coffee without my even asking. "Cream's in the
pitcher," she says. I'm one of the locals, suddenly. My name is Clyde
and I drive a Ford Ranchero. It's the blue jeans, I guess, and the
squashed hair and the blue-eyed lost cowboy look I've adopted for
times like these. "Pancakes for you today?"

"Sure. A short stack, with bacon. And orange juice, please."

"Coming right up, sweetie," she says. If she chose to pull me ten-
derly from the booth and hold me against her ample, motherly
bosom, I would not protest.

The air outside is still quite cool at seven-thirty. The gambling
casinos are open for business, and firemen are hosing down their
driveway. There's a long way to go down the Loneliest Road in
America before I arrive in Austin, the Loneliest Town in America. It
is near Austin that I must turn south, down a less substantial road to
Smoke Valley, home of the Loneliest Golf Course in America.

The vast wilds of Nevada are exhilaratingly beautiful, especially
with the morning sun behind me, illuminating the cedar and juniper
and sage, all of which exude an aroma so intoxicating that I drive
with the windows down. There's practically nothing to suggest
human influence on the landscape, and perhaps that's why the
terrain is so impressive. It's a remarkable thing to see a hardscrabble farm in the middle of nowhere; even windmills or dusty,
winding side roads seem anomalous. I'm very happy driving down
the cool, silver highway with only telephone poles to keep me company. I stop my car right on the road so I can pee, just for the pure

novelty of the act. There is so little traffic, and the vistas are so end-less, that I wouldn't hesitate to strip naked and run one mile up the road and one mile back. But I simply get back in my car and step on the gas.

I must overshoot the turnoff to Round Mountain Golf Club, whose claim to fame lies in the fact that there exists not one other course within a two-hundred-fifty-mile radius. Nor should there be one. I must refuel in Austin; get it while you can is the order of the day when you're cruising the boonies. The town consists of three or four modular motels, the obligatory casinos, the town hall, a seed store, a pair of gas stations, a church or two, a school, and a few houses, most of them ramshackle. The gas is excruciatingly expensive, but I don't exactly begrudge the station owner his profit. After all, I'm the only car at the pump, and it seems unlikely that I'll be joined anytime soon. There is a truck in the garage, presumably under repair, but there is no hydraulic lift; instead, there is a deep circular pit into which the mechanic descends by means of a narrow ramp. "How do you like living out here in Austin?" I ask Fred.

"Oh, I like it pretty good. Nobody to bother ya. Know what I mean? It's kinda bad in the snow, but we don't get that much."

"Not too lonely?" I ask.

"Oh, no. Everybody just gets along beautiful."

"Well, I'm off to the golf course," I tell him. "Ever been to Round Mountain?"

"Oh, I go by there on my way to Tonopah sometimes. But I'm no golfer, that I can tell ya. In fact, I'm supposed to deliver a clutch plate to a garage in Tonopah this afternoon. You couldn't . . ."

"Be glad to save you the trip," I tell him.

He scratches some pretty simple directions on the back of a blank receipt. "Can ya read my writing?" he asks.

"Sure can," I say. "I'll have it there by five at the latest."

"I owe you something for your trouble."

"Nonsense. It's right on my way," I tell him, and I shake his hand. I've never had occasion to shake the hand of a gas station attendant, but this is the Loneliest Town in America, and it seems a fitting gesture.

*   *   *

The drive to Round Mountain is nearly as lonely as the drive to Austin, and not nearly so beautiful. There are fewer trees, less contour to the land, and nothing to recommend the vistas except for the tall mountains off to the east and west. Occasionally, there will be a verdant oasis with a corral and a house trailer and a windmill and a wrecked car. But it's not a tourist mecca by any means.

Round Mountain is indeed a round mountain, bearing no particular relevance to anything but itself. Imagine a brown derby in a world of gray fedoras. There are no signs to the golf course, although I know I have penetrated the environs. I pull up to the gate of Round Mountain Gold Mine, the largest chemical-extraction facility in North America, for some directions, but I'm sent away by a uniformed security shrew whose duty it is to shame and scold me for failing to heed nonexistent signs barring unauthorized vehicles. "Where's the damn golf course?" I yell at her fat behind as she waddles back to her little booth.

She turns toward me, and I actually believe she is going to pull out a gun and shoot me between the eyes. "There!" she says, and points yonder. "It's over in Hadley. Other side of the highway."

I am in no mood to thank her for the info. If I could break wind in her direction, I would be tempted to do so. But there's no point. She's a watchdog, and I'm an intruder.

I crunch down to the highway, turn left, then right onto another gravel road, which seems to lead into a community of mobile homes and modular houses. Not one structure, including the schoolhouse, seems permanent. Then, out of the corner of my right eye, I see a flash of green. Then, a bit farther up the road, a small sign: GOLF COURSE.

With all due respect to the townsfolk of Hadley, I am not smitten with the aesthetics of this highly portable little burg. Flatbed trucks could relocate it, lock, stock, and cinder block in one busy afternoon, weather permitting. The town would look exactly the same, just a little bit more *elsewhere*. I turn right at the little sign and follow the narrow gravel road to a gravel parking lot behind a portable building. On the other side of the building is Round

Mountain Golf Club, which is surprisingly green and pleasant in contrast to the bleak surroundings. Off in the distance are the massive slag heaps from the gold mine and the scarred mountainside beyond.

A very pleasant woman named Judy greets me from behind the obligatory glass counter, where the obligatory golf balls and gloves and tees and divot forks are on display. There are sets of new golf clubs arranged neatly on racks set against the paneled wall, which surprises me somehow, given the sparse clientele and the forlorn golfing options available to them. "Would you like to play a round of golf?" she asks.

"Sure," I say. "Think there might be some unsuspecting souls who I could link up with?"

"Well, there's a twosome out on the tee, plus a girlfriend—I think that's who she is. They're just beginners though, so you might want to wait."

I assure Judy that I'm an equal-opportunity golf buddy, so off I go, solo, in my electric cart in quest of this pair of novices and the mysterious girlfriend. My egalitarianism is seriously challenged by what I encounter. A paunchy Native American fellow wearing a Buffalo Bills T-shirt and blue jeans stands stiff-legged over a yellow ball, his dusty work boots spread wide apart. At first I believe his legs are artificial, so I withhold judgment. His wild swing makes contact only with molecules of air, a source of amusement to both men and the female member of this peculiar threesome. The fellow on deck wears a black cowboy hat, a tank top, blue jeans, and Hush Puppies golf shoes. There is enough silver jewelry on their collective fingers and wrists to open a pawnshop. The girlfriend is entirely pink. The sociological opportunity presented to me nearly outweighs the obvious liabilities. Nearly. *Perhaps not,* I tell myself. *This is too much.* I sit in amazement while this group whiffs and duffs and chunks and shanks its way up the first fairway. God knows, they're enjoying themselves, but they've exceeded a boundary of tolerability I didn't know existed until now. Those crazy swoops and whacks and the general fall-down madness of their cavortings are fascinating, but they're not *golf.* I cruise back to the putting green to keep myself busy while I wait for any old Round Mountaineer to show up. Meanwhile, off in the distance, two golf carts carve wild circles in the fairway, perilously close to the ominous sinkhole.

The nine-hole course, Judy tells me when I duck inside to shoot the breeze, is a gift from the gold mine, sort of a consolation prize, really, for basically picking up the entire town of Round Mountain, renaming it Hadley, and moving it across the highway in order to excavate the land beneath the newly vacated site. It's a pretty strange setting for a golf course. There's the grade school and what might or might not be a church, depending on whether the curious pyramid atop the white trailer is indeed a steeple and likewise whether the metal thingamabob poking from the apex is a cross. If God exists, he exists here, surely, for they need Him. Trailers and modular homes border several of the early fairways; then the scruffy desert takes over. The sandtraps, on account of the strong desert wind (which even now whips at shirts and towels and underpants hanging from clotheslines), are not sandtraps at all; the gale-force winds don't discriminate between domesticated golf course sand and the desert floor. The sand, in either case, won't stay put. Instead, there are evil pot bunkers guarding the greens and fairways, and inside of these pits grows a brutal species of grass, maybe kikuyu, or possibly Zambezian spear grass. One is advised to avoid these bunkers at all cost because no golf club has yet been invented that will predictably extricate a ball from same. A large, grim sinkhole threatens the second fairway. The main punitive element of this harsh, very ugly hazard is, I believe, unutterable sorrow.

I've tried and failed to wangle a beer from the beerless clubhouse grill. I settle on a Coca-Cola and a hot dog, which I eat in the shade of my cart. It seems more and more likely that I will be playing this round by myself, which is a disappointment. The electric cart won't be necessary should I be relegated to playing the course as a single. But it's a long way I've come, certainly, to be marching the fairways alone. That may be what's brought me down into the trough of mild depression I feel sitting here in this dislocated golf venue. Golf should be integrated into the landscape, the community, connected to sister clubs, a stepping-stone up to or down from the course in the neighboring county or across town. But Round Mountain is only itself, painted like graffiti onto the foreboding nothingness—featureless, treeless, without sand, without any real contour. Its generic sensibility will test the soul of any golfer. Especially a stranger traipsing the windy fairways alone.

Soon, though, I am delivered. A very pleasant-looking, thick-bodied fellow tools around the corner of the clubhouse, captain of his electric cart. My aching heart soars. Perhaps . . . ! Alongside him is a pastel woman with her heavily bandaged leg propped up on the dash. Then, a young heavyset fellow wearing mirrored wraparound sunglasses plods onto the scene. I boldly glide up next to the cart. "Hi there," I say. "Could you tolerate another player in your group?" I'm suddenly a hooker, looking for a trick.

"Judy said you're the writer fellow."

"Yup, that would be me. Think I could tag along? I'm completely harmless. Your average Joe."

"Glad to have you," he says. "I'm Jim, this is my wife, Norma, and that's my son, Barry." I shake hands with everybody and tell them to call me Bill. "Norma's had an operation on her heel, so she's the copilot today," he says. He reminds me of my beloved Uncle Jim, my dad's brother, friendly and open and ever so slightly paunchy.

"Is this where you play your golf?" I ask.

He laughs at that one. "This is it. There's no place else until you get down to Bishop, California, and that's what . . . say, Barry, how far to Bishop, two hundred? Two hundred fifty miles!"

Barry, it so happens, is playing his very first round of golf. I'm pleased to be witnessing such a momentous occasion, considering the unforgettable nature of my first father/son golfing adventure. On the other hand, I feel as I'm intruding on some rite of passage. The presence of Norma undoes that little flicker of compunction, and I'm eager now to interlope. I invite Barry, who seems destined to hoof it around the course, to hop aboard, which he eagerly does. "What kind of book are you writing?" he asks. His spooky glasses make it hard to read any nuance into his question, so I throw caution to the hard-blowing Nevada wind.

"I'm going around the country trying to find people who play the game worse than I do, and then I libel them."

Barry laughs. It pleases me that he's got a good nose for irony.

And living here in the outback, I reckon he has a huge capacity for suffering and generally lowered expectations. He might just survive the ignominy of learning golf from the ground up on this queer little lonely course with its howling wind and killer grass bunkers. He plants his big white sneaker on the rubber dash strip, and off we go to the first tee.

"You a high school student?" I ask him. He looks like a beefy pulling guard to me. He informs me that he's twenty-one and a guard of a different sort at the Tonopah Correctional Camp thirty miles farther down the road.

Jim insists that I seize the honors on the first tee, so I load up a new Ultra and gaze at the red flag snapping in the wind, 385 yards away. With the altitude and the stiff breeze working to my advantage, I cream my drive at least 300 yards down the fairway. "Beautiful shot, Bill," Jim says. Barry, behind his freaky shades, is inscrutable.

Then Jim steps onto the tee and, without fanfare, employs a swing that only retired military types exhibit and cuts a slice that bows nicely over the perilous rough, then bends onto the fairway. "Bravo," I say. "Well struck." Alas, Barry, when he finally assumes his stance, seems to have been afflicted with fear-induced catatonia. "Relax your shoulders," Jim tells him. "Roll your grip a little more clockwise . . . that's it. Flex your knees. Keep your head down." *Cinderella! Cinderella!* Poor kid. It's a bewildering game. His backswing, if you could call it that, is truncated by nervousness; in its awkward, furious aftermath his head flies up in anticipation of the ball's flight. The sphere is unharmed, unmoved, perched cynically near his size fourteen shoes.

"Hey . . . Barry," I say, holding two golf balls against my eye sockets. "God is *watching*." Somehow, this goofy bit of twisted humor loosens the lad up, and his next shot lifts off into the stratosphere, high, but not very long.

Barry is all too aware that his foozles and whiffs and chunks will be recorded for posterity by the guy riding alongside him in the cart. "You know what . . . ?" I say. "Forget all the instruction-book stuff. Just take a nice loose grip on the club, then hit the crap out of the ball. Don't worry about all that instruction-book bull. That's for later. Right now, just keep your eye on the ball, and hit it right on the bazoot. *Capisce?*"

He looks relieved that the process can be that simple, which, of course, it isn't. But when you're just a beginner, and you're undertaking the most difficult single motion in all sport, it's best to address the basics and leave the rest for later. My old Scottish golf teacher used to scold me for overcomplicating my swing. "Take yourrr grrrip and let her rrrip," he'd say.

Jim and Norma pull up alongside my cart to witness the show. Barry's legs are still a bit stovepiped but he looks less terrified than he does resigned. "Watch where you're aiming," Jim says. Barry resituates himself, takes a few practice swings, then hauls off and slices the ball over a fence into somebody's yard. He hangs his head, a broken man.

"That's all right," I tell him. "You made good contact. You're just overswinging. Smooth it, okay? And follow through right at the flag." He skulks back to the cart for another ball, which happens to be a yellowed Acushnet Club Special, a relic from decades past.

Despair improves Barry's stance. His shoulders slump, his muscles surrender to the undeniable impossibilities of the game, and the intensity that fired his hulking attack on the golf ball has vanished. This time his swing is more temperate, and the result is a skulled shot that skitters up the baked fairway onto the apron, just shy of the green. "That's the ticket," I say. "See . . . direction is everything." A rejuvenated Barry plops into the cart beside me.

Jim sets up well left of the target and, using a modified Trevino chop, slices the ball high and right of the green; but wait . . . an invisible God intervenes. The ball miraculously curls back toward the dance floor, where it lands softly, twenty feet shy of the hole. "Birdie time," I shout. "Make that and we'll quit. I'll tell the world that you finished your round one under par." He's obviously pleased with himself for his little triumph. These fellows, when you come right down to it, are playing golf with a total stranger whose mission it is to immortalize this moment in which they are protagonists. I try to put myself in their shoes, imagining the pressure to perform well for the sake of posterity. I imagine the ribbing Jim would take back at the nuclear testing facility where he works if he were to reveal himself to be a golfing buffoon.

Several times per week, Jim and Norma make the drive up from Tonopah to play a game reduced to its lowest common denominator. The golf here is as straightforward as the treeless, windblown, unadorned landscape. The wind howls up the valley. The sun arcs across the sky. The grass grows west to east. The greens are hard. The kikuyu bunkers are akin to death. The blighted mountainside, ruined by the gold-mining operation, looms over the illusionary town of Hadley and the Round Mountain Golf Club.

My own game is subservient to the vagaries of Barry's trouble, and the dogged, miraculous competence of Jim's game. Barry is beginning to get the hang of things by the time we reach the fifth hole, a par three over an agitated pond. "Easy does it," I tell Barry. The tension melts from his arms, and he settles into an acceptable position over the ball. His backswing is short but adequate to the task. He nails a low screamer that skips across the little whitecaps, punches into the bank, and hops onto the green. "Whooooeee! You da *man*, Barry," I say. "Roll the freakin' cameras."

Jim and I also manage to loft our tee shots onto the green, but the real drama of the moment belongs to Barry, whose putting skills have proven to be seriously in doubt. He tends to drill ten-foot putts twenty feet past the cup. Twenty-footers roll ten feet past the cup, and the beguine begins again. I've putted like a goose all day. The crusty bent-grass greens yield nothing to my balky stroke, but I'm strangely unbothered today. "Now, Barry," I say, resting my hand on his beefy shoulder. "This is the climax of my narrative. I'm counting on you for some real drama. You can be a monument to yourself. You can make your father proud. The weight of the world is on your shoulders. We're all counting on you. This is your moment in the sun. But we *don't* want you to feel any pressure. Right, Jim?"

Jim gives me a who-the-hell-*are*-you grin, then bursts out laughing. "Hit the damn thing, Barry," he says.

Barry's exaggerated crouch transforms him into a human question mark. His grip shortens the putter by half, a curiously idiosyncratic adaptation that bears no explanation. After a painfully long delay, he gives the ball a solid whack, and, sure enough, it drools past the hole and keeps on going until it's once again twenty feet away from pay-dirt. But at least now the putt is uphill, a definite advantage to a man-handler like him. "Don't wimp out on us," I say. "Get it all the way to the hole." He gives Jim and me an *I'm trying, damn it* glance and hulks over the ball one more time. He spanks the gleaming orb, a loaner courtesy of yours truly, and this time the speed is right. The ball hustles toward the cup, equivocates at the lip, then, as an after-thought, falls in. "A par! A bona fide par for the young pro from Tonopah." I give him an exuberant high five. Jim pats his son on the back. It's a Kodak moment for sure, so I liberate my little Leica from the pocket of my bag. I pose them, father and son, right there on the green with the flag in the background and beyond that the slag-heap gold mine. "Smile like you just made a par," I say. "And take off those *Star Trek* glasses. Put your arm around your old man. That's it . . ." When he removes his shades, Barry looks like his father's son. They look happy together, like old golfing buddies. "Got it," I say.

Barry's par is the only one of the day for him. I play my usual par/bogey round, with one sneaky, wind-aided birdie on a par five. Jim is the real star of the show. He beats his handicap all to hell and back again. He's a god under pressure. But mostly, he's had a fine time watching his son knock the ball crazily around the course, delegating the onerous task of instruction to me and thereby preserving the deli-cate, loving, father/son relationship.

When the round is over, Jim buys me a tall, icy Coca-Cola from the grill, and we talk about nothing in particular. Then, I pose a question that yields a surprising response. "Jim," I ask. "How come you drive all the way up from Tonopah to play golf on this particular course. I mean, wouldn't you rather drive down to Bishop and play a championship course?"

"Well," he says, "the way I figure it, this is *my* course and that's *their* course. It's not much, I know. But it fits in right here. It's like those houses. They aren't fancy, but they keep you warm and dry and they're home to the folks who live in them. Here I can play the same holes every time and try to improve. The conditions don't vary too much, so I can really measure my progress. It's like taking the same test over and over again, and I like that. That's just about the long and short of it."

A damned good answer to an admittedly rhetorical question. And one whose depth I'll have to ponder as I make my way south and westward, through Bishop and toward the desert of California.

I wish Norma a speedy recovery and my friends Jim and Barry the best of luck. But I need to get my tires on the road if I'm to make Palm Springs before night falls.

"Keep your head down and your chin up, Barry," I shout before turning the corner of the clubhouse and leaving them behind.

CHAPTER 10

heat

As a child in Bowling Green, Ohio, I marked off the days on my calendar until the Fourth of July golf tournament, conducted every year at the country club, crosstown from the university golf course. There's nothing that delights a little kid more than watching a grown-up make a fool of himself, and it was almost a *fait accompli* that at least one competitor, drunk out of his merry skull and many, many strokes over par, would drive his electric cart into the quarry. It happened on such a regular basis that the club's trustees finally rerouted the cart paths and erected guardrails to prevent such eventualities. The delicious news of such occurrences would fly back to the clubhouse, where I was employed in the summertime as a scraper of spikes and a cleaner of clubs and a mopper of locker-room floors. I would then race to the terrace to witness the arrival of the soaked, inebriated fool who was generally greeted as something of a local hero. A cheer would go up, and the dripping passenger, betoweled and red-faced, would raise his hand with almost papal grace in acknowledgment of the adulation heaped upon him. On the fifth of July, frogmen would dive down fifty feet with hooks and belts so that a wrecker operator from the Court Street Garage could winch the vehicle from the depths. Having accomplished the major task, the divers would surface and resurface with the golf bags and irons that had gone down with the cart. Both events, the submersion and the extraction, were thrilling to a twelve-year-old kid like me. I was secretly disappointed that my father saw fit not to participate in this madness, but he was a nondrinker and a reluctant competitor.

Alcohol made philanthropists of tightwads, and I, the beneficiary of their sudden, patriotic munificence, earned enough in one day to buy a slightly used Bullseye putter and one dozen Worthington steel-center golf balls, which lasted me until September, when the arrival of the school year chased us kids off the country club course.

On the evening of the Fourth, the golf course was taken over by townspeople who spread their blankets on the fairways to watch the fireworks explode wondrously, just beyond and high above the first green. After piling into my dad's station wagon, we were transported crosstown to participate in the festivities. There was buttered popcorn, which we clawed from a grocery bag, and sodas, and Snickers bars. I would lie back on the blanket that was spread on the fairway, a fairway I regarded proprietarily, to watch the whistlers and bottle rockets that presaged the heart-thumping pyrotechnics to follow. Dad would make appreciative noises, and Mom would say, "Isn't that just *beautiful*."

Bishop, California, where I have spent a comfortable night in the Motel 6, is bedecked with American flags, banners, and patriotic storefront displays. Should I choose to malinger in this fine, robust town overlooked by snowcapped mountains and moistened by converging rivers, I would be witness to a parade featuring high school bands, drum and bugle corps, floats, horseback riders, and fire trucks. This is the first Independence Day I've spent away from loved ones. It's strange to be such an outsider on a day I so strongly associate with family and with the game I love the best. I'm half tempted to seek out a golf tournament, zigzag drunkenly from hole to hole in my battery-powered conveyance, maybe even drive the cart into a pond just to please the masses. I'd acknowledge the applause accorded me by onlookers, and I'd lavishly tip those clubhouse underlings kind enough to provide me with towels.

But I've decided, quite on the spur of the moment, to drive toward Palm Springs for a visit with Gillian's parents, hoping they might adopt me for this one night. I don't fancy skulking the fringes of a fireworks crowd alone, like a sad refugee. When I ring up Roslyn, Gillian's mother, she's surprised to hear that I'm only half a day's drive away. "It would be *wonderful* to see you," she says. "The house is a mess because we're moving. But if you don't mind boxes, we'd love to have you. Roger's in Washington state, so it's just me and Ellen. But please, do come." I'm elated to have a place to go, glad that I will again see familiar faces. Being away from family has taken its toll on the old psyche, I'm afraid. It would be infinitely pleasant to sit on an old army blanket to watch the fireworks with my son and daughter with Gillian at my side. I'd wrap my arms around Rachel and rest my chin atop her head. Gillian would drape her arm over my shoulder. Garth would allow Rachel to rest her plaster cast on his lap. A perfect family tableau.

Rachel's grandma picks up the phone when I dial her number in Highlands. "It's Bill," I say. "How's everybody?"

"Well, I'm stressed out," she says. "I've been awake for two nights, looking after Rachel. I wouldn't have it any other way, but I'm exhausted. Rachel's doing very well, though. She's been a trouper." I hear muffled coughing at the other end and sniffles. Cigarettes! "She's going to watch the fireworks tonight if she's up to it. We'll see."

I finally tell Rachel's grandma I'd like to speak to my daughter, She's come home from the hospital after only two days. A good sign. "Hi, Dad," she chirps.

"Hello, sweetheart," I say. "How's the wheel?"

"They've got me on heavy-duty painkillers, so it really doesn't hurt all that much until the medicine wears off. I've got crutches, so I can get to the bathroom. But I can't take a shower. And I *need* one." It does me good to hear her voice, although I can't help wishing all the more fervently that I was there to lend some fatherly assistance.

"Say, I got you a present the other day. In Moab."

"Indian jewelry?"

"My lips are sealed, but I think you'll like it. By the way, kid, have you heard from your brother? It's impossible to get in touch with him."

"Funny you should ask because he called here an hour ago."

"About your leg."

"Yes. He was upset, but I told him not to worry. He said he wants you to call him tomorrow at seven-fifteen his time. That's after supper but before his evening hoop-te-doo." She gives me a new number to call, one that might yield better results than the neglected hall phone in his dormitory.

I tell her of my plan to drive down to Palm Springs, and she's glad I won't be alone on the Fourth of July. We tell each other I love you and reluctantly hang up the phones.

The temperature at 10:30 A.M. in Bishop is ninety-five degrees. I can only imagine the heat in the Southern California desert, but into the furnace I must go if I'm to palliate my loneliness in the town where the glitterati and their rhinestone poodles dwell, if only in the winter months. So, after giving Iris a big drink of unleaded and checking her fluid levels, I bid adieu to this oasis town. It's a place where I could hang my hat if the need arose. A far cry from the generic, prefabricated trailer towns of southern Nevada.

The hot wind is blowing so furiously by noon that I must wrestle the wheel to keep Iris from flying into the oncoming lane. In Independence, California, a pretty little resort town, the banner hanging above the downtown traffic light is in tatters and the holiday streets are bare. My guess is that under better circumstances, the Fourth of July would be quite a big deal in this hamlet, and I wonder what happens to fireworks and floats and balloons when the wind is whipping at forty miles per hour. Just above Lone Pine, a live chicken blows across the highway and I swerve violently to avoid killing the critter. The Santa Ana wind, roaring down through the high Sierras, is making life tough for the likes of me. But ask me whether I would prefer driving at night, in the rain, on a strangely sinuous road. Give me a nanosecond to think it over and I'll get back to you.

I sip one purely medicinal Coors and listen to *Bob Dylan Unplugged* on the CD player, trying to imagine him explaining to his high school guidance counselor that he wants to be a singer. I blow my harmonica and pretend I've actually got some musical gift that just hasn't been properly wrapped. I actually believe I'm a better harp player when I'm wearing shades and have my shirt unbuttoned. It would help, too, if I weren't forced to grab the wheel with both hands when wind gusts knock the car halfway to sillyville. "Like a complete unknown . . . like a rolling stone." Stop it, Bob, 'cause your breaking my heart.

The howling gale lifts sand from the floor of the desert and scours everything in its path, including Iris, whose air filter must be feeling the effects. Poor girl. She's performed flawlessly from the time I left my driveway, but this gritty air has got to be bad juju for her pulmonary system, and I'll unbolt her filter for a quick perusal when I arrive in Palm Springs. On the outskirts of Ridgecrest, I stop at a combination Burger King/laundromat/filling station/curio shop. I pay for a burger, onion rings, and a Coke, then take my combo to a table where I can watch the rusty wind play havoc with the traffic signs and lift the skirts of old ladies who scurry from their Buicks to a heavy glass door they haven't the strength to wrestle open.

So here I am again, in direct physical contact with Formica. I'm trapped by wind in a way station just outside a city that isn't really a city at all so much as a sprawl of bleached-out cubes scattered across the rugged valley like numberless dice by an angry God. I can't even begin to conjure a green lawn or a humming-bird or a flower bed—or anything that might soften this feeling of exile, which is only exacerbated by the howling wind. I close my eyes and try very hard to superimpose a golf course onto the wind-blown purgatory. *Nada.* No luck at all. The concept is much too far-fetched.

A very unhappy-looking family pushes through the door, their hair riotous from the gale outside. The mother, apparently French, says to her red-eyed children, *"Nous allons à San Francisco, toute de suite." Je comprends, ma petite chou-fleur. Je comprends. Allez reservoir. Chevrolet coupé. J'ai mangé la fenêtre,* I say to myself in 101 French. Yes, I understand how the lush, foggy, oceanic beauty of San Francisco beckons, but I'm determined to brave the inferno. It's madness to allow a sentimental heart to rule the day. But there you have it.

* * *

A couple of hours later, after having followed a cavalcade of gawky
scaffolds strung with thick electric cables, I arrive in Adelanto, my
much-anticipated gas stop. The town is so grim that I just can't talk
about it, and I won't. Do not go there. Do not allow friends to go
there. I apologize here and now to the citizens of this town for perhaps leaping to conclusions. Maybe gentle souls abide somewhere
within its limits. Maybe the next Mother Teresa roams the littered
streets. God, I am sure, loves His Adelantonian children. But do not
go there. Do not for one moment leave your car unattended in this
town. Do not leave your doors unlocked and your collection of prized
CDs in view while you pay for gas and use the rest room.

I'm distraught. I'm sad. I'm mad as a pit bull. No more Big Walter
Horton, no more Crash Test Dummies or Dead Can Dance or Marley
or Jussi Bjoerling. Just Natalie, who was hiding inside the machine
when thieves did their hasty work. I love her all the more. She sings
me down from this heartless landscape, through turns that double
back on themselves like the convolutions of a snake. "I dream of a
circle . . ." she sings. Her voice is pure and clean and passionate,
antithetical to the world that has, just very recently, closed in on me.

Should I be sad in coming back to sea level from the continental
heights? Is sin diluted by thin atmosphere? Does virtue rise like a
weatherman's balloon?

San Bernardino gives me hope. Trees return, and billboards, and
traffic and malls. The furious gale has dwindled to a merely strong
wind, and I am a happy, happy man to be in the lap of civilization
with all its ills. I negotiate the northern loop of the bypass perfectly
and glide onto I-10, the very same highway that carried me across
Mississippi a couple of weeks back. That alone buoys my spirits. I
am one hour from a friendly doorstep and familiar faces.

I'm learning the hard way that some deserts are more beautiful
than others. Hard-core nature lovers would argue that beauty is in
the eye of the beholder. But my subjective opinion is that here are
objective truths that only *seem* subjective, one of them being the
relative beauty of the desert in this little corner of California. The
handsome shrubs, the sensuous rock formations that lean like gothic

buttresses against the shadowy early-evening mountainsides fill me with joy. Or perhaps it's the subtle presence of water, deep subterranean water, that imparts life and beauty to the natural elements at the surface. Aquifers, artesian wells, underground rivers, hot springs . . . the vital fluids that sustain the planet flowing abundantly beneath the desert floor.

I round a mountain bend and see before me a city that sprawls across a large, flat basin. Off in the distance, beyond civilization, thousands of white windmills turn fast against the rushing wind. Minutes now to Palm Springs, to Palm Canyon Drive, to Vista Chino, up to Hidalgo Way, where Roslyn and Ellen fill out their lame-duck tenantship of their coquina house with its red-tiled roof.

"Well, hello," Roslyn says. "Fancy meeting you here." She gives me a big hug and a kiss. "Come in. Welcome. So good to see you. I can't believe you're *here*." Roslyn is a very gigglesome middle-aged woman with cornflower-blue eyes and a soft Bronx accent. Her husband is a retired Air Force meteorologist, a military vagabond for whom packing and unpacking have become an art form evidenced by the perfectly stacked and cataloged boxes that fill the foyer. Their newest move will take them from Palm Springs, where Roger has worked as a long-range weather forecaster while Roslyn has been a teacher's aide in a remedial classroom. The last time I saw Roslyn, she was standing amidst a mountain of cardboard boxes in Fayetteville, North Carolina, waiting for the movers. "What can I get you to eat or drink? Some coffee [pronounced *kawfee*] maybe?" she asks. This has always been the final note of the opening bar of every encounter with Roslyn.

"Coke would be lovely," I tell her, and she hurries into the kitchen, apologizing again for the stacks of cardboard boxes and the general state of disencampment.

"Don't come in here," she says. "I'm embarrassed. We have absolutely nothing to eat, so I was praying you'd say you weren't hungry. You're so cooperative," she says over the humming of the fridge.

Ellen, Gillian's kid sister, pads up the hallway and into the living room, where I'm sitting with my feet propped up on a box. "Hi," she says, and gives me a demure hug. "Did you have a good trip down from wherever you were? Where *were* you?"

"I was at the loneliest golf course in America yesterday, but I spent the night in Bishop. The drive down to Palm Springs was despicably bad. Horrendifico. Barfo. *Muy malagueña.*" Ellen, like her mom, is an easy audience, and she kicks off an evening of unabated giggling with a fine spasm of laughter.

"We could order a pizza or pick up some Chinese, your choice," Roslyn says, settling my iced drink on a Jack Daniels box.

"How about I take you guys into town for some grub. Chinese, Lithuanian, Biafran, whatever's your pleasure. Or I could make some black beans and rice. How does that sound?"

A few minutes later, Ellen and I are walking through searing heat to the corner grocery store. The valley has been enduring record heat for a solid week, and there is no relief forthcoming. It's a new kind of heat for me—the difference between a sauna and a convection oven. We pick up onions, bay leaves, peppers, garlic, parsley, celery, black beans, Tabasco, hot sausage, chicken stock, a box of Uncle Ben's rice, French bread, and wine. For dessert we grab mint chocolate chip ice cream, which I quadruple-bag while I'm standing in the checkout line.

I'm looking forward to a meal that does not pour from a can, or come wrapped in waxed paper, or have the prefix "Big" or "Grand" or "Mega" attached to it. Back we go, through Dante's Inferno, past the sprinklers and heat-defying oleander, past the sturdy Saint Augustine lawns and cactus gardens and stockaded swimming pools.

Roslyn has excavated some forks and spoons from a box and set the table in anticipation of my Cajun feast. I admit it, I'm a one-trick pony. I have an affinity for Louisiana cuisine, due maybe to my time in Baton Rouge. I can do a passable stir-fry, and my bouillabaise is nonemetic. But I can make an oyster say *mama* and bring a crawfish to Jesus. My black beans and rice is a very windy entrée, for sure, but I seem to be sleeping alone on this trip, and tonight will be no exception.

Cooking for an audience is my one concession to ego. It's fun to brandish a chef's knife like a Cordon Bleu dropout, to nip onions and peppers into confetti with rapid, theatrically overstroked blade work. I create hillocks of sliced this and diced that, until everything is segregated into beautiful little factions on the large cutting board. I heat a puddle of olive oil in an iron skillet, then squeeze clove after clove of garlic into the sizzle, upon which the room fills with aroma. Next, pile by pile, I commit the various gratees to their fate. When the onions are *just* transparent, I add four cans of black beans, chicken stock, bay leaves, and Tabasco up the wazoo. I take a sip of beer, then pour a few fingers of it into the mix. "Ah . . . *c'est bon!*" I say. "*C'est magnifique, Monique,*" I say to Ellen. "*C'est la guerre. Haricot vert.* Jacques forgot his underwear." I'm beer-crazy and beside myself with joy. I'm in a house with people I care for, sipping beer, inhaling wonderful essences, speaking French, commanding the scene.

I'm stuck in a French accent from which there seems to be no escape. I lapse into and out of Charles de Gaulle, Edith Piaf, and Maurice Chevalier. Every so often, in the midst of my pre-intoxicated narrative one or all of us lifts the lid from the skillet and dips a wooden spoon into the simmering mixture. "That tastes amazing!" Roslyn exclaims.

I eat as if I own the patent on the activity. I fill and refill my wineglass. While I'm a caveman with manners, Ellen and Roslyn eat the black beans sensibly, but their praise is lavish. I'm feeling pretty pleased with myself when I realize that I've completely forgotten to call Garth. Just a few hours ago I was sitting in the Burger King at Ridgecrest watching French malcontents and chomping on fried potatoes while the appointed hour came and went. "Oh, damn," I say. "Rats! I was supposed to call Garth this afternoon and I completely forgot."

"Won't he just figure something came up?" Ellen asks. "Like you were driving in the desert where there are no phones?"

"Maybe. But I was really hoping to talk with him. It's been about ten days since I last spoke to him, and I miss him. Guess I'll set the

alarm and try calling him in the morning before he can get out of the
dorm."

Even the glorious fireworks we three watch from the fenced-in
backyard do not completely temper my unhappiness at having let my
son down. Through my own pure thoughtlessness, I've disappointed
him. Somehow, by feigning a pleasure I do not feel, I gradually
accommodate myself to the spirit of the event, and by the time the
last spectacular burst fades from the sky, I've let myself become
happy again. I'll call Garth's new phone number before his breakfast
tomorrow morning.

Roger has been in the Pacific Northwest for one month, studying
bicycle mechanics in hopes of beginning a new life in Florida.
Roslyn, I think, enjoys having an adult conversation for a change.
Ellen has gone to her room to read a book or clip her toenails or
maybe just to contemplate the upcoming move to the Sunshine State.
Her mom and I sit amidst boxes in the living room, talking about
Gillian and her upcoming graduate school plans, and *our* plans, hers
and mine, which are, as yet, unresolved. Relationships are difficult
when our lives are so divergent. But I do love her, and it's easy to
imagine us, a bit farther down the road, living a civilized life
together, maybe with a kid or two, just being happy with the world
we choose to live in. Gillian has no particular fondness for golf, but
neither does she have any aversion to the game. Once or twice, when
she accompanied me on a golf assignment for one magazine or
another, she putted a ball across the green to no avail. "This is it?"
she asks. But I soon eliminated that moral flaw as a criterion for a
meaningful relationship. And so, here we are. Three thousand miles
apart. She, biding her time in my waterside cottage three thousand
mile away while her bod makes happy small talk with her mother on
the fourth day of July.

My alarm sounds at four o'clock in the morning. I sit up on the
edge of the single mattress in the bedroom reserved for but never
occupied by Gillian. It takes me a minute or two, however, to
remember where I am and what it is that I'm awake for. Slowly,
detail by detail, the facts of my recent autobiography clarify, and I

realize that I must phone my son whose name is Garth and who is spending a few weeks in Winston-Salem, which is in North Carolina, my home state. Yes. And I'm in California, specifically Palm Springs, precisely a small bedroom at the end of the hall in a rectangular house on a cactus-and-pea-gravel street on the fifth day of July. Got it. I have slipped back inside my familiar skin, reconstituted my idiosyncratic self and summoned the wherewithal to make a phone call.

After a stop in the bathroom, I ease down the hallway to the living room, where I turn on one of the last unpacked lamps and sit on the sofa. The phone rings in Winston-Salem, and I'm hopeful. My slugabed son would surely be the dead-last soul to vacate his bed and tromp down the stairs to the chow hall. He would be malingering on his convict-style mattress, pondering the coil pattern of the top bunk, gauging its ingenious correlation to the configuration of the galaxy. A sleepy-sounding boy picks up the phone. "H'lo," he says.

"Good morning. This is Garth Hallberg's dad. Is he around?"

" 'S'minute," he says, and I hear the phone receiver twirling against the wall. Several minutes pass, after which my hopes dwindle to just above nil. Then, a familiar, albeit tired, voice comes on the line. "Dad," he says.

"How're you doing, Garth? Sorry I didn't call yesterday. I was driving through a windstorm in the middle of no-man's-land in California. Hope you didn't worry."

"I just figured you couldn't get to a phone. No problem. How's your trip?"

I give him the lowdown on a select few of my most salient adventures. He empathizes over the abduction of my CDs. He tells me he's been reading Kerouac and Ginsberg and Fariña and Kesey. Garth, given his open heart and curious mind, *would* have an affinity for the Beat poets and the counterculture crazies. "The approach to literature here is pretty provincial, so I try to leap the fence, I guess," he tells me. Good lad. *Buck the system, my fine, wonderful boy.*

We've been circling the more foreboding issues, he and I. Given his buoyancy, it seems wise not to dwell on bad tidings, except for some perfunctory clichés about how life chooses its own course despite our best efforts. That will have to do. He demands details concerning his kid sister, from whom he is all but inseparable. It's a bond I can identify with, so I shoot straight with him. It was a lousy, complicated break, yes. The growth plate, shattered. Metatarsals in disarray. Major bones snapped like kindling. Obviously, my report doesn't quite jibe with Rachel's more dismissive assessment of damage. "She'll be okay, Garth. You know Rachel. No more soccer for her, though. And no Irish jigs for a while."

The phone is silent at the other end. He's taking it all in, processing it, assembling a means of dealing with the information. "Why didn't you come back home, Dad?" My explanation seems to make more sense to him than it ever did to me. But he understands Rachel in ways I never can. He comes at her from a different, more accessible angle.

"Look, buddy," I say. "No more of this phone tag. Okay? I'll call you on Tuesday and Thursday nights at seven-fifteen. And I'll keep calling until I get through. I'd recommend you break wind in the phone booth a few minutes before the appointed hour."

"Hmmm," he says. "An amusing but strangely workable stratagem. Will do."

We say our good-byes and, using our own manly code, let each other know that we love one another.

I'm reconnected with this crazy universe; my role as father has been restored. In an act of pure rebellion, I determine that I will reject the Pacific time zone, thereby maintaining my allegiance to the eastern sunrise, which even now illuminates the foothills and mountains of the Appalachians. I quietly unlatch the front door and go out to my car, in whose trunk are the coffee and the Norelco percolator, which I seize, along with a one-pint milk carton from the cooler and a few packets of McDonald's sugar from the console storage compartment.

After having brewed a pot of java, I carry a cup of steaming brew to poolside, where I sit with my feet dangling in the water, waiting for sunrise to arrive in California.

It's odd to imagine that my son does not play golf. Part of me always imagined it was a genetic certainty that he would take up the game. Only once, however, have I golfed with him. I'd purchased a set of Ben Hogan Junior Apex blades and some chopped-down woods from a father whose own son had outgrown them. For days, I coached Garth on the basics of a golf swing, on the innumerable befuddling techniques of the short game. We putted balls across the living-room rug and verbally rehearsed various scenarios. Then, a few days later, we were standing on the first tee of a poorly maintained public course in a nearby town. I was brimming with the romantic expectation that this would be the first round of countless father/son rounds that would carry us to the very end of our earthly time together. But the experience was torture for him. He's a boy who can't stand to be defeated, who, in fact, rejects situations that imply victory or defeat. And the game simply defeated him. His earnest efforts produced wildly errant shots that resulted in protracted, fruitless searches through weeds and pine needles and flower beds.

But he dutifully maintains an observer's interest in the sport, the way he observes and appreciates music and literature and politics. The notion of unjustified suffering appeals to him, as do the curious lucky bounces that can change the course of fate.

Roslyn and Ellen appear simultaneously at around eight o'clock, just as I'm rinsing out the coffeepot in the sink. "Good morning," I tell them. "Shall I reload this machine?"

"I'll just drink instant," Roslyn says. "I actually prefer it, but don't tell anybody. And Ellen drinks juice."

"Gotcha," I say, the very emblem of ante-meridiem merriment.

"So, what are your plans?" Roslyn asks. "I know you have things to do, but Ellen and I are hopelessly bored if you want to entertain us."

"Actually, I was wondering if I could do a load of wash. In exchange, I could drive us to a mall and you can watch me buy some athletic socks and a polo shirt. Pretty exciting, eh?"

"I should have asked about laundry," Roslyn says. "Silly me. Of course. Help yourself to the washer and dryer. Do you need anything ironed?"

"I'm a wash-and-wear guy in a Sta-Prest world," I tell her, and she laughs.

After some quite meaningless traipsing through a mercifully air-conditioned mall in nearby Palm Canyon, I locate some thick cotton socks suitable for jogging, a cotton T-shirt, and some nylon Umbros, much more stylish than my LSU purple gym shorts. Then, jiggety-jog, we drive back home through the rising heat.

The record-setting heat wave afflicting the desert regions of California is predicted to continue through the week. My conscience urges me to conjure some golfing experience to justify my tangent to this netherworld.

I use the Yellow Pages to locate a public golf course where I might just find some golf nuts willing to play a round of heatstroke golf with me. In fact, a relatively new course called Desert Dunes is open to all comers, with special summer rates in effect. I call the pro shop, provide a slightly fictionalized account of my modus operandi, and wangle a gratuitous round on this highly regarded championship layout.

Sadly, I must pack if I intend to make Los Angeles by nightfall. I explain matters to Ellen and Roslyn, and they understand the way things are when you have a destination that summons you hence. I perform the arrival ritual, in reverse this time, and blow them kisses from the baking driveway. "Good luck with your trip," Roslyn says from the doorway. "We love you. Kiss Gillian for us when you get home."

"Will do," I say. "I love you, too. Thanks for everything."

I am reborn.

Desert Dunes has been victimized by the powerful desert winds. Greenskeeping assistants are busily raking sand back into the bunkers and collecting downfallen palm fronds and miscellaneous debris from the fairways. Otherwise, the course is amazingly green and beautifully contoured.

I park Iris in the crowded lot, grab my clubs, shoes, and a tan, leather-billed cap from the trunk. For the first time I am wearing shorts. This is no time to be a slave to my predilections, so I expose my Wonder bread legs to the nut-brown citizenry of the Golden State. After depositing my clubs at the bag drop, I go inside the cool clubhouse to greet my benefactor, a very young man with forearms like a poster boy for the Communist Workers Alliance. "Greetings," he says, when I introduce myself. "You've got a hot one to deal with today. Sorry about that. But we've got a threesome who said they'd be glad to have you join them." There is a beautiful photograph of the sixteenth at Cypress Point behind him.

"Ever play golf there?" I ask, gesturing toward the picture.

"In my dreams maybe. It's damn near impossible to get on. One of the members has to be bonking your sister or something pretty close to that."

"It's that difficult?"

"Yes, sir." So much for my little pipe dream. I had imagined making a persuasive phone call to the Cypress Point pro in which I gracefully introduce the salient elements of my professional résumé. Duly impressed, he extends an open invitation to play the most beautiful course on earth.

"Thank you *so* much for the free round of golf," I tell him. "This is beyond the call . . ."

"My pleasure," he says, and hands me a yardage booklet and a complimentary divot fork. "Enjoy yourself, but be careful. Drink lots of fluids, and keep your hat on. You have sunblock?"

"I'm pretty well slathered," I tell him, and shake his hand.

My playing partners are gathered in the shade of a palm tree behind the clubhouse. Kevin and Roy and Gil are entrepreneurs in the hot-tub industry. We shake hands all around and begin our obligatory complaining about the ferocious, breath-defying heat. Kevin, who has started his own business in the Bay Area, is quite a hefty, bearded fellow, his round face half hidden beneath a straw Chi Chi Rodriguez hat. Roy is a tall, taciturn splinter of a man, newly married and not much of a talker, it seems. The last member of our little group of survivalists is Gil, the wiry golf junkie. His bag is festooned with bag tags from courses all over the Far West, and his equipment is top of the line. He's been taking lessons from a pro in San Diego, and golf tees are tucked like reporters' pencils atop his ears. My demonic self wants to adopt the persona of a bumpkin who tees his ball on a mound of dirt, never takes a practice swing, never reads a putt, and generally mangles the lingo of the game. The idea swells inside a cartoon bubble in my golfer's brain.

The noonday sun bears down on us as we wait our turn at the tee of the par five first hole. They're over there by the ball washer; I'm over here by the Igloo cooler. "Who wants to golf the ball first?" I ask. "Is that the pennant for our hole up there?" I ask. The friendly chatter ceases. *Who is this fool?* they're wondering. "Shall I just go ahead and try to hit this ball onto the grass out there?" I consider letting a strand of drool trickle from the corner of my mouth. I lick my lips like a pug and toss an Ultra onto the neatly cropped grass between the blue tee markers. Without any preparation whatsoever, I belt the ball approximately two miles down the fairway, just right of center. I'm waiting for their discussion of space-age polymers and integrated flow patterns to resume, but it doesn't. "I guess that's good, huh? C'mon fellas. Anybody going to say 'nice ball,' at least?" I've put a real bug in their beer. Nothing. Just the rasp of a cigarette lighter and the jingle of pocket change. Gil looks at Kevin, who looks at Roy, who looks at Gil, and so on. I witness a couple of such revolutions, then pick up my tee and put it behind my ear

Maybe they'll open up to me as the round progresses. A couple of birdies, a hole in one, possibly setting myself on fire will bring them out of their collective shell. The best thing is to enjoy my new persona and see what sort of mischief I can get into. The beer wagon pulls up next to our group at the first tee. I give the fellow twenty bucks for eight frosty brews. "Two for each of us," I tell him. I figure that a burst of generosity will either break the ice or spook them totally. "Something to settle the nerves. Two for you . . . and two for you . . . and two for you, young fellow."

There is a friendly outburst ("Thanks, man—next one's on me."), but it's short-lived. In no time, I'm an alienated rube again. "Say, is

this your first day of golf in Palm Springs?" I ask Gil. A surefire
entrée.

"Played Indian Wells yesterday. Nice course."

"Is that an eighteen-hole course? Or nine?"

Gil gives me a funny look. "Eighteen," he says. "They're *all*
eighteen holes."

I'm sad to report that my partners are hackers, very avid hackers. They've dropped sixty bucks each to play golf in one-
hundred-twenty-degree heat, after which they plan to drive even
farther into the desert, where there is yet another green altar upon
which they can slay themselves. Gil, whose highly mechanized
swing bodes ill, has topped his ball fifty feet into the cactus patch
that separates the tee from the fairway. "Damn," he says, and
snatches up his tee. Then Roy launches a failed moon shot whose
end point is the cart shed, where it ricochets off an iron support
post and kicks into a patch of kikuyu. Kevin, our caboose, uses an
iron off the tee (always a bad sign), and his thinly struck ball
fades toward a high ridge that borders the fairway. "You guys
want to hit extra balls to see if you come out a little better?" I ask.
What I've failed to realize is that these guys are engaged in a
bizarre intramural competition that allows no mulligans, no gim-
mees, no free drops from scorpion nests. Maybe I'm just too
accustomed to an easy welcome into the fold. Or maybe I'm
feeling a little past my prime in the company of these generation
Xers. Or is it the heat that fouls my temper?

I abandon my cart and stand atop the ridge while my amigos
thrash on up the fairway. Roy and Gil lie three already, and they
haven't quite caught up to my drive, while Kevin's second shot rolls
to within a foot of my ball. When it's my turn to hit again, I scratch
my chin and stare into the sublime, blue sky. "Whaddya say, Kev.
Think I should use a metal iron or a wood club? Guess the wooden
one goes farther, doesn't it?" I place my beer can just an inch or two
from the Ultra, take a stance, and with no hesitation at all lash the
thing directly toward the green. Maybe this is how the game should
be played.

"Good ball," Kevin says. A breakthrough? A crack in the Berlin Wall?

Kevin hits a decent three iron toward the green. "That was very pretty," I say. "Probably I should have hit the same club." He shakes his head and smiles, as if he *might* be on to me.

As we're walking back to our carts, he asks me what I do for a living. "I write books," I tell him. "Golf books. I'm doing one right now, and you're in it."

"Aw, shit," he says. "Am I on *Candid Camera*?"

Kevin and I decide to keep our little secret from the others. Then, in the evening, over beers and fried wontons, he'll tell them, and they'll say, "No fucking way."

I've drunk my quota of beers before we even make the turn, so I make the switch to sixteen-ounce cans of iced tea. The air is so unbelievably hot and dry that the cans don't even sweat. The only relief from the heat comes when the cart is in motion; thus, I find myself driving aimlessly across the fairway like a wayward Shriner until it comes my turn to swat the ball again. My hit-and-run strategy, which began as a sort of ruse, has now become the order of the day. Standing beneath the hammering sun, I feel as if I might at any moment burst into flames.

In spite of my bad attitude, I am a seriously flashy one over par after nine holes, although I'm afraid that my weird behavior has unhinged Gil's robotic golf swing. He must feel a little foolish taking such pains, only to chili-dip his approach shots into sprawling bunkers from which there is no escape except on the back of a camel. "I don't know what's wrong with me today," he says, gouging his ball from one patch of sand to the next. "I just can't figure it."

"One of your spikes is missing," I tell him. "That might be it." He looks at me as if he'd like to take a divot out of my skull. Kevin has finally gotten into the spirit of things. I can hear him laughing over there in his shady golf cart.

At about the sixteenth hole, when the mercury has climbed into the overflow chamber of the thermometer, I begin to wonder if I shouldn't just drive my cart to the clubhouse, surrender the key, say my thank-yous, and hit the road. My legs are wobbly, and my eyes are sore from the dehumidified air. I feel drunk, although I shouldn't be. My oversoul has come unglued from my corporeal self, and it looks down on me, shaking its gauzy head. But I'm only three over par, with three holes to play. I feel as if I'm wearing lead divers' boots. Walking through the searing heat from cart to ball is so arduous that I don't even to notice the exotic plant life abounding in this wild desert region. I couldn't give a farmer's flip about the beautifully sculpted fairways and flawless greens. My hurried four-iron tee shot on the sixteenth plunges into a greenside pond, and suddenly a double bogey rears its gruesome head. But I don't really care. My second ball surrealistically floats into the shimmering sand, next to the green. I couldn't care less what Roy and Kevin and Gil do, except that they do it quickly. I want to run onto the tee and hit Gil's ball for him. I watch him tap his driver behind the ball, tap again. And again . . , and *again*. Then three practice swings. Two more taps. A short waggle and three longer ones. A voice inside my brain is screaming, *Hit the damn thing*. At long last he does, but the ball dives into a cluster of prickly pear fifty yards into the right-hand rough. I carve a sullen path to the green, my sand wedge at present-arms position. It's not exactly my turn to hit, but since the other three are foraging in the desert shrubbery, I dash into the trap and blast the ball onto the green. It dribbles to within a couple of yards of the cup.

When everybody has holed out, I add up the damage: a damnable *six*! I scratch the number onto my card. It looks lonely with all those threes and fours and fives.

But it is not lonely for long; my odyssey on number seventeen includes a side trip into the desert. Rather than take an unplayable lie and a one-stroke penalty, I try to punch the ball through a copse of sagebrush, to no avail. Finally, I dink the ball onto the fairway, which leaves me a long three wood to the green. *Some fun,* I say to myself.

Gil seems to like me better when I suffer. He tells me how glad he is that I could join them on this merciless day and invites me to go with them to Death Valley for a sequel to this madness. On impulse, I grasp his hand in an extremely friendly way. "I wish I could, but I've got to press on to L.A."

I can't help wishing the little guy would roll in the ten-footer

confronting him. This would be his first par, and it would redeem
many of the day's assorted abominations. "Looks pretty straight," he
says. My own read says that the grain will tilt the ball toward the
water, but it seems presumptuous to undercut him. Then a saintly
urge seizes me. My ball is diametrically opposite the hole from
Gil's. If I run my ball past the hole, he might just recognize the
right-to-left break, which *should* reveal itself as my putt trails off. I
knock my Ultra solidly down the line and watch it roll wistfully past
the cup, just as I had planned. Then, sure enough, it fades toward
the water.

"Hmmm . . . that thing seemed to bend a little when it cleared the
hole," I say. "I'll have to remember that on the comebacker."

Gil has gotten the message. He's aiming at the lip now, the correct read. When he strokes the ball, it runs perfectly true, as if it
will stay above the hole . . . but at the last gasp it curls directly
into the cup. "Great stuff," I say. "Excellent line. A nice damn
par." Gil pumps his fist in the air. He's just won the Masters. I'm
happy for the guy.

I complete my martyrdom by leaving my little comebacker
hanging on the edge of the hole—inexcusable, but oddly irrelevant to my happiness. "Tough luck," Gil says. "It just checked up
on you."

It would be a fine thing to relate how, on the last hole, my beautifully stroked fifteen-foot putt rolled into the cup for a birdie. And
how Gil and Kevin and Roy high-fived me and poured beer on my
head in celebration. Fact is, I made a decent, pedestrian par, which
earned me some muted praise from the trio of hot-tubbers, but not
much more than that. Their bogeys and double bogeys, were de
rigueur, and the round ended on that whimpering note.

I've failed once again to break eighty, but I content myself in a
host of rationales. The heat, the company, the early beers, the cru-
elty of fate.

I take a parking-lot photograph of my playing partners loading
their clubs into the back of an Isuzu Trooper. I snap one more of them
driving toward the road that will take them into the gates of hell.

After thanking the pro and his assistants once again for their kindness, I, too, must hit the road. I situate a fresh can of Coke in the beverage holder, slide Natalie Merchant into the CD player, adjust the rearview, and slowly make my way out of this blistering parking lot. I look baked, fried, and fricasseed. My face is fire-engine red. But what the heck. I'm headed for Tinsel Town, U.S.A.

CHAPTER 11

homeless

That's me leaning against a phone carrel in front of a Humpty Dumpty in a strip mall thirty miles east of L.A. I've got a pollution-induced bloody nose that may require cauterization if I'm to avoid total exsanguination. Blood has dripped onto my T-shirt, the fly of my jeans, the penny slot of my right loafer. I aim my face skyward and smush Dunkin' Donut napkins against my snout; we're looking at a serious nasal event here, and they're only a stopgap measure. What I need is some clean air, not this corrosive gas the Angelenos have come to accept. I imagine myself in a filling-station rest room doing an O.J. thing with my blood-soaked clothes, scissoring them into doilies and flushing them down the toilet.

Finally, finally, the bleeding subsides. Morning shoppers and paper-hatted bagel hucksters cringe at the sight of me, but they are way too busy to ask if maybe that bloody creature haunting the phone booth needs some medical assistance. I give them a tain't-nothin' shrug, which suits them just fine.

When I phone Susan's house at 8:45 A.M. and tell her that I happen to be in L.A. as part of my transcontinental golfing adventure, she is remarkably friendly and welcoming. Susan is the scriptwriter for the hypothetical, completely unrealized movie of my golfing novel. She lives just around the corner from Bundy Drive, where Nicole and Ron bought the farm. I've known her for a couple of years, but only as a voice at the far end of a long-distance phone line, although I admit

to having imagined her a thousand times, dark-haired, exotic, decorated with gypsy rings and puka shell necklaces. It's the dusky
unknowability of her voice, perhaps, that provokes these wild imaginings or else it's the mere by-product of cooking my own eggs for three
years too many. Her ex is a famous Hollywood producer of television
shows and blockbuster movies. Thus, my midwestern aw-shucks self
trembles at the thought of a face-to-face meeting with a woman who
has, for so long, been a luminous motif in my highly pedestrian existence. "Bill, is that really *you*?" she asks. Yes, she'd be delighted to
meet me in person. Yes, she'd be glad if I dropped by. Yes, she'd love
to have lunch with me. "Can you wait until around two o'clock,
though?" she asks. I tell her, "Sure. No problem," and my nerves
begin to jump the way they do when a long shot comes around the
clubhouse turn ahead by a neck.

Just up the highway is a Texaco station advertising CLEAN REST
ROOMS where I can rinse the gore from my kisser and slip into something less likely to provoke interaction with the constabulary.

After parking Iris next to the air pump, I skulk into the men's
room, where I wash my face and hands in a grubby pedestal sink
in a singularly filthy chamber whose single toilet has gone unflushed
through more usings than I care to talk about. I strip out of my blood-
splattered Levis and shrieking becrimsoned Rorschach *Sigmund
Freud Lives!* T-shirt and into something quite respectable—a
clean, gray polo shirt and khakis. I am so thoroughly respectable,
in fact, that I visualize myself sauntering into the locker room of
the BelAire Country Club to arrange a drop-of-the-hat eighteen-
hole match with Jack Lemmon and Tommy Lasorda and possibly
Cheryl Ladd.

I know I'm entering L.A. when I see a spandex Roller Blader gliding
down the berm of the Santa Monica Freeway, headphones clamped
on his ears, a fully loaded backpack hanging like a rhesus monkey
from his shoulders. Motorists toot their horns, but he's no threat to
them, and it seems arbitrary and rude that they would harass him.
But honk they do, and he flips them the casual bird without even
hazarding a glance in their direction.

A strange thing happens when I exit the freeway onto Wilshire

Boulevard. There before me is the sprawling VA Hospital complex and a commensurately big sign directing visitors to the various sectors within the compound. Do my eyes catch the words GOLF COURSE? I veer across two lanes and through the gate. I pull up to the sign. Yes, there it is . . . GOLF COURSE. Hmmm. An arrow points to the mysterious yonder of this vastly confusing village with its cypress and cedar, oleander and bougainvillea. My brain somersaults with images of amputees and cirrhotics and men who think they're Mrs. Miniver, all of them whacking white spheres in a billion directions until the sky is a cat's cradle of golf ball trails.

I park my car in a visitor lot near the chapel and am almost immediately greeted by a hulking security officer who tips his official black hat and smiles. "Help you?"

"Could you direct me to the golf course, please?" I ask him through my rolled-down window.

"I see you're a Tar Heel. You're military, right? Fort Bragg?" He leans on in and scopes out my junk-filled cockpit.

With my Santa Fe haircut, I could do a pretty good masquerade, but I decide not to risk it. "Well . . . ," I tell him, "I'm civilian, actually. I wanted to go to 'Nam, but the darn war ended before I got a chance to sign up. You know how that goes. Sheesh."

He thinks that's a pretty amusing concept. He takes off his cap, runs his fingers through his nonexistent hair, and chuckles. "Whatchew want with that little golf course, anyhow?"

"Well, I'm a writer, and I'm doing this coast-to-coast golf book . . . golf as it's played by the masses, rich and poor, the good, bad, and ugly. That's the basic idea, anyhow." It seems hugely pretentious to suggest that I'm trying to unearth the soul of the game, so I skip that part.

He looks over his shoulder as if somebody important might be eavesdropping. "Okay, tell you what. Anybody stops you, just say you got there on your own. Dig? I don't see how it can hurt if you jes' take a look around." After giving me totally confusing directions, he wishes me the best of luck and walks away shaking his head like I'm the craziest guy he's ever met.

Iris cruises past the psych unit and rehab facility and the residential quads and administrative offices. The nicely landscaped grounds

seem mysteriously uninhabited considering the vast patient population and the hundreds of support staff. The morning air is wonderfully cool, if smoggy, but it's a trade-off I can accept. Twice I stop my
car, hoping for more accurate directions. A voluminous Hispanic
fellow carrying a yellow five-gallon bucket and wielding a giant trash
tweezer aims the tool at a distant chain-link fence. "That's it, there,"
he tells me, and I thank him profusely.

The small adjacent parking lot is almost empty. I park Iris
in the shadow of a maintenance vehicle, then gambol toward
the unmanned white shack through whose open doors one must
pass in order to gain access to the golf course. A hand-painted
sign admonishes interlopers that the course is for PATIENTS AND
STAFF ONLY; since I am neither, I decide to wait for the attendant. On the battered wooden counter inside this structure is a
tray of primitive scorecards, some gnawed-at pencils, and a wire
basket labeled GOLF BALLS, which is completely bereft of same.
The rack behind the counter contains an odd assortment of
rusty irons and putters and a pair of lofted woods with blue-
laminated heads.

I'm the fellow standing in the shady interior of a ten-by-ten
shack, doodling on a scorecard, gazing out at the humble VA golf
course scraped onto a hillside overlooking the posh BelAire Country
Club. Below, millionaires in electric carts navigate emerald, sun-
dappled fairways. Up here, the only sign of human activity is two
guys kicking weeds along the fence, for what purpose I can't tell.
BelAire's Mediterranean clubhouse is a far cry from the peeling
equipment shack where I'm loitering. I'm the guy whose antiestablishment mood urges a foray onto the forbidden terrain, irrigated by
haphazard sprinklers connected to yellow hoses. I'm totally geared
to sally forth when a weathered-looking fellow in baggy jeans
and denim shirt leans into the doorway. "Where's all the golf balls?"
he asks me from beneath a very bushy red mustache. "Me and
Larry been looking all over hell and back for some damn golf balls.
How we going to play without golf balls?" He's clutching a sheaf
of mismatched irons in one hand; an unfiltered cigarette wafts
a spiral of smoke into the rafters of the shack. I shrug and smile as

disarmingly as I can. "We want to play golf, and there's no golf balls," he says in a softer tone. "You know where we can get some golf balls?"

"Sorry . . . I don't work here," I tell him, "but I can get some golf balls for you. Stay right where you are."

"Hey, thanks, man. Really appreciate that," he says.

I scurry back to my car and grab two unopened sleeves of Ultras and a clutch of loose ones and some tees from the side pouch of my bag. I also choose a few lofted irons and my putter. I've raced halfway across the parking lot when I'm struck by a realization. I hit the skids, throw everything into reverse, and run back to the car, where my Leica pocket camera is stowed inside a hiking boot. Then, posthaste again, across the pavement, through the shack, and onto the off-limits hospital golf course.

Larry, a balding fellow who looks like the guys you see running the Gravitron at the carnival, has now joined his friend at the little practice green. The newly mowed grass isn't really grass at all, but *Poa Anna*, a highly invasive weed that gives greenskeepers nightmares because it grows more quickly than bent grass or Bermuda, with obvious negative consequences. On his forearms, just above the plastic hospital bracelet, is a faded tattoo that might or might not be an eagle. I toss each of them a sleeve of pristine golf balls. "Here you go," I say. "A gift from me to you."

Larry says, "Wow, man, *thanks*. How about that, Dave? New ones."

"If you ain't staff, why you hanging around *this* place?" Dave asks.

"Just a gate-crasher," I tell them. "Not supposed to be here unsupervised, but as you see . . . I'm writing a book about how different people play golf, if you can believe that. I play with them, probe their brains, then write about them."

"Awesome," Larry says. "Whaddya think about that, Dave. We're going to be in a book. You and me, man. Characters in a book. Sure, you can join us. Didn't catch your name. What was it again?"

"Bill," I say.

"We'll have us a good time, Bill."

I pull some unbroken tees from my pocket and dole them out like antipsychotic meds to Dave and Larry. "Thanks, man," Dave says. "Wow. New tees."

The sooner we evacuate this all-too-conspicuous spot, the less my chances of being arrested and strip-searched by the VA Security Police. "Shall we get a move on?" I ask.

We three golfers shamble toward the first tee. Dave's knee is giving him some trouble, but he's too happy for complaining.

His weird stance is unique to beginners and inveterate duffers. I'm thinking of nearly catatonic Barry back at Round Mountain. Dave's legs and arms are completely rigid, and he's bent so far forward that a breeze would blow him over; his hand-over-hand grip is fine for pulping a mango—but not so hot for the striking of a golf ball. "Whoa. Stop the presses," I shout. "Hold it. Cut! You look like a *pederast*, Dave." I presumptuously arrange his fingers on the rubber grips just so, noticing in the process that the ring and pinkie fingers of his right hand are amputated at the second knuckle. With the toe of my loafer I nudge his heavy boots into a more conventional configuration. "Now, flex your knees a bit. *Just* a bit. Yeah. No. Easy. *Not* like you're taking a crap."

"Amazing, Bill. I can feel the difference," he says. "Thanks, Bill. Yeah, that's a helluva lot better, Bill. Yeah." Larry crouches down in order to get a better look at what's going on between Dave and me. They are wonderful students, totally attentive to every suggestion. It's sort of pleasant, starting them off from scratch this way. No bad habits to overcome, no preconceptions whatsoever. Any of my suggestions they see fit to adopt will be an improvement. "Listen, Dave, I want a nice loose grip. *Comprende?* And a limber backswing. Come on, let the club do the work. That's the ticket. Might help if you take that cigarette out of your mouth." He obediently flicks the thing in the general direction of a trash basket and takes a perfectly acceptable practice swing. "Okay," I tell him. "Now you're cooking with gas. How's about you give it a ride." He reverts slightly to his former self, but even so he's transformed. When he looks back at me for approval, there is genuine fear in his eyes, so I give him an encouraging nod. I can tell he's worried about letting me down. I doubt he's spent much of his street time pondering the technique of a proper golf swing, let alone trying to please somebody besides himself. I almost regret interfering with the little world they've created for themselves. It's conceivable that I've upset the delicate equilibrium of their care-free approach to the game, and that wouldn't be such a good thing. "Don't worry, Dave. It's all right. Just go for it," I tell him. He in-hales and exhales deeply, then takes a nice swing. His worm-burner tee shot scrambles along the dandelion fairway, skirts a small sand trap, and rolls toward the green, eventually pulling up dead on the frog hair.

"That's just amazing, Bill," he says. "Look at that. That's my best shot in two days. Thanks, man. Hey, you gotta try this, Larry."

Larry's approach is pure gung-ho. No practice swings, no waggles. He plunges headfirst into the task at hand. Although his first swing is a whiff, an air ball, a swing and a miss, he's absolutely undaunted. "That was your practice swing," I tell him. "But, Larry, my friend, you've got to keep your noggin down. Dave and I are going watch where your ball goes."

"Roger. Wilco," he says. This time, he hits the thing at its equator, inflicting what I know will be serious injury to his new Ultra. However, the ball is at least headed in the right direction . . . that is, until it takes a nasty kick left and rolls down the hill and away from the green.

"Tough luck," I say. "It was a pretty shot."

"It felt real good," he says. "Very good."

My nine-iron tee shot sails high into the smoggy sky and descends politely onto the green. My gallery is impressed. Larry says, "That's just awesome, Bill. Wish I could do that."

As we're hoofing our way up the first fairway, I ask Dave what it is that landed them here in the hospital. He tells me with no hesitation at all that he and Larry had been living on the streets of Los Angeles for a few years. He lost his fingertips to frostbite when he was home-less in Chicago ten years back. The bad knee is a souvenir from a rice paddy one hundred miles north of Saigon. They're recovering alcohol and drug users, both Vietnam vets, both of them casualties of the war. And strangers to one another until now. The hospital's outreach staff raked them off the streets a couple of weeks ago and put them in detox until their heads cleared. For two days straight they've been playing golf together, clean and sober, having the time of their lives. Neither of them had touched a golf club prior to this stint at the VA, and I can't help wondering if they will ever again play golf. But two more enthusiastic golf bums I've never seen.

"I wish I'd've known about golf a long time ago, Bill," Larry tells me. "I forget about everything when I'm out here. I mean it, Bill. Me and Dave, we've had a blast, even though we don't know shit about golf. But you guessed that easy enough, didn't you, Bill?"

"Yeah, I had a hunch you weren't too experienced."

"I wonder what would've happened if I'd've had golf waiting for me when I got back from 'Nam."

There's a part of me that suspects I'm being trifled with. They are so amazingly effusive and earnest and appreciative that my skeptical self can't quite take them seriously. Then, Larry's voice will crack with emotion, or Dave will shake his head just so, and one or the other of them will pat me on the back like an old friend. And then I'm ashamed of myself for doubting their sincerity. Probably no one has really taken time to attend to issues other than their addictions and their psych profiles and their survival on the streets. They are mere emblems of a sociological phenomenon with predictable symptoms and foregone outcomes.

Then along comes some fellow who gives them a few tips on how to play a game that will abandon them in a few days just as surely as the grass grows. And they fall all over themselves in their appreciation. The here and now of the game is crucial to them for reasons I can't understand. *Why* should it matter so? How could it? Until I came along, the game was just itself, something they invented. No expectations, no fussy little rules to bother with. Now, I've superimposed an unachievable ideal to which they gallantly, futilely aspire. Their inept game was surely a metaphor for something, *something*, even if they didn't quite know what that was. Metaphors can't hurl you into the cold or deprive you of hot food or a warm place to sleep. Maybe that's the beauty of golf. If the ball rolls down the hill, all the way to BelAire, what difference does it make? It's such a harmless little event. What happens beyond the chain-link fence is the real deal, not this crazy little game they play together. But Dave and Larry try *so hard* now to get it all just right. The grip, the stance, the swing, even the lingo. "Stiff to the pin, Dave." "Never up, never in, Larry."

Their days here are numbered, and they know it. Soon these two men will be returned to their lives on the street. So their happy banter drums inside of me with a poignancy I can't fully explain. Is their brand of golf a metaphor for the metaphor itself? I play the game and suffer theatrically, aware that I will be back again. The symbolism must be all the more precious for them because it ends right here on this humble patch of landscape. I can't help admiring them.

It embarrasses me to fly my tee shot onto the green because their admiration is so profuse. On the other hand, my praise for their every minor triumph is equally lavish. If they had tails they'd wag them. We've had a lovely time biffing each other on the shoulder, conceding impossibly long putts to one another. I've taught them every conceivable golfer's cliché, and they'll never be the same as a result. "Call the sheriff," Larry says when my putt lips out. "I peeked," Dave says when he tops his little pitch shot.

At the sixth hole Dave launches a beautiful seven-iron shot that lands at the geographical center of the green, just a few feet from the flagstick. "Unflippingbelievable, Dave!" I shout. I give him a high five and a low five and a gonzo forearm. Larry is whooping it up, too. We're a happy trio, reveling in Dave's triumph.

"Now, Dave," I tell him as we're marching up the fairway. "When we get up there, I want you to walk right up to that ball and knock it right in the middle of the hole. Don't try to read it. Don't think about it. Just *can* the damned thing. Got that?"

"You're the boss."

"I'm not your boss, Dave. I'm your guardian angel."

When Dave gets to the green, he limps toward his ball and looks at it admiringly. "Stop grinning and putt it," Larry says. So Dave does just that. He takes a nice crisp stroke, and the ball runs like a chipmunk right into the center of the cup.

"Birdie," he says. "A goddamned birdie."

"You're a god, Dave," I tell him. "A god, pure and simple."

Larry and I make bogeys, but we're so pleased for Dave's sake that nothing else much matters. And Dave himself is so puffed up that he can hardly get his tee in the ground at number seven.

Nothing much good happens amongst us happy linksters until we arrive at number nine, our last hole together and the longest hole on the course. In the middle of the green is an American flag and on either side of the green are pot bunkers, each as mean-spirited as anything down there at BelAire. Larry swears he's going to make a birdie. It's my "going-away present," he says. I close my eyes as he fidgets over the ball, wishing with all my soul that he would please, please nail one stiff to the pin. A frail hope, I know, but I'm wishing for it anyway. His lips are pursed, his grip on the golf club fierce. Suddenly, he thrashes the ball on a low trajectory over the ravine separating the tee from the far-off green . . . but the ball fades toward one of the pot bunkers and dives into the far bank of sand. He's disappointed, but it's a minor-league setback in the great game of life. He shrugs almost apologetically. "Tough break. Good effort, though. Just get it up and down and I'll love you forever." He lights a cigarette and blows a puff of smoke toward the green. Dave's shot is nothing too grand, but he's left himself a chip shot straight up the hill. "That'll work," I say. "Very acceptable."

My own seven-iron shot is a good one, so good that I'm only seven feet or so from paydirt. My credibility is at an all-time high as we click down the hill, a painful maneuver for Dave, then up the incline to where our balls rest in various states of suspended animation.

After Dave has chopped his ball onto the fringe, I wander over to where Larry's ball is buried in the sand trap. "Very, very ugly," I say. "A fried egg. Damn . . . damn . . . damn. Tell you what you're going to do. Borrow my sand wedge, and just beat the crap out of your ball with it, okay? I mean, dig your way to China. Get the picture?"

"Anything you say, captain," Larry says. He gently places his cigarette in the white sand a few feet off to the side, shimmies his feet into the stuff, and swings with all his might at the ball, which floats beautifully out of the trap and onto the green. It curls down a

swale toward the hole, and I'm almost ready to believe that the thing
is actually going to fall. "Roll . . . roll, you little bastard," I whisper.
But my psychokinetic powers are feeble. There's just not enough
mustard on the thing, alas, and it come up short. "Absolutely gorgeous, Larry. As good as it gets."

"Man, I wanted that birdie, Bill. You wouldn't forget *that*, would
you?"

"Tell you what, Larry. I'm going to remember that bunker shot
until I'm an old, toothless, drooling, piddling fossil. And Dave's
birdie. The two high points of my trip so far. I mean it."

"Really?" Dave asks.

"Damn straight," I tell them. "I wouldn't lie about something as
important as that." I concede Larry's two-foot putt and toss him
the ball.

They are more than happy to pose for me on the ninth green. Dave
holds the American flag and Larry stands alongside him, beaming.
Larry holds the flag, and Dave smiles next to him. They both hold
the flag, and I snap another picture. Then in a burst of creativity,
I set the self-timer, balance the camera just so on a golf club
tripod I've newly invented, push the release button, and dash
across the green. The three of us pose with our hands together
on the flagstick. Mount Suribachi it's *not*, but it's an image I will
treasure.

They know and I know that our time together is done. "I want you
guys to stay well after they turf you out of this joint. Hear me?"

We three stand for a while on the last green with the flag snapping
behind us, trying to think of something else to say that will have
meaning. I'm the writer. Words are supposed to be my currency, but
I'm flat broke when it comes to good-byes as painful as this one. I
hug them both and pound them on the back. "See you," I tell them,
and walk toward the white, uninhabited equipment shack. Part of me
wants to turn around for a last look at them, but they shouldn't see
me like this. The parking lot is such a blur that I can barely make
out Iris, nosed against the fence. The maintenance truck is gone, and
a couple of cars have replaced it.

Only after I've put my clubs away and backed out of the parking slot do I hazard a glance toward the golf course. Dave is at the first tee, waggling over his gleaming white ball, more or less limber and properly positioned to hit it toward the first green.

"You should have seen Susan's house," I tell Mom. I'm sitting on my Motel 6 bed in San Luis Obispo, just at dusk. The sky outside my window is all crimson and lavender, a good omen if the sailors' adage is true. "The place was sort of unassuming from the outside," I tell her, "then you walk in the door and it's just gorgeous. Lots of Native American rugs and statuary. Beautiful pottery and paintings."

"Was she pretty?" Mom asks. She hopes, even in her infirmity, that her son will find love there on the earthquake fringe of the continent. Her voice has lost the accents and intonations that would otherwise animate her conversation. The cancer has weakened her to the point of exhaustion.

"She was a total knockout, Mom. Blond, with funky cat glasses, denim overalls . . . *très chic.*"

"So you got along well with her then?"

"Absolutely. She was lovely to be with. Funny. Cute. And very, very rich."

"Do you think you'll see her again?"

I can't help laughing at her inquisitiveness. Wedding bells ring in her sleep. She worries that I'll be a lonely old goof if I don't act fast. "I doubt it, Mom. It was a onetime deal. Escape and fade. Eat and retreat."

"Oh," she says, a trace of disappointment in her voice. "Better say hello to your dad."

"How's he doing?"

"I'm concerned what will happen when I go."

"So don't go," I say, and she makes a noise that sounds like a little laugh. A wry little laugh. My guess is that she refuses to die for fear of breaking my heart, wreaking havoc on my career, possibly impeding my chance for love in the far reaches of the continent. She has a dim awareness of Gillian but voices concern about the age difference. My love-conquers-all attitude lacks credibility in her scheme of things, but I forgive her. She's my mom.

I detect a botched phone handoff in Bowling Green. There's some clatter and a good deal of beeping before I hear Dad's voice at the other end. "Hi, Bill," he says. "Where are you?"

"San Luis Obispo, California, Dad. I'm heading up to Monterey to play Pebble Beach tomorrow, weather permitting."

"Why are you doing that?" he asks.

"It's for this book I'm doing. You know, the golfing book."

"The golfing book. How's that going?"

"Pretty good," I tell him. "I'll be making the turn for home in a day or two," I tell him. "That'll be a welcome milestone."

"Are you at home now?" he asks.

"No, I'm in California."

"Oh, that's right," he says. "You just told me that, didn't you?"

"How's Mom?" I ask him.

"Very weak. She doesn't get up anymore." My heart pounds inside my chest for a moment, but then I tell myself that he might be mistaken about that. He's often mistaken. But it's a very precise statement from a man whose moments of clarity are generally significant.

"That's too bad," I say. "I want you to keep the faith, though."

"Oh, I will," he says. "I'm going to miss her."

"I know, Dad. I *know* you will." His weeping makes further talk impossible. It's very unlikely that he's holding the receiver against his ear anymore, but I pretend he is. "I love you, Dad," I tell him, as I always do at the end of our conversations. But there is no response, just the sound of muffled sobbing and Mom's admonition to her husband that he put the receiver back in its cradle.

The twilight hangs forever in the sky, unwilling to relinquish itself to the inexorable night. From my balcony I can see the lights coming on up and down Morro Bay. The sky darkens, the lights appear. A poetic equation, and a lovely one.

I walk across the parking lot, then zip across the busy commercial highway to a nearby McDonald's, where I order a large iced tea and salad with diced chicken. Quite a healthy selection by my standards.

That makes two salads in one day and no beers at all. I'm a prime candidate for sainthood.

I carry my healthy fare to a brightly lit table in the very center of the restaurant because, damn it, I'm a trifle lonely. With my flimsy plastic fork, I stab a cube of chicken and chew it as gracefully as I can. After all, I am a man in the spotlight at the center of a fast-food eatery three thousand miles from home.

CHAPTER 12

pebbles and beer

Seagulls are already squabbling in the Motel 6 parking lot when the phone rings at 6:30 A.M. My heart plunges into a cold cellar for a moment, but it's only a wake-up call from the insomniac desk clerk: nobody has died; Rachel is asleep on her grandmother's screened porch; Garth is dissecting Proust or composing a villanelle back in my home state.

I'm happy to be in San Luis Obispo on such a fine day. No more stifling heat to contend with, no more noxious smog. A chilly sea breeze fills my room when I open the door, tempting me to engage in some white-legged slob-jogging up and down the kelp-strewn beach; I decide to debut my new running costume a bit farther up the coast. Maybe tomorrow. Maybe not. Lightly sugared Kix and a cup of freshly perked black coffee are the order of the day. A sensible breakfast for a sensible man. No more Denny's for this Spartan. My life wants discipline, and I'm determined to make a new start. What inspires this determination is unclear, although I admit that I've been mentally juxtaposing my squishy pallor against the bronze muscularity of the Malibu surfers. Perhaps the moment of epiphany occurred as I stood like a cartoon figure on the boardwalk yesterday with my Topanga Bakery cream puff oozing its custard filling onto my chin. Just a nine-iron away, beach gods were riding blue-green waves with mad abandon.

By seven-thirty I'm showered, shaved, dressed, coffeed, and fed. Ready for the twisty shore-hugging road to Big Sur and beyond. Bear me off, Iris, to the rocky cliffs. To the land of Bing and Clint, Kesey, and Kerouac.

Because I'm a simple rube from the Carolina lowlands by way of the flattest stretch of midwestern corn country imaginable, the sight of green waves crashing against jagged palisades is almost too spectacular for me. Iris crosses the double yellow line more than once, and I must yank the wheel hard right to avoid becoming a casualty of the magnificent landscape. Again and again I succumb to yet another scenic overlook. Each time I vow, *this* will be the last, but the seething green waves and the brutal rocky spires are just too fine to ignore. I only wish there were somebody I could share my exclamations with. "Holy mother of God. *Look* at that . . ." I say. But, of course, there's nobody looking but me and some folks sitting in a Volvo with Iowa plates. The Pacific Coast Highway, a narrow shoelace of a road, winds through cliffs and over streams that tumble seaward from the Santa Lucia Range. As I close in on Big Sur, there are occasional lighthouses, majestic seaside pastures, and seal-covered granite islands lashed by the ocean. Behind me are summer-yellow, soft-shouldered hills threaded with hiking trails. Several of the wildly abundant flower species I know already—daisies, cornflower, Queen Anne's lace, Indian paintbrush—but others are fragile things, exotic and alien to me.

The ocean's vastness is more apparent here than on the Atlantic, which seems almost humble by comparison. The Pacific's waves, propelled by the westerly winds, are more forceful, too, more transparent, colder-seeming, and infinitely more sonorous. Enormous round pebbles grind against one another as the surf retreats into itself. It's a thrilling sound, the very essence of power.

I'm sitting on a granite shelf in a sweep of succulent ice plant on a cliff high above the ocean when two wonderful-looking college girls with backpacks and walking sticks climb the path toward me. I give them my handsome-bachelor look, and they smile amiably back at me. There's got to be something clever and hospitable one can say under such circumstances, but my mouth won't make the words, so I return my gaze to the endless blue horizon. "Hi," says the tall Viking girl. "Hi there," I say, noting the orange patch on the knee of her blue jeans.

"Would you like a granola bar?" she asks. I'm sure she's talking to her blue-eyed hiking partner, so I say nothing. "Last call." Finally it dawns on me that I'm being spoken to. She's looking down at me, haloed in sunlight like a saint.

"Oh . . . sorry," I tell her. "Didn't realize you meant *me*." She laughs, and tells me not to worry. I must be the most nonthreatening human being on the planet because they seem to have no fear whatsoever that I'm an escapee from Lompoc or an itinerant deviate with trouble in mind. Maybe they can tell I'm just a foolish romantic from the dreamy look in my eyes. Potential rapists don't generally carry binoculars and Peterson's *Field Guide to North American Birds*, I reckon.

"Well . . . ?" She tilts a foil-wrapped rectangle in my direction and jiggles it like a dog biscuit. *Arf*, says my pathetic alter ego.

"Why not?" I say. "Thank you very much." They uncinch their packs and sit on the rock with me. We introduce ourselves and peel the foil from our snacks. Like a dog, I sniff mine before eating it.

"You're from California," I say, as if it's a total certainty. But they're not from the West Coast at all. They're from the University of Maine, in fact. I've come to assume that everyone who is fit and brown is from California.

"We're hiking the coastal trail all the way up to Carmel. We started in Cambria," says Alice, who could make a fortune modeling anything she pleased. Her hair is pulled back in a ponytail, and her cheek is scratched just below her right eye. "What about you?"

It embarrasses me to admit that I'm writing a book because it sounds so much like a hokey come-on. I may as well claim that I'm a Broadway actor or a rock star or heir to the Kellogg fortune. They don't look like the type who would respond favorably to golfing tales. I tell them that I teach at a university in North Carolina and that I'm just traveling around for the heck of it. Killing off a summer.

"Cool," says Emily, sprawling now on the sun-baked rock, her head resting on the bedroll of her backpack.

Alice offers me a drag from her newly ignited bright-red joint, but I shake my head no. (Apparently I don't look like a narc, either.) It's not a solid *no*, but more of a *probably not*. "Sure?" she asks, using hardly a thimbleful of air for the utterance. I give the matter a once-over in my mind. Conclusion: negotiating the swervy roads is tough enough without sugarplum fairies dancing in my head. Misgivings: I will miss an infinitely pleasurable liftoff in the company of a flannel-clad angel. We might have explored the pseudoprofundities of love and loss together. We would probably have giggled ourselves to tears, then fallen asleep in the Platonic sunshine. But since I'm bound to make Pebble Beach by early afternoon, I must decline. And I do. Alice kicks Emily's boot and offers her a hit, which she takes like a pro. Alice asks nobody in particular a question she's maybe been tussling with since childhood. "Do American dogs," she wonders, "think in *English*?" It's a perfect nonsequitur. If I were stoned, it might float nicely on my own stream of consciousness, and we'd be into it. Dogs, windmills, the death of Elvis, sex in the after-life . . . fair game, all of it. But I'm destined to resist hallucinogens for the nonce, and having done so, I'm once again an outsider.

"Well, folks, I'd better shove off. Got to make Carmel by one o'clock. Maybe I'll see you there." I brush sand from the seat of my pants and shake their hands. "Good luck with your hiking," I say. "Nice to meet both of you."

"See ya, Bill," they say. "Take care."

I plod up the ice-plant slope to the gravel crescent where Iris is parked. I'm ashamed of myself for contemplating even abstractions of remote possibilities and the barest shadows of impossible sce-narios. I don't really know the real strength of my character or the power of my will; the demands of the day have simply won out this time. I can't help wondering what would have happened if . . . And suddenly I miss Gillian with an intensity that is almost unbearable. I haven't called her in several days, which is inexcusable. Something will be done to rectify that oversight.

In Seaside, just a mile or two from the gate of Seventeen Mile Drive, I stop at a large upscale grocery store to buy some Port du Salut cheese and a six-pack of Anchor Steam. A few doors down from the supermarket is a French bakery, where I purchase a dome-shaped loaf of peasant bread, which, with the cheese and beer, will make a fine picnic lunch. The thought of cold beer combined with the wind blowing in off the Pacific makes me shiver. The bank ther-mometer says sixty-two, but the bluster makes the air seem much

colder. I dig a thick wool sweater from my suitcase and put it on.
Even with a turtleneck shirt and a wool pullover, I'm so unused to
such chilly temperatures that goose bumps rise on my exposed flesh.

Back a few miles toward Big Sur is Port Lords Beach, a beautiful
expanse of coarse sand, untrammeled except for a woman and her
two black Labs. At the southern end of the beach looms a large rock
formation in whose lee I can make my picnic.

The beach sand is not so much sand as very tiny pebbles, hardly
bigger than sesame seeds. They creep inside my sandals and grate the
skin of my feet so fiercely that I'm forced to walk barefoot to my destination several hundred yards away. Off in the distance, across Carmel
bay, I see what I know is Pebble Beach, and I'm thrilled at the sight of
it. I'm no different from any American golfer. Ask him which golf
course he'd most like to play above all others and the answer will most
likely to Pebble Beach or its neighbor Cypress Point.

I sit on my wool blanket in the California sunshine eating my
bread and cheese while breakers tumble into the steep incline of the
beach. The pungent oceanic smell washes over me, and seagulls,
recognizing me as the tourist that I am, raise a terrible ruckus overhead. It's one of those rare moments in the life of a human being
when all his five senses are wide open. But my most active sense is
the visual, and the focus of my gaze is that emerald sward clinging to
the seaside rocks several miles across the bay.

One beer is all I will drink today. I'm maintaining my program of
austerity, true, but mostly I want to be sharp if I'm to have my
chance at Pebble Beach. Still, it's a lovely, biting beer that goes
wonderfully well with my hearty bread and cheese. After I've eaten
my fill, I walk back across the blustery strand to Iris, in whose warm
compartment I sit for a few minutes before departure. I want to
remember every single second of this day, including the intense
anticipation stirring inside me.

A rental Saturn occupied by a quartet of Japanese golfers precedes
me through the checkpoint at the gate of Seventeen Mile Drive, the
only access to Pebble Beach and Cypress Point. Judging from the
abundance of Asian tourists tooling up and down the Monterey
Peninsula, my experience on the links will be a cosmopolitan one,

which is okay with me. It is a little bit difficult, however, to imagine feeding my obsession at Pebble Beach if I've spent my adult golfing life launching fungoes into a practice net at a triple-deck driving range in downtown Tokyo. Still, I'm happy to tee it up with any hard-core surly-hearted golf junkie willing to drop a million yen and travel five thousand miles to worship at a holy shrine of American golf. On the other hand, I'd rather not be relegated to showing my teeth and making politically correct hand gestures to express my state of wonderment. I'll take what I get, though.

My Scottish grandfather's frugality gene is lighting up as I make my way past multimillion-dollar homes with views that no human being can possibly deserve, unless we all do. I'm more than willing to cough up the absurd three-hundred-dollar greens fee, having convinced myself that this is a once-in-a-lifetime experience that will validate me as a real golfer instead of a man who merely golfs. Rationalization is a lovely thing at a time like this. Because I haven't reserved a tee time, I will be shoehorned in wherever and whenever a slot becomes available. The fact is, I like the unpredictability of the adventure.

Pebble Beach is more than a golfing venue. There is, of course, the Lodge and myriad associated units with beautiful views of the outgoing and incoming fairways or not-so-grand views of the crowded parking lots and busy shops and restaurants. I park my car near the little par three nine-holer, used mostly by golfers who need to shake the starch out of their swings before confronting the painful beauties of the links itself. The grounds are bustling with well-dressed players coming off their rounds or heading out—or spouses of players, or their children.

I've never quite experienced such tangible excitement. Everyone seems reduced to grinning, either out of nervousness or joy or, more likely, a combination of both. Lest this seem judgmental, let it be known that I, too, am smiling uncontrollably. I'm happy as a man can be, knowing that as evening draws nigh, I will be striding up the final glorious fairway, wounded, perhaps, but triumphant.

In my mental scrapbook, I have countless snapshots of Pebble Beach. Hale Irwin's miraculous ricochet from rocks to fairway on the last hole of the U.S. Open. Tom Watson's astonishing chip-in winner at the seventeen. Countless untolled calendar images of the little windblown par three seventh hole . . . the death-defying leap across the chasm at number eight . . . the massively deceptive oak tree that beckons golfers to safety at the finishing hole.

Every January, after having suffered through a bleak, golfless, midwestern winter, I anticipated the weekend of the Crosby National Pro-Am, which kicked off the PGA golf season. By then, the curbs in my hometown were already piled with dirty snow and the temperature hovered in the teens. My father kept a bag of rock salt by our back door. But out there in Pebble Beach, California, men were *golfing* in the *sunshine* on *green grass*. I played and replayed those sunny Pebble Beach memories all throughout the winter, and they were my salvation until the snow finally melted and the first buds appeared on the trees. I recall even now a portion of Wordsworth's "Lines Written a Few Miles above Tintern Abbey," which Miss Mallory mandated we, her eleventh graders, memorize in order to fortify our midwinter spirits.

> *In hours of weariness, sensations sweet,*
> *Felt in the blood, and felt along the heart,*
> *And passing even into my purer mind*
> *With tranquil restoration . . .*

The TV camera invariably honed in on Jack Lemmon, sunk once again in a hopeless bunker. Or James Garner, bad knee and all, hobbling up the last fairway waving like a movie star. But it was Arnie and Fat Jack and the Merry Mex and Champagne Tony who commanded my attention. Every year, Dad and I sat immovably in the living room on that weekend, he in his easy chair, I on my private sofa cushion, oblivious to the mundanities rotating around our little theater. Sodas appeared on the coffee table before us, and sandwiches, which we masticated hypnotically while Billy Casper lined up his sixteen-footer. "Watch this one break toward the ocean," Jim McKay would say to his sidekick in the broadcast tower. "I don't think he's read this break." And, of course, the bent-grass green always made a prophet of Mr. McKay and a victim of whatever golfer failed to heed the proclivities of nature.

Now, clicking up the parking lot, nodding in that special way golfers nod at others in the know, I am becoming part of that landscape imprinted for so many years on my brain.

My first stop is the pro shop, where I wait in line for my assignment with two Japanese golfers and a rotund Georgian with a Bulldogs polo shirt. The shop is replete with monogrammed hats, shirts, umbrellas, bags, divot forks, ball markers . . . anything large enough to bear the imprint of Pebble Beach.

I'm assigned a three-forty tee-off, which should bring me up the eighteenth fairway at sunset, a lovely thing to contemplate. I'll be playing with three Japanese fellows, which might make things interesting.

Because there is time to kill, I rummage through several of the various gift shops, but the merchandise is not only very expensive but inconsistent with my birch-bark sensibility. I am drawn, however, to an antiquarian golf shop, specializing in books, photographs, golf equipment, and certain odd ornaments whose appeal can only be described as idiosyncratic. Wild Turkey whiskey bottles adorn a high shelf, and a curious assortment of inkwells and ashtrays and paperweights of dubious aesthetic value cover an entire display table. The far wall of the shop, overseen by a stout, graying fellow about my age, is covered with books, new, old, and very old. In a burst of ego, I search the shelves for my own books. To my surprise, there is a very fine first edition of *The Rub of the Green*, jacket to jacket with a copy of Holworth Hall's "Dormie One," a brilliant story treasured by aficionados. My pleasure is doubled by the very presence of my work on such hallowed grounds and, moreover, the placement of my book next to such a landmark of golf literature. My first edition of Hall's very long short story is one of the singular treasures in my modest golf book collection, and I'm tempted to purchase another copy merely for the novelty of owning two. Instead, I pluck out the less-expensive edition of my own book and carry it to the cash register. The stout fellow is processing my Visa transaction when it dawns on him that the name on the card matches the name on the book cover, and he hangs up the telephone suddenly. "You're William Hallberg," he says.

"Well, yeah, I am," I say, wishing for some dirt I can dig my toe into. It's slightly embarrassing to be purchasing one's own book.

"Can't find the darn thing anywhere these days. It's seriously out of print. Deeply passé. So I grab them wherever I find them."

"I've got two first editions at home," he says. "I loved that book. And your collection of stories, too. If you want a nice first of *Perfect Lies*, I can run home and get it for you."

"Love to have it, but I don't want you to go to such trouble," I say. But he's falling all over himself to be kind, and I hate to thwart his magnanimity. "What if I give you my address and you mail it to me," I suggest.

"Tell you what . . . I'll send you that copy and a couple of my own for you to autograph and send back. How does that sound?"

"Sounds like a deal," I tell him, and shove my Visa card back across the counter.

"You going to play the links today?" he asks. "Because if you are, I'll join you. You can be my guest. Gary can work us in, I'm sure."

"You're kidding. You can actually pull that off?" I say. "In fact, I'm playing Pebble Beach as part of a book I'm doing for a publisher in New York."

"Let's go, then," he says, and after hanging a BACK IN A MINUTE sign in his front window, he locks up and waves me to follow him back to the pro shop. "I'll call my associate in to cover for me."

When Gary sees my new friend—whose name I discover is Jim— and me loitering over by the necktie tree, he excuses himself to greet us. Jim introduces me to Gary and inquires about the chances of working us in. "*Him*, I can find a place for," Gary says, pointing at me. "But there aren't any spaces for two right now, and I doubt there will be. It's a busy day."

"Bill here is a golf writer. He wants to play the links as part of a book he's doing," Jim says. "How about we waive the greens fee."

"*That* we can do," says Gary, who scribbles something on a piece of paper and hands it to me. "Give it to the fellas at the counter over there. They'll take care of you," he tells me, and hurries back to his desk.

"Sorry I can't tag along," Jim says. "Maybe next time."

"Can't thank you enough for what you've done."

He shakes my hand. "Back to work, then," he says. "Have a great time." I can tell that he's a trifle disappointed not to be joining me. He looks a bit droopy walking past the front window of the pro shop.

I carry my fee waiver to the counter and hand it to one of the several busy young men who mastermind the well-oiled process of getting the right golfers to the right place at the right time. "Go get your clubs," he says. "Your group is on deck."

"I've got a three-forty already," I tell him.

"You speak Japanese?" he asks.

"Nope."

"Better hustle, then," he says.

That's William Hallberg, father, author, teacher, rank amateur golfer, scuttling between shops, hauling it across the parking lot to his gray Neon, chucking his sandals into the trunk of his car, grabbing some thick wool socks, putting them on, then his golf shoes, which he slides into without bothering to lace them up. He yanks his golf bag from the trunk. Also, a hat, an umbrella, a pocket camera. What else? He's calculating. Assessing. But not for long. Now he's dashing, fully loaded, back to the point of origin, where he's greeted by the starter, who, in a thick German accent, points his pencil at the group limbering up on the tee. "Zat's you," he says.

So here we are, a foursome, waiting for the fairway to clear. I strap my bag onto the back of a cart alongside the rented clubs belonging to Todd, who shakes my hand. "Glad to meet you," he says. We chat for a minute or two about the crazy circumstances behind our being here. He's a commodities trader from New Jersey, honeymooning at the Lodge with his new wife, who *insisted* that he seize the opportunity to play Pebble Beach. A good wife, indeed. "The older fellow over there is Frank, by the way," Todd tells me, "and the hefty guy is his son Carl."

Carl and his father will be riding in another cart. And then there's the entourage, consisting of Carl's wife, Cathie, and his sister Pam, who pilots the third cart, which is stocked with coolers and picnic baskets. A regular chuck wagon. Frank is a gray-haired man not quite five feet tall. Except for Cathie, they look Filipino to me, but when we introduce ourselves, I can't detect any accent at all. "Where are you fellows from?" I ask. Frank and his son are agricultural seed merchandisers from Salinas, one valley away from Monterey. Carl shakes my hand, then takes a few scary practice swings.

By all appearances, he's a very, very big hitter. Todd, on the other hand, has a nice rhythmic swing that looks as if it might just keep him in the fairway.

I hardly have time to contemplate the impossible truth of where I am and what I'm doing. Off to my right, waves crash against the rocks, to my left are million-dollar homes, and up ahead is the first hole with its transecting road at the far end of the fairway. This is it, then. A course I've played so many times in my imagination that the actuality and the dream seem like one thing. Cypress trees, almost too perfect in their exoticism, and meticulously groomed fairways lend a curious unreality to the moment. I remind myself that my feet are planted on the tangible turf. A palpable breeze animates the horizontal branches of the trees. I am Bill Hallberg, and this is the Pebble Beach Golf Links.

The acrid smell of Carl's cigarette smoke helps pull me back into the here and now. For the first time on this entire trip, I'm genuinely nervous. It's doubtful that I'll ever be here again to walk these fairways and greens, and I don't want to corrupt my romantic ideal with shameful play. We're all showing our nerves, except for maybe Frank, who is too wise to attach deeper meanings to the moment. Carl is on his second Camel in ten minutes. Todd is over there pacing the sidelines by the ball washer. I'm whistling "Yellow Submarine," twirling my driver, trying to think green thoughts until the moment arrives.

Todd and I lean on our titanium drivers and swap clichés while we wait for Frank and Carl to hit their tee shots. Twice, Carl has to back away from his ball to collect himself. He heaves a huge sigh, then settles over the ball once again. It's no small wonder he's feeling the pressure; Cathie is lying next to the tee marker, snapping photographs of her hubbie as he prepares to blast one down the fairway. My inclination would be to snatch the camera and hurl it into the sea. But Carl doesn't seem to mind. His drive is tremendous, but very crooked. The ball climbs into the stiff cross breeze, which carries it sideways toward the backyard of what looks like Windsor Castle, egregiously out of bounds. He shakes his head and tees up another ball, which, when he whacks it, sails high and left, but it lands softly this time and manages to stay on the happy side of the white boundary stakes. He lights another cigarette and stares angrily down the fairway while his father methodically bloops one straight down the middle.

Todd stands behind his ball to visualize a flight line, waggles the club head a couple of times, presses his hands forward a few inches, makes a decent take-away . . . then seems to lose control of his down-swing. The result is a yanked hook that squeals off the tee and dashes into the left rough. From that position he will be blockaded from the green by an encroachment of strategically located oak trees. It's an honest golf hole with a tangible system of rewards and punishments.

My strategy is to take care of the business at hand as quickly as possible, then tromp the gas pedal of the cart and beat a hasty advance down the fairway. My ego dictates that I establish credibility with the dozens of onlookers who are perpetually assembled near the first tee. To that end, I tee up a brand-new Ultra, take one perfunctory practice swing, then knock a perfectly decent but unspectacular drive down the center of the fairway. I'm relieved to have that one behind me so that I can finally relax and enjoy the various tasks awaiting me on this beautiful windy day at Pebble Beach.

Todd's lie offers him no options; he must chop the ball back onto the fairway and pray for a one-putt par. He negotiates the first task admirably. But his follow-up approach is fat and falls well shy of the green. Carl, the apparent subject of a photodocumentary, stands ankle-deep in fescue near an out-of-bounds stake. The greedy side of him wants to crush the ball over the row of cypress and onto the green. Then a mythical one-putt for a brilliant bogey. A piece of cake. But greed yields mischief in this game. His wicked thrashing swing produces a shot that never really gains altitude. It beelines instead toward the tangled branches of a tree and falls into the tall grass at the base. Discretion finally subdues valor; Carl dejectedly gouges his ball onto the short grass, stomps up the fairway, and, with his pitching wedge, pops a decent wedge onto the green. He tosses the golf club toward his sister Pam, who shrugs and smiles at her brother. It's a tough game sometimes.

Both Frank and I hit the small green in two, he with a five wood, I with a high-arcing seven wood. I've escaped my traditional first-hole nightmare, which makes me ridiculously happy. When we tally up our scores, Carl and Todd are badly wounded. Frank and I have escaped the scene uninjured.

The beer wagon arrives at the second tee. Todd buys a couple of Heinekens and offers one to me; I accept, but against my better judgment. Carl, meanwhile, palliates his suffering with a sixteen-ounce can of Budweiser extracted from a well-stocked cooler. He gulps beer between puffs on his cigarette. "Man, I'm so damned *nervous*," he says. "Got to calm down."

I figure that maybe some trivial conversation will help the cause. "What brings you to Pebble Beach?" I ask. Although he and his dad live within half an hour of Pebble Beach, this is their first round on the links, and I gather it's a gift of some sort. From his dad or his wife.

"I been waiting my whole life to play this course," he says. Cathie, it turns out, is taking a photography class at the community college, and Carl is, in effect, a homework assignment. "I hate messing up like this," he says. "Man, how many chances do you get to play Pebble Beach?"

"I know what you mean, brother," I tell him. "You only go around once, right?" Beer-ad clichés were made for situations just like this. "It doesn't get any better than this. Got to grab all the gusto while you can."

He takes a huge swig of Bud and nods, his eyes fixed on the far-off flag of the par five second hole. Thus far, the real character of the course has not quite come out from hiding; I *know* what waits around the corner, though. It's very important to get off to a good start because the seaside holes are upcoming and the ocean wind will likely play havoc with our games and with our minds.

After having hit a misguided fairway wood into a greenside bunker at number two, I manage a very lucky sand wedge onto the center of the dance floor, which affords me a decent run at a birdie. Unfortunately, my twelve-foot putt outsmarts me and draws toward the magnetic sea, just as Jim McKay would have warned. "Too bad," Todd says. "You got robbed." The ball hangs precariously on the lip. Perhaps God will dispatch His only son to march from the waves and nudge my ball with the toe of his dripping sandal. I await such a miracle, but nothing of the sort is in the offing, so I nick the ball into the cup with the back of my putter. I foolishly imagined that the stiff crosswind would counteract the break. But the lure of the sea and the grain of the grass prevail over wind, and even the tilt of the putting surface. Todd rebounds from his first-hole woes and makes a nice one-putt par, which earns him a pat on the back. We clink beer cans like fools. Carl's suffering continues unabated. Puffs of smoke issue from his cart, and there is an ominous rattle of empty beer cans rolling in the gear basket behind his seat.

I want to feel more involved in the vicissitudes of Carl's wild doings and the plodding bogeys of my cart mate. Even Frank's methodical approach merits my admiration. However, I find myself wishing I could simply chase everyone from the course for a few hours, during which time I could contest the issues without distraction.

The finiteness of my experience on this course at this time of my life fills me with a curious wistfulness that borders on sorrow. It's a crazy sort of incongruity, I know that, and obviously I'm making it way too personal. But I can't seem to help myself. Perhaps by selfishly indulging my childhood dream, by absorbing that ideal into my mad tangible world, I've become a little too keenly aware of the mortal truths that hobble and confine the people I love most. Do I feel guilty for being so privileged and so free? Or is it the *violation* of the ideal that upsets me . . . like a beautiful backpacker from Maine whom you enter into and exit from so tangibly that the myth of her evaporates into thin air. I wish I knew . . .

Probably the truth is easier than all that. This will very likely be my only try at Pebble Beach, and that, I suppose, is what brings me down. The links is magnificent and very difficult to engage for a less than stellar golfer like myself. I'm afraid of being defeated by a golf course that looms too large in my imagination. In a strangely existential way, I want this slice of time to be completely fulfilled, aesthetically, morally, and physically.

I'm doomed to work out the metaphorical implications in the presence of Carl and Frank and Todd and Cathie and Pam. They are perfectly nice people, and I must try to accept their presence and try to be congenial.

I applaud the achievements of my partners, and I commiserate with them when they struggle. Poor Carl was so intent on asserting himself that his game disintegrated on the first hole. It happens that

way sometimes. Todd, meanwhile, is becalmed in a place where
bogeys are the norm. Frank's short, highly ritualized game does not
adapt well to punishing fairways and strong winds and tiny greens,
but he's a stoic little man. On the other hand, this is a course where a
windblown Ohio boy can succeed, even if his name is not Nicklaus.

Standing on the seventh tee, pitching wedge in hand, I'm one over
par on a very windy day on a very tough course. This is the finest
short par three in the world and easily the most breathtaking. The
green sits on a shelf above the water, so close-seeming as to fool you
into scratching a premature par onto the scorecard. But the crosswind is always stiff here, and the rock-hard green is hardly bigger
than a bedspread. Ferocious bunkers surround the target, and any
misguided shot hit with a lofted club will bury in the wicked sand.
Which means a precarious bunker shot onto a hardpan green with
ocean beyond. It's a frightful little wonder of a hole. Mr. Neville, the
course designer, should have received a blue ribbon for conceiving
it—and then he should have been hanged!

I want to stand here forever like a figure on a Grecian urn, with
six respectable scores etched indelibly on his scorecard. Waves
boom against the rocks below, and the flag snaps in the wind. Even
the pelicans have a hard time making headway against it. I decide to
hit the ball from the turf rather than tee it up. My hope is to put as
much backspin on the ball as possible, which might help it to hold
the line. Furthermore, I'll need to get the ball all the way to the flagstick to avoid rolling backward onto the apron at the front of the
green. And this necessitates a gripper that will, even given the hard-
ness of the green, stick where it lands.

I flick the ball nicely off the tee toward the right half of the green.
The dimpled orb is perfectly obedient until a gust of wind grabs ahold
and tosses it disdainfully into the pot bunker to the deep left of the
green. I'm still shaking my head when Carl, without fanfare, hits the
green with his cut shot. But he's above the hole, not a prime location
for a man who needs a par. Frank's and Todd's shots become bathtub
toys for the sea lions that float in the tilting ocean.

My blast from the pot bunker lands miraculously above the hole
and trickles to within four feet. It's such dumb luck that I forgive the

Fates who scorned me just moments ago. When it comes my turn to putt, I manage to hole out for a nerve-racking par.

At the turn, Carl hands me a beer, which I happily accept. Cathie photographs the transaction and takes one of Carl tilting a can to his lips. Todd, who is well over par but enjoying himself immensely, also accepts a beer. I'm still smarting from a double bogey at the eighth hole with its diabolical, ball-gulping mid-fairway chasm. Despite that indiscretion, I've shot a thirty-nine on the front side of Pebble Beach. Better than I had hoped for.

The tenth hole is criminally difficult, and breathtaking. The buffeting wind takes the distance out of even a very good drive, and the long approach is an act of blind faith. When the flag is blowing stiff, away from the beach, one must float the ball out over the sea and trust the wind to haul it back home. After a strong drive, I'm standing thirty feet from a family of seals, trying not to fall into an ecstatic trance on account of the raw beauty that surrounds me. One of the ironies of playing a course like Pebble is the temptation to shift focus from task to topography, but it's a wonderful quandary. The trick is to take in everything subliminally so you can summon it from some dusty corner of the brain whenever you please. But woe unto him who stands in awe, for he shall be smitten.

I borrow too much from the sea, and my approach shot falls onto the rocks, forever lost. I drop my ball two club-lengths from the hazard and plop my wedge shot onto the green. Two putts later, I've earned myself a double bogey, a score identical to that posted by Jack Nicklaus in his 1972 final-round confrontation with the most difficult hole on the course. It's no consolation.

Now the golf course turns away from the ocean and burrows through groves of eucalyptus and Monterey pine and cypress. Because the scenery is more comprehensible here, it's easier to avoid distraction. On any other course, these would be considered signature holes. But this is not your ordinary golf course.

Carl's demise has been very well documented by his bride. She has assumed every position of the *Kama Sutra* in order to photograph her husband, waggling, hitting, following through, marking his ball, pulling the pin, grimacing, frowning, and begging the seven mad gods who rule the sea for some charity. Carl is very good-natured about his wife's activities, although she's bound to be a distraction to him. All those Budweisers and cigarettes have worked their deleterious magic, and he seems resigned to his fate, finally. When this acceptance occurs, he seems to play better, which says marvelous things about the quality of despair.

Finally, at number seventeen, the Pacific Ocean reappears in all its glory beyond the tiny green. The sun hangs low now on the orange horizon, and the air is much cooler than when we began our round. I'm glad to be wearing a sweater, although I feel sorry for Todd, who is in shirtsleeves. Carl, also sweaterless, is probably unaware of any drop in temperature. He stands next to Cathie, a cigarette in his left hand, a beer in his right, while I plant my tee in the ground. At six over par, I'm a bit too pleased with myself. And pride goeth before a fall. My chunked tee shot dives into the boomerang-shaped bunker guarding the front of the green. I can see the ball tucked under the far lip of the trap. I'm so upset with myself for losing concentration that I hardly notice what the others have done until, through the curtain of disappointment I've pulled around myself, I hear whoops and hollers. Carl's five iron is stiff to the pin. "Damned nice shot," I say. "Very, very good."

One among us makes par. The rest of us make double bogeys. My chance at breaking eighty is all but lost, but I'll go on living, I suppose.

The drive at number eighteen is probably the most dramatic in golf, with the possible exception of the par three sixteenth at Cypress Point or maybe the ninth at Turnberry. But the last tee shot at Pebble is surely the most famous. The optimal drive hangs out over the Pacific through most of its flight. Then, when it seems the ball will be consigned to the depths, the wind pushes it back to safety. Too much borrow, and you're wet. Too safe and you're stymied by a large oak tree.

The three tee shots preceding mine range from poor to miserable. Two balls are in the drink, and one is buried in rough at the far right of the fairway. This is the drive I have been waiting for since I was eight years old. I've played it over and over again in my sleep and in my waking hours, in study halls, at the Communion rail, behind the wheel of my car, under the covers of my bed. Always, the ball sails out toward the setting sun, then curves obediently landward. The scene is so familiar to me that I'm not in the least nervous. I take a couple of easy practice swings; then I lean into the ball with every-thing I've got. The ball is destined to obey the commands of fate. Out it soars, above the whitecapped ocean, toward the beach-ball sun until slowly, inexorably, the wind bends it toward the fairway. It's the finest drive I have hit in my life, I'm sure, and the fulfillment of my most impossible imaginings. I stand for a long time, watching the aftertrail of my shot etched upon the peach-colored sky.

That I have failed to break eighty at Pebble Beach is no shame. The battle was a standoff, well fought and fair.

It's taken me eighteen holes to understand what Dave and Larry, my friends from the VA Hospital, must have felt, knowing that their golfing adventures would soon end. The pleasure of the moment was, of course, all the sweeter because of it.

If I never return to this place, even in my old age, I'll take what I can recall of it, especially that one fine moment on the eighteenth tee at twilight with black pelicans struggling into the wind.

CHAPTER 13

the point

My sister Julie endures her illness week after week while doctors play Rubik's Cube with her chemo dosages. Novalbine mitigated with Zofran—intravenous for a month or two, then oral. When side effects (nausea, inappetence, neuropathy, anemia, dehydration, metabolic shutdown, depression) are too much, they juggle drugs and dosages. Dilaudid for pain, something even more powerful when the need arises. There's a curious, cruel poetry in the catalogue of means and methodologies employed by her team of oncologists. The drugs have names like towns in Faulkner's Mississippi. Then there are the periodic transfusions and infusions. Occasional confusions. When her swallowing mechanism shuts down, which it inevitably does, doctors open the portal with an inflatable balloon—esophagoplasty, they call it—whose efficacy diminishes with every such procedure. These peripheral symptoms of her cancer play a conspiratorial role in the drama. But the protagonist, of course, is the cancer itself, which lives and grows in the marrow of her bones.

"Hey, kid, how ya doin'?" I ask when Julie picks up the telephone receiver. I've returned to my Comfort Inn after having eaten a plateful of chicken fajitas—*"No cilantro, por favor. Cilantro no es bueno. Chilis, sí. Cilantro, no."*—at a cheap, brilliantly lit Mexican restaurant on the fringe of Monterey. I liked being the only Anglo in the place; I was a guest, a novelty for the locals who drank Miller Lite from bottles and let their brown babies sit on the tabletops. *"Mas?"* my waitress would ask, tea pitcher poised over my plastic tumbler. I ate until I was full, said *gracias* and *adios*, tweaked a baby on the cheek, and strolled out into the beautiful California night.

"Oh, I'm *doing*," Julie says, but I can tell just from the quaver in her voice that she's holding back something I won't want to hear. "How's your trip going?" Because it's the sixth day of July, I know she's just had an infusion of Novalbine, and while the side effects generally don't land until a day or two after the fact, she's obviously weary from the procedure.

"I brought Pebble Beach to its knees," I say.

"You *did*? Honest?"

"Sure. Then it got up and beat the crap out of me." I can hear her giggling at the other end of the line. My sister is a very easy audience. "I hit my career drive at number eighteen, Julie. Very dramatic. Right out there over the scrotum-tightening sea, back onto the fairway . . . quite suspenseful, really. Probably the coolest thing I've ever done with something longer than it is wide. The gallery went crazy."

"The gallery?"

"You know, the one in my brain. The more I think about it, I'd have to say that drive was the finest thing I've ever done on this earth."

"You're telling me your life is pathetic," she says.

"Hmmm . . ." There's some muffled coughing emanating from her end of the line, which tells me she's probably picked up another virus. A common cold is a life-threatening ailment for her, and I tremble to think what this symptom might portend. "What's with you these days?" I ask her. "Doctors treating you nice?" It's very difficult to elicit medical information from Julie gracefully. But this time she comes out with it.

"Well . . . my tumor marker went up from three hundred to five-eighty." There's a pause while she waits for me to assimilate this bit of bad news. "Nobody was very pleased about that, especially me, but the doctor says this is no time to panic. There are some other tricks up his sleeve. I'm getting a little tired of this, though." Just how long his sleeve is and what tricks are as yet unrevealed are a big question mark. "After I got the report, I came home and had a pity party for myself. Cried for a long time and got it out of my system," she says. "I'm better now. It's just the way it goes . . . you know? Sometimes you make birdies, sometimes you make bogeys, right?"

The whole world talks to me in golf metaphors, even my sister. It's an occupational hazard, I guess. "You deserve back-to-back eagles," I tell her. The empty-sounding cliché resounds inside my skull like a marble in a fifty-gallon drum. There's no real point in pursuing the issue further, so I let her rescue me from my foolish ineptitude.

"Well, where you headed to next?" she asks.

"I'd rather eat kelp than drive another five hundred miles," I say. "I need a break from the routine. Maybe I'll hike into the Santa Lucias tomorrow, maybe camp out under the stars in my bivvy tent. Howl at the moon. Pee wherever I please."

"What about Cypress Point?" she asks. "That would be a nice place to pee. Wasn't Cypress Point at the top of your priority list?"

"I'd cut off my *cajones* to play that course, but chances are nil. Yeah, sure, of course, I'll call the pro tomorrow morning before I head for the hills. I'm not holding my breath, though."

We talk for a while about Dad's ongoing difficulties and Mom's loosening grasp on the mortal coil, but it's a sad conversation and too hard to bear for either of us. So we content ourselves with talk about the weather. When the phone line goes silent at her end, then mine, we, at last, say good-bye to each other. "Keep the faith," I tell her. "I love you, kid."

"I love you, too," she says.

I spend the rest of the evening reading the novel I bought in Denver—or trying to. My mind drifts from the page time and time again. It floats around the room like a luna moth, alighting on the tangible emblems of my life on this planet. Golf clubs, laptop computer, Leica camera, golf cap, the shoe box full of photographs. Mine is an odd existence, really, furnished with such idiosyncrasies as these. I feel sadly lucky and rather foolish to be motoring around the republic, tilting against cartoon quandaries and meaningless issues of stroke mechanics, ingratiating myself with people who have their own little worlds to contend with. What does it matter that my damned tee shot finds the fairway alongside the bounding main?

And why, for that little moment, was I as happy as a human being can be?

I've got taco sauce on my watchband and sea sand between my toes. Should I therefore be deep in despair? That would make as much sense, as I now figure it.

At eleven o'clock I turn in, although I'm not especially sleepy. Lonely, yes, but not sleepy. Out there on U.S. 1, traffic whispers up and down the pavement. Car doors open and close in the parking lot below. Somebody's watching local news in the next room. Pipes chirp, hangers scrape on closet rods. Then relative silence.

After a sleepless, fretful hour, there comes the sound of quiet talk and laughter, just beyond the mirror wall opposite where I lie in darkness. Laughter, a young woman's laughter. "Yes," she says dreamily. "Yes. God. Yes. Oh . . . I *love* you, sweetheart. Oh, yesss." Wonderfully human sounds. Her lover is a good one and, I imagine, a thoughtful one. "Oh. Oh. Oh. Oh," she says. "Ohhhhhh . . ." The percussion of their lovemaking rattles my golf clubs, which are leaned against that wall. I'm so absurdly happy for both of them that my eyes fill with tears.

After having showered for at least twenty minutes, I eat breakfast in my room. Cold cereal, bread with Peter Pan, black coffee with too much sugar. The map spread out on the unmade bed shows dotted lines marching up the green mountains. I figure that the best approach is to backtrack to one of the state parks this morning, capture a tent site, then hike into the hills, which in person are more blond than green.

I've almost decided not to bother calling Cypress Point on account of my certainty that the quest is forlorn and foregone. I'm in no mood to grovel, but I phone the pro shop anyway on pure whim, then hang up after two rings. Something has plucked a thread of recollection way in the back of my brain, a fan letter written by a young San Francisco attorney years ago when my novel first came out. I was so flattered that I wrote back to him. Then, just before Christmas of that year, a friendly greeting card from San Francisco with a Cypress Point scorecard enclosed. "Whenever you're on the West Coast, let me know," it said. "We'll play Cypress Point. You wouldn't believe how beautiful." Why had I forgotten that until now? But his name. His *name* . . . ! Davis? Ellis? Hell and damnation, what's his frigging name? I flip through a make-believe Rolodex in a poorly lit corner of my cerebellum. I make a round-trip through the alphabet. A San Francisco attorney named . . . *what? EVANS!* His name is Evans. There is no first name forthcoming, but Evans will work. The rest will be easy. Brilliant, wonderful William Hallberg. Nothing wrong with *his* brain.

The operator tells me that there are four attorneys named Evans listed in the directory. The very first name on her list is David. David Evans. Of course. *David* Evans. "Hot *dog*. That's him," I tell the operator. "Can I please have his number?" She tells me that there's no home phone, but she has his law office.

Only now, when the tiny light glimmers at the bottom of the gray valley of despair, do I admit to myself how set my heart has been on this one impossible destination. I vow not to leave this spot on the map without turning over every rock, round or jagged, in my search for any old key that will get me through the door to Cypress Point.

The phone rings in San Francisco, and a young woman picks up. "No," she says. "David's been out of town. He's expected to come in a little bit later this morning. Would you like his phone mail?"

"Please," I tell her, and wait for the connection. David's voice comes on, followed by the obligatory beep. I leave a breathless message. First, my phone number . . . a sly invite to play some golf on the peninsula . . . and my solemn oath that I will wait by this phone until checkout for his call.

At ten-ten the phone on the bedside table rings. "Bill Hallberg?"

"David Evans?"

"Good to hear your voice, Bill. I'm awfully sorry to ask for a raincheck on the golf. That would be a real treat for me," he says. I tell him it's no problem, but my heart has sunk into a cold well. "I'm afraid I *just* got back in town, and there's no way I can work it in this time around. My father died last week. I flew him down to Hawaii for a father/son golf vacation. On the same day we were to fly back home, he had a heart attack and died. So there's been the funeral and all that to contend with."

"Oh . . . gosh. David. What terrible news. I'm really sorry to hear about your dad. It must be awfully tough to lose him so suddenly. I don't even know what to say. It sounds almost poetic to me, though . . . the way he went out, I mean. I'm sure it meant a lot to him, being with you on those beautiful golf courses."

"That's the saving grace, Bill. Honestly. We had just a super time out there together, sharing something we both love. We just totally rejuvenated our relationship. And I'm grateful for that."

"I can really relate to . . . I wish I could . . ." There's something I want to say about my own father, but I just can't do it.

"Listen, Bill. You've *got* to play Cypress. Whatever it takes, do it. Tell them you're Clint Eastwood's bastard son. Anything. If I were a member, I'd get you on somehow. Unfortunately, the fellow we would have played golf with, Gary Van deWe, is out of town for the next few weeks, and he's the only member I know. Damn it to hell. Sorry, man. I'd give anything to get out there on the peninsula and play some golf with you. But if you come to Frisco next week and want to play Olympic, give me a ring and I'll see what I can arrange."

We chat for a while longer about this and that, upcoming books, golf movies, titanium drivers. Finally, he's got to get back to work. Clients are waiting, work has piled up . . . "Great talking with you," I say.

"You, too, Bill. Best of luck with everything."

It takes me a while to catch my breath after my conversation with David. I'm envious of his communion with a dad who lived for golf. Although I love my own father, there has never been any real catharsis to bring our souls together, at least not in the way I've always imagined it happening. In my mind's eye, such a moment occurs on an elevated tee, high above an emerald fairway on a windblown golf course hard by the Irish Sea. The bluster brings tears to our eyes, or maybe it's the raw beauty of the land around us and the poignant mortality of the links in the great scheme of things. Cruel gray waves lash the rocks, grasses blow horizontal in the wind, the dunes shift underfoot . . . and there below is mankind's brave little attempt at asserting itself against the inexorable forces of nature. A beautiful green monument to man's transitory existence on the planet. We will succumb, both of us, and ultimately the green fairways as well, to those winds that blow the grasses sideways and hurl black shadows over the intermittently bright fairways. Standing side by side, knowing that common truth, is the moment I yearn for.

Now, of course, it's too late. There are only those odd lucid moments that quickly evaporate into the cosmos. My love for Dad is broken into tiny puzzle pieces scattered and lost in the riddlesome thing we call a relationship.

"Jim," I say to the head professional. "This is Bill Hallberg. I know that I'm asking the impossible of you . . ." The poor man listens, probably from behind a glass counter, while I give him a feverish autobiography. "Anyway," I tell him, "a San Francisco attorney was going to join Gary Van deWe and me for a round of golf at Cypress Point this summer, and . . ." The blatant name-dropping causes a serious thud at the pit of my stomach. But on I go, concocting clever, self-deprecating rationales for my feeble supplication. "It would certainly be a highlight of my golfing career, let alone this golfing odyssey."

After a long, extremely uncomfortable pause, I hear a submissive sigh. I've drowned him, I think. He just can't fight the current I've sent rolling in his direction. "Why don't you show up tomorrow morning at eight, and we'll see what we can work out for you."

"That would be just *wonderful*," I say. "I just don't know how to thank you."

"See you at eight, then."

For the rest of the day, I'm a jovial oaf. While Natalie Merchant sings about "Stockton Gala Days," Iris rumbles along an unpaved road that climbs the coastal hills past cattle ranches and truck farms to Jamesburg, a speck of a town with a general store and a gas station. Here I buy a very cold beer, which I drink in the shade of an oak tree. It's good to wear shorts and hiking boots instead of khakis and polo shirts and the like. I feel as if I've reclaimed some of my identity, real or imagined. The rugged outdoorsman, that is, with a sweaty T-shirt and a knapsack on his back. A cow-hocked beagle sashays across the road in search of human kindness, which I happily provide. I share a peanut butter sandwich with the old fellow, and scratch his rib cage until his spindly hind leg kicks air. "Ride your scooter, fella. Thataboy. Ride your scooter," I say to him.

I leave my car in Jamesburg and pick up the hiking trail that ascends into Los Padres National Forest. In my knapsack are granola bars and Snickers and peeled carrots in baggies, peanut butter sandwiches, and two warm cans of beer. Around my neck are the Leica range finder and my compact binoculars. Alas, I've forgotten my Mannlicher elephant gun and my Sherpa guide.

My spirits are so high that I greet oncoming hikers like first cousins. "How is it back in the woods? Beautiful, I'll bet, huh?"

"Very beautiful. Lovely. Wonderful," they say.

Okay, I have to admit that part of me hopes to encounter two New England girls backpacking, coming down the trail toward Carmel. In my mind I've been subliminally calculating the time frame. Unless they have taken the coastal trail, which was not their plan, Emily and Alice will be coming out of the high hills either today or tomorrow, depending on how frequently they commune with nature and their degree of debilitation. Exactly what might theoretically happen after the nonfact of a hypothetical encounter is only a frothy abstraction that sloshes against my hypothalamus. Occasionally, however, a crisp heartbreaking image floats to the surface, at which point I gaze bathetically skyward and whimper like a lonely beagle.

Despite the surprising number of backpackers traipsing through the shady forests and wildflower meadows, there are no chance encounters with beautiful hiking college girls today. And it's really okay. What I needed more than confusion and sexual torment is some time away from the highways and fairways of America. I don't even mind the horseflies that follow me for miles, orbiting my head without ever landing. There's time now to recalibrate my affection for family and friends, any one of whom would be welcome company right now. Relative isolation makes the preoccupations of love and duty more bearable somehow, as if, again, the Hallberg Principle of inverse proportionality pertains.

The town of Carmel has no special allure for me, but any trip to the Monterey Peninsula would be incomplete without . . . and . . . So here I am, fondling Peruvian knitwear and copper weathervanes and jade indoor fountains. I snap up a few Take One bonbons from an upscale sweetshop, but they make me slobber like a basset hound, so I spit them into a fancy iron trash receptacle near the square. Across the street, Le Café Français beckons like a Parisian whore. But frankly, coquilles Saint-Jacques is quotidian fare for a bon vivant such as myself, so I'm not seduced by the aroma issuing from the redwood slats that ventilate the sidewalks. Already today, I've eaten *un* Snickers and *un sandwich beurre de peanutte*. Plus, two *bierres. Alors . . .*

The cynical me superimposes the Wausau Yodeling Club onto the posh street corners. Or a shirtless Australian rugby squad. Or a rasher of Krishnas with brass bells and tambourines. Shake up the troops a bit. Crackle their linen. In all fairness, I do find a pretty cotton lap robe for my mom in a sundries shop, and I use my Visa to pay for it.

Inevitably, my wandering steps lead me to the strand overlooking Carmel bay and Pebble Beach Golf Links beyond. It seems years since my drive floated out over the sea. Forever ago. A dream. An impossibility.

Tomorrow, tomorrow, the inner sanctum of American golf, barely visible beneath the setting Pacific sun.

My wake-up call occurs while I am showering the dust and sand from my hair and toes. Sleep has been a rare commodity of late; I've been awake most of the night, hitting tee shots through the darkness of a forty-dollar motel room. The exception to my insomnia took place sometime during the wee hours, when Gillian slid briefly beneath the covers and took me ecstatically away. This vaporous erotic fantasy will probably be the extent of my romantic adventures for a while, so I do my best to replay it over and over again in my love-starved brain.

I dress in my best blue wrinkle-free pleated slacks, a black shirt, and a teal blue wool sweater. It's quite a costume, and I can't help feeling like a cutout doll upon whom some whimsical child has hung whatever adornments stir the imagination. It's a far cry, anyway, from the tank-top, tube-sock nightmare from days of yore. Breakfast is out of the question (it's nerves), and one cup of coffee is my limit today. My typical three or four doses of caffeine might compromise my already skittish putting stroke.

For the last time, I pay the gatekeeper at the entry of the peninsula drive. "Cypress Point?" he asks incredulously when I tell him my destination.

"Yup," I say. "Yeah, me and Clint have a score to settle. He's going to make my day for me."

Very hefty guffaws ensue, and a *Be gone, silly boy* wave. He doesn't believe me for a minute, but I don't give a monkey's bum; I'm on my way to glory.

The driveway leading to paydirt is nothing like I had imagined it. There is no gate at all, and the modest white stucco clubhouse is almost immediately visible through the cypress trees. My heart gallops into tachycardia and stays there as I maneuver Iris carefully up the asphalt path toward the small parking lot, which is framed on three sides by a boxwood hedge.

I am loath to change into my golf spikes there in the parking lot. I would sooner take off my shirt, whack the flesh of my hairless belly, and belch at the morning moon. This is church, and I am bound to behave myself. At this hour, there are just a few cars in the parking lot, all of which seem to scoff at my dirty Neon with its oodles of napkin wads and crushed beer cans and rumpled road maps.

The beautifully manicured putting green is vacant. In fact, there is nobody stirring as of yet. The course, too elegant for pretense, belongs entirely to me; the small nearby driving range, the square tee box of number one, the empty green-painted bag drop . . . all *mine*.

I push through the white screen door to the clubhouse, where I'm greeted by a friendly assistant pro who stands behind the obligatory glass counter. My acquisitive self takes in all the logoed paraphernalia, some of which I would dearly love to own, if only to convince nonbelieving friends that I have indeed achieved nirvana. But I demur, fearing that the tawdry exchange of cash is beneath the moment. Jim, the head professional, has yet to arrive, but his assistant has been expecting my arrival, and all the various preparations have been made for an interloper like me. "Just leave your clubs at the bag drop," he tells me. "Your caddie, Tim, will take care of everything after that. Go ahead and use the locker room to change into your spikes."

I hustle out to the parking lot and quickly extricate my golf bag and my scruffy shoes from poor Iris's trunk. After stashing my clubs at the bag drop, I carry my spikes into the locker room, a green-carpeted sanctuary with comfortable, slightly threadbare furnishings. On the coffee table, surrounded by leather sofas and chairs, is a basket filled with books of matches imprinted with the Cypress Point monogram. I pilfer a few, fearing they will be my only tangible souvenir, then wander over to a bench, where I change into my golf shoes.

I'm in command of the quiet locker room, squished into a comfy chair, smoking an imaginary cigar, mulling over the vagaries of a mythical bond market when a club member pushes open the heavy wooden door and smiles at me. "You've got a beautiful day to play golf," he says in a curiously resonant voice.

"Couldn't ask for a better one," I reply. We're just a couple of gents, this aristocrat and I, swapping pleasantries before tackling the links.

Tim is waiting just outside the clubhouse door, my golf clubs slung over his shoulder. "Hello, Mr. Hallberg," he says. "So you're going to take a run at it, eh?" He's a nice-looking fellow about my age with an unmistakable midwestern accent. On his feet are red-soled rubber boots, into which he has stuffed the cuffs of his trousers. He grins at me from beneath a navy blue visor. "You've got the run of the course this morning. We're first on the tee."

"You mean I'm playing as a single?"

"Consider it an honor. Guests rarely play alone. You won't have any distractions to worry about." The putting green is now populated by a foursome of handsomely sweatered golfers, two women and two men. "Take a few putts," Tim says. "Get a feel for the speed of the greens. You'll discover that they're very fast and extremely true."

I take a few very nervous strokes on the practice green. Indeed, the surface is unbelievably slick, especially with the grain, which grows unerringly toward the sea.

"Ready," I say. It's clear that there will be no time for hitting practice balls at the driving range. My destiny is to get up and running as quickly as possible, so as not to hold up any club members with early tee times.

"You sure?" Tim says. "Take your time."

"Let's go," I say, and follow my caddie to the first tee, which is in plain, proximal view of both the clubhouse and the putting green.

Only once before have I been attended by a caddie, a singularly nightmarish occasion when, as a teenager playing Toledo's legendary Inverness Club for the first time, I hooked a golf ball through a row of elm trees and kneecapped a comrade of my club lugger. The friendly relationship I'd enjoyed with Bobby (a name etched indelibly in my memory) up to that point dissolved into a sullen silence, during which he handed me any damned club he pleased and I hit it. But Tim is a different breed altogether. He's bright and slightly wry in his manner. He's probably seen enough millionaires in his day to recognize me for what I am, and that seems to put him at ease.

He surely detects the whiteness of my knuckles as I warm up at the first tee. "No need to be nervous, Mr. Hallberg. It's just a golf game. Nobody's going to die if you hit a bad one. So just relax." His reassurance actually has a calming effect on me. I take a last moment to survey the scene in panorama. Everything about the place is wonderfully low key and unutterably beautiful. I'm thinking of the Disneyesque pretensions of downtown Carmel and the clamorous confusion of Pebble Beach. The fairways, moist from the retreating fog, the prim hedge over which I must aim my tee shot, the distant eerie cypress that commands the unseen first fairway. "Hit your drive toward that tree, please," he says. "Nice easy swing."

The world is so quiet around me that I can hear cigarette paper burning when Tim takes a drag on his Marlboro. *Nice and easy,* I tell myself. I'm trying to imagine Beethoven's Fifth, the three preparatory notes followed by the powerful downstroke. Part of me knows how important this drive is to the sentimental archive where I store such memories. Without my even being fully aware, I feel myself taking the club back into the notch, then dropping my hands into the chute and pulling the club head through the imaginary swing plane. The titanium face meets the ball solidly, and soon I'm tasting the wool of my sweater arm, which means that I've managed to keep my head in the proper position. When I look up, my ball is sailing perfectly over the intervening boxwood hedge, straight and true in its flight toward the lonesome cypress tree.

"Absolutely perfect," Tim says. He takes the driver from me, towels off the head, replaces the leather cover, and slides the club carefully into the bag. "Well, how did *that* feel?" he says. "Were we a little bit nervous?"

"We were nigh onto conniption," I tell him, and he laughs. When I ask him to please call me Bill, he agrees, but I have my doubts.

We walk side by side, Tim and I, down a shell path that skirts the seaward extreme of the hedge, talking like old pals. The hedge serves as a sort of curtain beyond which the drama unfolds. My caddie is, as I suspected, a midwesterner, by way of just about everywhere. A good Catholic boy from a big Illinois family. We've gotten just about that far in his biography when we arrive at my ball, which is in perfect position, as I was assured it would be. "About one seventy-two," he says. "Pin is back left. Bunkers front left and front right. Go long and you're dead. What's your pleasure?"

"Seven wood?" I ask.

"Might work," he says, and hands me the club. "Aim just left of the flag. The wind will bring it back. Nice and smooth, please," he says.

I'm all set to hit my ball, all cozy and comfortable, when the truth of my situation lands so forcefully upon me that I have to back away for a moment. It's very hard to hit a shot properly when you're grinning like a duffer's golf ball. "Amazing," I say. "I just can't believe I'm standing on the first fairway of Cypress Point."

"It's a special place," Tim says, and I know he means it. "Not many golfers get a chance to play here. They're missing something, aren't they?"

"They sure are," I say, and settle over my shot once again.

"Easy swing, please," he says, and I oblige his request. The ball makes contact with the center of the club face and soars into the blue morning sky. "Perfect," he says.

I'm standing over a ten-foot birdie putt, concentrating on a discol-
ored grass blade only an inch above the hole, when a deer tiptoes
across the fairway just a few yards shy of the green. The creature
seems to understand how important this putt is to me because it
pauses momentarily while I stroke the ball, rather feebly it turns out,
toward the hole. "You were watching that deer, weren't you?" Tim
says, and laughs.

"Yup," I say.

My golfing friends back home have heard me say it time and again:
I'd rather eat sod than wait behind a group of lollygagging hackers
who haven't the common sense to let faster players through. My game
disintegrates when a golf shot becomes disassociated from its immediate ancestors and its as-yet-unborn descendants. Today, however, I
want to slow everything down. I don't want to wait on my shots, but
neither do I want to scurry through this breathtaking landscape
without really taking it properly into my soul. There are no excuses to
be made for bad play this morning. The pace is mine to set, and Tim
seems more than willing to afford me all the time I need.

Number two is a rather long par five that, like so many of Dr.
Mackenzie's golf holes, requires a tee shot long enough to carry a
stretch of sandy hummocks overgrown with sea grass. A topped drive
or even a low-flying shot will rendezvous with misery. "Same drive
as number one, please," my caddie says. "Right over the crest of the
far dune."

Again, I knock a drive so perfect that I simply can't believe it's
me inside these clothes. "Thank you," Tim says. "You'll enjoy the
outcome."

We've got a long, circuitous hike around the fragile ecosensitive
dunes, which gives me a chance to catch my breath. "So, Tim, how
in the heck did you wind up caddying at Cypress?"

"The short version is that I came back from Vietnam all screwed
up. Spent time in VA hospitals, on the streets, you know . . . a bad
time any way you cut it. I wound up here in Carmel, drunk, broke,
all shot to hell." Tim pauses for a moment to pick up a gum wrapper.
He shakes his head in disgust. "Then I met a guy who caddies here
at Cypress, and he told me I ought to give it a whirl. I said, 'What

have I got to lose?' and I came on out. The pro, Jim, took me under his wing, taught me the ropes, and I've been here ever since. He's been sort of like a father to me ever since, if you know what I mean." Of course, I can only dimly imagine exactly what he means, but I nod anyway.

Once again, my ball is in A+ position. However, the next shot is the key to success. Dr. Alister Mackenzie, the famous architect of this masterpiece, was apparently in a grumpy mood when he laid out this fairway; the landing zone ahead is flanked by amoeboid bunkers, either one of which is dedicated to ruining my fun. The whole raison d'être is to force golfers like me to use our brains. Luckily, my brain is standing next to me with a seven wood in his hand. "Lay it up short of the bunkers, please," he says. "You'll have a nice easy eight iron home."

"Okay," I say. My very tall fairway shot lands just short of the right-hand bunker, in good position for a relatively short approach. Had I followed a similar line with my four wood, I'd need a backhoe to dig my ball from the steep face of the trap.

The ensuing eight-iron shot is a scalded thing that yelps its way up the damp fairway and leaps onto the putting surface, where the grain takes command of the ball and guides it benevolently toward the flagstick. "Whatever works . . ." Tim says, and I can tell he's amused by my luck.

"Will ya look at *that*," I say. "There *is* a God."

"Guess he wasn't paying attention," Tim says.

My new best buddy in the world tells me to aim my putt exactly one and one half inches above the hole. "Nice and smooth, please," he says, and I obey. The ball makes a lovely clattering sound at the bottom of the cup. "Perfect," he says, and spears the ball with two fingers. "Now you've made a birdie at Cypress Point. Not many people can say that. That makes you one under after two. Want to quit now?"

As I climb the redwood walkway up to the eighth tee, I am one stroke above par due to a foolishly overstroked lag putt back at number five. Not since I was a Young Turk with a roundhouse backswing have I played as well as I'm playing on this day. Whatever happens from here on in will be pure denouement, or so I tell myself as I waggle over the ball from the eyrie notched onto the edge of a forested ridge. "You're in for a treat here," Tim says. "But you've got to hit your drive first. So aim just left of the tallest dune, please."

I've let myself get distracted for a moment by the prospect of something memorable. Thus, my drive is a wicked right-to-left bender that curls across the horizon and dives into the unforgiving sea grass bordering the fairway. "Oh, *fart*," I say. "Fart, fart, fart!"

"Remember," Tim says. "It's only a game. Nobody died. Right? I've got a good spot on it so we'll just track it down. You punch it back onto the short grass, and we'll go from there. Whaddya say?"

I tell him, "Sure."

No sooner do Tim and I round the cluster of sand hills than the Pacific appears before us, obscured by an imposing dune that shelters the green from the elements. There it is, finally, the endless sea and the first taste of a brisk wind that will only strengthen as the morning passes on toward noon. The view is so magnificent from my spot in the fairway that my knees buckle slightly from pure romantic ecstasy. There is exactly nothing I can say to anybody that can convey the thrill that comes from tasting the very same salt wind that torments the churning waves.

Tim's optimistic script comes nicely to life. He finds my ball quickly, but the lie is barely playable. He hands me a sand wedge. "No heroics, please. Solid contact is all we're looking for here." I slash the ball onto the fairway, and Tim pats me on the back. "Here's your nine iron. Hit it hard, please, just left of the flagstick."

A mediocre approach shot and two putts later bring me to two over par, a score I maintain through number eleven, an impossibly hard four par that I manage to subdue by means of a twenty-foot putt, charted and choreographed by none other than Tim.

There will be a polite demurral from any discussion of abominations as they pertain to number twelve. Shall we instead say that I have leaped from a gaudy two over par to a merely handsome four. As Tim continues to remind me, however, nobody has died and dogs are still humping in the back alleys of America. Of course, he's right, but the wounds smart mightily and I need to heal quickly if I expect to remain standing when I achieve the finish line.

The real glory of Cypress Point lies before me now. Perhaps the four best consecutive holes in North America await my arrival. In each case, the ocean whispers bad cues in the golfer's ear, and he must gain command of the situation by defying his own instincts and outwitting the forces of nature. Or else he must have a caddie like Tim, who knows what's what at any given moment.

By virtue of a couple of respectable wind-battling shots, I manage a "routine" par at number thirteen, which culminates on a crest just above the cliffs.

"And now the fun begins," my caddie tells me. He lights a cigarette and exhales a ribbon of smoke that disappears as soon as it leaves his lips. "See that?" he says. "That's the enemy from here on in. You can't see it, but you sure can feel it." Number fourteen rides along the edge of the cliffs, shawled by purple ice plants that inflict misery upon any golfer whose shot strays even slightly toward the sea. The wind dares you to hit the ball out over the rock pinnacles that climb like Greek gods from the waves. "Got to trust the force," Tim says. "Aim it toward downtown Carmel and let the wind do its thing. Same swing as always, please."

My drive is a prizewinner, so well placed that I simply can't understand what saintly virtue has possessed me today. Unfortunately, the devil returns to scorn my approach, which defies the crosswind and stays right; the ice plant has eaten my ball, damn it, and while Tim finds the thing quite easily, I'm faced with an unplayable lie. Suddenly, I'm hitting *four*, with an intervening bunker and a pin tucked close to its edge on the high side of a green that slopes away from me. "Aim left and avoid the far bunker. You'll have a chance that way," Tim says.

I cut a nice wedge shot off the crisp turf, and it lands just beyond the extreme right edge of the near bunker, then tracks quickly to the cuff on the far side. It's the very best shot I can make, maybe the best of the day. My caddie Tim hands me the putter and tells me to please aim the ball at his right toe. "Play it like a level putt, please. You're with the grain." My putt runs directly at the red sole of a rubber boot, then shrinks to the right when it loses speed. For a moment both Tim and I are sure that I've holed out, but the ball hangs on the edge, just as it did prior to yesterday's deus ex machina. Alas, the wind is working against me today and there's no hope, so I nip the ball into the cup with the toe of my Ping B61. Still, a double bogey.

One of the vast oversights in my lifelong preoccupation with Cypress Point is an underappreciation of the short par three fifteenth hole, with its microscopic green and necklace of evil bunkers. Once again, the golfer must carry the tiny pulsating inlet and the far cliff with its ice-plant blanket. Tim hands me a seven iron, and I take it without hesitation. If he handed me a spatula I'd swing it, no questions asked.

"Try to hit it in the deep right trap, please. Nice and easy."

Yet another par for me. Which makes me very, very nervous. By this time in any given round I'm usually leaking oil all over the course. My wheels have come off, and flames shoot from my wrecked tailpipe. Today, however, I've conceded all the thinking to Tim, who charts coordinates while I merely handle the controls. It's a fine brand of symbiosis because it eliminates the weakest part of my game, which happens to be my vulnerable intellect.

I am nervous because I am now standing on the tee overlooking the very best golf hole in the history of the sport. At the risk of losing momentum, I hand my pocket camera to Tim so he can immortalize me standing at the edge of the seething maw that opens wide between this tee box and the far-distant green, hardly bigger than the surface back at fifteen. My poses are grandiose, histrionic, Napoleonic. But what the hey. Look where I am. That's me with the green in the deep background, grinning as if I've won the Open. There I am again, squatting near a patch of ice plant. Over my shoulder are dozens of seals basking on the sun-baked rocks. The green does not appear in this picture. Just me and the ice plant and the seals and the ocean beyond. I take one of Tim, who mugs magnificently. There will never, never again be a moment to equal this one in my golfing life. Joy and sadness swirl together in the hard-blowing wind. I have to remember the lesson taught to me by Larry and Dave back in Los Angeles. It's all here and now. That's what counts. Make plans, remember the past, but enjoy the here and now.

"Here's your driver," says Tim, smiling. "Ever hit a driver on a par three? Aim for the rock shaped like a derby. See it there?" He points with the shaft of my putter. Yes, I see it, but it's too wide of the target. Way too much borrow. "Aim at that rock, please, and . . . Mr. Hallberg . . . don't hold back."

For only the second time all day I'm utterly and absolutely trembling. "Give me a drag off that cigarette. Please," I say.

"Hit it solid, *Bill*," he says. I exhale a huge lungful of smoke-free air and position myself according to instructions. Then, without wasting any time, I take a swing that feels almost otherworldly in its disconnection from my physical self. The ball flies somehow toward the target rock and I'm waiting, waiting, waiting for the wind to grab hold. The ball gleams against the blue sky, true and invulnerable to the fierce onshore wind. Finally, the ball begins to move, subtly at first, then more and more determinedly toward the hole. It lands somewhere near the target, but the concavity of the apron hanging from the chin of the little green obscures the outcome. "That sir, was a wonderful golf shot," Tim says. "You just couldn't have gotten there today. Wind's too stiff. But you should be able to use your putter and roll it right up to the hole from there."

I want to do cartwheels down the walking path all the way to the green. I want to throw my arms around Tim and kiss him on the lips like a Russian war hero. "I'll bet you like your job," I say.

"Best job in the world," he says. "I'd be dead in a gutter somewhere if I weren't here. I was so far gone only *this* could save me. This place has powers."

"Yes," I say. "It sure does."

"Now, I want you to split the green with your putt, please. Hit it three quarters. Grain will carry it to the hole."

"Yes, sir," I say. His wish is my command, and I obey it to the letter. The ball trickles toward the hole and stops within a foot of the cup. A tap-in par on the hardest par three in golf.

That I made bogey at number seventeen is of no special significance. I simply happened to find a greenside bunker on my approach, and that was that. Then, on the finishing hole, my blind approach shot from the slope of the hill landed twenty feet from the pin. Two putts later and this round was, alas, a chapter in my golfing history.

But I have broken eighty on Cypress Point in the howling wind, and that is my triumph. Perhaps I will play as well again someday. Maybe at St. Andrews, or Troon, or Pebble Beach, or here again.

But if such luck should never again come my way, I've got the scorecard to prove my mettle and a friend to vouch for me.

While Tim hurries back to the eighteenth tee to retrieve a missing head cover, I duck into the pro shop to shake hands with Jim, the pro who so graciously allowed me this chance to play his golf course. "Our pleasure," he says. "I'm glad you enjoyed yourself. Come back sometime."

I've already loaded my clubs in Iris's trunk when Tim reappears with my leather head cover. "Well . . ." I say. "*That* was an adventure. Don't think I've ever had a better time." I transact the awkward business of paying him for his services, which seems a terrible sacrilege, at least to me. He quickly tucks the bills in his back pocket, as if he also wants to get that over and done with.

"I enjoyed caddying for you. Hope we can do it again."

"Me, too," I say, and shake his hand. He gives me a meaningful tap on the elbow, and I biff him on the shoulder.

"Be careful on the road, please," he says.

"I will. Thank you," I tell him.

CHAPTER 14

clear cut

It has taken me two and one half hours to play Cypress Point, only half as long as my contest with Kiawah . . . Lord, how long ago? A year, it seems. So, just what does one do on the heels of something so grand as my morning round on the shore of the Pacific Ocean? I haven't made any decisions on that score, except for my determination to pilot Iris toward the Northwest as speedily as possible.

Snowcapped mountains and crashing streams are less in command of my imagination after these days of waves and salt air, but I reckon all that will change when the smell and taste of Cypress and Pebble sift through me. Or so I tell myself as I pound up the coastal highway toward San Francisco, which seems, even in my mind's eye, too compressed, too busy for my soul to bear. The simple concept of forward motion has considerable appeal at this moment—the blur of yellow landscape, the sound of radial tires turning beneath the car, the knock of expansion joints, the onrushing green signs announcing this highway or that bridge to anytown U.S.A. That's all I want for now. I know that I must return soon to a less epic version of the game, but I can't wrap my mind around the imagery of a commonplace par five that tracks alongside pretentious housing developments.

I pick up Highway 101 near Salinas, home of my Pebble Beach amigos, and let the road take me toward the unavoidable urban barrier looming between this milepost and an unencumbered escape route to the very corner of America. Under other circumstances, I'd allow myself a few hours in the City by the Bay . . . maybe a beer or

two on Fisherman's Wharf, an obligatory cable car ride up Powell
Street, a whiff of incense in Chinatown. However, I now see San
Francisco as a mere glimmer in my personal history, a perfunctory
snapshot in my mental album. An opportunity lost perhaps. But
there you have it . . .

After an hour of scenic turnoffs and artichoke farms, I join the
noonday city traffic, which passes by neighborhoods of narrow,
pastel row houses with tiny front yards swimming in oleander. This
is my only humane glimpse of San Francisco; the rest is industry
and warehouse and tenement and geometric sprawl that begs
escape.

I glide onto the Oakland Bay Bridge exit and follow traffic
across the water toward Berkeley, where I head north again. My
speedometer needle tilts far to the right; I'm in serious danger of
arrest, but it's a chance I take. There are lots of other corpuscles,
streaming along this meandering artery, northward, away from the
heart of the city. I trust in the power of anonymity.

Finally, the countryside returns, shimmering beneath the inland
heat. Vineyards and pastureland, truck farms and roosteries. When
the highway connects with Interstate 5, my blood pressure drops and
my mind clears. I'm Bill Hallberg again. A grass-stained fellow with
golf tees and books of Cypress Point matches in his pocket.

In Willows, a clean little town hours north of the city, I pick up a
six-pack of Anchor Steam and some ice at an IGA on the main drag.
Five of the beers are relegated to the cooler, but one sits on the passenger seat next to a box of Triscuits. I have eaten exactly nothing
today; I'm not even vaguely hungry. However, my responsible self will
not allow the consumption of even one beer on an empty stomach. So
it's a solitary cold brewski with a Triscuit buffer; it's Bill's Rule of the
Road, my compromise with legality and common sense.

There are half a dozen little kids waiting in a Caprice station
wagon alongside where I've parked Iris in front of the grocery store. I
pull two golf tees from my pocket, slide them beneath my upper lip
like tusks, and snarl at the little buggers. This act of pure lunacy
provokes wild laughter inside the baking confines of the automobile.
So I snarl again.

*   *   *

North of Redding the tall mountains and evergreen forests make a dramatic appearance. Mount Shasta, king of the Cascade range, crowned with snow, dominates the landscape. It's a beautiful mountain, illuminated by the western sun. At a little town called Dunsmuir not far from Shasta, I exit the highway long enough to eat a peanut butter sandwich alongside the Sacramento River, which is swift and clear at this high altitude.

Picture me sitting like a troll beneath an iron bridge, chomping my pathetic Peter Pan supper, an icy Anchor Steam balanced on a nearby chunk of asphalt. Who would imagine me here among the weeds, my toes dangling in the cool water? The very same guy who trod the elegant, nearly inviolable fairways of Cypress Point now occupies a gravelly bank beneath a rusting bridge in a dinky town way, way up there in the state of California. I nibble the crust from my sandwich, press the sweating beer bottle against my aching head, and daydream of my own humble front porch. Golf is only a cartoon flicker in the theater of my imagination.

I seize the advantage of endless daylight to pound northward through the beautiful mountains into Oregon. It's my first venture into the Pacific Northwest and one of the last unvisited states in that catalogue I harbor in some corner of my brain. The snowy peaks and blue-black evergreen forests are unmistakably different from anything I've ever seen. The trees are taller, more symmetrical than those in Colorado, or the Smokies for that matter. Rockefeller Center Christmas trees multiplied by billions. They climb the sweeping mountainsides until altitude forbids their growth, and there the tree line ends suddenly, like the fringe of hair around a friar's head.

Finally, as night begins to fall, I check into my Motel 6 in Grants Pass, a pleasant resort town tucked into the Rogue River valley. I note the presence of a Denny's only one block from my motel. One peanut butter sandwich, two carrots, two beers, and a handful of Triscuits aren't quite enough to offset a four-mile hike along the fairways and seaside cliffs of Cypress Point, not to mention a full day behind the wheel of a compact car. I know I'll be hungry in the morning, and I have a hankering for lipids and saturated fats.

Gillian picks up the phone after only one ring. It's late in North Carolina, but she's a night owl by nature, so I have no qualms about the hour. "Hello, sweetie," she says. "I miss you."

"Miss you, too. How are you and the pups doing? Any calamities?" My vital organs swap places beneath my skin. A subtle something in her voice tells me that worrisome news is around the next bend of our conversation.

"Pups are fine. You forgot to pay the cable bill, so I used the rabbit ears for a day or two. Otherwise, the domestic scene is well in hand," she says. Then, "Bill . . ." It's here that I flop back on the king-sized bed, from which vantage point I can see the face of Babe Ruth—or is it Gertrude Stein?—in the textured ceiling. Now for the dreaded unknown news. "You should call the hospice supervisor tomorrow. There's some sort of problem in Bowling Green," she says. "I doubt you'll have to rush home or anything like that. Sounded *mildly* urgent, though," Gillian tells me. "Anyway, she suggested you phone her tomorrow morning." And there it is . . . a little something to sleep on. A nightcap to soothe a troubled soul.

There's no use in bringing Gillian down, so I shift the subject to my own recent exploits at Cypress Point, my escape from California, my proximity to Denny's, the clarion alarm bell for my vegetarian girlfriend. "I want you back here. *Soon*," she says. "I want to do very bad things to you."

"As in . . . ?"

"It's a big surprise," she says. "Dairy products and pheasant plumes. That's as much as I'm going to reveal." This is hyperbole, I know, but worth a tumble in my imagination.

After I hang up, I know she's going to make herself a cup of herbal tea; flanked by the dogs, she'll sit on the leather sofa and her eyes will fill with tears. That's her way, and it has always been her way. By the time the cup is empty, she will be okay again.

I surprise myself by sleeping deeply, dreaming of golf holes cut onto diabolical downslopes. My putt rolls past the cup without so much as a sidelong glance, and races like a lemming to a seaside cliff and tumbles into the ocean. Then just slightly after the sun appears above the eastern slopes, I wake up. I take a quick, boiling-hot shower, brush my teeth vigorously with the pink Oral-B number I bought to replace a lostling back in Palm Springs, then phone Sue, who oversees the volunteers who care for Mom. "Hi, Bill," she says. "Sorry to interrupt your trip with a worried phone call, but I thought you should know the situation in Bowling Green."

"The situation," I say.

"We need to get some more help in there," Sue says. "Your dad just can't manage things after the helpers go home in the evening. We're all afraid he'll burn the house down or break his back again trying to lift your mom out of bed. We need twenty-four-hour assis-tance, and that's all there is to it."

"And he's bucking the idea. Right?"

"Precisely. It just has to be done, though. He'll agree to it on a Wednesday, but by Thursday he's negative again. He even forgets his opinions." She laughs good-naturedly.

"So we nail it down on a *Wednesday*, when he's agreeable. Could you possibly arrange some extended home care for both of them?" I stand up suddenly next to the bed; I need some intellectual traction to deal with this troubling stuff.

"I already did that, Bill. Just wanted you to know what's hap-pening. Your mom is much worse than when you saw her last. She's way below one hundred pounds, and with these ischemic attacks her mind is often very confused."

"Mmm . . ." I say. With a soda straw, I'm poking perfectly circular holes in a slice of Wonder bread on the night table. "Think she'll hold on until I get back to Ohio next week?"

"I think so. I don't want to worry you. But you should know the score. I don't want to bother Julie; she's got her own problems."

"No. Wouldn't bother her with any of this just yet. We can manage it. Sorry you have to bear the brunt, but I'll be in Bowling Green in a week or ten days."

"Well, don't rush your trip," she says. "Just stay in touch, okay?"

I pull on my thick athletic socks, then my nylon running shorts, a T-shirt, and, last, a pair of Nikes. My watch says six-fifteen, although the morning sun is well above the eastern peaks of the lower Cascades. Clutching my motel key tight in my fist, I jog across the parking lot to an access road, which passes beneath the highway, then bends up a hillside. There are just a couple of gas stations on that side of the road. After that, the scene looks more promising—a few rustic houses and a trailer or two perched on the bank of a swift stream, but mostly it's thick stands of spruce and fir trees.

Just past the last filling station, beyond public scrutiny, I begin to run, furiously, past Looney Toon cabins, past cartoon trailers, mailbox to mailbox, one more and one more . . . up the steepening road, up the struggling incline, until I feel myself pouring into a dark red ocean of pain. My heart roars like surf inside my skull; I hear neither the tumbling stream nor my footfall on the gravel road. Too much Denny's. Too much beer. Too much time behind the wheel of my car. My lungs burn from effort; my legs grow rubbery and weak. Still, I push through the pain, laboriously up the tilting landscape until a vast cosmic ache and pure exhaustion crowd everything— death, disease, fractured limbs, mental depreciation—from my mind. Only *then* do I stop. I lean on a rural mailbox while fireflies twirl through my field of vision. When the terrible wave of nausea sweeps over me, I sink onto the shoulder of the road, which swims in and out of focus like a silver eel.

After I've caught my breath, the town below comes clear. Not so far away. A mile, tops. Not much to show, really, for my effort.

I do not breakfast at Denny's. Instead, I grab a drive-through coffee and a container of orange juice from McDonald's on my way out of town. Whether Gillian would approve or disapprove of this newfound asceticism, I do not know. But my appetite is nonexistent at present.

My map of Oregon indicates a gray road meandering through the Klamath Mountains between Grants Pass and the coast. If I golf today, it will be a by-product of my journey along the shore. It seems ridiculously important that I simply explore with no ulterior purpose in mind. Yes, golf today will be by pure accident.

* * *

Lumber trucks roar past me every minute or so. It's an impossible thing for the mind to grasp. So many trucks heading inland from wherever the chain saws are running. Every other valley is scarred by timber harvesting. I'm confronted time and time again with eroded mountainsides upon which grow stunted saplings clinging to the rocks. It's such a sickening juxtaposition, this unending parade of trucks rolling fully loaded through the clear-cut hills and mountainsides, that I want to scream for them to stop. I want to enjoy the beautiful moist valleys and the gorgeously rounded mountains that make up the Klamath range, but I can't abide the scars that result from the clear-cutting of these magnificent trees. My love affair with golf courses, some of which necessitate the removal of large stands of trees, seems tainted in light of this all-out assault on the verdant forest. We all need our houses and our Kleenex and our legal pads, and I suppose we golfers learn to love nature through our experiences on the beautiful wooded courses of America. There must be a better way than this, though.

In the logging-camp town of Agness, on the fringe of the Siskiyou National Forest, I stop to buy a Coke and a tank of gas at a one-pump filling station, which also sells myrtle and redwood gewgaws—clocks, kiddie toys, birdhouses with bark roofs. My wounded conscience won't allow me to succumb to a beautiful chessboard made of myrtle redwood squares. There's an overalled old pauncher sitting on a metal folding chair beneath the Coke sign. "Pick it up and look it over," he says. "You won't find a nicer'n than that." It would make a wonderful gift for Garth, but damn it, I'm mad at the people who allow the old-growth trees to fall so people like me can buy chessboards and whimmie diddles and redwood cat clocks with roving myrtlewood eyes and willow tails. I put the thing back on the display bench and tell the fellow no thanks. I then squeeze ten dollars' worth of fossil fuel into the tank of my proletarian automobile and hand over the money to this fellow, whose lapdog nips at my fingers. Having asserted my moral authority, I climb back inside Iris for the drive through the wooded hills to the coast.

What has possessed me I can't say, but I find myself listening to Rush Limbaugh as I cruise through the wilderness toward the coast. He's blathering away about the liberal mind-set when it occurs to me that the target of his diatribe is the "ecocrazies," as he calls them. He's not too concerned about the plight of endangered species, nor of global warming, nor of the depletion of the world's resources. I find myself hurling insults, screaming obscenities, whacking my innocent dashboard in anger and disgust. It dawns on me that I'm in a rather bad frame of mind today. I am badly in need of a mood-altering liquid refreshment to rescue my sensibility for the day ahead. There are five unopened Anchor Steam beers bathing in an icy bath in my Igloo cooler. I stop at the mouth of a logging trail, exit my car, open my trunk, grab a beer, find a tree stump, plant my butt on it, and swallow frosty lager from the sweating bottle. A westerly wind, so strong as to rock the high overhead branches of the pines, blows my Santa Fe haircut sideways like sea grass.

When I look down, in that way thinking men do when they're sitting on tree stumps, I see that my sandaled feet are resting on pure white sand. Very odd, considering I'm twenty miles inland. I scrape the stuff into little mountains with the edge of my soles. As a golfer, the bane of my existence has been sand. Even at Cypress Point, my double bogey at twelve was the by-product of sloppy bunker play. Hmmm. A *brainstorm*. I fetch my Hogan Special from the golf bag inside Iris's trunk and a few golf balls. I drop the balls onto the little beach there by the stump and pick out a pinecone near the road and draw a ten-foot circle around it. I lay the blade wide open behind ball number one and concentrate on taking a smooth backswing and a complete follow-through. I imagine the club head meeting the sand a few inches behind the ball and splashing it toward the target.

That I look ridiculous out here in the woodsy boonies, honing my game, matters not one bit. When a truck rumbles by, I tip my imaginary visor and shimmy my feet into the warm sand. "Fore," they yell, and shake their heads. Invariably "Fore." It's what truck drivers yell when they see a blond guy hitting golf balls in the middle of a wilderness. I hit dozens of sand shots, some good, some bad. One bladed shot flies into the deep woods across the road, but dignity will not allow even a perfunctory search. After I've managed to land three successive shots within the large circle, I pack up my equipment, slug down the rest of my beer, and resume my place behind the wheel.

The coastal road, which appears on the map as a shore-hugging route, only intermittently nudges the sandy beach. Mostly, it dodges inland through pleasant but relatively undistinguished farmland and humble agricultural towns.

All of that changes when I come to Coos Bay, a handsome, bustling town that brings to mind a Maine fishing village. There are picturesque marinas along the bay and boardwalks fronting the historic waterfront buildings, most of them converted into shops.

I park Iris in front of the Tourist Information Center and walk inside the clapboard building to pick up a map and maybe some details on the golfing scene. A stout, jolly woman hands me dozens of brochures promoting boat rides and fishing museums and water skiing exhibitions. I am a tourist, after all. Nearly lost in the stack of pamphlets is a trifold listing the various golf courses in the state. "*This* is the one I need," I tell her, and place the others on the counter between us. She looks so hurt that I pick up a couple of others merely to placate her. "Oh, and these two," I say. She's okay again, happy to be of service.

The nearby deli sells takeout sandwiches, so I order a Reuben (minus the highly caloric sauce) on rye and a dill pickle. I munch on the former as I drive across the handsome iron bay bridge and leave Coos Bay behind. After I've snapped up my sandwich, I unfold the golf brochure against the hub of the steering wheel to see what might be in store for me. The centerfold photograph catches my eye, a rolling seascape that, upon closer examination, reveals itself as a beautiful golf course, Sandpines Golf Club, couched amidst the tall, white sand dunes. An hour away, perhaps, and a likable destination.

My mind has already turned the corner toward home. It's as if I've entered a kind of gravitational field that exerts itself so powerfully that I can barely keep the car on the road. Perhaps it's the force of the strong crosswind that pushes me eastward, but it's more likely that the troublesome issues clouding the domestic landscape have cast their shadow over my journey up the Oregon coast. The sky above me here is azure blue, and the mammoth, piney dunes, so reminiscent of the Michigan dunes of my childhood, give some comfort. But golf seems a queer preoccupation right now, and I can only hope that once I slide into my spikes and wrap my hands around the grip of a titanium driver, a Pavlovian response mechanism will kick in and all will be right with the world. I'm salivating, to be sure, but it's the damned pickle that's the culprit.

I lack the motivation to call ahead for a tee time at the golf course. Instead I will show up unannounced and entrust myself to the whims of fate.

The young woman behind the tee-filled fishbowl in the Sandpines clubhouse checks out my freaky windblown hair. "It's really gusty out there, isn't it?" she says. "It's been like that for a few days now." The wind sock attached to the flagpole on the back patio is fully tumescent, and there are little whitecaps on the pond that folds around what I suspect is the number ten green.

"I love the wind," I say, affecting a ridiculous Scotsman's brogue. "Arrrh." She laughs at my strangeness. "I'm looking for some poor masochists who might wish to brave the gale with me on this fine day." I can't stop myself. I'm Angus McTavish with a snootful. I finally feel ashamed of myself and I reveal my true identity—the golf odyssey, the book, yadayadayada—to this lassie whose Ping visor keeps her own brown hair tidy.

"There's *nobody* out there," she says.

"They've blown away," I gather.

"Maybe so," she says, and takes another look at my roostered-up hair. "I think Jim is going to be back from lunch pretty soon, and I know he's playing this afternoon with his friend Steve. I'm sure he'd be glad for you to join him."

"And Jim is . . . ?" I ask.

"Oh, he's the pro. Sorry. Meant to tell you that," she says. "If you want, you can use the putting green or the driving range until he gets here. I'll send him out to get you."

"Thanks," I say. And shake her hand. "I appreciate everything."

The wind is so powerful that on even the slightest leeward incline, the balls roll of their own volition until they reach the cuff. The wind is distressing in a way I can't quite describe. I press my golf cap over the dome of my skull and tighten the adjustment strap like a tourniquet. I envision myself loping, a crazy vaudevillian, across the pine barrens for a runaway chapeau. The chilly wind makes my eyes water, and my nose runs like a spigot. Some fine day for golf.

The first few holes at Sandpine are hidden in the sheltering evergreens. Thereafter, it's pure links-style golf, modified by the evil July bluster. Only once, at Royal Dornoch in the north of Scotland, have I encountered golfing conditions even remotely as windy as these. This wins the trophy for sure. I envision a kind of novelty act unfolding this afternoon—something like mud wrestling hybridized with nude cliff diving. My two-hundred-fifty-yard drives will shrivel against the gale and stretch to kingdom come heading the other way. God only knows what the crosswind will do to a lofted wedge.

I'm slamming my lag putts into the teeth of the tempest when a shadow intervenes between my ball and the cup yonder. It's Jim and his friend Steve, here to greet me in advance of our upcoming adventure. Jim is a burly fellow, completely bald, yes, but more in the sense of the shaved-head linebacker than your standard baldy with a pocket protector and Hush Puppies. It suits him, somehow, and furthermore, his hair won't be blowing ten ways to Sunday. Steve is an older fellow, hale and cheerful. "You're writing a book, I hear," Jim says. "What brought you to Sandpines?"

"I could say that the wind blew me here and it wouldn't be far from the truth," I tell him. "Mostly, I wanted to play one more links course before I swing inland. It's the Celt in me, I guess."

"Well, it's always windy as hell here," Steve says. "Maybe not as windy as *this*, but windy. Always. Until the fall. Now, *that's* the time to play Sandpines."

"We got flooded this past winter, and now with this wind, the course isn't quite what it could be," Jim says. "Sand's been blowing right out of the traps, the sand from the dunes has been pouring down on the course. It's been a hell of a July."

"I'd play during the Apocalypse if God gave me leave to do it," I say.

Jim makes a grunting sound and rubs grit from his eyes. *"Jesus,"* he says.

I have this funny feeling that were it not for my presence here, Steve and Jim would be playing poker in the back room instead of engaging in this survival contest. But I'm grateful for the companionship and tell them so. "We're glad you decided to come here on your tour around America," Jim says.

Steve belches loudly, then apologizes. "Damn cheeseburger's backing up on me."

Jim and Steve have time for only nine holes of golf, which is really all right with me. Golf will be work today especially since my mind isn't quite riveted to the task at hand. After the round is finished, I will, for the first time in weeks, be heading in the general direction of home, a very large preoccupation for a guy on the verge of a very challenging round of golf.

I'm at the helm of my own private golf cart, which has a plastic windshield to protect passengers from the tempest. An odd assortment of trash has blown from God knows where onto the fairway before us: pink insulation, the funny papers from Sunday's edition of *The Oregonian*, a plastic garbage can, a bird's nest, and what may or may not be a partially deflated balloon. Jim zigzags up and down the right-hand rough, picking up the stuff and stowing it in the equipment basket of his cart. I know Jim's a mite peeved by the sight of all this debris on his ordinarily pristine fairways, but I don't hold him accountable for the relentless wind.

We're about to toss the tee to establish honors, and we're smiling at each other, wondering who the stalking-horse will be. A forty-mile-per-hour wind is smack in our kissers, and driving the ball will be a vast experiment. "Hit away, Bill," Jim says, laughing. "You're the guest."

"Thanks a helluva lot," I say. Twice my ball blows from its little wooden perch. Finally, I decide to hit the thing off the turf, which might help keep it low into the wind. My drive, though, is a mallard duck, which quacks and flaps and craps its way onto the flank of an adjacent sand dune. "Mulligan?" I ask.

"Hit till you're happy," Steve says.

I finally get the bright idea of spitting on the tee before attempting to balance the ball on the little concave dish at the top. The experiment is a success. This time, I'm able to hit the ball squarely, and relatively straight, but no more than one hundred fifty yards into the wind. "Mother of *pearl!*" I say. "Will ya look at that? It'll take three good shots to make the green."

"That's right, Kimo Sabe," Jim says, dropping his Titleist nonchalantly onto the turf. Without fanfare he kills his ball, which defies the wind for as long as possible, then nose-dives onto the fairway, forty yards past mine. "I can't hit it any harder," he says. Steve also wastes no time in teeing off. His drive is a bit crooked, but there will be no mulligan for him. I realize immediately that I've waded into an ongoing money game between these two fellows. My presence among them is so much a nonsequitur that I may as well be a hood ornament on their golf cart.

"Fire when ready," Jim says to me from his cart. I clobber a four wood straight at the green, but after a promising start, the ball falls from the sky like a dead pheasant. Almost immediately afterward, Steve drills a three iron up the fairway, well short of the green. Then we're off to the races, three golfers on Dexedrine. Jim bolts from the cart, two iron in hand, and smacks his ball forthwith into a greenside trap. Into the cart with him, down the fairway. I give chase, laughing myself stupid at the absurdity of this scenario. I quickly get into the spirit of things, however. I grab a seven wood for my third shot, which can't be more than 125 yards. No practice swings for this automaton. Zap! A lovely high-altitude number that parachutes onto the green from the cerulean sky. Into the cart, then, and sideways onto the concrete path at maximum warp speed. Giddyap. By virtue of pure dumb luck, my ball is a mere six feet from the cup and downwind to boot. A totally makable putt, but who the hell cares?

When all the chips are gathered in, I have made the only par amongst us. This game is way, way too easy for a fellow of my capabilities.

"Nice par," Jim says.

"Thanks," I say. "Pure luck."

"Don't think so," Jim says.

"Me neither," says Steve.

"Hmmm," I say. Perhaps these two hustlers have decided to include me in their reindeer games. I stare at the green that hides at the far end of a pond whose pregnant belly intrudes on the landing area. This time we're traveling with the wind, although there's no point in letting out shaft. It's a conspicuous layup, even with a gale-force tailwind. Considering the conditions and the pin placement, any tight approach will be nearly impossible. My 230-yard seven wood stops just short of a merciful bunker placed on the near edge of the pond. Jim leaps from his cart and knocks a five iron clear to kingdom come, high and dry and right of the pond. Perfect. Then Steve pulls a black something or other from his bag and strides to the tee. I'm witnessing a *Zorro* rerun, a replay of *Beat the Clock*. Steve's hasty worm burner flees directly into the fairway bunker. "Damn it," he says and leaps into the cart.

I would, of course, dearly love to probe the innermost souls of my golfing partners, but after three holes Jim is kicking Steve's butt from the Klondike to Kabul and the stakes are going up. Bets are being doubled. This is no time for cathartic revelations, let alone genial autobiography. I'm that guy—whatshisname?—over there in the blurry windblown cart. The guy whose drives range anywhere from 125 to 350 yards in length.

My frantic game slides into the sewer at the sixth hole after five of the best pars I've made in my life. I finish the front side by making a snowman on the par five seventh, a shank-cursed triple on the par three eighth hole, and a kamikaze double bogey on the clubhouse ninth, a four-hundred-seventy-yard bruiser directly into the wind. Jim, at the conclusion of nine holes, has places to go, things to do, people to see, and Steve needs a nap. We chat for a while over Cokes in the clubhouse, but we've got our antennae on different frequencies. They're perfectly fine fellows, and I've enjoyed my peripatetic demiround of golf with them. Sandpines is a lovely course, extremely challenging on the best of days. I much prefer the company of pleasant, albeit speedy, gentlemen to ignomious solitude any old day. "Well, Bill, I've got to run," Jim says. Steve's expected home forthwith, so I shake their hands and thank them for braving the gale force winds with me.

My own competitive self emerges as I sip coffee and pretend to read a golf magazine in the clubhouse. I commit myself to the objective of playing the back side for all it's worth. On the back nine, I'll be a hard-nosed sumbitch from the get-go, a gonzo kick-butt, mofo, samurai bastard from hell.

After ditching my electric cart behind the clubhouse, I plunge into the fray on the back side by dinking my tee shot onto the sixteenth tee, dislodging a testicle from its moorings in so doing. A lovely way to begin my comeback. A highly pissed-off, wind-aided four wood ensues, but it's a Christmas ornament bound for the high branches of the pine trees parading down the right-hand rough of the tenth fairway.

I'm totally ruined after that hole. A triple bogey, my third in the last four holes. My game has gone totally Kevorkian. But I stay on life-support for few more holes, until I realize that I'm having no fun at all. My eyes burn from the sandblasting effect of the wind, and I'm simply tired of the struggle. So, after my double bogey at number twelve, I pull the plug on this stinking round. Except on those rare occasions when lightning or downpour have chased me home, I have only once before in my life walked off a golf course before my round was complete. Jimmy, the Scottish pro who manned the humble clubhouse at Bowling Green Country Club, tilted his head back and regarded me through his bifocals. "So you're a quitter, eh?" he said. I wordlessly reversed course, and resumed my dismal round exactly where I had abandoned it. Now, thirty-some years later, I stand alongside this green for a few minutes, a Baggie plastered against my ankle by the wind. The whole day seems to have been conjured up, like a daydream run amuck. Nevertheless, it's a shameful thing, quitting mid-round. There was a time when I'd pray for days like this one, but now, playing alone with nobody to commiserate with, it's just work. There's absolutely nothing to prove to myself, after all, and God comprehends my mortality . . . so I plod, shoved along by a tailwind, toward the clubhouse like a sad soul from *The Grapes of Wrath*. *Go Home*, the wind seems to say, and I'm in no mood to argue. I'd rather not show my face in the clubhouse; that would be a clear admission of defeat. Instead, I march up the homestretch hill to the parking lot, throw my clubs in the trunk of the car, slide into a pair of loafers, and climb behind the wheel.

This is a moment worth pondering. Here I am, parked behind the clubhouse of a seaside links course on the coast of Oregon, a few thousand miles from home. The very instant I put Iris into gear and ease up on the clutch pedal, I will be heading homeward. *Here we go*, I say. Gravel crunches beneath my tires, and I'm on my way.

CHAPTER 15

where it's not

At the main traffic light in Florence, just moments from making the turn toward home, I lean my forehead against the steering wheel and close my burning eyes. I've just spent two hours as the headliner in a theater of the absurd production of *Golfer Bill's Holiday Adventure*. A very bizarre anticlimax, for sure, to my week on the Pacific coast, especially after driving so far to get here. *Maybe*, I tell myself, if the wind hadn't been howling like misery today the golfing masses would have made the scene, e.g., duck-hooking defrocked priests, chili-dipping cheese mongers, dog trainers with terminal yips . . . *then*, at least, my dignity would be intact. But it was a day for fools, and I was the paragon of fools. *So what?* I ask myself. *Is it the end of the world? Relax, Bill. Qué será será.* My little consolation party is interrupted when an oaf in a pickup truck leans on his horn; the light has turned green, and the natives are restless. I take a deep breath, turn the steering wheel hard to the left, and depress the accelerator. I'm on my way home.

The road inland from Florence follows the Siaslaw River for a good twenty miles before the two part company, after which the road, according to my tourist map, forges on alone through open farmland, all the way to Eugene. The river is clean and brown. Its smooth surface is creased every now and then by pleasure boats coming from and going to the ocean. It's a daunting thing to consider . . . the miles I must travel before arriving in familiar territory once again, but I'm the happiest I've been in weeks, excluding some magnificent moments on the links, of course.

The winds decrease as Iris bears me farther and farther from the coast, and the temperature rises degree by degree until at the junction of Interstate 5, just east of Eugene, the Third Federal Fiduciary Bank thermometer blinks ninety degrees. Here I must travel north to Portland before I can turn permanently and decidedly eastward. It's a brief interruption, really, and a fairly pleasant one; the fat cows, the silos and windmills seem so familiar that my mind plays tricks. I'm a twenty-year-old kid again, driving a pink microbus past Ohio cornfields and dairy farms to Bowling Green for a visit with my folks, both of them healthy and happy.

It's hard not to daydream when you're driving cross-country in an empty Neon with many miles to travel and no particular dot on the map you can point to and say, "I'll stop . . . *here*." There's almost too much room in the imagination; thus, the past wants to furnish the vacant chambers of the mind. Of course, a lot of my personal history begs to be called back for revision—arguments and falsehoods, omissions and commissions—but the scores have been indelibly posted for all to see.

It would be a fine thing if I could finally sit down with my dad and tell him what I've learned on this journey. That I'm much less a cynic than before. Less afraid of the world. Less prone to temptation. More disciplined. More tolerant. Maybe more capable of love. Many of these lessons I've learned on the golf courses I've traversed with other souls not so different from me. That I'm a much better player now seems almost irrelevant to the real meaning of what I've experienced. I'll tell Dad all of it when I see him next. And for *that* moment he'll *know*. I'll remind him and remind him of who I am *now*, until the fact of it takes hold in his mind.

This northbound highway loops eastward around Portland, then hooks up with Interstate 64, the same road that whistles past my sister's house in Virginia Beach, three thousand miles away. I could conceivably drive from here to Julie's backyard fence without making a single turn. Almost subconsciously, I press the gas pedal closer to the floorboard and reset the cruise control.

At first I fail to notice the twirling blue light in my rearview.

"Damn it," I say, and pull onto the berm. "Damn it to hell." But the patrol car whizzes past me in pursuit of some other poor soul whose mind is adrift.

The Columbia, which mirrors the meanderings of the highway, is the most beautiful big river I've ever seen. I can't help recalling a muddy rope called the Mississippi, along whose leveed banks I lived a dozen years ago, and how disappointed I was when I first saw it crowded by decrepit warehouses and rusty barges in dry dock. But now, here, pristine green mountainsides plunge to the very edge of the road, occasionally throwing the asphalt surface into dark shadow. The river itself is profoundly green and glassy and populated by sensuous rock formations reminiscent of sculptures by Henry Moore. Little agricultural settlements crouching on the shadowy upslope of the river basin, far off in the distance, seem like artists' make-believe conceptions of towns. The quality of the late-afternoon light lends an eeriness to the landscape, as if we travelers are all tiptoeing through a vast museum. I'm sorry that my Brahms Violin Concerto is among the CDs stolen from my car in Adelanto; that music would be playing softly now, rising and falling with the landscape, the notes glistening like the river. I'm pretty much stuck with John Lee Hooker, Natalie Merchant, and the Chieftains, so I content myself with silence.

The dots on my road map grow tinier as I push upriver toward the bridge at Umatilla, a couple of hours ahead. Just a ways beyond this bridge, the Columbia, after flowing hundreds of miles southeast from the high Cascades, doubles back on itself for the inexorable westward run to the sea. Common sense dictates that I stop before long to reserve a motel room somewhere within striking distance. I have no intention of driving through the darkness.

As soon as I've filled my tank with gas at the BP in Hood River, I use a pay phone to dial the toll-free reservations number for Motel 6. I'm in luck. Two hundred miles ahead, in Pasco, Washington, I'll find exactly what I'm looking for—a cheap room with clean sheets and a hot shower. I tell the agent to keep a light on for me, and she says she'll do just that. Before abandoning the phone booth, however, I make one more call, this one to Rachel, who may be wondering what has become of her father since last we spoke. After less than one full ring, she picks up at the other end. "Hello?" she says.

"Hi, sweetie. It's me."

"Dad. Where are you? I *miss* you."

"I'm golfing my way back home, Rachel. Right now I'm standing on the banks of the Columbia River on the very tiptop of Oregon. Soon I'll cross over into Washington."

"That's awesome, Dad. I'm jealous, especially since I'm pretty much stuck in a little room with a TV that gets two channels. I've got crutches to get around on, but my leg hurts if I don't keep it elevated. So anyway, I stay in my room, mostly. Kind of a drag."

"You lonesome?" I ask.

"I want you to come home soon," she says. "I miss the pups."

"I hope you miss me, too."

"Well, I already *said* I miss you. That's kind of a given, don't you think?"

"Mm-hmm," I say. "Guess what. I played Pebble Beach and Cypress. Incredible. There were seals and baby deer."

"Since I can't play soccer now, you can teach me how to golf."

"I'd love to teach you. I've got a host of bad habits I'm dying to pass along. But shouldn't you take lessons from a pro?"

"I don't want lessons from a pro. I want *you* to teach me."

"Agreed, then. Done and *done*," I say, aware that my time is running out. "Listen, kiddo, I'm going to be home in a little over a week. Can you hold out until then?"

"I *guess* so," she says, and I feel guilty again for being away for so long. I'd give anything if she was in the car with me, drinking in all this miraculous scenery, laughing at my preposterous jokes, climbing into the backseat every now and again so she can better dig her little claws into my shoulders when I need a massage. "But hurry, okay?"

"I will, honey. I sure do love you."

"I love you, too, Dad," she says.

She has meticulously avoided any questions concerning her Aunt Julie or her grandma and grandpa in Bowling Green. Rachel is one of those children who leaves the room when sad images fill the TV screen. One glimpse of a starving child and she's in tears. It's an endearing trait, but none too practical, considering . . . So we dodge the dreary family issues, she and I: "Discussing it won't change anything, Dad. So what's the point?" she always says.

Since Garth's interest in golf is, at best, vicarious, Rachel's new enthusiasm makes me happy. She's the family athlete, an incredible give-it-all hustler with a shelf full of trophies, and now she must abandon her soccer and basketball. I wonder how I would feel if I could no longer play the game I love. I'd grieve for a good long time, I imagine, and I grieve for Rachel's loss as well, although I suspect that she'll dive into golf with everything she's got and practice until her fingers bleed. That's Rachel for you.

When all is said and done, golf may mean salvation for both of us. The world, it seems, is filled with strange poetry.

I stop briefly at a Colonel Sanders in The Dalles for some Golden Roast chicken, coleslaw, and an iced tea. It should be pointed out that the William Hallberg resting his elbow on the Formica tabletop is a more streamlined man than he was at the outset of his journey, due mostly to starvation coupled with miles and miles of walking. The high-rise biscuit and the little tubs of butter included with the meal are banished to a corner of the orange tray, where they taunt me while I dismantle a breast quarter with my plastic implements.

For dessert I drink a cold beer in the KFC parking lot, a sordid bit of imagery, I know, but my heart-stopping brush with the highway patrol has made me cautious.

According to my calculations, Pasco is about one hundred fifty miles ahead, and I have two meager hours of daylight to work with. So I gulp down the last few inches of beer, slide the bottle under my seat, and exit the scene.

The landscape is far less dramatic now. Beautiful, yes, but less dizzying than before. The verdant mountains are now treeless brown mesas whose contours are thrown into relief by the sliver of a sun just visible above a jagged silhouette to the north. It's a strangely lonely stretch of road now, with dozens of miles tripping off the odometer between exits to invisible towns. The speed limit is seventy, but I push the needle to seventy-five and set the cruise control. I'm beginning to regret having passed up lodging in The Dalles; darkness descends swiftly here due to a distant wall of mountains that steals the final throes of a sunset from me.

I fix my mind on sun-splashed fairways hovering above the ocean cliffs. My caddie Tim shades his eyes to better witness my tee shot. Then I'm imagining Carl's wife, Cathie, posing us all for a group photograph alongside a gaping Pebble Beach bunker. Then, I'm lying on a fragrant rocky cliff with Alice and Emily while waves crash against the palisades and gulls squabble overhead. But the surrounding gloom overtakes me anyway. I slide Natalie Merchant into the CD changer and try singing along with "Noah's Dove," but I don't know the words. Wordsworth's poem comes to me briefly, but the lines evaporate before I can extract even a modicum of comfort from them. How utterly strange I must look, traveling the vacant highway with my dome light illuminated against the gathering darkness.

There they are, in the distance, the lights of Umatilla. I race toward the town and the hint of a bridge spanning the black river. Lights, however, are deceptive, and ten minutes pass before the green exit sign directs me off the highway. I roll onto a side road where there's a McDonald's. I park Iris near the side door and go inside for a cup of coffee and a respite from the dark.

My hands shake so badly that steaming java sloshes from my Styrofoam cup. "Could you pour some of this out, please?" I ask the lipsticky counter girl. "It's a little too full." She does a Betty Boop thing with her mouth, then scoots over to a stainless-steel sink with my coffee.

"Are you all right, sir?" she asks.

"Fine," I say. "A bit road weary is all."

"I can relate . . ." she says and rolls her eyes.

After I've composed myself, I climb behind the wheel of my car and drive across the gleaming bridge into the state of Washington. I steel myself for the twenty-mile sprint to Pasco, where I will again cross the Columbia River. "I'm doing this for Rachel," I mumble. I try to picture her in bright sunlight, gripping the golf

club just so, taking the club perfectly back to parallel, then
releasing gracefully into the ball. Iris hurls through the mysterious
black night like a riderless horse while I replay the scene again and
again.

I lie awake in my motel room for a while, methodically stowing all
my worries, one by one, in little pigeonholes, each with a little door I
can close to seal them in. It's a relaxation technique taught to me by
a counselor whose hourly fee was so burdensome that it, too, became
one of the worries I pigeonholed. This latest bout with night fright,
scarifying as it was to my psyche, is more easily set aside than past
episodes. I didn't plunge into the bowels of hell, after all, nor did
eternal dark wrap its hoary hand around my throat. It's easy to laugh
at myself in the aftermath, but I'm laughing with all the lights
burning and the TV playing.

At ten o'clock at night I feel my body, heavy with the weight of
sleep, settling like a boulder into the mattress. On some days there's
just so much to think about that your mind simply surrenders to
oblivion. And today is one of those days.

The eastern sky is dark when I wake up in the morning, rested and
refreshed by a good night in the arms of Morpheus. I sing Jimmy
Reed songs in the shower and Neil Sedaka while I towel off. I can't
help checking out my new torso in the mirror above the bedroom
desk. Full frontal. In profile. Over the shoulder. Narcissus with a
farmer's tan.

Breakfast is a cup of Pasco Burger King coffee and a whiff of
somebody else's Croissandwich. Then, at exactly six-o-five in the
morning, with dawn breaking over the decapitated mesas of eastern
Washington, I'm on the road again.

On the outskirts of Spokane, I allow myself a McDonald's muffin,
which I consume on the fly. It's a messy critter, though, especially in
the midst of morning rush-hour traffic. There's a straightforward
midwestern feel to this city, with its familiar architecture and tree-
lined streets—a brave commentary considering my vantage point,
which happens to be the slow lane of an elevated highway that

merely skirts the business district. Billboards advertise classic rock radio stations and Heineken beer and men's clothing stores.

Straight ahead, obviously trapped between the concrete walls of the elevated highway, is a black mongrel dog. The little fellow stares into the oncoming traffic like a forlorn hitchhiker. I click on my emergency blinkers and ease to a halt just a few feet from him. He looks as if he might run away when I get out of my car and walk slowly toward him, but he stays put; the blaring car horns are a lovely complement to my rescue operation. "Go to hell," I shout at any commuter who gives me a look.

"Hey, boy. What're you doing out here?" I say to the dog. I offer Fido the back of my hand, which he sniffs nervously. When I'm sure he's not going to bite me or bolt into traffic, I snag him around the rib cage, carry him back to my car and toss him into the backseat. "Stay," I say. He immediately leaps into the front passenger seat, again to the backseat, then to the front, again and again, shredding Washington and part of Virginia in my *Rand McNally*. He piddles on the upholstery and mushes his wet snout against the windows. All this before I can even put Iris into gear. "Sit," I tell him. "Sit, please, damn it!"

What to do with a collarless stray dog in a strange town is a question I must now come to grips with. I take a downtown exit and pull into the first filling station I can find while my sidekick ricochets like a Superball inside my car's cockpit. I tote the dog like a bag of groceries to a phone booth and dial 411. The operator gives me a number for Animal Control, which I immediately dial, only to hear a recorded message informing me that I've got half an hour before they open for business. I explain my plight to Bob, the gas station attendant, who agrees to put the dog in the cab of his tow truck until the shelter opens. "Don't worry. I'll give 'em a ring," he says. I offer him ten dollars for his trouble, but he laughs and waves away my offer. "You were nice enough to save his little black ass," he says. "Least I can do is finish the job for you."

I shake his hand and thank him profusely. "Good luck," I say.

"Might just keep him," Bob says. "Seems like a good dog."

"I'm sure he is," I say.

One hour later I'm hauling through Coeur D'Alene, Idaho, home of a golf resort featuring a floating green, access to which is accomplished, most likely, by jumping out of a low-flying aircraft. I reject the temptation of yet another mind-blowing acid-trip adventure in favor of highballing it down the pretty highway, which threads through a vast national forest. For the first time since North Carolina, I enter wooded mountains unscarred by loggers and developers. I shouldn't take the abominations of the timber industry so personally, but I have to admit that old growth forests have an incredibly uplifting effect on me. Smokey the Bear hugged me at a Cub Scout jamboree when I was a little kid. That might just explain it.

About an hour past Coeur d'Alene, just below the interstate highway, lies a beautiful little mountain town called Wallace, where I spend a good hour walking up and down the old main street. I wonder if I'm just too naive to comprehend that the atmospherics have been rigged to seduce me or whether this hamlet, with nothing but itself to offer tourists, is as authentic as I think it is. The picturesque Seed n' Feed store is frequented by overalled ranchers and farmers who drive pickups and pitch fifty-pound bags of cattle feed into their truck beds. There's an old movie theater, too, which happens to be showing *The Andromeda Strain*, a moldy flick from the early seventies. Few of the shops seem oriented toward tourists, and, indeed, I'm one of the few outsiders roaming the town's sidewalks. On the upper tier of this terraced village are picturesque Victorian houses, snug against a mountainside. I haunt the store windows for a while; then, when I remember the miles I have yet to travel, I buy a highly caloric hand-dipped mint chocolate chip ice-cream cone from a soda jerk in a dime store with a hammered tin ceiling. I hike carward past the saddlery and the farrier's shop, licking away at my single dip, scoping out the humble townsfolk, half afraid that I'm going to wake up and find that I'm still in a Motel 6 in Pasco, Washington.

After my ice cream lunch, I'm on the highway again, cruising at a high rate of speed past the clear-cut mountainsides of western Montana toward Missoula, the end point of a college road trip that culminated with my making awkward, icy love inside a cramped flannel sleeping bag in the backseat of a Ford Cortina in a blizzard at the foot of Lake Apgar in Glacier National Park. My hitherto Platonic love

partner Cheryl, and I, having shrunk our wet boots to unwearability in
the heat of a blazing campfire, and having lost our matches in a snow-
bank, and our tent to the blizzard, and our only hope for a battery jump
with the departure of the last foolish campers, allowed ourselves the
romance that cruel death was inevitable. So we gave our bodies frantically to one another as the elements raged outside the car windows.

Of course, the rangers found us shivering and disheveled the next
morning. They dug out our tent for us, towed us onto a cleared park
road, jump-started the Cortina, and bade us a fond farewell. Cheryl
and I drove back to Missoula in our stocking feet.

The here-and-now highway whisks past Missoula with hardly a
nod and on down to Butte, where, on my return trip to Ohio with
Cheryl, the Cortina gave up the ghost, necessitating a very acrimo-
nious Amtrak train ride to the Buckeye State.

Today will be a golfless day. There will be no putting on the motel
carpet. No practice pitch shots, turd to turd, in the pet exercise yard.
Even the thought of a six-foot putt clangs in my mind. This day was
made for racking up the miles. To that end I push ahead at Mach 1
through the ever less picturesque, ever more rugged and inhospitable scrubland of Montana, all the way to Billings, where I again
seek shelter in my totally reliable, insanely mundane, relatively
comfortable Motel 6. I ponder whether I should explore downtown
Billings. But this would require my getting into the driver's seat of
my car, so I opt for a swim. The pool is empty, and it takes me
only one exhilarating second to see why. *Uffff,* I say, when my
head breaks the surface after my illegal dive into the frigid water.
Ooojeeze. I spit water and clamber up the ladder.

After stripping out of my sopping trunks in the motel room, I
scrupulously avoid even a haphazard glance at my naked self in the
mirror. I take a very long hot shower and slip into my sweatpants and
a T-shirt.

Within the hour, I'm sound asleep on top of the bedspread with
the TV playing and the bathroom light on.

I awaken eight hours later, facedown, with my head at the foot of
the bed and my toes resting on motel pillows. At first I can't remember
where I am. California maybe. Or Santa Fe. Then, slowly, the world

comes clear to me, and I realize that I've come a long, long way in two days.

The motel is surrounded by warehouses and fenced-in compounds filled with semitrailers, past which I jog, stiffly at first. My temperamental right heel aches at every footfall, and my lungs are sore from the intake of absolutely cold air. Not cool, nor brisk, but *cold*. However, just beyond the masonry supply store, my muscles cease their rebellion, and my lungs adapt to the air temperature. I enjoy chasing down the plumes of gray fog issuing from my mouth and listening to the quiet clop of my Nikes on the asphalt road.

After a pancake breakfast at the Holiday Inn restaurant in downtown Billings, a spotless, Cubist cityscape with frontier museums and avant-garde fountains, I launch myself onto the never-ending highway. The optimistic farmland east of town gives way to an inhospitable stretch of arid, rocky terrain that occasionally yields up a struggling ranch or an embattled cluster of ramshackle houses that call themselves a town. When I've despaired of civilization, another thin tributary of the Yellowstone River up north will quench one more humble settlement. These villages have quaint grocery stores and hardware stores and shops selling sundries. There are the obligatory chain restaurants catering to travelers. Each town is basically the same. Near Hardin, an hour east of Billings, I see the sign for Little Big Horn Battlefield National Monument. I've done precious little sightseeing on this odyssey of mine, so the proximity of Custer's Waterloo lures me off one highway and onto another, which will eventually require some creative backroad detours if I expect to reconnect with I-94.

At Crow Agency, I pick up Route 212 for just a few miles . . . and there it is, just up a winding asphalt road, Little Big Horn. I park my car near an uninhabited ranger outpost and walk up the path to the crest of the hill where General Custer met his doom at the hands of the Cheyenne and the Sioux and the Arapaho warriors. Maybe it's the early hour, or the remoteness of the site, I couldn't say, but there is only one living soul here at the top of this windblown hill, and that's me. I stand next to the granite obelisk, my back to the chilly wind, and take in the endlessly yellow barrenness of the landscape.

A shiver climbs through me, maybe because of the wind, although I doubt that. I try to imagine Custer, the poor arrogant bastard, staring in fearful wonderment as fighters from the three tribes amass on the brink of the surrounding hills. But, it's really more than the mind can take in. The wind makes a whistling sound up here, and shadows sweep like fleet ghosts across the grassland toward the rocky outcrops miles in the distance. After half an hour of solitude, I decide to hit the road again. I walk slowly down the path to where Iris awaits. Along the way, I encounter a dark-haired young woman carrying a twin-lens reflex camera and a tripod. We smile at one another in a funny, sad-to-have-missed-you way and continue on our separate paths. Her license plate is from Illinois. A bumper sticker is affixed to the trunk of her Civic: MY KARMA RAN OVER YOUR DOGMA.

I drive through the beautiful, rugged landscape of the Crow Reservation, blighted periodically by impoverished trailer communities like Busby and Lame Deer. The sorrowful fact of these little settlements brings me down, despite the awesome fineness of the layered rock formations and the piney hillsides that climb from the grass plains. It's hard to ignore the triviality of my golfing exploits when I contrast them with the hardscrabble truths before me.

In Colstrip, a relatively prosperous little island in an ocean of poverty, I fill up my tank with gas and extract my last Anchor Steam from the cooler. Perhaps I can dilute my guilty soul with a tall, cold brew—a frail bit of logic if ever there was one. Still, I'm a thirsty middle-aged bleeding heart who just plain wants a beer. And have one I shall—legal, illegal, ill-advised or not.

On the northern fringe of this town, tucked into a rockbound notch in the hills, is a treeless nine-hole golf course, practically overrun with electric carts and brightly clad foursomes with hand trollies. This is such a wondrous bit of frivolity that I pull off the road to witness it. I'm leaning on the fender of my car, blatantly sipping forbidden beer, wishing I was out there with them. It's just the fix I need to reestablish a habit that seems to have atrophied under the welter of travel brochure imagery. Down below, a bruiser in Bermuda shorts and a cowboy hat sinks a monster putt from the fringe at the first green. His hollering echoes against the canyon wall. I want to clap for the guy, and, but for the beer bottle in my hand, I would.

Hooray for you, you meaty boy.

Up the gray road I go until I intersect with I-94 again, near the town of Forsyth. My golfing hormones are suddenly percolating, so I venture into the business district to inquire about the existence of a golf course where a golf junkie can get his fix. A young woman in a Texaco Pantry store directs me to the crosstown route that passes by the country club.

The golf course is surprisingly green and inviting. There are plenty of hills and willow trees and ponds to make life interesting. When I enter the clubhouse to make my inquiry, I discover that the pro shop is abandoned, although the adjoining bar, lighted only by neon beer signs and garish jukeboxes and flickering pinball machines, is hopping. It's nine-thirty in the morning, but the beer flows copiously from ivory taps behind the counter. Some old whiskey-drinking gents at the bar give me the once-over. "Excuse me," I say, adopting my innocent contralto tone of voice. "Is the pro shop open?"

The barmaid informs me that a tournament is under way and that the course is closed to public play. "Sorry," she says. I thank her for the info and nod congenially at the bar fogies, for whom I'm a singular amusement. I'm tempted to wander out onto the course anyway so I can follow the fortunes of locals who are apparently competing for cash prizes. But the player in me argues in favor of a venue farther down the highway where I can actually tee it up in pursuit of par.

I discover in short order that nearly every little town in eastern Montana has its own golf course, mostly humble nine-hole tracks, completely bereft of architecture. Imagine a flat three-hundred-yard runway bordered with scruffy saplings, culminating in an unguarded ground-level green; or a five-hundred-yard rifle shot to a perfectly circular target with the pin poking from the bull's-eye; or a one-

hundred-fifty-yarder—just a tee box and a green, really, with a fairway in between.

In a little town called Fallon I've actually parked Iris outside a
large barn (which triples as an equipment shed, a saloon, and a
meager pro shop). My spikes are laced up, and my hand is on the
strap of my golf bag; but I just can't bring myself to go through with it.
I empathize with these farmers and their wives who hike up and down
the humble fairways, and I appreciate their fondness for the game.
Part of me wants to engage them in some convivial interaction if only
to prove my humanity. But at the very last moment, I put my sticks
back in the trunk, hop behind the wheel, and, without removing my
golf shoes, drive back toward the ramp leading onto the interstate.

At noon, I stop in Glendive, Montana, to pick up the makings for
a turkey and cheese sandwich. The checkout lady tells me that there
is indeed a very nice golf course just up the way. "It's real nice," she
tells me. "You're bound to like it."

And I do like it, maybe too much. I'm wishing, when I pull up to
the modern clubhouse of the Cottonwood Country Club, that I had
taken my chances back at one of those rural tracks laid out by a
local farmer on his day off from grinding silage. Here the tight fairways are lined with cedars and hardwoods; the greens are guarded
by sand traps thirsty enough to gulp down a golf ball or two. I
gander at my map of Montana and determine that I have only two
pencil-point towns before the border of North Dakota, and I have
this foolish notion that Montana is too big a state not to at least
take a divot from. But I've eaten a lot of white bread in my day, and
this course just seems too predictably mundane, too much like the
little club where I learned to play the game. I've decided to cut my
losses and pound on into North Dakota, which looms eerie and
remote in my imagination, when two lady golfers of retirement age
wave at me from the first green as if they somehow know who I am.
I'm reckoning that the chances of their having connected me with
the jacket photo on my novel are roughly nil, as are the chances
that they are one of the chosen few to own a copy. What possesses
me I can't say, but I grab my camera and stroll across the first

fairway to the second tee, where the ladies are laughing at some private joke.

Their delight withers to disappointment as I approach their cart. At a distance, I may have been a dead ringer for some nice fellow who fills their prescriptions or boards their poodles. But up close I'm a space alien from the planet Zebulon. "Hi," I say. "Sorry to interrupt your round."

"That's okay. We're just kind of poking," says the copilot, who is munching on a sandwich that might be egg salad. I don't know for sure. "Beautiful day, isn't it."

"It's a *wonderful* day," I say. The driver of the cart sizes me up from beneath her black visor, fearful perhaps that I'm going to ask her if she *really* knows Jesus Christ. "I *know* how weird this is going to sound," I tell them, "but I'm a writer, and I'm doing this cross-country golf book for a publisher in New York . . ." Skeptical looks are coming at me in stereo. The driver has her toe on the accelerator, and I'm in danger of having one of those awkward moments like when you discover that you're talking to an empty phone line. I give them the blah-blah-blah details of my venture, to which they patiently listen. "So . . . would you mind if I sort of walked around with you, took a few pictures, asked lots of impossible, and highly personal, questions . . . ?" Squirrels are fighting overhead, and a car backfires in the parking lot. I'm nigh onto the knuckle-sucking stage of embarrassment, when the smaller woman, the passenger, says, "I'm Marian, and this is Elna. I hope you're not expecting pros."

"Nah, pros are a dime a dozen," I tell her, and shake hands with them. Ice has been broken. Flesh has been pressed. "I'm Bill."

"Glad to meet you," says Elna. "Where are you from?"

"Zimbabwe," I tell them. "Near the coast."

"Never been there," says Marian, who wears a score tabulator on her wrist.

"I've never been *here* either," I say. "Until now, I mean."

We continue to make small talk while Marian finishes off her sandwich and takes a sip of water from a paper cup. She wipes her mouth on a golf towel, and both women exit the cart to hit their tee shots. Marian is a wiry, cigarette-smoking little woman. She bloops her tee shot into the left rough, snatches up her tee and dashes back to the cart. "I'm making you nervous," I say. "Ever try to putt with a giraffe watching you?"

"You're not from Zimbabwe," she says, and blows a plume of smoke toward the scorecard. "I know the accent, and that's no Zimbabwe accent. You're trifling with us." Marian cranks the ball washer very, very slowly, eyeing me like the stranger that I am.

"You're right. Exactly right. I'm just tired of giving everybody the same spiel."

Elna regards me disapprovingly. "So what brings you to Glendive? You selling something?"

"I'm an author. Honest. I'm doing this book on the soul of American golf."

"What on earth does *that* mean?" Elna asks, and eases the cart forward, forcing me to dogtrot alongside. "You're pulling my leg, aren't you? Start again. Where are you really from?"

"Seriously . . . ? I'm from North Carolina, and I'm out here in Montana trying to get beneath the game. To figure why it's become so important in people's minds."

"I think I'm ducking my shoulder. That's what's on *my* mind," Marian says, inspecting her ball for cleanliness. The cart stops suddenly, and she dismounts just long enough to chop her Pinnacle another fifty yards up the fairway. "Crap!" She clicks the tabulator on her wrist. Elna waits until Marian is aboard, then slams the accelerator to the floorboard, leaving me to the dandelions. Before I can catch up, she's corked her ball onto the fringe of the par four second hole.

"Beautiful," I say. She shrugs bashfully and climbs behind the wheel. "So, are you going to ask us personal and embarrassing questions?" she asks.

"Don't ask about our love lives," Marian says. Her laugh trails into a coughing spasm.

"He's no author, Marian. Ask him what books he's written."

"Well," Marian asks. "Any best-sellers, Mr. Zimbabwe?"

"Nope," I tell her. "Couple of minor successes is all. Earned enough to pay off my Visa. That's about it."

"Now I believe you," Marian says, and scrapes her third shot into the bunker. She looks to me for help. "Come on, what am I doing?"

"You're not breaking your wrists," I say. "And you're peeking."

I'm traipsing along behind their electric conveyance, wishing for some histrionics here in the outback of Montana. Marian, for instance, hurling Elna's perfectly driven golf ball into the center of the frog pond.

"What the hell was *that* all about?" Elna asks, hands on hips. "What's come over you, Marian? My word!"

"Illegal ball," Marian says. "I can't abide cheaters, and you, Elna, are a *cheater*. That was a Wonder Ball and you know it!"

"That's pure horse drizzle," Elna says. "As I live and breathe, it was a *Pinnacle*."

"False," says Marian. "It was a Wonder Ball. You've got square grooves, too. Outlawed by the U.S.G.A., *as* we both know."

"Marian, I can't believe this. How long have we been playing together. Ten years?"

"Yeah, and I've finally had it up to here with you, you *hussy!*" Marian yanks Elna's visor down over her eyes, tears the scorecard into confetti and sprinkles it on Elna's bean. Elna and Marian tumble from the cart, and tussle like angry cats in the fairway grass, pulling great hanks of gray hair from each other's heads. Finally, Elna uses her size and weight advantage to subdue her opponent. The culminating image of their battle finds Elna sitting on top of Marian, pinning her arms to the ground.

This, of course, is just the fiendish machination of a tired brain. Elna, whose own game is ploddingly competent, praises Marian's minor triumphs and commiserates with her carefully tabulated failures. "I've got a son about your age," Elna says. "How old are you?"

"Twenty-six," I say. "Almost twenty-seven."

"And we're *forty*, right Elna?"

"Marian dear . . . what I wouldn't give . . ." Elna says.

They're playing dime-a-hole skins, although I suspect that Elna could buy a yacht with the earnings she's accumulated over the years they've played together.

"The soul of American golf, eh?" Elna says, after tapping in a six-inch putt at the fifth hole. "Want to know what *I* think that is?" She pauses a minute for dramatic effect. "I think it has very little to do with hitting a golf ball into the hole. I got started playing golf after cancer surgery about ten years ago . . . to keep from going out of my mind. I met Marian here, and we've been golfing partners ever since and I love her like a sister. We just play golf together. No cards. No movies. Just golf every day on this same little course. We know each other better than we know ourselves, I swear."

"That's true," Marian says. "The best friends you can have are golfing friends. Now don't ask me why that is. You're supposed to figure that out, aren't you? Why do you suppose that's true?"

"I need to think about it," I say, and I do need to roll it around in my mind.

Marian is having a very bad day, but she notches her scores faithfully, putts out everything, and doesn't let the problems get her down. Elna, on the other hand, is a bogey machine.

"I *would* like to make one par so this young man can write about it," Marian says. "He must wonder why I don't just stick to knitting. Right, Bill? Don't you just wonder how I can enjoy this . . . obscenity?"

"You just need some minor adjustments."

"Honey, they need to overhaul me. I've just got too many miles on my engine. There's the plain and simple fact." Marian lights a Salem and takes a tiny puff.

"Marian can play very well," Elna says. "Her game is temperamental, that's all. She's high-strung."

"What does *that* mean, Elna? I'm certainly not high-strung." Marian pokes her tee in the ground, takes a wiry stance, and hits her best shot of the day onto the green at the short seventh hole.

"She's not high-strung," Elna says to me, and smiles. Even after her tee shot sails into the greenside bunker she's smiling.

"I'm going to get your dime on this hole," Marian says. This time she inhales more deeply, and blows out a never ending stream of smoke. "High-strung."

Elna cuffs her ball out of the trap and onto the green, but well shy of the hole. "I'm still away," she says. She takes a good look at the contour of the green. "This one moves right a little bit," she says. "I've had this putt a few times in my life." She takes a good whack at the putt, which races directly toward the hole and disappears.

"You *would* hole the thing," says Marian. "She likes the spotlight, Bill. Looks like I need to make mine if I'm going to be in your book. Right?"

"That or you'll have to do something totally insane. Like throw you clubs in the pond or cuss a blue streak."

"Oh, she can *do* that," Elna says.

"Silence, please," Marian says, and looks over her twenty footer from both sides. When she's got it figured, she situates herself over the ball, glances back and forth from cup to ball, ball to cup, until the beak of her visor points straight down and stays there. She draws the putter back slowly and jabs the ball toward the hole; it skitters across the bent grass green, hellbent on its target. As the ball rolls inevitably toward the cup, the slumbering fates awaken just in time to blow the ball ever so slightly off course. Her immaculate Pinnacle hangs on the lip, its shadow falling into the hole.

"Pick it up," Elna says.

"Beautiful roll," I say.

Marian shrugs, clicks the gizmo on her wrist a couple of times, and scurries toward the cart. Elna follows and slides behind the wheel. She puts her arm around her friend and gives her a sisterly squeeze, just enough to provoke a grudging smile.

I can't imagine Elna and Marian anywhere else than here. Kiawah would be wasted on them. Pebble Beach would swallow them whole. This golf course suits them, and they fit the landscape as surely as the trees. Playing golf here must be like coming home every night to the same easy chair and the same soft sofa. You eat off the regular dishes and sit around the familiar dining table. At night, when the world is buried in snow, you climb into your own bed and dream on the same old pillow. There's something to that, I guess. And I can understand the loyalty Elna and Marian feel toward their golf course.

Still, it's a hard thing to imagine ... these fairways in mid-January, buried under snow so deep that golf dreams suffocate beneath it. I'm spoiled by living in a part of the country where this green sport is a year-round phenomenon. On the other hand, I have a wistful feeling about Cottonwood Country Club and these two good friends who play their daily golf together. It's not the sort of feeling you can throw a rope around either. Just a sense that for them the game has to do with how our days wind on toward the end. I imagine them playing their last round together in the sparsely inhabited plains of Montana, with the first chill of autumn descending. They would know that an end had come to their golfing days. They would concede their last putts, maybe have a cup of tea in the clubhouse grill, then do the final accounting of their betting game. I hope that day is years and years away.

After the round, Elna and Marian invite me to join them in the grill for a Pepsi. Elna insists on treating me. We sit on bar stools at the counter while the wall-mounted TV flashes green fairways and brightly clad golfers. Elna asks me about my kids, and my adventures on the road. I tell her and Marian about my experience with Dave and Larry back at the VA in Los Angeles. "That's marvelous," Elna says.

"So," Marian says, "you've seen lots of golf courses on your trip. How do you think this one measures up?'

Now why that question touches me so powerfully I don't know. Everybody, I guess, wants reassurance that their world is valid and credible. It would break her heart if I demeaned something so integral to their existence, and these are two people whose hearts I would never wish to break. "It's a *perfect* golf course," I tell her. "I judge a course on how well it suits its world. Cottonwood feels absolutely right."

"I agree with you one hundred percent," Marian says. "We're very proud of our golf course, and our pro is just a splendid fellow."

There is nothing but ice in my glass, and although Elna offers to buy me a refill, I politely decline. She leaves five dollars on the counter, and we three walk out the side door into the sunshine. "Well . . ." I say. "This has been such a pleasure. I *needed* something relaxing and intimate after two hard days of driving. It was a wonderful afternoon. Thank you both very much."

"Listen, honey," says Marian. "It was *our* pleasure. We look forward to reading your book."

"I'll make sure you get a copy," I tell them.

I give Elna and Marian farewell hugs just like I would any of my dearest relatives at the end of a long visit. "I'm off to North Dakota," I say.

"You be careful, now, Bill. And stay in touch."

"Oh, I will," I tell them. But I know that lots of hard winters will come and go before chance brings me back to this remote part of the country.

As I'm backing Iris out of the shady parking slot, Elna and Marian give me a wave, as if they know who I am.

CHAPTER 16

golf on the
moon

Marian's pioneer toughness and Elna's openheartedness have been a comfort, although in the aftermath of my hours with them, I feel homesick. They are transplanted reincarnations of my two straw-hatted great-aunts, Emily and Esther, who, with their ten-foot cane poles, pier-fished together for Lake Michigan perch and whistled like canaries and listened to the Tigers on the radio. For a long time to come, I'll think about Marian and Elna the way I think of Esther and Em, as women without pretense, and good as God can make them.

More than ever, I want to see my mom again before her time comes. There are things I need to tell her about this quest undertaken by her prodigal son; she deserves a full accounting. And Dad needs a man to keep him company while he watches the Tigers on TV. If the weather is kind to us, maybe we'll try one more round of father/son golf on the flat, plainspoken university course in Bowling Green. Even if it takes him two hundred strokes to get to the last hole, that will be okay by me. The point, after all, is to hit the ball, then hit it again, right? To disconnect the ball from the earth for a moment or two, until the forces of nature bring it home. I'll pat him on the back at every turn and tell him the old clichés that ring like a curious liturgy in the mind of true golfers. "Tee it high and let it fly, Pop. Never up, never in."

* * *

I'm almost but not quite in the Midwest, and I can feel its proximity as surely as I can feel anything in this world. The soft-edged topography and endless horizons typifying this chunk of the world untangle the tensions of a long journey; my old familiar self has crawled back inside my skin and I'm no longer just a persona with golf clubs in his trunk. I'm Bill Hallberg, Michigander by way of Ohio and North Carolina. A wolverine nourished on buckeyes and pecans.

That I'm in North Dakota, the outback of my imagination, seems almost impossible to fathom. I should be home lying in a hammock, dreaming my golf dreams, visualizing the perfect, poetic follow-through. Here I am, though, surrounded by the finest links-land one could possibly imagine. There are hillocks and hummocks, swales and shallows, and enough grass to make a bed for all the gods in heaven. In short, it's the quintessential turf for a grand irrelevant golf course played by lonely tourists and existential wanderers like me. Alas, the prerequisite sea retreated from this region eons ago, and there are absolutely no golfers here, Irish or otherwise, to merit the magnificent links with which I overlay the barren landscape. Instead, there are only lonely cattle herds and Erector Set windmills to break the brilliant monotony of the plains.

Sometimes pure impulse subdues common sense. Here I am, driving Iris through the Missouri National Grasslands, surrounded by thousands of square miles of land upon which no golfing fool has made his mark. The hills roll like green sea swells for as far as the eye can see, interrupted here and there by schooner-shaped rock formations becalmed on the horizon. I park my car on the shore of this imaginary sea and pull my driver, one perfect golf ball, and a tee from my bag. After climbing a barbed-wire fence alongside the road, I wander through the grassy dunes to the tallest among them. The grass atop the hillock is thinner than in the swales, so it's not impossible to find a reasonable place to tee up the ball. After all, I don't want to flatten the grass or uproot it just to prepare my personal tee box. "There's a good lad. The grass never harmed *you* after all," my old

Scottish pro Jimmy tells me. "All right, young William. Look for a
target now. Ay. A good choice, that. Now, hold it in your imagination
while you focus on the dimples, just *there* on the hindquarter of the
ball." Jimmy seems to tickle the back of my Ultra with the rubber
grip of his omnipresent five iron. I sight on a distant rock formation,
settle the driver behind the ball, take a full backswing, and smack
the thing as hard as I possibly can. "Fore! Fore, all you bastards of
the world!" I yell. It's a fine thing, watching a golf ball hang above
rolling prairie, only to land in terra incognita. This land, let's face it,
demands to be golfed upon; I'm just the first man to listen. The drive,
a black dot floating forever above an ocean of grass, is as memorable
as any I've hit in my life; no shot precedes it, and none will follow; it's
only itself and nothing more. I plod back out from the dunes, reclimb
the fence, slide my driver into the bag, and slam the trunk.

The route across North Dakota is a west-to-east rifle shot, which
tempts one to crush the accelerator against the floorboard and
lead-foot it across the state at one hundred miles per hour. I'm no
saint, and my homing instincts are irresistible, so I exceed the
posted speed limit by a careful nine miles per hour. Iris com-
plains, but she does as she's told. Just inside the border, I stop at a
welcome station to take a simple pee. I confess to having had
ample opportunity back in the dunes to address this perfunctory
matter, but the act seemed sacrilegious in that setting. Maybe the
place was too holy for something so trivially human. Or maybe I'm
a fool.

A funny thing happens as soon as I open the welcome center
door and enter the warm confines of the building. I am verbally set
upon by the two blond, blue-eyed young women who work the
lonely info counter. *Where do these girls live?* I wonder. In a sod
prairie hut, maybe, in one of those flyspeck towns one finds on a
road map. They treat me to a detailed discussion of the grassland
habitat—all of it—the prairie dogs, the Indian wars, the Swedish
settlers, the devastation of the buffalo herds by the "long rifles."
"Sometimes," the one with the name tag reading Hildegaard says,
"the winter temperature can reach fifty below. Your spit freezes

before it hits the ground." Fascinating minutiae to be sure. I'm much more interested in the capacity of a human bladder. I lean palms-down on the counter and cock my head to simulate curiosity. "Hmmm . . . that cold, eh?"

Hildegaard's not-quite-identical twin, Dahlia, twiddles her name tag. "When it's that cold we do what we always do. *Nothing.* Or else we watch videos. Lots of videos." A bitter child, this Dahlia.

"Do you golf?" I ask. "In the summer, I mean?"

"Golf?" asks Dahlia, pruning up her face like I've dropped two Balinese humping slugs onto the counter.

"*You* know . . ." I say. "Like . . . are there courses around here where somebody like me can play golf?"

"Just a minute," Hildegaard says again, and fishes through some brochures captured in a big cardboard box. "Here," she says. "It's all the golf courses in the state. The nearest one is, let's see . . . Dickinson, I think. Yup. Dickinson."

"Dickinson. *Okay*, then," I say with finality.

"You like to fish?" Dahlia asks. "There's lakes in Dickinson. Good fishing."

"If you want to golf, I'd go to Bismarck," Hildegaard says. She drags her red-lollipop-colored fingernail down a column of listings. "Let's see. There's Apple Creek and Briarwood."

"If you like to fish, those lakes in Dickinson are full of bass," says Dahlia. She unwraps a pink Hostess Sno Ball and takes a bite out of it.

"Excuse me," I tell them. "I'm going to just duck in here for a minute if you don't mind. And then I'll be on my way."

"Okay," says Hildegaard. "You help yourself."

After I've finished in the restroom, I say "See ya" without looking over my shoulder and dash into the waning North Dakota afternoon.

The farther east I drive, the more farms and pastures appear. The grasslands have reluctantly yielded to fenced acreage with barns and flocks of scraggly sheep and wire corncribs. The agricultural smells take me home to Ohio, where corn is shoulder high by now and where golf courses abound. I've always imagined North Dakota as a sort of doomsday landscape with year-round snow halfway to the sky and odd Scandinavian survivalists braving the elements marshaled to subdue them. When I was growing up in Ohio, Bismarck was the all-purpose conversational metaphor for exile: "If you don't buckle down, Billy Boy, you'll wind up selling banjos in Bismarck." That's what Miss Underhill used to say to me when I snoozed through her interminable blather on Emily Dickinson. "You'll be selling banjos in Bismarck, young man." Now, however, the North Dakota landscape seems soft-hearted and warm and Bismarck looms as a pleasant destination on the horizon of a romantic daydream.

I check into the Motel 6 at eight P.M., with two hours of daylight left in the sky. The proximity of said motel to Taco Bell presents a temptation that overwhelms a cosmopolitan male like me. Nothing is quite so grand as eating a burrito supreme from a gooey waxed paper square while watching *Wheel of Fortune* in your underwear. But there I am, replicating this scene precisely. It's wicked and decadent, I realize, but occasionally sin is good for the soul.

Later in the evening, while the burrito works its way through my gut like a pig through an anaconda, I ponder whether I should explore downtown Bismarck. Fact: doing so requires getting behind the wheel of my car—anathema to a man whose butt is now congruous to the bucket seat of a Neon. A resounding *no* to that idea. Instead, I hole up in my room and read *Snow Falling on Cedars*, which carries my imagination to a far corner of the Pacific Northwest, just beyond the reach of my travels. It's a fine, engaging novel, with characters, Scandinavian fishermen and Japanese strawberry pickers, whose faces I see and feel as vividly as those of the men and women who have populated my world for the last month.

The novel is wistful and a little sad, which fills me with longing for familiar voices from the real world I left behind. It's too late to call Mom and Dad, and Julie generally gives out before nine o'clock at night. Garth, on the other hand, rarely goes to bed before the bewitching hour, ergo, figuring a two-hour difference in time zones, he might still be roaming the corridors of his residence hall. I ring his dorm phone, knowing full well that some sleepy-headed kid will answer. My son is most likely singing blues songs on the campus courtyard with a few of his buddies. "Eric here," a voice says.

"This is Garth Hallberg's dad. Is he up and around?"

"Yeah. I'll get him. Hold on," the kid says. I can hear the receiver twirling against the plaster wall.

"Dad! Hi," Garth says in a voice much deeper than mine.

"Hey there, you young whippersnapper. What's going on with you these days?"

"Same old same old, mostly. I'm reading 'Kaddish' by Ginsberg. Incredible poem. And I've made some cool friends, but this is a strange experience. Kind of a detour from my career ladder. What about you, Dad? Did you find the Grail or true and infinite wisdom?"

"Ran over Bugs Bunny in Montana. Now I'm in Bismarck—mostly for the scintillating nightlife. Hookers, tabletop dancers, bathtub champagne, chain-saw jugglers. What a town!"

"So you're just a few days from home. Bet you're glad," he says. "Don't quote me on this, but I've really missed you and Rachel."

"Well, I admit that I've been conceding myself thirty-foot putts lately just to hurry things along. That's a bad sign, isn't it? Guess I must smell the oats in the barn or something."

Garth agrees to meet Rachel and their grandmother in Winston-Salem on Saturday. From there, my offspring will drive back to our house and link up with Gillian. A few days later, we will be reunited, one and all. It feels good, making these plans, and my spirits are lifted all the way to the textured ceiling of this fine bargain-basement room.

When I wake up in the morning, I almost believe that I've merely dozed off for a few minutes after a late-night shower. "Good Morning America" is on TV—a total impossibility. But the proof of dawn glistens on the rain-soaked parking lot outside my room. Morning has broken in the Midwest, and I'm filled with energy that defies explanation. On pure impulse, for the second day in a row, I attire myself in running shorts and the other assorted accoutrements of a jogger. I snatch my room key from the bureau and hurl myself out the door, across the parking lot and onto the road that fronts the motel. There isn't much traffic at this early hour, so I jog toward a middle-class housing development at the crest of a shallow hill. Perhaps my spirits are soaring this morning, or maybe the contours of my route are more congenial this time around . . . Whatever the reason, the brick and Masonite houses swoop benignly past me, and the mailboxes look nothing like hives of malevolence. I actually enjoy this jaunt into an anachronistic world where, years ago, I lobbed rolled-up *Daily Sentinel Tribune*s onto the neighborhood lawns before racing to the golf course. Mr. Simmons salutes me from his front porch on State Street in Bowling Green. "Hiya, Mr. Simmons." The Ferringers' evil poodle nips at my ankles. "Beat it. Scram, ya little pecker!" It's a lovely wave of nostalgia that sweeps over me on this Sunday morning, and I want it to go on forever.

Of course, my stamina fails me, and I walk the last mile or so, but I accept the shortcoming with good cheer.

My eagerness to make tracks across North Dakota catapults me wet-haired into the cockpit of my Neon. Iris deserves a bag of oats and a sponge bath at the earliest opportunity. Except for an oil change in Palm Springs, she has been maintenance free. No coughs, no sputters, no weird comas that might strand her pilot in no-man's-land.

The countryside east of Bismarck is dotted with little water-tower villages—Grand Rapids, Montpelier, Napoleon, Hastings—Ohio names, Michigan names, everywhere names. I roll down the car windows and suck in the delirious grassy smell of the land; what does it matter if Kleenex and gum wrappers spin in the windy vortex? I'm sailing toward the rising sun, by God. And if this tumbling green landscape flows like a dream into corn and soybean counties, so much the better. I stop for a fuel-up in Eldridge—which, when winter comes, will surely disappear beneath all-encompassing snow. Now in midsummer, it is a charming cluster of white prairie houses and brick buildings and train stations and grain elevators. No golf courses that I can see. I imagine that the verdancy of the landscape makes golf less vital to the mental health of the local citizenry than to the townsfolk in Glendive, or

Colstrip, or Forsyth. For them, the golf course, however humble, is the hub of the universe.

Valley City is a simple town only one hour or so from the Minnesota border. There's got to be a government-issue golf course here where I can link up with another pagan. This is a very strange part of the American landscape, and it's an even stranger golf course I've conjured in the recesses of my brain. Something with rubber greens and Astroturf tee boxes maybe. Or a golf course where sheep crop the fairways, as in olden days. I want to golf with dwarfs or acromegalics or Afghani refugees with pseudonyms and fake beards. I nibble a McDonald's lemon poppyseed muffin while I case the town for selfish purposes. To the sound of tolling church bells, I roll like a heathen wanderer through Valley City's unassuming residential streets, hoping to spy any old golf course, where I can meet up with some locals for a waltz around the links. There's a distinct possibility that my game has atrophied from lack of practice. God knows what bad habits I may have developed in the gale-force winds of Oregon— an overly wide stance, for starters, and a truncated backswing contrived to maintain balance. I visualize my old ways, but the wind howls so strongly in my imagination that I can't quite succeed.

The small-town businesses, the IGA, the Valley City Ford dealership, the True Value hardware are clones of those found in Bowling Green, or Washington, North Carolina. I roll down my car window in front of the Lutheran Church, where a trio of parishioners are whacking each other on the back and laughing. "Excuse me," I say, "but I'm looking for three virgins to deflower." Or at least you would *think* that's what I've said, given the expression on their faces. In fact, I have merely inquired as to where a heathen can find a game of golf on this Lord's day. Maybe they're just bitter at having spent this beautiful morning pressed onto a hard pew beneath the resounding palaver of a soul-saving reverend. Finally, the heaviest amongst these three Christian men takes pity on me. "Get back on ninety-four and go back one exit and get off there. Go under the highway, and drive about half a mile south. You'll see the signs for Bjornson Park."

"Thanks very much," I say. "Have a scrumptious day."

Sure enough, a simple wooden sign leads me onto a side road that crawls beneath the interstate, then up a shallow hill. Soon thereafter, a larger sign: BJORNSON PARK MUNICIPAL GOLF COURSE. I take a gravel road that culminates in a large gravel parking lot next to the clubhouse, alongside which is a horse barn and a corral. After parking Iris, I fetch an apple and a limp carrot from my cooler. A sway-backed mare clops over to the fence separating her from me and hangs her shaggy head over the barbed wire. "Here you go," I say. She squeezes the apple between her Scrabble-tile teeth until juice drips onto the dirt at her feet. Then she takes the fruit into the cavern of her mouth by means of some clever manipulation of her black lips. Even while she devours the apple, she keeps her eye on the carrot. She eats that, too, when I give it over, and whinnies in such a way that I know she wants more. "Sorry, old girl," I tell her, and pat her velvet snout.

The clubhouse is one of those familiar cinder-block structures, functional but a bit sad. Although, or maybe *because*, it is Sunday, the parking lot is empty. It's probably a little bit harder to skip church in favor of the links in a town so small as this one. The clubhouse attendant is a young man in his twenties who looks the part of a golfer. "Beautiful day," I chirp. "Where is everybody?" There is the usual assortment of clubs and hats and shirts on display against the walls and on metal racks. There is a Coke machine and some round metal tables, and not much else by way of amenities. This is, after all, a public golf course and not a country club. The greens fee is only twelve dollars, plus two dollars for a pull-cart, which I happily pay to the young man.

"At around noon, *after* church lets out, you'll see a lot of cars in that parking lot. We have a very low divorce rate in this town."

I explain my mission to this fellow, and he tells me that if I hurry on up to the first tee I will catch up with Lynn and Joe. So I hustle up a goat path toward the elevated first tee where a middle-aged fellow and his son are taking practice swings. Out there beyond the tee is a beautiful green ridge with grazing cows and a scattering of photogenic willow trees. If those cows were sheep, and if the sky were suicide gray, this could be a pastoral from the Yorkshire countryside. It is a beautiful, moist morning, so calm that the lowing of the cattle carries across the valley. "Come on and join us," the father says before I gather the nerve to ask. He's much shorter than his son, and a bit bandy-legged, but all in all a very pleasant-looking chap. His son, a typical young galoot with a backward baseball hat, has obviously played a lot more golf than his dad, judging from the easy grace with which he wields his driver. "I'm Lynn, and this is my son Joe," he says. "Joe here's the golfer. I'm just a hacker . . . but I have fun."

I'm wondering what will happen if I tell Lynn and Joe that I intend to immortalize them. My instincts suggest that they will feel more at ease laboring in ignorance of my motives. On the other hand, it might be fun to witness the effects of such weird tidings. "I ought to warn you fellas I'm writing a cross-country golf book about people just like you. It'll be in every bookstore in America, so you better make a lot of birdies."

Lynn gives me a very funny look, then bursts out laughing. "Man, you're in for a big disappointment. I won't break sixty for nine holes."

"Actually, that's my fervent prayer," I say. "Of course, you will be disguised as Sicilian cabdrivers or male strippers if it gets *too* bad, so don't worry about embarrassing yourselves." If it were me in their shoes, I'd be nervous as a cat at the idea of being freeze-framed in my incompetence. I gather that Lynn is pretty nonplussed by the concept, but Joe's eyes tell me a different story. I know he wants to prove something to me.

"So, are you any good?" Joe asks. He's leaning on his golf club, watching me take my practice swings.

"I played the tour for a couple of years . . . before my lobotomy," I tell him. "Now I hit everything left of center."

"Oh," Joe says. His eyes go unparallel.

"Yeah, I won the Yerflize Open ten years ago," I tell him. "And the Chrysler Mixed Singles Invitational."

"Hey, Joe . . ." Lynn says. "I *think* he's pulling your leg."

"Oh, jeez," Joe says, and butts his noggin with the heel of his hand. "Your *fly*'s open. I get it."

I give Joe a friendly biff on the shoulder and tell him to hit away.

He sets up nicely over his ball, takes a few obligatory waggles, then swipes mightily at the ball, which rockets into a row of holly bushes way out at the turn of the dogleg. He hurriedly tees up another, then wallops a perfect clone of his first shot. "We'll find them. Maybe you got lucky," I say. He shakes his head, sits on the bench, and stares at the grass between his large white shoes.

Lynn takes a couple of brisk practice swings with a four wood, which he hoods to prevent a world-class slice. He finally takes a swipe at his ball, which sails far, far left of center, then bends ferociously back onto the fairway, short but playable. "A shrewd use of alien airspace," I tell him, and he laughs.

I'm totally relaxed when my turn comes. There's nothing to prove; I've made all the disclaimers that will excuse whatever might befall my Ultra DPS. When I hit the thing, it beelines obediently down the middle of the fairway, and I almost believe that my lifelong habit of choking on the first tee seems to have been broken this summer.

I feel very lucky to have bumped into such nice fellows as Lynn and Joe. I could very easily be flying solo this morning, a sad prospect when I consider how starved I am for companionship. Lynn's accent is pure midwestern, and very comforting to me. When I close my eyes, I can hear Uncle Jim or my dad or any number of Swedish ancestors who have entered and exited my life from time to time.

We three golfers probe the prickly branches of the holly bushes for Joe's errant drives. We circumnavigate them, we get on hands and knees to examine the dark domain beneath. We prowl the weedy perimeter on the off chance of a ricochet. No luck. "I'll just drop one," Joe says. Such sad words on the first hole of a round of golf.

He holds his arm out straight and drops the ball into the thick rough. Poor kid is staring down at a duck egg in a grassy nest. "Drop it again," I say. "That's an impossible lie." Lynn and I stand aside while Fate works her evil spell on Joe. He takes a couple of thrashing practice swings, then goes after his ball. His six-iron recovery shot is no recovery at all but a wicked shank that dives into the holly bushes once again. He looks skyward, rolls his eyes, snatches another ball from his bag, and drops it, hastily this time, in the shallow rough. I look at Lynn and shrug. We both sense the smell of a blown engine. The kid has thrown a rod on the first turn, and there's no pit crew to rescue him. "He's nervous," Lynn says.

"I know. He's trying too hard, isn't he?"

In deference to Joe and his place in golfing history, much of the ensuing mischief shall go unreported. Translated from the original Celtic, "bogey" means "between the devil and the deep blue sea." Not surprisingly, Lynn and I share the misty flats of mediocrity on the first hole; Joe has tumbled headfirst into the pit of despair. I promise to put a Groucho nose and mustache on him when it comes time to write about our adventures on the hilly links of North Dakota.

An anonymous young man, cleverly disguised as Groucho, scuffs down the path toward number two. "Joe's really a very good golfer," Lynn says. "What'd you shoot here last week, seventy-seven?"

"Seventy-*six*," Joe says, kicking pebbles.

"I couldn't play worth a crap if I knew that some oaf was going to take notes on my golf swing," I tell him. "Keep in mind that I have poetic license. I can make you into a prom queen if I want to. I can give you a birdie on the first hole. Think I will."

"That's okay," he says. "Don't worry about it."

My drive on the second hole is a high fade that climbs partway up a grassy slope paralleling the fairway. I make a goat noise and pick up my tee. "Na-aaa-aaa."

Lynn's slice carries his ball into the thatch with yours truly, which leaves a nice open fairway for Joe. I will tell you only this about Joe's drive: I have *no comment*.

Black, steaming oil drizzles down his thighs. Acrid smoke pours from both ears. "Joe, you're experiencing a severe case of humanity. Suffering makes you lovable, right, Lynn? Chicks dig a man who goofs up once in a while." Joe gives me a cockeyed smile.

There's a slight holdup at number three on account of a foursome, two of whom are deep in the woods. We three sit on a green wooden bench with morning sunshine pouring down on us. I tell Joe about the time I made a fourteen on the second hole in a qualifier for the Ohio Junior Amateur in Toledo. My tee shot had skittered under a Christmas tree, and my horizontal swipe at the ball yielded only pinecones and brown needles. Six swings later, the ball finally emerged from its hiding place. I finished the hole with tears of frustration and rage rolling down my cheeks. "I *knew* my dad would be ashamed if I walked off the course, Joe, so I kept playing. But I *wanted* to quit, believe me. I shot one hundred and ten that day and failed to qualify. Some days things just don't work right."

"If I'm going to be in a golf book, I'd at *least* like to play decent," Joe says.

"Well, I'm counting on some hot damn golf from here on out. Dig?"

Lynn is the service manager at Valley City Ford, and Joe is on summer vacation from the University of South Dakota. "How often do you get to play together?" I ask Lynn.

"I'm so damned busy . . ." he says, running his hand through his gray hair. "Not as often as I'd like. I'm going to start playing more often, though. I enjoy it. Joe here plays just about every day."

After the third hole, Joe's misery is compounded by a very bad case of the shanks. The worst place to cure this disease is on the golf course in the middle of a round with a stranger whose good opinion you would like to earn. The physical symptoms of the shanks (anger, fear, flop-sweat, self-loathing) only compound the problem. I here confess that I'm a reformed shanker. My golfing past is strewn with scarred two-by-fours and bricks and strips of inner tube and Jerry Barber shankless golf clubs—all the devices that might train the mind away from this dreadful habit.

I want to tell Joe, "Relax. Think green thoughts. Loosen up." But there is no hope for a golfer with the shanks.

"This is a beautiful little course," I say. "There's so much to work with . . . the river, the ponds, the hills and trees. The architect did a nice job with the layout." Any course designer worth his turf would kill for terrain like this. At number six is a perfect cattail pond, teaming with slippery green frogs that leap in a mad panic into the water when I approach the bank. Somewhere beneath the surface of that pond is my own shanked approach shot. I have been infected with Joe's disease. I know the cure, however, and I'm not worried.

"Sorry," Joe says.

"Hey, we're mortals, right?" I say.

Lynn smiles at me. He probably suspects that I've purposely shanked my ball into the drink to palliate his son's suffering. I regret having announced my purposes here. Except for my presence, Lynn and Joe would be enjoying a rare father and son morning. Joe would be just a few over par, and Lynn would derive vicarious pleasure in his son's talent. I've undone the delicate armature of their time together, and for that I'm sorry. Joe is a very nice kid with an admirable sense of pride, dented by poor play. It happens. It's happened to me again and again, even on this adventure of mine. On number seven, I see them over there in the trees looking for Joe's shanked approach shot. Lynn puts his arm around his son's shoulders for a moment, then pats him on the back. The beak of Joe's hat moves up and down. Maybe I'm just a crazy sentimental fool, but for a minute or two my jaws ache with emotion and I can hardly take in a breath of the delicious morning air.

In the wake of my humiliation on that Friday morning in Toledo, after my triple-digit round of golf, I heard my dad telling his neighbor Ernie how proud he was of me for hanging in there when I could easily have quit. My dad wasn't always the greatest when it came to expressing his feelings about me or my sisters. We knew, though, albeit secondhand, how he felt. Hearing him utter those words, "I was damned proud of him," was almost, *almost* worth the abject humiliation I suffered as I knelt, grass-stained and dirt-splattered, next to that diabolical spruce tree at Sunningdale Country Club decades ago.

Nothing remarkable occurs on the last few holes. Joe's shanking problem persists. Lynn makes his bogeys and double bogeys. For pure comic relief, I take three shots to get out of a deep bunker at number eight. A cloud of windblown sand billows back over me. Half a cup of sand finds its way down my shirt collar. Granules creep into my underwear. "That was some fun," I say, brushing myself off.

We're walking up the last fairway of the day. Joe has nailed a massive drive straight down the middle. Joe's dad and I have managed decent drives, but nothing for the record books. Lynn leaves his approach shot well short of the green, and my own seven iron settles on the fringe on the wrong side of the flag. "Let's see a par, Joe," I say.

"You got it," he says. He pulls out a wedge and drops his golf bag onto the grass. He takes a few practice swings that look promising, then settles into a slightly open stance over his Titleist. I can see his grip tightening. The little muscle at the corner of his jaw bulges with determination. *Don't wait too long*, I say to myself.

Joe takes the club steeply back and hurls it down and into the ball, which exits stage right and dives suddenly into a loop of the Sheyenne River. He slams his club into the moist turf and shakes his head. He looks at his dad, then at me.

"Oops," I say, and give him a sort of hayseed bucktooth cartoon grin, just enough to open a floodgate at the back of his brain. Joe begins to laugh, tentatively, almost wistfully at first. "I *suck*," he says. "I just *suck*." Then he's a goner. His hilarity is grandiose, voluminous. It sweeps me up and Lynn, too, until we're buckling with hysterics. Imagine three golfing fools huddled mid-fairway somewhere in North Dakota, hooting, guffawing, choking, roaring with laughter. Leaves rattle in the trees, the river reverses course, and two million crows flap in wild feathery frenzy in the azure sky. If this were Colstrip, Montana, our laughter would echo forever in the canyon.

We mercifully end our suffering on the ninth hole, park the flagstick in its socket, and walk wordlessly across the footbridge toward the clubhouse. Joe is smiling; he has survived his ordeal and even transcended it. Lynn loves his son all the more for his noble suffering. And I, by the pure vicariousness of the experience, love my own dad in a new way that I can't even hope to describe.

In the parking lot we shake hands and trade addresses. I pose father and son next to the putting green. "Put your arm around your boy," I tell Lynn. "Pretend you love him." I click the shutter and capture them forever in their pose.

The noonday sun floats above us, and the cows have relocated to a shady side of the distant hill. "Well . . . that was a lot of fun," I say, "but I'm aiming for Wisconsin, so I'd better hit the road. Lots of miles to cover."

"Godspeed," Lynn says.

"Yeah, good luck," says Joe.

"You'll be hearing from me before too long," I tell them.

"Looking forward to it," Lynn says.

I shake their hands and carry my clubs over to where Iris is parked near the horse barn. After depositing my clubs in the trunk and changing into loafers, I give the horse one more carrot, then climb behind the wheel of my car for the next leg of the journey.

the north woods

Ever since Cypress Point, my passion for golf has dwindled into a Platonic funk, in which each shot is only itself, without heat or urgency, overtone or consequence. If my putt hangs on the lip, well, *c'est la vie*. There's an explanation for this, I guess, which has something to do with yearning for the unattainable ideal so nearly realized on those seaside links courses where every shot was part of a contest, with all the green gods of golf huddled in opposition. But now that the Pacific Ocean is fifteen hundred miles behind me, the gods lounge in their heavens, eating chips and playing poker like fat winter duffers from the snowbelt.

Not that I haven't enjoyed my hours on the humble prairie courses . . . the camaraderie, the plainspoken topography; I *have*, but always in a vicarious way that doesn't quite give me the fix I need. The emotional hold of those magical seaside links *will* probably fade over time, and I'll once again appreciate the here and now of all the familiar courses laid out before me. But at the moment, closing in on Wisconsin, I'm a jaded fellow, to be sure.

During my sophomore year of college in Ohio, I fell madly in love with Turi, a Wisconsin girl, whose very name caused my heart to fibrillate. Together, we rode a Honda scooter up and down country lanes, frequented the abandoned nighttime fairways of the local golf course, drank cheap wine on the bluffs behind campus, danced in the dusky basements of fraternity houses, embraced beneath the porch lamp of her dormitory (our breath vaporizing in the cold January night), and argued sometimes over matters of no consequence. She wore a red scarf around her neck in those days, and ate her pizza with a fork, and hummed in my ear as we tooled around campus on that gray motor scooter. Exactly when and how we broke up, I can no longer recall. I suppose we just wandered apart over a minor misunderstanding one summer because in September, when the autumn winds blew leaves across the campus sidewalks, our candle flickered and died. Still, for years following the breakup, nobody else would do but Turi, who by then had found a new fellow and a job in Chicago and a maturity I never quite achieved.

Last May, in the midst of writing a novel, I needed a few tidbits of information regarding the landmarks of northern Wisconsin. So, on pure whim, I phoned directory assistance in Wausau to see if Turi still lived there, figuring, what the hey, she might just be able to help me out with the info. If there was an ulterior motive to this gambit, I wasn't conceding it to myself. She wasn't in the Wausau directory, but her parents *were*, so I rang them up and extracted Turi's number from her mom. For days afterward, I felt foolish and impulsive. More than once I picked up the receiver, punched all the right buttons, then hung up before the phone had a chance to ring in Wisconsin. It was all very adolescent, I thought, this silly game I was playing with myself. When, a few days later, the phone finally rang in Minocqua and I heard her heart-stopping voice at the other end of the line, I had no choice but to tell her that it was Bill Hallberg.

"My God," she said. *"Bill Hallberg!"*

Minneapolis is the crossroads where I must decide on a route home. I can accept an abstract but sincere invite to visit Turi and her husband, Jim, way up in Minocqua (impractical but tempting), or I can angle down toward Chicago, which sits on the hypotenuse to Bowling Green. *If* I spend a day or two in the north woods of Wisconsin, I would be almost morally obligated to cut across the Upper Peninsula of Michigan to Traverse City, my old stomping grounds at the top of the mitt, where I could try one last time to wangle a round on Frankfort's Crystal Downs, the forbidden treasure of American golf. Like Cypress Point and Augusta, it's an Alister Mackenzie masterpiece tucked into the windy reaches along Lake Michigan.

Suddenly, my golf hormones are percolating again. Of all the places in America for a magnificent golf course, there is none finer than the grassy lakeside dunes—excepting, of course, the Monterey Peninsula.

William Hallberg has flipped a coin in his brain, and it has come up heads. He will drop in on Turi and Jim for a day or two, then hightail it across the U.P. to the Mackinac Bridge, which separates Lake Superior from Lake Michigan. From there it's a beautiful, easy drive on down to Traverse City in the state of my birth.

Of course, there's no way I can make Minocqua before nightfall, so I set my sights on Rice Lake, only because it's in bold print on my map of Wisconsin—and I know I can get there before nightfall. Besides, there is no Motel 6 until Rhinelander, and I don't fancy barreling through deer habitat at night with dark angels howling in my ear. So, Rice Lake it is.

One hour beyond St. Paul, just inside the Wisconsin border, I exit the freeway at Baldwin, the start of a sidetrack through quaint Germanic towns, each with its own lake and yodeling club.

This is the first significant change in landscape since the linksland of North Dakota. There's an intimacy here that one can only find in the north woods. The pastures are now small pockets of exquisite green rather than endless acres of grazing land. The black-and-white cows are more inclined to find their own individual turf here—less of the herd mentality, maybe on account of the boundless, luxurious grass that covers their stockaded habitats. But these little farms are an isolated phenomenon, really. Mostly, I'm driving through hardwood forest of oak and maple, and birch, whose white trunks stand out like skeletons against the darker columns phalanxed alongside a two-lane road that bends around lakes and through the lowlands flanked by round, forested hills.

Rice Lake is a handsome resort town, big enough to have a Wal-Mart and the usual fast-food joints, none of which will get my business. My stomach no longer recognizes hamburgers as food or tacos or waffles or anything fried in batter. Lettuce it can comprehend, and black beans and yogurt and stout-hearted breads—not to mention beer. And Wisconsin is the beer capital of the universe. *Bitte, ein Bier, danke. Ja, gut Bier. Ach, du lieber!* After I find a place to rest my road-weary bones for the night, I will scope out the local *Brauerie* scene. If no local beer maker is to be found, I will haunt yon Super Valu for Augsburger or Point or any beer brewed within one hundred miles of this tourist town.

I am not a drunkard. I am, in fact, a very careful drinker of beer. For the most part. Usually. But tonight, my desire is to find a lakeside bench within staggering distance of my motel, where I can watch the sun go down whilst I quaff many bottles of hoppy amber fluid until my soul quivers in delight. But first I must nourish myself with the broiled flesh of indigenous fishes, preferably something from the trout family. Rainbow, brown, brook . . . any of that trio will suffice. Fish, corn bread, a healthy salad, and a mug or two of hearty ale.

All right, another confession is in order: my obsession with beer results from nervousness at the prospect of seeing Turi; after all, we have lived our lives once over since we saw each other for the last time . . . was it on the steps of the library? Or at the counter in Tuffy's Café? On the slant walk? Why can't I remember? I'm sure we've preserved in amber the images we have of one another, and I'm not totally sure I want to replace mine of her just yet.

I pay for a night in an AmericInn and carry my suitcase and clubs down to my room, which is nicely appointed and comfortable.

The TV picks up forty-seven channels, and the towels are as thick as Berber carpet. After a stinging shower, I dress in my last clean clothes and throw everything else into a pillowcase. My grandiose plans for the evening have shifted into a much lower gear. Instead of eating rainbow trout in a knotty-pine restaurant (followed, of course, by the hypothetical drinking of beer on the shore of Rice Lake), I sip Coke in the steamy motel laundry room to the sound of clothes sloshing in the jumbo Maytag. It occurs to me that I ought to call Turi's number in Minocqua, just to let her know I'm in the vicinity, so I use the pay phone bolted to the wall next to the detergent vending machine. It's almost a relief when Jim picks up. "This is Bill Hallberg," I say. "How are you, Jim?"

"Hey, *Bill*. You're still alive. Where are you calling from?" I tell

him that I'm reading a *Seventeen* magazine in the coin-op laun-
dromat in the AmericInn motel, that I'm in Rice Lake, just a few
hours away.

"Now why on earth didn't you drive on up to Minocqua? We've
got a guest house with your name on it. No need to stay in a motel."

I could explain that I've got a bad case of night terror, that I'm
haunted by shades of evil, that the dark Wisconsin back road is the
tunnel to purgatory. "Gosh, that's a kind offer, Jim," I tell him, "but
I just couldn't have driven another mile. So I stopped here."

"Turi won't be back until the wee hours of Tuesday morning. But
we want you to stay with us for as long as you can. We won't take no
for an answer. Turi's dying to see you."

"You *sure*?" I ask. "That's a pretty big imposition."

He gives me some simple directions to his tool-rental business,
and I jot them down on the back of a paper plate. We may, he says,
have time for a quick round of golf in the afternoon, if Jim can get
away from his shop for a few hours. But lunch, at least.

When my clothes are acceptably dry, I roll them up and stuff
them back into the pillowcase, which I carry like Santa Claus back
to the room. There I ditch the whole mess and leave the motel.

The Super Valu has a nice selection of indigenous brews, so I
pick up a six-pack of Augsburger lager, a bagel, a packet of
Philadelphia cream cheese, and a can of Off, then hike to the lake-
front with my purchases. The sky is now black, but the light from
cottage windows winks a million times over on the surface of the
water. It's a fine romantic image, especially for a pensive man sitting
cross-legged on the pestiferous sand with a twelve-ounce bottle of
beer and a cheese-slathered bagel. I'm wondering how Jim really
feels, knowing that an echo from Turi's past has rebounded off a distant wall and returned years later, altered by time and travel, but
mostly intact. He must be a good man, this Jim, to accept my arrival
with such grace. He would feel easy if he knew how pleased I am
that she is happy and well and fulfilled in her life with him. It's an
almost noble thought, but the pesky, undaunted mosquitoes soon
chase me from the empty public beach and onto the sidewalk
leading back to the motel.

* * *

"Hello, love," I say to Gillian when she answers the phone down there in North Carolina. "I'm on the homestretch. Wisconsin, to be exact. It's *so* Teutonic here."

"Hurry back," she says. "I miss you. The dogs miss you, too." There is the faint sound of a whimpering wirehaired dachshund in the background.

"How was your trip across the Great Plains? Worthwhile, I hope."

"Sort of a pleasant change of pace, actually. Not very dramatic, but, hmmm . . . solidly American. How's that?"

"Isn't that the whole idea?"

"Guess so," I say. Two sumos are knocking bellies on the television screen. "Any news from Bowling Green or Virginia Beach?"

"Well . . ." Gillian says. I can hear her taking in a deep breath. "Sue called this afternoon. Your mother isn't doing very well at all. She's not eating, and the doctors think she's had a series of small strokes, which accounts for her confusion. Sorry, sweetheart. Not what you wanted to hear, is it? I haven't heard from Julie in days, though . . . but no news is good news, right?"

"Sure . . ." I say, and fire a pair of rolled-up socks at the two porky Japanese grapplers. "I guess that's right." The rest of our conversation will go unreported, as it delves into physical mysteries and base human impulses best left to the imagination. I confess that *my* end of the discussion has less heat than it should because my heart is divided by troublesome circumstances. "See you in four or five days," I tell Gillian. "I love you."

"Love you, too," she says.

What in the hell am I doing? It's a question that roars in the corridors of my brain. My mind can't couple the swarming homefront realities with the concept of hitting a dimpled sphere toward a pin planted onto a circle of mowed grass. Would I, after all these years, see fit to insinuate myself into the well-joined world of an ex-girlfriend who probably hasn't given me a thought since graduation day at Miami of Ohio? There's a good one for you.

The six o'clock wake-up call jolts me out of a sound sleep, but I know I'll never return to my dream, which finds me stroking a golf ball down a country road, one shot followed by another. In the dream, I'm hitting the ball out of corn-stubble fields, and weedy banks of roadside ditches, and dirt driveways of farmhouses. I only know that with a nine iron I must scrape the ball from a rural town to a far-distant city where I will be judged. The strokes afforded me are limited, and the consequences for failure are dire. It's a foolish dream, and a bit too conspicuously symbolic for my taste, so I rub the sleep from my eyes and pad into the bathroom, where I peel out of my sweatpants and T-shirt. I shampoo my hair with the little packet provided free by the motel, and I lather up using the free bar of Dove. There are probably rules prohibiting the sorts of liberties I take with the hot water supply, but I indulge myself anyway for twenty minutes beneath the steaming spray.

The drive from Rice Lake to Minocqua takes me through hardwood wilderness punctuated by small lakes (ponds, really) and smooth-running green rivers with seven-syllable names. Those few towns along the way are nothing more than log-cabin saloons with gas pumps out front. There might be a little clapboard house flanking this rustic watering hole, a superette, or a bait shop (NIGHT CRAWLERS AND WIGGLERS BY THE CARTON!), or a snowmobile/chain-saw/outboard-motor dealer, but usually nothing more than that. Deer graze amongst the roadside ferns, and fearless buzzards eat the meat from the inevitable roadkill. These birds yield no ground to passing cars; thus, they, too, provide carrion for other single-minded buzzards.

The first and only sizable town on State Route 70 is Minocqua itself, which seems to have all the amenities of a resort. Finding Lakeside Rental requires only that I pass through one traffic light and turn left into the designated parking lot. I imagine myself as Jim, welcoming my wife's ex-boyfriend with open arms, a dagger or a poisoned quill secreted up my sleeve. However, when I walk through the open doorway into the shop, Jim, who is at the customer counter joshing with his employees, recognizes me immediately and reaches across to shake my hand. "Hey, Bill. Great to see you. I've heard so much about you, and, of course, I know you from reading your book."

"I've heard wonderful things about you from Turi, Jim. How ya doing?"

"You didn't come here to steal her away, did you?" he asks.

I laugh, *ha, ha, ha*. But a cartoon image flashes on a screen at the back of my brain: a goggled, leather-hatted Hallberg leans over the handlebars of his Harley with Turi's arms wrapped tightly around him. They are roaring toward Baja to begin their new life together.

We sit on barrel stools in a corner of the store while customers fondle giant chain cutters and jackhammers and rototillers. Jim is a nice-looking fellow with a big shock of gray hair and blue eyes. He's not as tall as I'd imagined him, nor is he the lean athletic demigod my mind's eye had conjured. Instead, he's a pleasant, straightforward middle-ager with some girth and an easy laugh he's able to sustain even while sipping coffee.

"Well, here's the plan," he says, finally. "You follow me out to the house, and get yourself settled in. Then, when you're ready, you come on back to the shop and we'll grab some lunch. By then I'll know whether I can sneak away for golf. Sure would be nice if I could . . . damn it."

I get behind the wheel of my car, and Jim climbs into a red pickup, which I follow across the highway and down a side road lined with cottages fashioned of skinned oak logs and indigenous stone. We meander over one-lane bridges and past a man-made dam that traverses a channel connecting two small lakes. Soon thereafter, it's up a gravel driveway to a beautiful Germanic lake-side cabin trimmed in green and dark red. So . . . this is where Turi has been nestled these past decades; life *does* go on beyond our ken. All those years of her waking up every morning to a shimmering lake and a nice husband and a couple of kids. Hard to conceive of, but there's the evidence. The picture window, beneath which is a large boat port, overlooks Lake Minocqua, a sand-bottomed sprawl of green water. I'm escorted to a small cabin detached from the main residence. "You can have the run of this place," Jim says. There are golf trophies on the shelves and golf memorabilia and photographs of Jim and his son from a prior marriage grinning broadly in front of a putting green. The decor is absolutely right for a cabin in the north woods. Wool blankets folded nicely on the Adirondack trunk. Heavy, unpretentious furniture. A very far cry from the sameness of the Motel 6 regimen. "Just make yourself comfortable, and when you're ready, come on back and get me. Okay?"

"I can't thank you enough. This is a wonderful place."

"You should have seen it before Libby and Jamie cleaned it up. Those kids can really make a mess. Come on over to the house and I'll introduce you to them."

Libby is making a grilled cheese sandwich in the pine-paneled kitchen, and Jamie is lying on a braided rug in the living room, cutting the pages of a magazine into slivers with scissors. "Kids, this is Mr. Hallberg. He went to college with your mom, and he's an old friend. He'll be staying in the bunkhouse."

I shake hands with them and give them a big fatherly smile. "So you're the chef, eh?" I ask Libby.

"Yes, sir," she says, and flips over a charred rectangle in the iron skillet.

Jim walks me back to my quarters, then hops into his truck. "See you whenever . . ." he says through the rolled-down window.

I bring some things in from my car and plant them in a corner, then change into khakis and a black golf shirt, just in case. I can't help picking up a framed childhood picture of Turi, skinny-legged and big-toothed. But unmistakably herself even then. It's odd, but I feel incredibly happy after having met Jim. Turi's life here is nearly perfect, and her husband, under other circumstances, would surely be a great friend of mine. He's a comfortable soul, and rock solid. I imagine him dealing cards at the Moose Lodge or piloting the motorboat with his kids water-skiing between the green wakes. I see Turi alongside him, her red scarf tied beneath her chin. Good for them.

I walk past the main house to the dock and sit there on the gray planks for a while, taking in this world of boats and cottages and nautical flags that ripple atop flagpoles planted in the middle of lakeside lawns. A coot surfaces near a swimmers' raft, then dives beneath the surface again. It's all so far removed from the sort of chaos that looms in my near future. I can't help feeling slightly envious of the tranquillity of this place, the utter smoothness of the lake, the blue, trouble-free sky.

* * *

An hour later, Jim is saying a quick good-bye to his desk crew and walking with me to the parking lot, where all the rental trucks are lined up and ready to go. His business schedule prohibits his joining me for golf, but he's set me up with a tee time at the Trout Lake Golf and Country Club in Woodruff, twenty miles north of Minocqua. "Better take two vehicles over to Tula's," he says. "That way you can take off right from the restaurant without having to come back here." I can tell I've caught him on a busy day in the busiest season of the year. He couldn't be friendlier, but he walks quickly to his pickup and drives at a fast clip back down Route 70 to the strip mall where Tula's Café is located. After parking next to each other in front of Trig's Grocery, we push through a glass door into the restaurant, a typical strip-mall luncheonette with booths and counter stools and busy uniformed waitresses. We sit opposite one another in a booth and toy with our menus. "You hungry?" he asks.

"As a horse," I say.

We settle quickly on our orders and replace the menus between the sugar dispenser and the wall. "So, how long have you been on the road, Bill?" he asks.

"Seems like a year. I can't keep track of everything I've seen because there's just so damned much of it. When you travel, you usually go to one place. You know, the Bahamas or Grand Canyon. I've taken in the whole country in one gulp."

"Ready to get back home, I'll bet," he says, and I nod.

There isn't much time for transition; I just come right out and ask him how he met Turi. It's not such a complicated story. He was newly divorced and living in the same D.C. apartment complex as Turi. They started going out together, fell in love, and got married. Simple as that. I expected something slightly more flamboyant. Turi thrashing in the icy Potomac and Jim diving in to save her. Jim choking on a cube of prime rib and Turi executing a perfect Heimlich maneuver. Turi, as I think on it, was always an up-front and honest person, so I should have expected an uncomplicated romance. During our college fling, I was swept away by my idealism. While I was handcuffed to the door handle of the ROTC building, she was studying for her exams in the library. Maybe *that's* why our relationship ended.

"You know I was crazy about your wife back then," I say.

"Who could blame you?" he says. "She's a special person."

"She *is*, Jim. You're a lucky fellow. You've got beautiful kids, and a wonderful house, and, of course, Turi."

I tell him all about Rachel and Garth, about my life in North Carolina, my mutts, my twenty-five-year-old girlfriend. I find myself competing to prove that my life is just as happy and fulfilling as his. I avoid mention of the more troubling elements of my recent autobiography, as if I'm ashamed of them. Then I'm ashamed of being ashamed of things beyond my control. "Garth's much smarter than I am," I tell Jim. "I've been losing arguments with him since he was three. And Rachel is so darned beautiful that I can't deny her anything."

"Turi showed me pictures of your kids," Jim says. "Rachel's a showstopper."

We're halfway through our sandwiches before the subject finally gets around to golf. "I'm a complete hacker," Jim says. "I'm working so hard these days that there's not much chance to play. But I'm flying out to California in the winter to play golf with some old buddies. I'll see my son Justin out there and maybe play a round or two with him. Now *he's* the golf nut in the family."

"Sorry you can't join me this afternoon."

"Me, too," he says. "You know, it's hard to separate you from your protagonist in *The Rub of the Green*. I'd be nervous as hell playing golf with that guy."

"Well, I'm not nearly the golfer he was. He was wishful thinking on my part."

"I'll bet you're a scratch golfer."

"Well, I understand the game better than I understand myself. So I'm constantly thinking my way into mediocrity. It's been ever thus, I'm afraid."

"I don't believe you," he says.

After lunch, Jim and I head in separate directions—he to his shop and I toward Trout Lake Golf and Country Club. "I'll bring back some beer. I expect you to help me drink it," I say.

"We should be getting home at about the same time," he says. "We'll have a beer or two, then dinner at Bosacki's on the lake. You'll like it."

It's a short drive to Trout Lake. Just an easy poke past clusters of Kozy Kabins and lodges and stores selling rustic furniture and boat shops. I pass through little villages like Woodruff and Arbor Vitae before the woods take over again. Here is where I'm to begin looking for the sign to Trout Lake Golf and Country Club. Finally, a blue billboard directs me up a gravel road into the deep woods.

The golf course clubhouse is a very large chestnut-colored log cabin with a glassed-in porch overlooking the first tee and the eighteenth green. This course has been around since the Depression and has only recently been refurbished by some wealthy investors.

I leave Iris to graze on the yellow grass at the edge of the parking lot and enter the clubhouse through a screen door. Inside, men and women are sitting at round tables, drinking beer and playing cards. The television, tuned to CNN, goes unwatched by the beer-drinking crowd. Just beyond this hub of activity is the pro shop, which is nothing more than a split-log counter with glass shelves beneath. A young woman wearing a visor greets me from behind the register. "You've got a tee time?" she asks.

I tell her that Jim has phoned in on my behalf, so she looks up and down the ledger for my name. "You're the author," she says, and shakes my hand. "Thought so. You look like an author. It's the wire-rimmed glasses, maybe. Anyway," she says, "there are three groups ahead of you. Why don't you have a beer and relax for half an hour. Or use the putting green if you like."

"I'll just putt around for a while," I say. "How much do I owe you?"

She waves her hands as if she's parting an invisible curtain. Then she wiggles her fingers at me. "Skedaddle," she says. "Our treat. Enjoy."

"That's awfully nice," I tell her. "Thanks." I give her my best authorial smile, then retrace my steps past the lounge. I like the atmospherics of the place. Even the cigarette smoke seems appropriate to the scene, in which everybody is laughing and coughing and having a hell of a good time.

Today I want to play by myself. I need to think about the game and what it means to me before I lose meaningful contact with it. Furthermore, if by some miracle I can figure a way to play golf at Crystal Downs, I want to be at my best. That course, whose rolling fairways I trespassed as a little kid, deserves the best I have to offer. Trouble is, I can't quite tell where my game is right now.

A young couple with JUST MARRIED written all over their faces, is waiting on the first tee when I arrive. "You go ahead and hit," the fellow says. "We'd hold you up."

"Thanks," I say, and without so much as a warm-up swing, I knock my tee shot over the weedy river and into the left rough, well on toward the green. "Good luck," I say, and shoulder my golf bag.

I don't mind having hit a mediocre shot off the tee. The point is, I'm out here on a beautiful day with all the opportunity in the world to work through the problems that have plagued me of late.

Trout Lake is probably the greenest course I've ever played, due perhaps to the heavy rains that have fallen nearly every day this summer. The fairways are very heavy and the fescue roughs are extremely lush. My Ultra, only a few feet wide of the fairway, is barely visible in the tall grass.

The salvation of the planet depends on my success. It's the game I used to play as a kid. If I didn't make par on this hole or that hole, Toledo would explode and all the animals in the zoo would die. A birdie on the par five meant that Dad would win a million dollars and buy a ranch in Idaho. Here and now, I vow that I will deliver Mom and Julie and Dad—and even Rachel—from their torment by shooting seventy-eight or less from the championship tees. No mean feat on such heavy fairways on a strange course after what amounts to a weeklong layoff.

I have 135 yards to the flagstick from my patch of spinach. The smart play is to take a more lofted club than the distance would suggest, tighten the grip a tad, move the ball a few inches toward the back foot, and come down at a slightly steeper angle, making sure to contact the ball before the blade cuts into the turf. My thrashing practice swings pitch long blades of grass over my left shoulder. Finally, I settle over the ball, relax my shoulders, and take a good sturdy swing. The ball leaps from its nest and flies up toward the green, just short of the bunkers guarding the front side. A good shot, all things considered. From that position I have three options: a cut wedge, a pitch-and-run up the slope, or a putt. I'm out of practice, but I'm determined to use the shot that best suits the circumstances. The greens are nearly as soft as the fairways and should hold the ball quite well, so I pull my Hogan copper wedge from the bag. This is my backyard shot. The delicate wedge shot over the tomato garden, onto the lawn in front of the birdbath, and tight to the plastic batting helmet. Lawn golf. This time, though, the sharp blade sinks into the soggy turf, and the ball barely makes it onto the front edge of the green, thirty feet short of the pin. The putt is uphill and straight as a laser, but the health and well-being of my family depends on my success. So I line it up from every angle, newlyweds be damned, and detect a very slight break dictated only by the influence of the grain. However, when I stroke the putt, it drifts right of the hole. A tap-in bogey. "Aw, crap," I say. "Crap!"

On the second hole, my drive fades into a well-placed fairway bunker, where it buries in the face, only a foot below the lip. This poses a bit of a problem for a man who does not pack a shovel in his golf bag. The best I can do is dig in with my feet, open the blade, and swing through the sand with all my might. Which I do, but the ball catches the overhang and rolls into the wet basin at the center of the trap. I'm lying three already, and newlyweds are watching me suffer. The lie this time is clean, allowing me to hit a conventional wedge shot out of the bunker and onto the fairway, one hundred yards shy of the dance floor. I'm hiking up the green runway toward my ball when I realize that my lip is bleeding. Not since I was a kid have I had this problem, born of intense concentration. Taking a mathematics test, gluing the wings on a model airplane, playing golf . . . anything requiring concentration would cause me to bite so hard on my lower lip that I would injure myself. Now, thirty-some years later, I've lapsed into childhood, all on account of a buried lie in a fairway bunker on the second hole on a resort course in the bowels of the north woods of Wisconsin. I wipe off the blood with my towel and take three or four deep breaths to relieve the tension. I'm taking this game way too seriously, although I admit that it's reassuring actually to suffer again after a week of relative apathy. I accept my double bogey and move on to the third hole.

I stick a seven-wood tee shot tight to the pin on number three, which, for the moment, stops the figurative if not the actual, bleeding. But something passing strange occurs on the fourth hole, when I assert the age-old right ascribed by King James to all male golfers. What can be the problem, then? After all, it's a nicely secluded hole framed by dense forest. Growing in the dark shadows beneath the trees are mushrooms, which makes a fine target for a man answering the call of nature. Suddenly, out of nowhere, a problem. A very *big* problem. They appear like ghosts, two teenage girls and a little boy, the latter carrying a mesh sack half filled with golf balls.

"Dear God!" I shout. There's a good deal of activity thereafter. Shrieking, followed by the metallic sound of clenching zipper teeth, the rustle of underbrush, the pounding of size-ten golf shoes aiming toward daylight.

I slash a very hasty five iron down the fairway and jog after it, my clubs clicking noisily with each footfall.

Strange things happen to the competitive instinct on the heels of such occurrences. Which is to say that it shrivels into a little cocoon, that blows away at the first gust of wind. I play the next few holes numbly in the freshening wind, under a gray foreboding sky.

I'm standing at the eighth tee, within four hundred yards of a hot dog stand, when the first rumbles of thunder roll across the golf course. I hit my drive quickly and walk after it, keeping one eye on the ever-blackening clouds overhead. Then it happens. A huge streak of lightning creases the horizon, followed by an earth-shattering explosion that climbs through my skeleton and ricochets inside my skull. I am cartless and alone on the eighth fairway when the first big drops of rain tumble from the sky like liquid marbles. From behind me I hear someone shouting. It's the handsome Tab Hunter and his beautiful bride. "Climb on!" he says. I dash back to the electric cart and squeeze in next to his beloved, who, even in this mad, drenching frenzy, smells wickedly of sin. Her bare legs are stippled with goose bumps, and her white halter top is soaked through. "Son of a *bitch*! Can you *believe this*?" the fellow says. "Hells-a-poppin'."

"You said it," I shout above the pelting of raindrops on the fiberglass roof of the cart.

My new best friend in the whole wide world tilts through the fairways, ignoring NO CARTS placards posted near the greens. Electric carts are bottlenecked at the bridge over the stream at number one, but when our turn comes, we sail across and under the metal awning where the carts are stabled.

"Now *that's* a rainstorm," he says. Then to his wife, "You okay, honey?"

"I'm soaked is all," she says.

I tell them, "Thanks a million for the rescue," flip open my umbrella, and walk through the downpour to my car. I toss my dripping golf bag into the trunk, slam it, unlock my door, and climb inside. Only then do I collapse the umbrella with which I've been fending off the downpour.

It makes sense to cut my losses. The police are probably waiting in the clubhouse to arrest me for indecent exposure ("But officer, I was just answering the call of nature!"), and the golf course, already a muddy track, will not soon recover from this drenching. I put the car into reverse, back out of my parking place, slide the shift into first, and bid a fond adieu to Trout Lake Golf Club.

Jim is already home from work when I return from my adventure. "Thought I might see you walking through that door a bit early. You're a drowned rat. Why don't you go take a hot shower, then come on back and we'll have a beer."

"Capital idea," I say. "Think I'll do just that."

We sit in front of the living room's picture window, which overlooks the lake. Jim and I are drinking Augsburgers, talking the way men do about beer and love and cars and houses, moving in and out of our subjects, gliding back and forth, mixing them together any old way we please. Jim is, as I guessed, a very well educated fellow, who gave up a professional career to buy a small business in Minocqua so that Turi could live in her childhood home here on the lake. It's a noble thing to have done, and I admire him for it. I wonder what I would have done. It's not an issue past knowing, and I can only guess at my degree of selflessness, and I'm ashamed at the outcome of this little inventory of the soul.

Jim, the responsible father, has consumed only one beer to my three. Our plan is to go to Bosacki's for dinner with the kids. I've eaten precious little over the last few days, and the prospect of an oval plate mounded with hush puppies and slaw and trout and pickerel and fries looms like a deliriously happy dream in my hungry man's imagination.

Into the truck we go, Jim and me and Libby and Jamie, then along the lakeshore until we arrive at a rustic tavern with a long, covered porch. We enter through the noisy, pinball, cigarette smoke, brass rail bar, then make our way to the dining room, which commands a handsome view of the lake. The waitress materializes and Jim orders two Point amber lagers, one for him, and one for me. "So," I say to Libby, "You're engaged to be married?"

She rolls her eyes behind her glasses, but I can tell she's secretly amused. "Yeah," Jamie says. "Libby's getting married." Libby gives him a quick elbow shot to the triceps, which Jim catches out of the corner of his eye.

"Kids," he says. "Settle down."

"My fault," I say. "False accusation."

We eat fresh pickerel and baked potato and a terrific house salad. The light fades from the sky over the lake, and the lights come up on the little marinas and in the windows of the lakeside cottages. "So," Jim asks after the kids have dashed off with a roll of quarters to the pinball machines, "how long did you date Turi?"

"A year or so, I guess. I saw her a lot after we broke up, and I think we had one kind of wistful date about a year after the fact. But I always thought she was terrific. Too terrific for me."

"And now look at you. A writer. Doing well for yourself."

"Hmmm . . ." I say, and look out at the moon clinging to the trees, now barely discernible along the far shore. "I'll tell you something, Jim. I really had no intention of coming here to steal Turi's heart or anything like that. Honest. I think I wanted mostly to reassure myself that she was okay after all these years. She was the first girl I ever loved, and I just wanted to know . . ."

"I understand," Jim says. "I'm glad you came."

"Turi's in good hands," I tell him.

"I really appreciate your saying that. I hope things work out well with you and Gillian. She sounds just great."

"She's pretty great, all right."

I'm lying in bed awake in the bunkhouse. It's probably three o'clock in the morning, and I hear tires crunching on the gravel driveway leading up to the cabin. I hop out of bed and feel my way over to the window. It's Turi, back from her four-day rotation as a flight attendant. She's only a silhouette, really, but I recognize the way she moves, even in the darkness. My heart tilts sideways inside my rib cage, then rights itself and clutches hard against itself. *There she is*.

In the morning, after my shower, I slide into clean blue jeans and a khaki-colored T-shirt. My Santa Fe haircut is still a blight in my estimation, but then again, my level of self-scrutiny is at an all-time high. My lower lip bears the wound from yesterday's frustration, and there are dark half circles beneath my eyes. I am at least fifteen pounds lighter than I was at the outset of my journey; for that one blessing I am grateful. I take a cup of home-brewed coffee with me out to the dock and strike a thoughtful pose in anticipation of Turi's appearance.

After only a few minutes, I hear a screen door clap shut. I turn around in time to see her coming up the dock, clutching a mug of what I know is Twinings tea. "Well, who's this?" she says.

"Wow," I say. "You look just the same, Turi." And she does. There are a few gray hairs mixed in with the brown. But the eyes are the same bright eyes from years ago, and the smile, and the shoulders. She's as trim and fit as a girl.

"You look great, too, Bill." She gives me a big squeeze, and we sit down together on the dock.

For a while, I struggle for words. I want to tell her that I've thought about her often over the years, that on those rare occasions

when I try to pray, I include her, that I'm sorry things fell apart
between us the way they did. She tells me about finding my novel in
a bookstore in Chicago, reading it in one night, imagining my voice
coming through the pages. I'm pleased that there exist, through time
and space, those filaments that connect us.

Mostly, we talk about topical things—our kids, our mutual friends
from college days, our houses, our vacations, her life in the Friendly
Skies, mine on the unfriendly fairways. It's okay, though, because
thrumming beneath the banter are unstated words and suppressed
emotions that we're too shy to reveal on such short notice. I know
that, and she does, too. "Jim's great," I tell her. "And your kids are
wonderful, except that they can go through a roll of quarters in
nothing flat. Anyway, I'm really happy for you. I can stop worrying."

"You worried?"

"Maybe I shouldn't have, but I did."

"I wondered about you, Bill. But I never worried."

Turi's folks are going to be arriving later in the morning, and I
have a long way to travel, so I tell her that I'd better get a move on.

"You just *got* here," she says.

"Sorry. It's the life of a famous international author."

"You're still a nut," she says.

Jim appears on the sidewalk only long enough to shake my hand
and wish me good luck on my book and with my life in general. We
invite each other to bring our kids to our respective necks of the universe and all the other perfunctory pleasantries associated with reluctant farewells. Then, coffee mug in hand, he slides behind the wheel
of his truck and waves good-bye.

Turi walks me to my car, which is loaded and ready to go. I give
her a long look, hoping I can preserve her image in the amber of recollection. Then I put my arms around her and give her a long good-
bye hug. All the memories of those college days come crashing
home. It wasn't so awfully long ago, really. Was it? "Don't let anything bad ever happen to you. Do you *hear* me?" I whisper.

"You either," she says.

I climb yet again behind Iris's well-worn steering wheel and start
the engine, which sounds none too healthy at this point in my

journey. I wave good-bye, and with perfectly poetic foolishness, I turn in the exact opposite direction from my intended destination.

"Bill!" she shouts. I see her in the rearview, waving her arms. "*That* way!"

I do a three-point about-face, put Iris back on course, hold an imaginary gun to my head, and pull the trigger. She laughs hard at me, and we wave one last time. "See ya," I shout.

"Good luck," she says.

CHAPTER 18

final fairway

Within an hour, I'm in my native state of Michigan, cruising eastward on Highway 2. It's a great road for a thinking man. A few lumber trucks, a lonely pickup, a fox, a deer carcass, a possum, a careless skunk. Just enough to remind you that there's a road under your tires.

I'm thinking specifically about how I would have enjoyed playing golf with Jim, a curious hypothetical chapter in the book of love: the ex-boyfriend plays golf with the loving husband in a subliminal duel to the death—winner gets the girl. But I already have a girl, whom I love and who seems to love me in spite of all the obstacles that she must surmount in order to do so. And, of course, Turi loves Jim. In retrospect, I'm happy to have stopped in Minocqua, to have engaged in something so mysterious—and so wondrously poetic. It pleases me to imagine we'll all be friends in the future, even if that only means a card at Christmas or a note to announce something momentous . . . a new grandchild, a graduation, a change of venue, a death. The point is . . . the *point* is that the well-being of Turi and Jim and their kids will matter in a new, more poignant way than before. And I will be something besides a crazy college boy who grew up to be an author, or the alter ego of a character from a golf novel. I'm that middle-aged guy Bill, with the golf clubs in his trunk and the wire rims and the bad haircut and the injured kisser.

Nobody knows how happy I am to be in Michigan, although the Upper Peninsula is as alien to my experience as North Dakota or

Idaho or Nevada. It's Michigan, though, and there's no denying it.
The forest is thinner in the peninsula, maybe due to logging, maybe
on account of the sandy soil blown ashore by the prevailing onshore
winds. Whatever the reason, I know I'm in terra cognita again. If I
wanted to, I could drive straight home to Bowling Green and be there
before nightfall. But I have one more sentimental journey to take.

If I can find a way to play Cypress Point, I can surely finagle a round
at Crystal Downs, the most majestic heartland course in America. And
perhaps the most private and the most pedigreed. I'll rent a kilt and a
sporran and a bagpipe if that's what it takes. ("That's rrright, laddie.
I'm the grrreat grrrandson of Doctorrr Mackenzie himself, heeere forrr
the sake of Auld Lang Syne.") Between his work on Cypress Point and
Augusta, Alister Mackenzie nestled this masterpiece into the dunes
that tower above Lake Michigan. The character of the course is that of
an Irish links, with wild grasses and native sands and indigenous
flowers and trees only in for poetic accent.

In Escanaba, a weary, tapped-out mining town clinging to the shore
of a bifurcated Lake Michigan harbor, I stop at a KFC for lunch. The
natives' accent is unlike anything I've ever heard. "Whatcha tink,
Walt? Let's chust lock the kits in the grodge and we cun go inta town
an pick up sum Strose peer." I order a breast quarter of Golden
Roast, some mashed potatoes, and coleslaw. A feast for a starving
man. Seated at the table across from me are an old fellow in bib
overalls with voluminous hair growing from his ears, a child twelve
years of age, maybe, in a JESUS IS LORD T-shirt, and a bonneted
woman of about thirty who, if I'm not mistaken, is mother to the girl
and wife to the old man. They are praying so fervently over their food
that I feel a little bit strange shoveling mashed potatoes into my
yawp. But when you're a hungry heathen, immediate gratification
wins out over piety seven days a week.

The Mackinac Bridge connects the U.P. to the Promised Land.
On the west side of the bridge are the waters of Lake Superior and on
the east, Lake Michigan. When, at the far end of the bridge, I catch
my first glimpse of Fort Michilimackinac, a totally restored outpost
from the French and Indian Wars, I know I'm in God's country

again. I exit the highway at Mullett Lake, twenty miles past the
bridge, to refuel. A celebratory beer is in order, and the gas station
cooler is stocked with Stroh's and Frankenmuth. For old times' sake,
I purchase a six-pack of the former and stow five of these fellows in
the cooler; one of them is riding up front with me. It's a violation of
the law, I know, and a bad example for the youth of America, but I'm
disciplined enough to stop after one tall cold one. So go ahead, arrest
me, you blue-clad rangers of the Michigan highways.

At Indian River, I cut westward on Highway 68 to Petoskey, where
Hallbergs twice and thrice removed still reside. Steep-roofed frame
houses and sturdy homes constructed of round Lake Michigan pebbles
line the main street. Now there are attractive restaurants catering to
tourists, and gift shops and big yellow B & Bs, and shops specializing
in semiprecious stones harvested from the big lake. Thirty years ago,
this was a quiet, threadbare community with Swedish civic clubs and
downtown diners catering to the locals. But with the death of the mills
and the mines and the fishing industry, tourism is Petoskey's only
means of survival. I try to imagine my grandfather driving his Packard
up from East Jordan with four little kids in the backseat and my grandmother riding shotgun.

Beyond Petoskey is Lake Charlevoix, the first of the Caribbean
blue lakes I've struggled for years to describe. Along its shores are
myriad wooden cottages, relics of the 1920s, most of them tiny, most
of them white, some of them hidden amongst the birches that grow
in profusion. The town of Charlevoix has also given itself over to
tourism. An outlying stretch of farmland that just a few years ago was
a ferny, cornflower meadow, is now a golf resort with tennis courts
and spas and riding trails. It's sad to see it happen, and I find myself
resenting the presence of golf courses that compromise the terrain so
embedded in my memory.

At the main intersection in downtown Charlevoix, I make a spon-
taneous decision to turn left onto Route 68, which will take me to
East Jordan, where my mother was born. On my mantel at home in
North Carolina is an old sepia-toned photograph of my mother and
her sisters standing in front of their home in East Jordan. I have a
vague recollection of having seen the place when I was a little kid,

but, except for the echoing clang of the nearby foundry once owned by my great-grandfather, I remember very little of that excursion.

The meadowland between Charlevoix and East Jordan is what sets Michigan apart from anywhere else in America. Except for a few pockets of fertile ground, the sandy soil in this region will not sustain crops for more than a few seasons. Thus, there are open grassy meadows that sweep up the hillsides until they collide with birch and maple forest. When the farms can sustain grazing, however limited, there is bound to be a stone barn or a clapboard monster big enough to house the cattle and sheep when the snows come.

East Jordan is tucked into Michigan ski country. But the town is just itself, an old Victorian settlement with street after street of reclaimed clapboard houses with gingerbread bonnets and filigreed skirts. In the midst of these shady neighborhoods sits the East Jordan Iron Works, the old family business, long since sold and updated. Still, it's a foreboding, gray fortress beyond whose corrugated walls are smelters and forging molds configured in the shape of manhole covers and ships' anchors and fire hydrants. I don't know on what street my mother's birthplace is located, but my mind's eye holds the photographic image, and I find myself superimposing that transparency over the reconstructed faces of these dozens of refurbished frame houses. Then, when I've all but despaired of succeeding, I see a house that might be hers, but I'm no more certain of that than I would be if I were to walk into a retirement home with a childhood photograph of the oldest resident, hoping to make that vital connection. But the sharp peak is the same, and the double window beneath the dormer, and the oddly gabled front porch. I stop next to the curb and climb out of the car. It *must* be the very house because she's standing there, flanked by her sisters and her maiden aunts, Esther and Emily. "Say cheese," the photographer shouts, but only my mother complies.

The all-encompassing shadow of the ironworks creeps toward me from across the road, and sparrows skitter from branch to branch overhead. Without my quite realizing it at first, my eyes cease to focus and the house before me becomes a blur. I swallow hard to keep the emotion from welling out of me in some publicly embarrassing way, but I can't quite stop it. It's times like these when a man wishes he had a sleeve or a Kleenex at least. But I don't, damn it all, and my tears splash on the sidewalk.

The summer light is fading quickly, and I must make Traverse City before dark, so I take my own photograph of the house, toss my camera onto the passenger seat, and drive away toward the highway that will carry me to my destination.

Traverse City is no longer a sleepy bay-side community. I come into town from the east, past motels and miniature golf courses, past cineplexes and outlet malls. It's nigh onto darkness when I arrive, so I choose any old motel that looks affordable, in this case a humble wooden sprawler with German siding and a slightly compromised view of Grand Traverse Bay. I fork over fifty dollars to a college kid, son of the proprietors, who can't quite figure how to make change or how to operate the room phones so that yours truly can make his nightly calls. He's nice enough to call his sister in Mancelona, who has more experience in such matters than he, and she apparently gives him the word, which he in turn gives to me. "Thanks a bunch," I tell him. Already, the Michigan vernacular is creeping into my language pattern. Now, how often in my life have I said "Thanks a bunch"? (A) Once. (B) Never. (C) Not too damned often, but sometimes. It's either A or B. Definitely *not* C.

First order of business is to phone Rachel, just to let her know where her old man is and to tell her that I'll be seeing her in four days exactly. She seems more than ready to come home when I talk with her. Garth, I remind her, will be meeting her at the performance hall at Salem College tomorrow. "Thank God," she says.

"Can't wait to see you, sweetie pie," I tell her.

"Ditto," she says. Such a romantic child. *Ditto.*

Although I'd rather not face the task, I am duty bound to phone Sue, the hospice coordinator, to find out what's happening in Bowling Green. I dial 6 for an outside line, then 00 for an operator, who notches in my calling card number and the number I'm calling. It's a byzantine process, but it seems to work because after two rings I hear Sue's voice.

"Hello," she says. "Wood County Hospice."

"It's Bill Hallberg calling from Traverse City. Just got in."

"Hi, Bill. I guess you got my message from Gillian. I was hoping you'd call last night, but I guess you were afraid of calling too late in the evening."

"Yeah, I was in the Central time zone, and it would have been a heart-attack phone call. What's the latest?"

"You need to get home as soon as possible, Bill. I don't mean immediately, but as soon as you can. Your mom is going downhill fast," Sue says. "I'm going to check on things tomorrow morning. But I don't think you should risk waiting *too* long."

"How is Dad holding up?"

"Not very well, I'm afraid. He's terribly undone by all this, as if he wasn't already struggling. She's really the one who keeps the ship on course, and now she's having these ischemic attacks that muddle her thinking. The time is coming fast, Bill. Sorry."

"I'll be there tomorrow," I say.

"Good!" Sue says. "Good."

I sit on the edge of the bed and stare at the painting of mallards rising in furious flight from the cattail marsh. Do they know an oil-paint hunter from the adjoining canvas is intent on blowing their feathery behinds to kingdom come? That's the way life goes sometimes; you get up a good head of steam and somebody with a double-barreled shotgun terminates you with one blast.

Over the course of ten hours, my KFC lunch has descended into my socks. I could eat the bark off a birch tree, but my soul can't abide sitting down in a restaurant with waitresses and silverware and 15 percent obligations to fulfill. Nor can I handle another fast-food experience. Not for the rest of my natural living days. I lock the room behind me and shamble down to the Meijer supermarket, where I buy a bag of premixed salad, a jar of Kraft ranch dressing, and some of Mrs. Callandar's croutons. Then I return to my room at the Sunset Motel, where I pour a few tablespoons of ranch in with the greens and shake up the bag for a minute or so until every constituent is coated with dressing. I chuck in a handful of croutons and eat the salad right out of the bag with my camp fork. I wash down this mess with four—count 'em—Stroh's beers. It's a pathetic image, a grown man with a family who loves him, hitting the bottle like this, and I'm ashamed to report the fact, but we're in a crisis situation here, and a little bit of understanding is in order.

My fantasy concerning Crystal Downs has gone a-glimmering, I'm sorry to say. Instead, I'll tackle that little afterthought of a golf course in Frankfort, where I played golf as a little kid vacationing with my parents on Crystal Lake. It's a place with nostalgia going for it, if nothing else. The hell of it is, a well-nailed drive could sail from there, over the mediating birch forest, and onto the hallowed fairways of Crystal Downs. It's a tantalizing and blatantly frustrating juxtaposition, but *quoi faire après tout*? What's a body to do?

After eating the entire bag of salad (a family-sized portion) and quaffing the aforementioned palliative beers, I take a hot shower and slide stoically into my sweatpants and sour-smelling T-shirt. I flip out all the lights, slam my head on the sponge pillow, and will myself to sleep.

I'm awakened by a car wreck out on Highway 31. One of the guests at my motel has pulled out of the driveway and into oncoming traffic. Nobody's hurt, but I envision a long, frustrating day for the old fellow, whose Buick is very much the worse for wear. The middle-aged woman, bleached blond and befangled with heavy jewelry, is blowing smoke in the man's face, stomping a high-heeled shoe on the pavement, and generally giving him hell. Her Honda Accord will need the same kind of reconstructive surgery that she, no doubt, has undergone from time to time.

Using a plastic drinking cup, I wet my hair under the sink, then brush my teeth and get dressed in blue jeans and a white polo shirt. I've slept much later than I'd anticipated, and I have at least an hour's drive to Frankfort.

I follow Highway 31 westward between the canal and the bay shore. All the downtown shops face in the opposite direction, so I'm looking at dumpsters and loading docks and billboards painted onto the brick posteriors of the various businesses. There's a trade-off, however, which is the bay itself, sky blue in the morning light. The shuffleboard park whizzes past, as do the Traverse Bay Woolen Mill and myriad public beaches with swing sets and volleyball nets. Then the highway dives southward, past the anachronistic neighborhoods whose streets, unpoetically, are numbered—1 through 20. My dad's aunt Elsie lived on 9th Street as I recall, in a white house with an iris garden out front. Or was it roses? Farther down, on 6th, Great-uncle Oscar and his wife, Agnes, occupied a two-story frame house, also white, until Oscar died and Aunt Agnes was relegated to a nursing home, where she herself died within a year of her husband's passing. Everyone goes, and where they have gone we are all going.

Between Honor and Beulah is a little mineral shop where, year after year, I purchased Petoskey stones, or pumice and polishing cloths to shine up the specimens my sisters and I collected from the shore of the big lake. I stop once again and buy a big clunker, all honeycombed with fossilized *Hexagonariae*. It's a fifteen-dollar item, but it's a last hurrah and a gift certain to please my dad, who treasures gifts with biological overtones. The scientific part of his brain seems to function quite well. Ammonites, trilobites, a *hexagonariaria*. He can still excerpt his lectures, some of which date from the Paleozoic era.

One of the finest sights in Michigan is that of Crystal Lake, which shows itself wildly cerulean between the rounded grassy dunes that guard its easternmost reaches. The first raw glimpse of it, with the sun still low behind me, is thrilling, even after all these years. I pull the car onto the roadside, and, standing knee-deep in Queen Anne's lace and clover, I snap a keepsake photograph to glue into my album. "Amazing," I say out loud.

Wouldst that I could stand there in a nostalgic swound for hours, but I must drive halfway around the lake to arrive at Frankfort Public Golf Course.

The highway connects with Crystal Drive in Beulah, a tiny resort town at the eastern shore of Crystal Lake. Right at the IGA, left at the mysterious vacation compound ordained for mysterious CEOs of unnamed corporations. Then, it's a meandering drive past Depression-era cottages interspersed with contemporary houses with decks and balconies and oddly angled roofs. The older cottages have names—The Warren, Seagull, Sand Castle—or hand-painted signs with misplaced apostrophes—The Baxter's, the Lundquist's. The lake is impossibly blue, then bluer still after the drop-off a quarter mile from shore. On the right, up a tiny road, now paved, Crispell's Cottages, where I spent many summers in the pine-paneled bungalow tucked amongst the birch and hemlock. Now the cottages belong to a corporation, which has added decks and carports and basketball goals. For a while, the road creeps away from the shore, into the woodsy hills, past lavish year-round homes of recent vintage. Just here, on the right, the stone gates of Crystal Downs, where, once, years ago, I stood on the fourth tee and hit one illicit drive, short and crooked, into the punitive, exquisitely yellow rough.

Farther on, a humbler entry, this one to the Frankfort Public Golf Course. One should not scoff at such a course. Because of its age, which is considerable, and because the cedars and hardwoods lining the fairways have grown large over the many decades since their sapling days, the fairways are tight and the trees an ever-present danger. The parking lot outside the wooden clubhouse is nearly empty at this still early hour of the day, which means that there won't be much holdup to contend with. The clientele here is not often your low-handicap crowd but, rather, patrons of the lucrative club-rental business conducted within the confines of the little white building.

There is a sign bolted to the wall behind the heavyset fellow who sits on a stool with his elbows on the scarred, heavily varnished counter. "Help you?" he asks.

According to the sign behind him, the greens fee is ten dollars for nine holes and fifteen for eighteen.

"Could I pay for nine holes, then give you five more dollars if I want to play eighteen?" I ask.

He ponders the variables for a moment, makes a mental calculation, then issues a sort of resigned clucking noise and nods. "That'll be fine," he says.

I give him a ten and a couple of quarters for a pack of tees. "Not much business today," I say.

"Oh, it'll get crowded yet. You'll see."

I emerge from the clubhouse just in time to see two kids hiking down the steep incline of the first fairway. I dash to the tee, drop my clubs, and holler down to them. "Mind if I join you?" They look at each other as if maybe I've asked which of them is Queen Elizabeth. They shrug almost simultaneously, then wave me to come on.

I hurriedly tee up my ball, then, while they hide amongst the cedar trees, I hit a terrible, howling thing that desecrates the game I'm trying to play here. "Mulligan," I yell. This time the ball stays on the fairway, but there are still overhanging branches to contend with. I grab my clubs and gallop down the grassy slope, only to discover that the taller of the two kids, who is a head shorter than I am, has knocked his drive ten yards past mine. The little fellow, praise the green gods, is well back in the fairway, but dead center. "I'm Bill," I tell them. "Who are you?"

"I'm Chip, and this is my brother Jeff. We're staying over at the Congregational Camp. You know, the assembly or whatever."

"The Congregational Summer Assembly. Kind of a mouthful, isn't it?" I say. "Hey, are either of you guys any good?"

"My brother is," Jeff says. "I stink." Chip is wearing a cabretta golf glove, and the clubs in his canvas bag are Ping ISIs, the very latest, high-tech, big-dollar equipment.

"I'm not *that* good," Chip says. He's got his hat on backward, and he carries his clubs like a pro, with his skinny forearm draped over the hub of the bag.

"I'm not either," I tell them. "So what are we playing for . . . ten bucks a hole sound good? Twenty?"

"Get *real*," Jeff says, taking a dinged-up five iron from his bag of rented clubs.

"Okay, a nickel. Me against you guys. Double bops for birdies. Carryovers."

Chip sniffs at the proposition, then relents. "Okay," he says. "We'll take you on."

My approach shot requires a low fade if I'm to avoid some leafy tentacles that threaten from above. First, I must witness Jeff's five-iron shot, which jumps only a few feet up the fairway. He hits it again, but it races sideways into the woods. Poor kid. "Use your three wood," I holler back. He looks at me as if I'm a meddling fool, then accedes. This time, his ball sails down the fairway, just short of the traps guarding the green. "Good one," I say. "You're lying two right there."

"Six," he says. "I'm lying *six*." He's one of *those*. I could tell him that my first eighteen-hole score was 176. That I counted every stroke, including four complete whiffs.

My punched long iron clips some leaves in transit toward the green, which throws it off line just enough to plant me in one of the tiny greenside bunkers. "Boogers," I say. The perfect expletive, given the company I now keep. "Monkey snot."

Chip hits a high-flying wedge shot that looks as if it wants to sail all the way to Petoskey, but it surrenders in midair and drops onto the green. His divot is a clean-edged green toupee, perfect for a Mohawk Indian. "Bravo," I say. "Well played, my man."

Jeff's chip shot jumps into the trap next to mine, which gives me a chance to be didactic. "You actually *like* this game?" I ask.

"Mmm-hmmm," he says.

"Well," I tell him, "if you want it to like *you*, you'll need to choke down on your irons a wee bit. You're not a big drink of water like your *frère* over yonder." I must have scored points by suggesting that three-wood from the fairway because he drops his hands down the grip a few inches, which automatically brings them closer to his zipper, always a plus when you're nigh onto adolescence. He chops the ball nicely onto the green.

It's all I can do to match the success of my pupil, but somehow I extricate myself from the Lake Michigan sand that fills the traps.

Jeff is farthest from the hole, so he gives his ball a good thump with his crappy little putter, but the putt is much too strong. He's away again. I can see frustration building into that thin film that now covers his eyes, which are the exact color of Crystal Lake. "It's okay, Jeff. That's the scenic side of the hole. You get a nice view of the lake from over there. But enough's enough. Whack the gumball into the hole, will ya?" Why am I suddenly talking like Dizzy Dean? A golf embolism, perhaps. This time he slides his hands subtly down the grip until the tip of his right pointer finger touches the metal shaft. *Good boy*, I say to myself. The ball does not drop, but it threatens the hole in passing and stops within a few feet of its target.

I make a duffer's bogey on the hole, and Chip wins the nickel with an easy two-putt.

"So, who taught you to play golf, Chip?" I ask. "The pro from Dover?"

"My dad," he says.

"Shouldn't he be out here, so you can kick his butt?" He gives me a funny look, shakes his head, but doesn't answer my question. I'm expecting a shadow to fall over us there on the tee. "Sorry," I say.

"It's okay," he says.

Nobody says much of anything for a few holes, just perfunctory golf babble. Nice shot. That'll play. Nice shot. That's good. I'd give anything for a beer right about now. Not to drink, but so I can conk myself on the head with the bottle half a dozen times.

At the fifth hole, the match is all even. "Okay," I announce. "I'm changing the bet. Me and my buddy Jeff are going to tear you apart, right, Jeff?" Jeff shrugs. "I take that as a yes. Okay, Chip, tee it up."

Par on this course is only thirty-two. I've made one lucky birdie, a par, and a flock of bogeys. Chip stands over his ball at number six tee with his front teeth sunk into his bottom lip. He's on his own now, challenged from two sides. His backswing this time is quick, and he yanks his drive into the ever-present trees. For the first time all day he's smiling. "What's so funny?" I ask him.

"Here's where it gets interesting," he says.

Jeff hits his best drive of the day. It overshoots the slope like a hyped-up Norwegian ski jumper and lands all the way down on the flat of the fairway. I high five him. "Killer stuff, dude."

"Was that fun, Jeff?" Chip asks.

"Yup," says my playing partner.

My drive is no better than Chip's. I may actually have brained a squirrel or any species of arboreal mammal stupid enough to show his furry head when I'm on the tee. "It's all on your shoulders, Jeff. You've got to carry the ball. By the way, hit your three wood again."

"I was going to," he says.

Chip's ball is a goner. I manage to find mine in a patch of down-fall from a towering hemlock tree, but I'm definitely in jail with nobody to bail me out except for the little wheezer standing out there in the fairway, mocking me. I punch my ball onto the fairway, or try to, but it ricochets into deep, dark trouble. "Hit your damned shot, will ya?" I holler.

Jeff hits another beauty straight down the fairway. Chip has taken a drop. Lying three. I hack my way out of the forest and onto the fairway. My irrelevant seven-iron approach is my best shot of the day; it lands like a dart five feet from the hole. "Beautiful shot," Chip says. "Nice tempo. For once."

"Whaddya mean . . . for *once*?" I ask.

"You hurry your backswing. Every time but that one."

"Where were you when I needed you, Mister? As in way back there on the first hole?"

"We're playing for money."

"Then the bet's off," I say.

"Not yet," my partner says. He then hits a very neat seven-iron shot that lands on the apron and runs up close to the hole.

"You make that one and I'll write a book about you," I say.

And he does make it, for a par, his only one of the day. I give him a big fatherly hug and turn his hat backward so he looks like his brother. "Good job, partner," I say.

Chip gives him a high five and a low five and an elbow jolt. Jeff is one happy little clam, and I'm happy for him.

We play the last few holes for fun. Chip puts my grip in proper alignment and lengthens the arc of my backswing slightly. The results are sensational, and I'm very willing to give the kid all the money in my wallet. "*Who* did you say taught you to play this damned game?"

"My dad," he says. "I already told you."

"I know. I just think it bears repeating, 'cause that's a heck of a gift he gave you," I say.

Jeff and Chip will be playing golf for the rest of the day, of that I'm certain. But I have pressures weighing down on me, and I really should be on the road. I buy them each a twenty-ounce Coke from the cooler inside the clubhouse. "I'm going to make you guys famous," I tell them. "I'm writing a golf book, even as we speak."

"If you're a golf writer, how come you're not a better golfer?" Jeff asks, then belches like a stevedore.

"Don't *have* to because I can write about it."

"Can we get the book when it comes out?" Chip asks.

"I'll send you an autographed copy." He scribbles his address on a scorecard and hands it over. "That's my mom's apartment."

I give my pals a handshake and a slap on the shoulder. "Got to go and write this book, fellas. It's been great."

"See ya," Jeff says.

"Bye, guys," I say, and watch them click toward the number one tee for yet another tour of the nine-hole course.

I always come into Bowling Green from the east; that way I can pass by the university course where my dad and I played so many rounds together. Today, the rains have arrived and nobody is on the course, except for two men in slickers who are crouched over a large iron pipe valve of the sort manufactured in East Jordan. The old university course I played as a child has been replaced by residence halls and parking lots, beneath whose foundations are innumerable orphaned golf balls lost and abandoned by hackers and duffers and run-of-the-mill players like myself. In the gray rain, the motel signs and music store windows and neon-ringed beer clocks seem less bright than I remember them. Just past the intersection of Main and Wooster, heading west toward the hospital, is my alma mater, now a junior high school. Left, finally, onto Western Avenue, a quick right on Pearl, then on down Martindale to Clark Street, *my* street from time to time.

I park on the blacktop driveway next to the garage, and, without knocking, I go on inside. "It's me. I'm home," I say.

Dad, who has undoubtedly been sleeping in his easy chair, leans out over the footstool to catch a glimpse of me when I come through the kitchen into the family room. "Hi, Dad," I say, and I give him a big squeeze.

"Hi, Bill," he says. "When did you get here?"

"Just now," I tell him.

"How's Mother?" he asks.

"Let's go down and see," I say. He shuffles ahead of me, down the hallway to the back of the house. I say hello to Sue, who's in the bedroom with Mom. She gives me a smile and tells me that Mom is doing better. But better is a relative term, and Mom is far worse than when I saw her in early June. CNN is blaring on the television, and Sue snaps it off. "Hi, Mom," I say, and crawl halfway across the bed so I can give her a kiss.

"Hi, honey," she says in a voice that isn't quite hers. She gives me a wan smile from beneath her covers.

Dad's eyes fill with tears, but by some miracle not one droplet trickles down his cheek. "She's holding on, isn't she," I say to nobody in particular.

"She didn't want to interrupt your trip across the country," Sue says. "She was pretty emphatic about that." Then, in a voice that is almost a shout, she says to Mom, "Bill's back from his trip. He's all finished."

"Did you get what you need?" Mom asks.

"Sure did. It was wonderful from beginning to end," I say. This shouting is something that will take adjusting to. It's very hard to smile when you're talking loudly, and I want her to see my smile. I can't think of anything quite appropriate to say. "I *love* you," I shout.

"I love you, too, honey," she says. It's all I can take. One more syllable and I will succumb completely to the ache that grows like a tumor inside of me. "You go back to sleep," I manage. "I'll come back down in a little while."

Dad follows me into the living room, where I've gone primarily so I can compose myself. He's such a short fellow now. Gravity has given him a good working over in the last ten years. He shrugs his shoulders, as if to say, *What can we do to stop this?* "You want a soda?" he asks.

"Sure," I say. He meanders into the kitchen, then ducks into the garage, where the cans of soda and beer and mixers have always been kept. He returns, finally, with a Miller High Life.

"Thought you'd prefer that to a Pepsi," he says.

"You're a gentleman and a scholar," I tell him.

"Some people think I'm neither," he says. It's one of those crisp bolts that emanates from the clouds every now and then. I laugh so hard that he laughs, too. Shyly, I suppose, because he might have forgotten the source of my laughter.

"*Salut,*" I say, and take a healthy slug of slightly skunky beer.

I can see him flipping through a mental index in which most of the cards are blank. I'm sort of expecting something off the wall—*Sieg Heil!* for instance. "Down the hatch," he says. He knows he's on a roll now, and he's a happy fellow.

Sue comes into the living room when she hears us laughing, but I can't really explain what's so awfully funny. "Your mom's asleep," she says. "She's glad you're here. That was the last thing she said before she dozed off. I hope you didn't sacrifice part of your trip to get back home."

"Not at all," I tell her. "It worked out perfectly. I'm glad to have it all behind me."

"Where were you?" Dad asks.

"I was in Traverse City for this book I'm doing, Dad."

"Oh," he says. "That's right."

Sue moseys on into the kitchen to fiddle with a casserole dish she's brought down from home. She's the casserole queen of North America, capable of catering a Moonie wedding on short notice. Unless I eat soon, I'll be gnawing the legs off the table. My food intake today consists of one tall can of liquid bread and nothing else.

Later in the evening, after Sue has gone home, I leave Dad to his Tigers game and walk down the hallway to visit Mom. She opens her eyes when I speak to her and smiles. "Well, hi," she says. "Did you get some food?"

"Sue made a Mexican casserole. It was scrumpdillyisious. Are you going to have some?"

"I'll come out there and eat," she says.

"You sure?" I ask.

She nods and says, "Mmm-hmmm." When I lift her out of bed and ease her into the wheelchair, she seems almost weightless, and I feel as if this were the moon and if I wanted to I could bound into the living room, covering twenty feet at a hop.

"Off we go," I say, and I pilot her up the hallway and into the family room. "Look who's here," I say.

"You must be feeling better," Dad says.

"Little bit," she says. I park her chair at the end of the dining table, and Sue brings out a small plate of food, a can of Ensure, and a small tray of medications. "This looks good, Sue," she says, then looks at me. "Your sister's an angel."

"I know. So is dad." I sit at the table with her while she eats, a difficult proposition for someone whose nerve ends are frayed like a hemp rope from all the chemotherapy. I tell her all about my trip, and she nods. "I want to hear more about that," she says when I tell her about the homeless fellows in Los Angeles. "I think I need to go lie down now," she says. I walk her down to the bedroom.

I get Mom comfortable under the covers again, and I tune the TV to CNN so she can watch Larry King. When I kiss her forehead, she pats my cheek and says I'm a good boy. Her strange, middle-aged boy. "How's your girlfriend?" she asks.

"At present, lonely. But otherwise she's doing great. Working at a plant store until her semester begins in Chapel Hill."

"You shouldn't be alone," she says.

"I won't be, Mom. I promise."

"You run along," she says, and closes her eyes. Then, suddenly she opens them again and studies my face as if committing it to memory. I sit with her for a while, until I know she's asleep, then I go into the living room.

"Say, Dad. How'd you like to play golf tomorrow? Sue will be here to take care of Mom. What do you say?"

"I'm no good anymore," he says. "I need some lessons."

"Nonsense," I say. "We'll learn as we go."

"You're a pro," he says.

"Dad," I say. "I'm a goof."

"A goof," he repeats, and laughs.

In the morning, I remind Dad that we've got a golf date, but he already knows, somehow. Maybe Sue reminded him or else he's

managed to grasp that singular concept on account of its familiarity.
"How do I look?" he asks.

"*Très chic,*" I say. "You've got the plaid/stripe thing working for
you. Very daring."

"Should I change?"

"Maybe just the shirt."

We load Dad's clubs, then mine, into the trunk of his Buick Park
Avenue, which, after three years, has only ten thousand miles on it.
It's an odd feeling, steering this big boat out of the garage, searching
futilely for a nonexistent clutch, grasping for a shift that isn't there.
The car is a veritable mastodon, but we cruise through Bowling
Green as if we own the town.

My dad has maintained his membership at the university course
for as long as I can remember, and he's a well-known figure in the
clubhouse, even given the infrequence with which he makes his
appearances. "Hi, Dr. Hallberg," says the young girl working the
counter. "You're going to play some golf, huh? Good for you."

"This is my son. He's written several best-selling books," he says.

"Not quite best-sellers," I say. "My friends bought copies."

"I'm sure you're being modest," she says.

Because it is a weekday, and because the university happens not
to be in session, there are only a few golfers on the course when we
glide out to the first tee in our topless electric cart. "You want to play
the back tees?" Dad asks.

"Not on your life," I say. "Whites for me. Unless *you* want to play
the championship tees."

He smiles. "No."

"Warm up before you hit your ball," I tell him. "Get nice and loose."

"If I was nice and loose I wouldn't be old," he says. I really don't
remember him being so funny as he's been lately. It's as if that part
of his intellect has floated to the surface of his mind while the rest
settles toward the bottom. He's a far more lovable fellow than I've
given him credit for. And, despite his own difficulties, he has been
gallant in his care of my mother. For that, if for nothing else, he
deserves to be honored and loved, which, of course, he is.

When it finally comes time to hit the golf ball, Dad's cramped swing sends the ball skittering into the rough, just off the tee. "Hit another one," I tell him. His hands shake so badly that it's hard for him to get the ball to balance on its perch. The mulligan ball glances off the heel of his graphite driver, into a row of spruces. "Jeez," he says. "That's terrible."

"You're just rusty," I tell him. And I tee up a ball for him, this time as tall as I can. "Kill it," I say.

He makes a better pass at the ball this time, and it sails down the middle but trickles into the ditch. "Good hit," I tell him. "It's not your fault the ditch is there. You couldn't hit it any better."

Our golf goes on this way for most of the afternoon. I try giving him pointers to counteract his myriad difficulties, and my heart aches that his game has faltered so. But how do you give pointers to a man who has broken his back twice in the last several years, falling off the same forbidden ladder, whose right wrist is all but fused, and whose mind can't fully calibrate the nuances of a golf swing? But he tries, and he revels in his meager triumphs.

On the fairway near the man-made pond at the heart of the course, Canadian geese munch on the lush, rain-fed fairway grass. They leave droppings in their wake, which puts a new spin on the "lift and clean" rule. But they're beautiful, notwithstanding their bad habit of crapping where they shouldn't. "They've come back from Mexico," he says. "I killed one with my drive a long time ago. Or maybe that was Ernie who killed it. Or was it a dove he killed?" I clap my hands and yell "Shoo," but they're brazen in their foraging. Only one cowardly honker flaps onto the muddy pond; the rest stay put.

At the little par three fifteenth hole, his drive makes the green, and he two-putts for a par. I slap him on the shoulder and tell him "Great going, Pop. Good stuff." He fights to keep from laughing, he's so pleased by the adulation.

"It's a beautiful day," he says.

"It *is*," I tell him. "Just a beautiful day."

I'm reluctant to report what transpires on the last hole of our interminable, but altogether pleasant, afternoon together. It's far too poetic to be believed, and my primary witness may not have the wherewithal to attest to my credibility. But setting aside the potential ridicule of a world of doubters, I'm willing to swear that what I say is true. Number eighteen at the Bowling Green University course is a five-hundred-yard par five. Dad has fuddled his way up the fairway to my ball, which is within inches of the sprinkler head marking the halfway point between the tee and the green. On what could conceivably be the last hole I ever play with my father, I wish like crazy to go out as poetically as possible by doing something nearly metaphysical in character. I take advantage of the year-round winter rules applicable to the clover fairways at this golf course and nudge my ball onto a barely perceptible mound. I decide to use my space-age driver from the fairway, a brave but risky choice, considering the ditch that parallels the fairway, then take a right-hand turn across the front of the green. "Better watch this one," I say to my dad. "It could go anywhere." I take a few practice swings, which at this stage of the game feel pretty loose, settle the club face behind my ball, and take a swing that I would like to repeat in my dreams from now until the end of time. The ball streaks straight down the fairway, over the obstreperous ditch, between the guardian bunkers, and onto the eighteenth green, twelve feet from the cup.

"Did that go on the green?" Dad asks. "I didn't see it."

"It sure did. Dumb luck."

"It takes more than dumb luck. It takes skill," he says.

Dad chops his way onto the green. Who knows how many strokes it takes him to get there. Everything's a six anyway. Always, he says he's made a six, even when it's a five. He holds the pin for me while I line up my putt, which is a left-to-right breaker. I think I've got a handle on it, but who knows what evil lurks . . . "You knock that in and I'll buy you a Coke," he says.

It's an offer too good to pass up. So I roll the ball directly into the hole. "That's an eagle, Dad."

"How about that. An eagle." He chuckles at the thought.

I wind up buying both of us Cokes. We sit at a picnic table beneath a large oak tree in front of the clubhouse. Old friends of my dad's greet us, but sometimes he can't bring to mind their names. But they understand and happily fill in the blanks before Dad has a chance to get embarrassed. "Well, shall we . . . ?" I say at last.

"Okay," Dad says, and we walk around the clubhouse to the car. "Thanks for taking me out, Bill. Probably wasn't much fun for you."

"Dad, I wouldn't trade it for the world."

Soon after Dad and I return, the hospice volunteer departs, leaving Dad and me to handle things on our own. Mom is sound asleep in the bedroom, with the TV tuned to C-Span. Mom's newshound tendencies persist through her direst infirmity.

"I wish I could do more to help her," Dad says.

"You've done your part," I say. "I don't know what else you could do besides what you've done. I'm proud of you."

"Mom says you're an angel," I tell Dad.

"I lose patience," he says. "It's been a long struggle."

"Soon to end," I say.

"It would be a blessing for her, wouldn't it?"

That night, while Dad is watching the Tigers, I sit at the foot of Mom's bed and recount the salient details of my trip. I leave out the part about Rachel's ankle, figuring Mom's got more immediate concerns. "I thought about you all the time," I tell her. "I worried that I wouldn't see you again." There are a million other things I want to tell her, but I can't string the words together without coming apart. Furthermore, she's lying under an electric blanket and there's a serious risk of electrocution for both of us. "You're the best," I say. "I know you've hung on for me, Mom. Sue told me."

"I wanted to see you again."

"Well, here I am," I say.

"Thanks for taking your dad out golfing," she says. "That meant a lot to him. He forgets almost everything, but he won't forget that." Her eyes flicker a bit, and I know I've worn her out.

"You need to get some sleep?" I ask.

"I'll go to sleep now," she says. "When are you leaving in the morning?"

"Early. You just sleep in. Don't get up to see me off. I'll come in and kiss you good-bye."

"*No!*" she says. "You come and wake me up."

"Okay, I promise I will. I love you."

"I love you," she says.

Dad is sound asleep in his easy chair when I return to the family room. I tap him on the shoulder, and he wakes up with a start. "Where's your mother?" he asks.

"She's in bed, asleep. Why don't you go down and join her? You had a big day."

"Think I will," he says, steadying himself on the console of the Magnavox as he makes his way toward the hallway. "I'm pretty tired."

"Good night," I say.

"When are you leaving?" he asks.

"Tomorrow morning," I say.

"Oh dear. I forgot. Come and wake me in the morning before you go," he says, and takes a few more steps. Then he turns and smiles at me. "That was a beautiful eagle you made at number eighteen."

"Thanks," I say. "It was for you, Dad. My going-away present."

In the morning, after the alarm sounds, I take a hot shower in the front bathroom then don my blue jeans and a clean T-shirt and my sandals. Only after I've loaded everything into the trunk do I knock softly on Mom and Dad's bedroom door.

"I'm leaving now," I whisper. "Stay in bed. I'll just kiss you where you lie. Like Romeo did to Juliet."

"We're getting up," Mom says. "Get me my housecoat, would you, Bill?" Dad flips on the swag lamp, and both of them wrestle on their morning robes. Dad and I help Mom into her wheelchair. "I want to see you off, same as always," she says.

Dad rolls her toward the back door, and I walk at a snail's pace alongside her chair. When we get to the door that opens onto the driveway, she makes a supreme effort and rises from her chair. I give her a huge hug, knowing that I could easily wrap my long arms twice around her, and I kiss her good-bye. I give Dad a hug, too. "I love you both," I say. "More than you'll ever know."

I open the storm door and hop down the steps like an elf. I wave to

them over my shoulder and climb behind Iris's gray steering wheel
yet again. Although the sun is on the verge of showing itself in the
east, I turn on the headlights, start the engine, throw the gearshift
into reverse, and slowly back out of the driveway. I take one last look
at the illuminated glass panel, and there they are, side by side,
waving and smiling.

the nineteenth
hole

It's a thirteen-hour drive from Bowling Green, Ohio, to Washington, North Carolina, from wistful sadness to pure joy. I make it in eleven and a half hours. I'd love to report that as I travel that last leg home, I've taken stock of my various adventures, rolled them over in my mind, sorted them out and drawn profound conclusions. But for now, I can only conclude that there are plenty of people to admire on this planet, and that golf provides a fertile setting for love in all its manifestations. That one realization will have to sustain me until I can assemble the millions of pieces that comprise this puzzling, wonderful adventure.

At exactly five-thirty in the afternoon, I turn the knob on my front door and walk inside the house. Gillian and Garth and Rachel are eating spaghetti at the kitchen table, unaware of my arrival until I burst into the kitchen. "Here I am," I say.

Gillian and Rachel (who is propped up on crutches), bound across the floor to greet me. They are the recipients of huge hugs and many kisses, although Rachel's bulky cast necessitates some careful maneuvering. Garth gets a manly handshake and a healthy squeeze, meaningful but under control. In his doggy joy, Louie pees on the kitchen floor and Ceilidh does pirouettes on the Congoleum. "You want to know the strangest thing that happened on the whole trip?" I ask.

"Tell," says Rachel. "Do tell."

"I made an eagle on the last hole, while playing with my dad," I tell them. "So let's hear it for me, huh?"

My journey ends with a round of applause, slightly cynical, to be honest, but what the heck, I'll take it any way I can get it.

© Kevin Amos

ABOUT THE AUTHOR

WILLIAM HALLBERG is the author of the golfing novel *The Rub of the Green* and editor of an anthology of golf short stories entitled *Perfect Lies*. His writing has appeared in *Golf Magazine*, *Golf Digest*, and the USGA centennial commemorative edition, *Golf: The Greatest Game*. An ardent golfer from earliest childhood, he has played the game with actors and rock stars, top-rated pros and old hackers, wild-eyed prodigies and gerontian Scottish ladies. He lives and golfs in Washington, North Carolina.